The Slave Community

The Slave Community

Plantation Life in the Antebellum South

REVISED AND ENLARGED EDITION

JOHN W. BLASSINGAME

New York Oxford
OXFORD UNIVERSITY PRESS

Library of Congress Cataloging in Publication Data

Blassingame, John W 1940-
The slave community.

Bibliography: p.
Includes index.
1. Slavery in the United States–Southern States.
2. Plantation life–Southern States. I. Title.
E443.B55 1979 975'.004'96073 78-26890

ISBN-13 978-0-19-502563-7 pbk.

For Teasie

PREFACE TO THE SECOND EDITION

Intriguing, complex, opaque; these are descriptive terms easily applied to American slavery. The more the student of the peculiar institution reads, the more the conviction grows that antebellum Southerners persisted in deviating from the beliefs and behavioral patterns historians have ascribed to them. The most incongruous stories appeared in the press. In 1859 the *African Repository* reprinted one of these accounts from a Tennessee newspaper:

> On Lynn Creek, Giles county, Tennessee, there is a Hardshell Baptist Church, supported by a number of wealthy communicants of that "persuasion," who for several years past have had for their regular pastor a negro man, black as the ace of spades, named George—known as *"Bentley's Old George,"* and belonging to the estate of one Matthew Bentley, deceased. George is said to be a most excellent man and a good preacher. Sometime ago, he had a noted public discussion, lasting four days, with a white preacher, on the subject of baptism, from which the white man is said to have come off (if any difference) "second-best." The Church wants to buy George, but he is unwilling to be sold out of his master's family, and is withal a regular Southern pro-slavery parson. George is the "preacher in charge" of a large congregation, nearly all of whom are slaveholders, and who pay him a salary of $600 to $700 for his pastoral services.

This book had to be revised because of George Bentley. I first encountered George in 1961 when I was working as a research assistant for Professor Elsie Lewis of Howard University: the story of his ministry appeared frequently in the abolition newspapers I read that summer. Little in the story made sense to me then; I escaped from the dilemmas it represented by rationalizing: it might have been a hoax; it *must* have been. But George would not go away. A few years ago when I began compiling a book of slave documents, the account of George Bentley's ministry virtually leaped out of the pages of the *African Repository* at me again. If observers were perplexed by nineteenth-century blacks being described as "conservative," a bondsman who was portrayed as "a regular Southern pro-slavery parson" was clearly a mystery wrapped in an enigma. And what of those Tennessee planters who believed that one of their slaves could lead them to Heaven? Had many more of the Africans and their descendants been so thoroughly acculturated, Americanized, and christianized that they were able to teach their masters?

The questions raised by George Bentley were innumerable. I found answers to a few of them in books, dissertations, and essays published since 1972. But in the main I turned to new primary sources for data on Southern religion, the evolution of the black church and the role of the minister in it, and the African impact on American language, religion, folklore, agricultural practices, folk customs and sexual attitudes.

The white church quickly emerged as the key institution which had to be analyzed in order to understand the most crucial aspects of Southern antebellum society. The pervasiveness of guilt among planters, the acculturation of the bondsman, the evolution of marriage and family life in the quarters, the education, treatment, and personality development of the slave all hinged, to some degree, on the activities of Southern white churches. At first my examination of Southern churches led to almost as much confusion as light. Then, I decided to follow the suggestion of the Reverend Charles C. Jones, who observed in 1842: "It is not good to measure ourselves by ourselves. One opportunity of faithful comparison, will shed more light and carry more conviction into the mind, ofttimes, than volumes of facts and arguments. The only danger to be apprehended from such comparisons, is that, becoming acquainted with that which is *worse,* we may rest satisfied with that which is *bad.*" My comparison of the activities of the Catholic church in Latin America with those of churches in the South made clear many facets of Southern life I had initially perceived dimly.

The Reverend Jones's observations led me to other comparisons.

How, I wondered, did white men and women enslaved in Africa react to bondage? Did their personalities disintegrate? In many ways whites enslaved in Africa faced the same problems blacks encountered in the Americas. Both groups had to learn a new language, incorporate or reject elements of a new culture, work, and accept or resist bondage. Examination of slavery in the British West Indies also suggested some of the new avenues I explored.

Since George Bentley's activities had been chronicled in abolitionist and colonizationist journals, I read them systematically in an effort to uncover more data on Southern society. Living in an age when the practice of writing letters to editors for publication was one of America's favorite pastimes, Southern planters, overseers, ministers, politicians, businessmen, and reformers often corresponded with Northern journalists. Antebellum Northern editors not only published the missives they received, they also reprinted letters, editorials, and news accounts from Southern periodicals. Data on slave resistance, accommodation, and treatment, the impact of bondage on white planters and non-slaveholders, Southern anti-slavery sentiment, religious attitudes, and social and economic philosophies rarely found in other records appeared regularly in abolition journals.

In addition to trying to solve the myriad dilemmas posed by George Bentley, I have attempted to answer the questions raised by students, colleagues, and reviewers since the first appearance of *The Slave Community* in 1972. Especially important in this regard was the session at the 1976 annual meeting of the Association for the Study of Afro-American Life and History where Eugene Genovese, Herbert Gutman, Leslie Howard Owens, George Rawick, and Earl Thorpe challenged some of my conclusions. Since I do not enjoy the polemics of historiographical debate, I have incorporated some of their suggestions and those of James Anderson, Ralph Carter, John Henrik Clarke, and Stanley Engerman (published in a book of essays edited by Al-Tony Gilmore) without long protestation or argument. Sometimes, of course, the changes diverge so markedly from the suggestions giving rise to them that provenience is not easy to trace.

Some colleagues have persistently asked such penetrating questions that the changes I made represent in many ways a continuation of dialogues with them. Mary F. Berry of the Department of Health, Education, and Welfare, Mae G. Henderson and C. Vann Woodward of Yale, and David Bishop of North Carolina Central University insisted that I consider alternative perspectives, urged me to write history with an essayist's economy of words, and exhorted me to develop the creative artist's appreciation for human diversity.

Inevitably, while contemplating the larger issues raised by reviewers, friends, and critics, I was also led to reconsider some of the minor details. Some of the changes I have made, therefore, only extend discussions of black and white insanity, slave secular songs, courtship rituals, sexual attitudes, rebel leaders, African cultural survivals, slave women, children, and drivers, and white perceptions of bondsmen. On occasion I have responded to questions about some of the assertions I made in 1972 by presenting more proof of them in the notes. But since the point of diminishing returns is reached rather quickly in such operations, I tried to restrain myself. It was not always easy. Historians suffer from a chronic temptation to expand their citations *ad infinitum* in vain efforts to clinch arguments over essentially emotional issues largely immune to logical proof. Facing such controversies, the scholar can only present what evidence he or she thinks is sufficient and, in the words of Carter G. Woodson, "weep like the minister who felt that his congregation consisted of too many to be lost but not enough to be saved."

Whatever the mix of reviews, critiques, and suggestions leading to specific changes, I appreciate all of them primarily for the light they shed on George Bentley. While George is less of a mystery to me now than he was in 1961, he is still elusive: he apparently wrote no autobiography and gave no interviews, the records of Giles County, Tennessee yield few glimpses into his character, and his master was an extremely obscure figure.

J. W. B.

New Haven, Connecticut
September 1978

PREFACE TO THE FIRST EDITION

This book describes and analyzes the life of the black slave: his African heritage, culture, family, acculturation, behavior, religion, and personality. In terms of emphasis, it breaks sharply with American historiographical tradition. Even a cursory examination of the literature shows that historians have never systematically explored the life experiences of American slaves. Southern planters, on the other hand, have had an extremely good press in the United States. Historians have analyzed practically every aspect of the planter's behavior, ideology, social and economic position, customs, and politics. Although the 3,954,000 black slaves greatly outnumbered the 385,000 white slaveowners in the South in 1860, the slave has generally been shunted off to the wings on the historical stage.

By concentrating solely on the planter, historians have, in effect, been listening to only one side of a complicated debate. The distorted view of the plantation which emerges from planter records is that of an all-powerful, monolithic institution which strips the slave of any meaningful and distinctive culture, family life, religion, or manhood. The clearest portrait the planter has drawn of the slave is the stereotype of Sambo, a submissive half-man, half-child. Such stereotypes are so intimately related to the planter's projections, desires, and biases that they tell us little about slave behavior and even less about the slave's inner life, his thoughts, actions, self-concepts, or personality.

Any examination of such a new topic as slave life must rest securely on an analysis of new kinds of sources viewed from different angles. The utilization of psychological theory is the first step in this direction. The new insights gained from psychology are useless, however, if they are applied to stereotypes and restricted to traditional sources. Instead, an investigator of the personality development of slaves must depend largely on the personal records left by the slave, especially autobiographies. This is all the more necessary because historians have deliberately ignored these sources. Consequently, a great deal of emphasis has been placed on non-traditional sources in this study in an effort to delineate more clearly the slave's view of bondage and to discover some new insights into the workings of the system.

While relying heavily on those black autobiographies which pass the tests commonly applied to historical sources, I have also systematically examined several hundred white autobiographies, plantation records, agricultural journals, and travel accounts. This approach permits us to view slave life through the eyes of three witnesses. Two of them, the planter and the slave, give an insider's view of the plantation. The third witness, the traveler, views the relation between slave and master from the outside. Although there are no absolute guarantees of truth, this three dimensional picture of the plantation at least reveals the complexity of the institution and, hopefully, gives us a close approximation of the interaction between masters and slaves.

The inescapable conclusion which emerges from an examination of several different kinds of sources is that there were many different slave personality types. Sambo was one of them. But, because masters varied so much in character, the system was open at certain points, and the slave quarters, religion, and family helped to shape behavior, it was not the dominant slave personality. Rather than identifying with and submitting totally to his master, the slave held onto many remnants of his African culture, gained a sense of worth in the quarters, spent most of his time free from surveillance by whites, controlled important aspects of his life, and did some personally meaningful things on his own volition. This relative freedom of thought and action helped the slave to preserve his personal autonomy and to create a culture which has contributed much to American life and thought.

Like most scholars, I have accumulated many debts in the course of my investigation. I could write much about all of those historians whose published work influenced my thinking, but I hope that the footnote citations and the bibliography truly reflect what I have learned from them. The burdens of research and writing have been lightened by a summer grant from Yale University and the aid of several people. The probing questions raised by Mack Thompson of the University of California at Riverside during an institute at Carnegie Mellon University in 1964 about my first efforts to deal with the topic have continued to influence my thinking. Similarly, Richard Morse's criticisms of an essay I wrote on slave personality during my first year of graduate study at Yale helped me to identify many of the topics I have developed in this book. David B. Davis, Edmund Morgan, and C. Vann Woodward of Yale University, Louis Harlan of the University of Maryland, and John Hope Franklin of the University of Chicago, read several drafts of the manuscript; Joseph Logsdon of Louisiana State University at New Orleans, Thomas Holt, Jerry Thomas, and Lawrence Powell of Yale University, and Nicholas Canady of Louisiana State University at Baton Rouge, commented on the early drafts; Mrs. Dorothy Porter, Curator of the Negro Collection at Howard University, and the staffs of the University of North Carolina and Louisiana State University helped me find many sources. I am deeply indebted to my research assistants Barnett Rubin and Miss Mae Henderson for the hot summer they spent uncovering material on antebellum planters, to Miss Fran Drago of Wesleyan University for helping me to refine my psychological concepts, and to David Robinson of Yale for sharing his knowledge of Africa with me. Mrs. Anne Granger, Mrs. Janet Villastrigo, and Mrs. Rebecca Davis, who had the unenviable task of deciphering my script, cheerfully typed several drafts of the manuscript.

Dedication of this book to my wife is, as only she knows, poor payment for her sacrifices.

J. W. B.

New Haven, Connecticut
March 1972

CONTENTS

1 Enslavement, Acculturation, and African Survivals, 3

2 The Americanization of the Slave and the Africanization of the South, 49

3 Culture, 105

4 The Slave Family, 149

5 Rebels and Runaways, 192

6 Plantation Stereotypes and Institutional Roles, 223

7 Plantation Realities, 249

8 Slave Personality Types, 284

Appendix I: Comparative Examination of Total Institutions, 323

Appendix II: African Words, Numerals, and Sentences Used by Former Slaves in Georgia and South Carolina in the 1890s, 332

Appendix III: Statistics on Slaves and Slavery: Observations and Tables, 336

Critical Essay on Sources, 367

Selected Bibliography, 383

Index, 403

ILLUSTRATION SOURCES

Frontispiece	*Century Magazine* 31:813
Figure 1	Cornell University Library
Figure 2	Cornell University Library
Figure 3	Library of Congress
Figure 4	W.P.A., *The Negro in Virginia* (Hastings Publishers, N.Y., 1940, copyright, Hampton Institute)
Figure 5	Library of Congress
Figure 6	*Harper's Weekly* 4:344
Figure 7	*Harper's Encyclopedia of United States History*, Vol. 8, New Edition. Revised and Enlarged by Benson John Lossing (Harper & Row, 1915)
Figure 8	Historical Pictures Service of Chicago
Figure 9	Library of Congress
Figures 10, 11	*American Anthropologist* 10:plates XL, XLI
Figure 12	British Museum
Figure 13	
a	The Papers of Benjamin Latrobe, Maryland Historical Society
b	Curt Sachs, *Les Instruments de musique de Madagascar* (Paris, 1938, copyright, Institut Ethnologie, University of Paris)
c	Bernard Ankerman, *Die afrikanischen Musikinstrumente* (Berlin, 1901)
d	The Papers of Benjamin Latrobe
e	Jean-Sébastien Laurenty, *Les Tambours à fente de l'Afrique Centrale* (Tervuren, Belgium, 1968, copyright, Royal Museum of Central Africa)
f	Laurenty, *Les Tambours à fente de l'Afrique Centrale*
Figure 14	
a	The Papers of Benjamin Latrobe
b	Sachs, *Les Instruments de musique de Madagascar*
c	Stephen Chauvet, *Musique Nègre* (Paris, 1929, copy-

	right, Société d'éditions geographiques, maritimes et coloniales)
d	The Papers of Benjamin Latrobe
e	Ankerman, *Die afrikanischen Musikinstrumente*
f	Ankerman, *Die afrikanischen Musikinstrumente*
Figure 15	Hamilton W. Pierson, *In the Brush* (New York, 1881)
Figure 16	Muriel and Malcolm Bell, Jr.
Figure 17	Muriel and Malcolm Bell, Jr.
Figure 18	National Maritime Museum
Figure 19	John Ogilby, *Africa* (London, 1670)
Figure 20	Pierre Dan, *Historie van Barbayen* (Amsterdam, 1634)
Figure 21	Louis A. Berbrugger, *Algerie historique, pittoresque et monumentale* (Paris, 1843-45)
Figures 22, 23	*American Anthropologist* n.s. 10:plates XLII, XLIII
Figure 24	*Century Magazine* 31.808
Figure 25	*Century Magazine* 31:525
Figure 26	*Century Magazine* 31:524
Figure 27	Peter Schnapp. Copyright, Peter Schnapp—*Realités*
Figure 28	The New York Public Library Astor, Lennox and Tilden Foundations
Figure 29	*Harper's Encyclopedia of United States History,* Vol. 8, New Edition
Figure 30	*Harper's Encyclopedia of United States History,* Vol. 8, New Edition
Figure 31	Hampton Institute Library
Figure 32	*Illustrated London News* 38:139
Figure 33	Library of Congress
Figure 34	The Chicago Historical Society
Figure 35	James S. Buckingham, *The Slave States of America* (London, 1842)
Figure 36	Culver Pictures
Figure 37	William Wells Brown, *Narrative of William W. Brown, A Fugitive Slave* (Boston, 1847)
Figure 38	Henry Bibb, *Narrative of the Life and Adventures of Henry Bibb, An American Slave* (New York, 1849)
Figure 39	William Still, *The Underground Railroad* (Philadelphia, 1872)

Figure 40	Culver Pictures
Figure 41	Still, *The Underground Railroad*
Figure 42	Library of Congress
Figure 43	Solomon Northup, *Twelve Years a Slave* (London, 1853)
Figure 44	Northup, *Twelve Years*
Figure 45	*Century Magazine* 31:520
Figure 46	*Harper's Monthly Magazine* 15:440
Figure 47	*Harper's Monthly Magazine* 8:456
Figure 48	*Ballou's Pictorial* 14:49
Figure 49	*Harper's Monthly Magazine* 8:457
Figure 50	*Harper's Monthly Magazine* 8:459
Figure 51	*Merry's Museum* 6:111
Figure 52	The New York Public Library Astor, Lenox and Tilden Foundations
Figure 53	*Harper's Encyclopedia of United States History*, Vol. 8, New Edition
Figure 54	*Putnam's Monthly* 10:447
Figure 55	*Harper's Encyclopedia of United States History*, Vol. 6, New Edition
Figure 56	*Harper's Monthly Magazine* 19:729
Figure 57	Frederick Douglass, *My Bondage and My Freedom* (New York, 1855)
Figure 58	Austin Steward, *Twenty-two Years a Slave, and Forty Years a Freeman* (Rochester, N.Y., 1861)
Figure 59	Northup, *Twelve Years*
Figure 60	*Harper's Weekly* 7:429
Figure 61	Moses Roper, *A Narrative of the Adventures and Escape of Moses Roper from American Slavery* (London, 1840)
Figure 62	Library of Congress
Figure 63	Wilson Armistead, *A Tribute for the Negro* (New York, 1848)
Figure 64	Bibb, *Narrative*
Figure 65	James A. Bear, Jr., editor, *Jefferson at Monticello*, University Press of Virginia (Charlottesville, 1967)

The Slave Community

I

Enslavement, Acculturation, and African Survivals

Middle Passage:
    voyage through death
        to life upon these shores.
"10 April 1800—

Blacks rebellious. Crew uneasy. Our linguist says their moaning
is a prayer for death,
ours and their own. Some try to starve themselves.
Lost three this morning leaped with crazy laughter
to the waiting sharks, sang as they went under." . . .

Voyage through death,
    voyage whose chartings are unlove.

A charnel stench, effluvium of living death
spreads outward from the hold,
where the living and the dead, the horribly dying,
life interlocked, lie foul with blood and excrement.

Deep in the festering hold thy father lies,
the corpse of mercy rots with him,
rats eat love's rotten gelid eyes.

But, oh, the living look at you
with human eyes whose suffering accuses you,
whose hatred reaches through the swill of dark
to strike you like a leper's claw.

Robert Hayden

The chains of the American Negro's captivity were forged in Africa. Prince and peasant, merchant and agriculturalist, warrior and priest, Africans were drawn into the vortex of the Atlantic slave trade and funneled into the sugar fields, the swampy rice lands, or the cotton and tobacco plantations of the New World. The process of enslavement was almost unbelievably painful and bewildering for the Africans. Completely cut off from their native land, they were frightened by the artifacts of the white man's civilization and terrified by his cruelty until they learned that they were only expected to work for him as they had been accustomed to doing in their native land. Still, some were so morose they committed suicide; others refused to learn the customs of whites and held on to the memory of the African cultural determinants of their own status.

To argue, as some scholars have, that the first slaves suffered greatly from the enslavement process because it contradicted their "heroic" warrior tradition, or that it was easy for them because Africans were by nature docile and submissive, is to substitute mythology for history. The enslavement of Africans was intimately related to the history of Indian-white relations in the New World and certain historical and anthropological principles. In regard to the latter, historically it has been almost impossible to enslave members of societies who are nomadic food gatherers, herdsmen, hunters, or fishermen. Consequently, Europeans in North America either exterminated the war-like hunting tribes or worked the simple food gatherers to death. Neither group made effective slaves. On the other hand, and in spite of the myths surrounding the "noble red man," when Europeans encountered Indians of a higher culture accustomed to systematic agricultural labor and sedentary habits (as did the Spaniards in Mexico and other parts of South America), the Indians were reduced to slavery or something closely akin to it.

Initially, the English in North America were so outnumbered by the war-like Indian nations and Confederations surrounding them that they rarely systematically attempted to enslave the red men. This was especially true of their immediate neighbors. When, however, inter-tribal wars or conflicts with whites resulted in Indian captives, they were enslaved. Even so, it was unsafe to keep an Indian slave in the neighborhood of his nation; most of them were sold out of the colonies in which they were captured. The more peaceful Indians succumbed so quickly to European diseases (smallpox, typhus, measles, influenza, and syphilis) or had an economic system so alien to the plantation regimen that they did not make suitable slaves. Because of the many problems an alien people faced in enslaving men in their native land, Europeans turned to Africans to supply their labor needs.[1]

In Africa the whites encountered some of the same problems they did with native Americans. Like many Indians, African hunting, pastoral, and fishing peoples were too nomadic or warlike to be captured. As a result, most of the Africans brought to North America were members of agrarian polities in West Africa, accustomed to hard, continuous labor and a sedentary life. A majority of them belonged to the Ibo, Ewe, Biafada, Bakongo, Wolof, Bambara, Ibibio, Serer, and Arada peoples. Members of the large, well-organized African states like the Yoruba, Dahomey, Ashanti, Fulani, Kom, Mandingo, and Hausa, with their centralized governments, fast moving cavalries, or disciplined standing armies, rarely fell into the slave trader's hands. It took the British, even with modern weapons, until the first decades of the twentieth century to conquer some of these states. On occasion, some of the centralized states became so weak that large numbers of their citizens were captured, as happened with the Oyo Yoruba after 1750. For the most part, however, these peoples were almost immune to enslavement. In fact, these were the nations which made war on their more peaceful (or defenseless) neighbors and sold them and the peoples who fell under their political, economic, military, and cultural hegemony into bondage. Approximately ten million Africans were brought to the New World between the sixteenth and the mid-nineteenth century.[2]

1. Wesly Frank Craven, *White, Red, and Black: The Seventeenth Century Virginian* (Charlottesville, 1971), 73-75; W. Robert Higgins, "The Geographical Origins of Negro Slaves in Colonial South Carolina," *South Atlantic Quarterly* LXX (Winter 1971), 34-47; Almon W. Lauber, *Indian Slavery in Colonial Times Within the Present Limits of the United States* (New York, 1913).

2. J. F. Ade Ajayi and Dan Espie, *A Thousand Years of West African History* (London, 1965), 157-60, 318-29; M. M. Green, *Ibo Village Affairs* (New York, 1964 [1947]), 32-48, 61-77; J. D. Fage, *A History of West*

The ethnic origins of the first slaves are important primarily in relation to the extent to which native culture and economic organization prepared the African for one facet of plantation life: systematic labor. While the customary labor of certain peoples made it relatively easy for them to adapt to agricultural labor in the New World, it is not at all clear that there was a close relationship between docility and rebelliousness among slaves and their ethnic origin. For example, although South American masters of the sixteenth and seventeenth centuries obtained most of their slaves from what they considered the most "docile" of African peoples, these slaves rose in rebellion after rebellion during the colonial period. In other words, it was not the contrast between the African slave's warrior past and his dependency on the plantation which was primarily responsible for determining his behavior, but rather the interaction between certain universal elements of West African culture, the institutionalized demands of plantation life, the process of enslavement, and his creative response to bondage.[3]

Although a few chiefs sold their own subjects, household slaves, or criminals, most African slaves were prisoners captured in wars or kidnapped by slave raiders. After their capture, the Africans were tied together by a rope and then marched hundreds of miles while suffering from thirst, hunger, and exhaustion. Consequently, many either died along the way or were reduced to a very weak and emaciated condition by the time they reached the sea coast. On the coast, the Africans were made to

---

Africa (London, 1969), 81-95; Daryll Forde and P. M. Kaberry, *West African Kingdoms in the Nineteenth Century* (London, 1967), 37-39, 72-73, 90; Basil Davidson, *The Growth of African Civilization . . .* (London, 1965), 173-233; Philip D. Curtin, *The Atlantic Slave Trade: A Census* (Madison, 1969), *passim;* Walter Rodney, "Upper Guinea and the Significance of the Origins of Africans Enslaved in the New World," *Journal of Negro History* LIV (Oct. 1969), 327-45.

3. On the economic life of West African tribes, see: Madeline Manoukian, *Tribes of the Northern Territories of the Gold Coast* (London, 1951), 13-23; P. Amaury Talbot, *Tribes of the Niger Delta* (London, 1932), 273-84, 294; Madeline Manoukian, *The Ewe-Speaking People of Togoland and the Gold Coast* (London, 1952), 11-12, 15-20.

jump up and down, had fingers poked in their mouths and their genital organs handled by a doctor. Those chosen by the Europeans were then branded.[4]

Taken on board ship, the naked Africans were shackled together on bare wooden boards in the hold, and packed so tightly that they could not sit upright. During the dreaded Mid-Passage (a trip of from three weeks to more than three months) the slaves were let out of the hold twice daily for meals and exercise, and women and children were often permitted to spend a great deal of time on deck. The foul and poisonous air of the hold, extreme heat, men lying for hours in their own defecation, with blood and mucus covering the floor, caused a great deal of sickness. Mortality from undernourishment and disease was about 16 per cent. The first few weeks of the trip was the most traumatic experience for the Africans. A number of them went insane and many became so despondent that they gave up the will to live. Slaves in the latter condition were described as having the "fixed melancholy."[5]

Africans were not, however, totally immobilized by shock. Often they committed suicide (especially while still on the African coast) by drowning, or refusing food or medicine, rather than accept enslavement. One captain made it all the way to the West Indies before the Africans began a mass suicide attempt. He asserted that he

> thought all our troubles of this Voyage was over; but on the contrary I might say that the Dangers rest on the Borders of Security. On the 14th of March we found a great deal of Discontent among the Slaves, particularly the Men, which continued till the 16th about Five o'Clock in the Evening, when

4. Elizabeth Donnan, ed., *Documents Illustrative of the History of the Slave Trade to America* (4 vols., Washington, D.C., 1930-35); Daniel P. Mannix and Malcolm Cowley, *Black Cargoes: A History of the Atlantic Slave Trade, 1518-1865* (New York, 1962), 1-49, 100-130; W. O. Blake, *The History of Slavery and the Atlantic Slave Trade* (Columbus, O., 1860), 93-142; John R. Spears, *The American Slave Trade* (New York, 1900), 1-82.

5. Mannix and Cowley, *Cargoes*, 104-30; *An Abstract of the Evidence Delivered Before a Select Committee of the House of Commons, 1790-91* (London, 1791), 39-44; Spears, *Trade*, 68-81; Blake, *History*, 126-42.

Figures 1, 2, 3, 4. The Shock of Enslavement

to our great Amazement about an hundred Men Slaves jump'd over board, and it was with great Difficulty we sav'd so many as we did; out of the whole we lost 33 of as good Men Slaves as we had on board, who would not endeavour to save themselves, but resolv'd to die, and sunk directly down. Many more

Figure 5. Into the Hold

> of them were taken up almost drown'd, some of them died since. . . .[6]

Many of the Africans resisted enslavement at every step in their forced emigration. Conscious of the wrongs they suffered, they began trying to escape on the long march to the coast. Failing this and suicide attempts while still in sight of their native shores, the Africans often mutinied while being transported to the New World and killed their white captors. In spite of their chains and lack of arms, they rebelled so frequently that a number of ship owners took out insurance to cover losses from mutinies.[7] In their study of the slave trade, Mannix and Cowley uncovered

6. Quoted in Darold D. Wax, "Negro Resistance to the Early American Slave Trade," *Journal of Negro History* LI (Jan. 1966), 9-10.

7. Wax, "Resistance," 1-15; Lorenzo J. Greene, "Mutiny on the Slave Ships," *Phylon* V (Fourth Quarter 1944), 346-54; George Francis Dow, *Slave Ships and Slavery* (Salem, 1927), 83, 175, 207; Joshua Coffin, *An Account of Some of the Principal Slave Insurrections* (New York, 1860), 14-15, 33; Donnan, *Documents*, I, 463, II, 232, 266, 397, 460-86, III, 37-42, 51, 119,

Figure 6. Middle Passage

fairly detailed accounts of fifty-five mutinies on slavers from 1699 to 1845, not to mention passing references to more than a hundred others. The list of ships "cut off" by the natives—often in revenge for the kidnapping of freemen—is almost as long. On the record it does not seem that Africans submitted tamely to being carried across the Atlantic like chained beasts.[8]

318; Harvey Wish, "American Slave Insurrections Before 1861," *Journal of Negro History* XXII (July 1937), 299-320; Spears, *Trade*, 31-35.

8. Mannix and Cowley, *Cargoes*, 111.

Early records indicate that the Africans continued to resist even after they landed in the New World. Many eighteenth-century travel accounts, memoirs, and slave notices show that a number of the newly imported Africans almost literally ran away as soon as their feet touched American soil.[9] A North Carolina advertisement of 1775 is typical of many:

> ELOPED from the Subscribers on Wednesday the 26th Inst. two newly imported Men Slaves KAUCHEE and BOOHM, about 6 Feet high, and, perhaps 30 Years of Age.—They absconded in Company with three other Slaves about two Months ago, and were taken up at Broad-Creek, about 10 miles off, and brought back by William Gatling of that Place, who has since purchased a Wench who was imported with them; from which it is supposed they are lurking about that Neighborhood.

Even when they did not run away, the Africans were often obstinate, sullen, and uncooperative laborers. An English traveler observed in 1746 that an African born slave, "if he must be broke, either from Obstinacy, or, which I am more apt to suppose, from Greatness of Soul, will require . . . hard Discipline . . . you would really be surpriz'd at their Perseverance; . . . they often die before they can be conquer'd."[10]

The psychic impact of what they had undergone was so great that a majority of newly imported Africans, exhausted from the journey which often lasted more than six months from the time of their capture, offered little resistance to their masters. For most

9. John Brickell, *The Natural History of North Carolina* (Dublin, 1737), 272-74; Alexander Hewatt, *An Historical Account of the Rise and Progress of the Colonies of South Carolina and Georgia* (1779), in B. R. Carrol, ed., *Historical Collection of South Carolina* (2 vols., New York, 1836), I, 331-32, 348; Hugh Jones, *The Present State of Virginia* (Chapel Hill, 1956), 76; Harriet Martineau, *Retrospect of Western Travel* (3 vols., London, 1838), II, 98; Bernard Romans, *A Concise Natural History of East and West Florida* (New York, 1775), 73; Garnett Andrews, *Reminiscences of an Old Georgia Lawyer* (Atlanta, 1870), 10.

10. Quoted in Wax "Resistance," 11; "Observations on Several Voyages and Travels in America," *William and Mary Quarterly*, Ser. 1, XV (Jan. 1907), 149.

slaves in the seventeenth and early part of the eighteenth century, the shock of enslavement was crucial in determining their behavior. Captured and brought to America under the most painful and bewildering conditions, the seventeenth- and eighteenth-century Africans were taken from a society where their status was assured, and thrust into one where customs and languages were totally different and where their prior status was of no import. The African who survived the Mid-Passage, however, had one important advantage, for the experience he was about to face was not entirely unfamiliar to him. Generally, both men and women were accustomed to agricultural labor in Africa and knew of the existence of slavery. In fact, the frequent wars represented a constant reminder of the threat of capture. Even so, enslavement was an unparalleled shock.[11]

Historians have few sources on the initial reactions of Africans to their bondage. From the sketchy accounts which have survived, however, it is possible to obtain a more or less clear idea of their reactions. Fortunately, there were a few African-born slaves who lived to recount stories of their enslavement. One of these, Venture Smith, born in Guinea in 1729, was brought to the United States when he was eight years old.[12] He remembered that his people raised sheep, goats, and cattle. Polygamy was practiced, but apparently a man could not marry an additional wife until he obtained the consent of his other wife or wives. When Venture's father, a wealthy prince, took a third wife without his mother's consent, she left him, though she soon rejoined him. Venture remembered his father as "a man of remarkable strength and resolution, affable, kind and gentle, ruling with equity and moderation." He recalled most vividly and painfully, however, his father giving cattle and goats to assuage the avarice of African slave raiders, the raiders breaking the bargain, de-

11. Green, *Ibo*, 32-48; Forde and Kaberry, *Kingdoms*, 268-69; Francis Hall, *Travels in Canada and the United States in 1816 and 1817* (London, 1818), 432.

12. Venture Smith, *A Narrative of the Life and Adventures of Venture, a Native of Africa* (New London, Conn., 1798).

Figures 7, 8
Landing

stroying the village, and torturing his father to death: "The shocking scene is to this day fresh in my mind, and I have often been overcome while thinking on it."[13]

The most famous and revealing account we have of the process of enslavement was written by Gustavus Vassa, or Olaudah Equiano.[14] The son of an Ibo tribal elder, Olaudah was born in 1745 in a part of the Benin empire (located in what is now Eastern Nigeria). Industrious agriculturalists, the Ibos produced corn, tobacco, cotton, plantains, yams, beans, spices, and pineapples and traded for guns, dried fish, and beads. Land was held in common, and everyone worked in the fields. Bullocks, goats, and poultry were also raised. The women wove calico cloth and made earthenware while the men made hoes, shovels, spears, shields, and swords. They had an organized marketing system and used small iron anchor-shaped coins as money.

Often parents promised children in marriage while they were quite young, and the marriage was consummated when the girl came of age. Since the girl became the "property" of her husband's family, her own family was compensated for her loss by gifts from the groom's family. In order to get the new couple started in life, all of their friends and relatives gave them gifts. The girl acquired a new belt to indicate the change in her status, and the marriage ceremony ended with a great feast.

The family was rigidly patriarchal. Olaudah asserted that the marriage bed was so "sacred" and men so jealous of the fidelity of their wives that adultery was punishable by death. The women were bashful and chaste. According to Olaudah, the women were "uncommonly graceful, alert, and modest to a degree of bashfulness; nor do I remember to have ever heard of an instance of incontinence amongst them before marriage."[15]

Within the patriarchal system, women played important roles. They made the clothes, served as warriors, did the marketing, and worked in the fields alongside their husbands. The care and

13. Smith, *Narrative,* 11.

14. Gustavus Vassa, *The Interesting Narrative of the Life of Olaudah Equiano, or Gustavus Vassa, the African* (London, 1794), 1-61.

15. Vassa, *Narrative,* 14-15.

training of the children were primarily the responsibility of the women. As a result, a deep bond of affection developed between mothers and children. Olaudah was especially favored in this regard because he was the youngest boy: "As I was the youngest of the sons, I became, of course, the greatest favorite with my mother, and was always with her; and she used to take particular pains to form my mind. I was trained up from my earliest years in the arts of agriculture and war: my daily exercise was shooting and throwing javelins; and my mother adorned me with emblems, after the manner of our greatest warriors."[16]

The Ibo religion was a complex synthesis of magic, nature worship, and belief in a Supreme Being. The Supreme Being, or Creator, lived in the Sun and governed all events, especially death and captivity. Ancestors, who guarded one against evil spirits, were revered: there were frequent nightly prayers and oblations of the blood of freshly sacrificed animals at their graves. Some Ibos believed in transmigration of souls, and all honored the priest. The priests, succeeded by their sons, foretold events and discovered jealousy, theft, and evidence of poisoning. In addition to their religious duties, the priests were also physicians. Upon the death of a priest, his body, along with his earthly possessions, was buried, after the proper sacrifice of animals, at the end of the day. Some snakes were considered as omens of future events and were not molested.

There were several noteworthy Ibo customs. The chief men or elders decided all disputes and meted out punishment for crimes. The people were cheerful and enjoyed music and dancing. According to Equiano, his people was "almost a nation of dancers, musicians, and poets. Thus every great event such as a triumphant return from battle or other cause of public rejoicing is celebrated in public dances, which are accompanied with songs and music suited to the occasion."[17] Children were often named after some spectacular event which occurred at the time of their birth. The Ibos bathed frequently, practiced circumcision, and had no knowledge of swearing. Fearful of being poisoned, the people al-

16. Vassa, *Narrative*, 31.
17. Vassa, *Narrative*, 7.

ways kissed fruit or tasted food to show a friend or stranger that it did not contain poison.

European contact with Africa almost destroyed the society Olaudah knew. After Europeans gained a foothold on the coast, wars, frequently started by avaricious chiefs to obtain slaves, became endemic. Traditionally, prisoners of war had been either returned for ransom or kept as slaves who were treated like, and did the same work as, other members of their master's family; they could even own property. Equiano's father owned many slaves, and his people traditionally sold some of their war captives to African slave traders. Europeans changed this by encouraging raids which frequently led to the kidnapping of Ibos in the area by black slave traders.

Olaudah and his sister were kidnapped when he was eleven. At first, they comforted each other. When they were separated, Olaudah cried and refused to eat for several days. Traveling for many days, he was finally sold to a kind African goldsmith. Although his labor was light, he had "an anxious wish for death to relieve me from all my pains." Constantly looking for a way to escape, he was pressed down with grief. He was, he recalled, "quite oppressed and weighed down by grief after my mother and friends, and my love of liberty. . . ."[18]

Olaudah was sold to European slave traders seven months after his capture. Arriving on the coast, he was terrified by the strange ship and the white men with "horrible looks, red faces, and long hair." The boat was a veritable devil's pit. The whites were "so savage" that he was sure they were going to kill and eat him. When he saw a pot of water boiling on the deck, he fainted. The billowing sails and the ability of the whites to make the ship start and stop at will filled him with wonder and convinced him the white men were evil spirits. The groaning men, shrieking women, galling chains, and nauseating, suffocating smell made the hold of the ship "a scene of horror almost inconceivable." On the way to Barbados, two slaves, chained together,

18. Vassa, *Narrative*, 35. For an overview of the staggering variety of slave systems in Africa, see: Suzanne Miers and Igor Kopytoff, eds., *Slavery in Africa* (Madison, 1977).

jumped overboard and drowned. Although he was anxious about his fate and terrified by the whites, Olaudah was consoled by some members of his own ethnic group who were on board. Still, the constant flogging of black slaves and white sailors and men dying daily were oppressive. "Every circumstance I met with served only to render my state more painful, and heighten my apprehensions and my opinion of the cruelty of the whites." The voyage was a nightmare; the hold a den of horrors.[19]

When the boat docked in Barbados, a new series of horrors began for Olaudah. Immediately the blacks were painstakingly examined by the eager merchants. Again, the haunting fear of the cannibalistic tendencies of the whites returned, and Olaudah asserted: "there was much dread and trembling among us, and nothing but bitter cries. . . ."[20] This continued until some slaves came on board and explained that the Africans had been brought to the island to work for the whites. Taken off the ship and herded into a stockade, they were amazed by the brick houses of the whites and the horses they rode. The amazement turned to terror a few days later when the Africans were sold by the "shout" or "scramble." Olaudah described the spectacle in the following words:

> We were not many days in the merchant's custody before we were sold after their usual manner, which is this: On a signal given, (as the beat of a drum) the buyers rush at once into the yard where the slaves are confined, and make choice of that parcel they like best. The noise and clamour with which this is attended and the eagerness visible in the countenances of the buyers serve not a little to increase the apprehensions of the terrified Africans. . . . In this manner, without scruple, are relations and friends separated, most of them never to see each other again.[21]

Most of the Africans were sold in Barbados, but a small group, including Olaudah, were taken to a Virginia plantation. Soon

19. Vassa, *Narrative,* 47, 49, 52.
20. Vassa, *Narrative,* 54.
21. Vassa, *Narrative,* 61.

Figure 9. Selecting Parcels

Olaudah was the only newly imported African left on the plantation. He was mortified by his inability to converse with anyone: "I was now exceedingly miserable, and thought myself worse off than any of the rest of my companions; for they could talk to each other, but I had no person to speak to that I could understand. In this state I was constantly grieving and pining, and wishing for death, rather than anything else."[22]

On the Virginia plantation he weeded grass and gathered stones for a few days. Then, called to the mansion to fan his master, Olaudah was terrified by the iron muzzle on the face of the black cook, mystified by the ticking of a clock, and convinced

22. Vassa, *Narrative*, 70-71.

that a portrait on the wall watched his every move and would report any of his transgressions to his master who was asleep. Consequently, he performed his task "with great fear." He spent "some time in this miserable, forlorn, and much dejected state without having anyone to talk to, which made my life a burden," until an English sea captain purchased him.[23]

The narrative of Olaudah Equiano details the process of enslavement and some elements of the cultural baggage Africans brought with them to the New World. The general outline of these elements must be described in order to understand the nature of acculturation. Acculturation in the United States involved the mutual interaction between two cultures, with Europeans and Africans borrowing from each other. When the African stepped on board a European ship he left all of the artifacts or physical objects of his culture behind him. In Africa, as in most societies, these objects were far less important than values, ideas, relationships, and behavioral patterns.

The similarities between many European and African cultural elements enabled the slave to continue to engage in many traditional activities or to create a synthesis of European and African cultures. In the process of acculturation the slaves made European forms serve African functions. An example of this is religion. Most Africans believed in a Creator, or all-powerful God whom one addressed directly through prayers, sacrifices, rituals, songs, and dances. At the same time, they had a panoply of lesser gods each of whom governed one aspect of life. Publicly supported priests, sacred festivals, funeral rites, dirges and wakes, dances and festivals expressing joy and thanksgiving, sacred objects and images, and charms and amulets for protection against evil spirits were the usual elements found in traditional religions. Funerals were especially important to Africans, and often were expensive, drawn-out affairs involving a long period of mourning and the burial of personal objects with the deceased. All the

23. Vassa, *Narrative,* 71. At this point, Olaudah Equiano's story merges into English and West Indian history. He led an eventful life. Taken to England in 1757, he worked with Granville Sharp to free English slaves and, in 1788, presented a petition to the Queen calling for the abolition of slavery.

friends and relatives of the deceased visited his family for a month after his death, delivered their condolences, and periodically arranged great feasts with much singing, dancing, and drinking to prevent the family from brooding over their loss. The merriment was also indicative of the African belief that upon dying one went "home."[24]

Christian forms were so similar to African religious patterns that it was relatively easy for the early slaves to incorporate them with their traditional practices and beliefs. In America Jehovah replaced the Creator, and Jesus, the Holy Ghost, and the Saints replaced the lesser gods. The Africans preserved many of their sacred ceremonies in the conventional Christian ritual and ceremonies: songs, dances, feasts, festivals, funeral dirges, amulets, prayers, images, and priests. After a few generations the slaves forgot the African deities represented by the Judeo-Christian gods. Still, it was a long time before some blacks completely forgot their gods. One group of Africans, for example, still remembered the names of their tribal deities fifty years after they were brought to Alabama. Whatever the name of the deity they worshipped, in many facets of their religious services the slaves retained many African elements.[25]

The whole question of African survivals in slave culture is so controversial and so limited by inadequate research that one must analyze the primary sources carefully in order to arrive at some tentative conclusions. The debate over this can only be approached by a comparison of African cultural forms with those

24. A. B. Ellis, *The Tshi-Speaking Peoples of the Gold Coast of West Africa* (London, 1887), 9-22, 119-48, 222-43; G. T. Basden, *Among the Ibos in Nigeria* (London, 1966 [1921]), 112-34; David P. Gamble, *The Wolof of Senegambia Together with Notes on the Lebu and the Serer* (London, 1957), 71-72, 102-3; Northcote W. Thomas, *Law and Custom of the Timme and Other Tribes* (London, 1916), 29-40; M. J. Field, *Religion and Medicine of the Ga People* (London, 1937), 4-25.

25. Charles C. Jones, *The Religious Instruction of the Negroes in the United States* (Savannah, 1842), 125; Charles A. Raymond, "The Religious Life of the Negro Slave," *Harper's Magazine* XXVII (Oct. 1863), 676; Zora Neale Hurston, "Cudjo's Own Story of the Last African Slaver," *Journal of Negro History* XII (Oct. 1927), 648-63; Robin Horton, "African Conversion," *Africa* XLI (April 1971), 85-108.

of the antebellum slaves. Whenever the elements of the slave's culture more closely resemble African than European patterns, we can be relatively certain that we have identified African survivals. Because there are so many universals in culture, however, this procedure almost inevitably leads to an understatement of the African survivals. Then, too, since the slaves had to preserve many of the African elements in their master's language, many Africanisms will be missed because the European equivalents are too obscure for the modern ear to detect. On occasion the Africanisms can be established because of the frequency of such elements in slave culture when compared to European culture.

Several aspects of West African culture are so distinctive that it is relatively easy to discover their presence or absence among Southern slaves. Dances, folk tales, music, magic, and language patterns are susceptible to this kind of analysis. Music was central to African culture. Drums, guitars, flutes, piccolos, whistles, and horns were the principal instruments and were played on many occasions. Fast changes in tone, intonation, pitch, timbre, and impromptu variations were characteristic of African songs. Skilled instrumentalists enjoyed a high status, songs accompanied work in the fields and set the pace for rowers. Group participation, improvisation, call and response, rhythmic complexity, and percussions are constant in traditional African music. Often hand clapping or stamping of the feet supply the percussion accompaniment to songs.[26]

Perhaps the most distinctive feature of traditional African music is its rhythmic complexity. In this area the African is far superior to the European. While European music is based characteristically on one rhythm, African tunes often contain three or more patterns. An Englishman who studied traditional African music concluded:

> African rhythm is so complicated that it is exceedingly difficult for a European to analyse it. . . . Broadly speaking, the dif-

26. J. H. K. Nketia, *African Music in Ghana: A Survey of Traditional Forms* (Accra, 1962); W. E. Ward, "Music in the Gold Coast," *Gold Coast Review* II (July-Dec. 1927), 199-223; Ellis, *Tshi,* 325-28; Basden, *Ibos,* 185-93; Gamble, *Wolof,* 76-77.

> ference between African and European rhythms is that whereas any piece of European music has at any one moment one rhythm in common, a piece of African music has always two or three, sometimes as many as four. . . . From this point of view European music is childishly simple. . . .[27]

In traditional African dances there was little separation of sacred and secular performances. Usually held in the open air, the dances were elaborate, exhausting affairs. African dances differed greatly from the traditional, stylized European dance between couples. Instead, women and men danced in separate lines, moving back and forth toward each other. Traditionally, the African dance was one of display, involving "seductive" and rapid movements, and leaping to the furious rhythm of the drum. Sometimes a large group of people would form a circle around two dancers while clapping their hands. On other occasions the dance might involve sinuous movements of the upper torso without moving the feet.[28]

European dances were generally unsuited to the most adulterated African rhythm. The uniqueness of the traditional African dances was indicated by an amazed Englishman among the Ibos:

> The dancers range themselves and begin slow rhythmic movements, unconsciously swaying their heads in time with the music. As the dance proceeds they appear intoxicated with the motion and the music, the speed increases, and the movements become more and more intricate and bewildering. . . . The twistings, turnings, contortions and springing movements executed in perfect time, are wonderful to behold. . . . For these set dances . . . the physical strength required is tremendous. The body movements are extremely difficult and would probably kill a European.[29]

One of the most important cultural forms in West Africa was the folk tale. Throughout the region story-telling was an art form

27. Ward, "Music," 214.
28. Ellis, *Tshi*, 222-43, 325-28; Basden, *Ibos*, 127-34; Gamble, *Wolof*, 76-77.
29. Basden, *Ibos*, 131-32.

including acting, singing, and gestures that served as the favorite evening entertainment. In many ways traditional African folk tales were similar to those found in early European societies in their attempts to explain natural phenomena and various animal traits, giving animals the power of speech and containing gods and heroes, creation legends, magic, witches, and morals. Often accompanied by drums and responses from the audience, West African tales showed that the people valued family ties, children, and knowledge.[30] Animal stories are constant throughout West Africa. The trickster figures—the Nigerian tortoise, the Ghanaian ananse or spider, and the rabbit—are ubiquitous. Congenitally weak, slow moving, or looked down upon by the stronger animals, the tortoise, spider, and rabbit are wise, patient, boastful, mischievous, roguish, guileful, cunning, and they always outwit their stronger foes and triumph over evil.[31]

Regardless of his previous culture, upon landing in the New World the African-born slave had to learn the language of his master. Taught by overseers or native-born slaves, the African acquired a few European words in a relatively casual and haphazard fashion. He began by recognizing his own name and that of his master in his "adopted" language. While they generally had to learn their master's language in order to understand his commands and to communicate with other slaves, many Africans refused to accept a new name.[32] For instance, a Georgia newspaper described two recaptured fugitive slaves in these terms:

30. Elphistone Dayrell, *Folk Stories from Southern Nigeria, West Africa* (London, 1910), vii-xvi, 1-6, 20-38, 64-72; Alta Jablow, ed., *An Anthology of West African Folklore* (n.p., 1962), 29-39; Ellis, *Tshi,* 331-43.

31. William Owens, "Folklore of the Southern Negroes," *Lippincott's Magazine* XX (Dec. 1877), 748-55; Basden, *Ibos,* 278-83; Northcote W. Thomas, *The Ibo-Speaking Peoples of Nigeria* (4 vols., London, 1913), I, 139-40; Amaury Talbot, *Tribes of the Niger Delta* (London, 1932), 336-44; G. T. Basden, *Niger Ibos* (London, 1966 [1938]), 424-36.

32. Allen Walker Read, "The Speech of Negroes in Colonial America," *Journal of Negro History* XXIV (July 1939), 247-58; William R. Bascom, "Acculturation Among the Gullah Negroes," *American Anthropologist* XLIII, n.s. (Jan.-March 1941), 43-50; "Eighteenth Century Slaves as Advertised by Their Masters," *Journal of Negro History* I (April 1916), 163-216.

> Run aways. . . . TWO NEW NEGROE YOUNG FELLOWS; one of them . . . computed eighteen years of age, of the Fallah country, slim made, and calls himself Golaga, the name given him here Abel; the other a black fellow . . . computed seventeen years of age, of the Suroga country, calls himself Abbrom, the name given him here Bennet.[33]

While some remarkable Africans could converse in English after only eight months in the colonies, it took most of the older ones several years to add a few English words to their vocabulary. Children and younger Africans acquired a knowledge of the new language with relative ease. One Maryland native reported in 1822 that a group of African "boys have been three months only among the English and they now speak it better than most of the blacks in these Southern states."[34] If the African had been "seasoned" in the West Indies, he usually arrived in the South with some knowledge of the English language.

Some Africans consistently refused to abandon their linguistic tie with their homeland. Samuel Hall's mother, captured in Liberia, was typical of many stubborn and proud Africans: "The mother would never work after she was sold into slavery, but pined away, never even learning the language of the people of this country."[35] When newly imported Africans were on large plantations where they had little contact with whites and thus little need to use a European language, they were remarkably successful in retaining elements of their native language.[36]

33. Read, "Speech," 251.

34. P. J. Staudenraus, ed., "Victims of the African Slave Trade, A Document," *Journal of Negro History* XLI (April 1956), 149.

35. Samuel Hall, 47 *Years a Slave* (Washington, Iowa, 1912), n.p.

36. John W. DuBose, "Recollections of the Plantations," *Alabama Historical Quarterly* I (Spring 1930), 66; Marcel (W. F. Allen), "Negro Dialect," *Nation* I (Dec. 14, 1865), 744-45; Marguerite B. Hamer, "A Century Before Manumission: Sidelights on Slavery in Mid-Eighteenth Century South Carolina," *North Carolina Historical Review* XVIII (July 1940), 232-36; Albert H. Stoddard, "Origin, Dialect, Beliefs, and Characteristics of the Negroes of the South Carolina and Georgia Coasts," *Georgia Historical Quarterly* XXVIII (Sept. 1944), 186-95; Sarah H. Torian, ed., "Ante-Bellum and War Memories of Mrs. Telfair Hodgson," *Georgia Historical Quarterly* XXVII (Dec. 1943), 350-56; Samuel H. Chester, *Pioneer Days in Arkansas* (Richmond, 1927), 41-42.

The acquisition of European languages was an extremely slow process for the Africans, especially during the seventeenth and eighteenth centuries.[37] Eighteenth-century travelers and clergymen frequently observed that African-born slaves throughout the American colonies did not understand English. The Reverend John Bell of Virginia wrote in 1724 that there were "A great many Black . . . infidels that understand not our language nor me theirs. . . ." The same year the Reverend James Falconer asserted that the adults among the Africans imported into Virginia were "never . . . able either to speak or understand our language perfectly."[38]

As the number of American-born slaves increased, a patois containing English and African words developed in the quarters. For example, the English traveler J. F. D. Smyth in 1773 declared that in conversing with Virginia slaves he could not "understand all of them, as great numbers, being Africans, are incapable of acquiring our language, and at best imperfectly, if at all; many of the others speak a mixed dialect between the Guinea and English."[39]

In many areas this pattern continued well into the nineteenth century. Whites in several states, for example, remembered native Africans who often counted or prayed in their native language and gave African names to some of the objects around them.[40] Joseph Cobb recalled that when African natives in

37. William S. Perry, ed., *Historical Collections Relating to the American Colonial Church* (5 vols., Hartford, 1840), I, 264, 280, 344, IV, 197, 222, 224, 305; James B. Lawrence, "Religious Education of the Negro in the Colony of Georgia," *Georgia Historical Quarterly* XIV (March 1930), 41-57; Marcus W. Jernegan, "Slavery and Conversion in the American Colonies," *American Historical Review* XXI (April 1916), 518-19; Frederick Dalcho, *An Historical Account of the Protestant Episcopal Church, in South Carolina* (Charleston, 1820), 105, 279; Mary F. Goodwin, "Christianizing and Educating the Negroes in Colonial Virginia," *Historical Magazine of the Protestant Episcopal Church* I (Sept. 1932), 144; Edmond Gibson, *Two Letters of the Lord Bishop of London* . . . (London, 1727), 5-6.

38. Perry, *Church*, I, 282, 293.

39. J. F. D. Smyth, "Travels in Virginia in 1773," *Virginia Historical Register* VI (April 1853), 82.

40. Joseph Le Conte, *The Autobiography of Joseph Le Conte* (New York, 1903), 28-30; Henry W. Ravenel, "Recollections of Southern Plantation

Georgia became excited in the 1820s "they would involuntarily slide into the dialect, or rather *lingo* of their native country. . . ." Around 1830 in Maryland, Frederick Douglass found one group of slaves whose language was a patois which was "a mixture of Guinea and everything else you please . . . there were slaves there who had been brought from the coast of Africa. . . . I could scarcely understand them, so broken was their speech."[41]

The survivors of two of the last slave ships to land in the United States, the *Wanderer* (1858) and the *Clotide* (1859), demonstrated the longevity of African languages in the black community. When the anthropologist Charles Montgomery interviewed the survivors of the *Wanderer* in 1895, they gave him a clear portrait of the Africa they had left thirty-seven years earlier. Still using their African names, many of the former slaves recalled the names of their villages, chiefs, and spoke "fluently their native language, and remember much of the life of Africa." From seven Georgia and South Carolina informants, Montgomery recorded the African equivalents of Ninety-one English words, One hundred numerals, and Twenty-nine sentences. The words included zola (love), gooba (peanut), mano (teeth), doky (devil), mauna (baby), and nlilly (cloth). Among the sentences were "Ukola?"—"How do you do?"; Quer quenda?"—"Where are you going?"; and "Vo vonda ngondo"—"Kill that alligator." The 116 Africans imported in the *Clotide* in 1859 came to be known as "Tarkars," and the twentieth-century survivors were often interviewed. Nine of the Africans resided in an area near Mobile, Alabama, in 1913 when they talked with Emma Langdon Roche. Insisting that Roche use their African names when referring to them, the survivors of the *Clotide* still retained many of

Life," *Yale Review* XXV (June 1936), 775-77; "Reminiscences of Charles Seton Hardee," *Georgia Historical Quarterly* XII (June 1928), 158-76.

41. Joseph Cobb, *Mississippi Scenes* (Philadelphia, 1851), 175; Frederick Douglass, *My Bondage and My Freedom* (New York, 1968, [1855]), 76-77; Chester, *Pioneer Days*, 41-42; J. Ralph Jones, "Portraits of Georgia Slaves," *Georgia Review* XXI (Spring 1967), 130; George P. Rawick, ed., *The American Slave: A Composite Autobiography* (31 vols., Westport, Conn., 1972-77), II, pt. 1:30; (Supplement) III, 261, 322, XII, 268-69; New Orleans *Picayune*, Aug. 28, 1840, April 8, 1842.

Figures 10, 11. Survivors of the Slave Yacht "Wanderer"

their African customs and, "Among themselves they speak the Tarkar language."[42]

The center of African linguistic survival was along the Georgia-South Carolina sea coast, where the slaves had little contact with whites. John W. DuBose, a planter in the 1850s, declared that "These low country South Carolina negroes, living through generations of small contact with whites have hardly learned to speak intelligibly. . . . 'Wha um d?' means where is he, she or it to be found? A pronoun or a sex is unknown to them."[43] The South Carolina clergyman and editor William P. Harrison reported that in 1855 there were hundreds of slaves in

42. Charles J. Montgomery, "Survivors from the Cargo of the Negro Slave Yacht *Wanderer*," *American Anthropologist*, n.s. X (Oct. 1908), 611-23; Emma Langdon Roche, *Historic Sketches of the South* (New York, 1914), 125; Appendix II; Tom H. Wells, *The Slave Ship Wanderer* (Athens, Ga., 1968); Hurston "Cudjo," 648-63.

43. DuBose, "Recollections," 66.

the state who "still jabbered unintelligibly in their Gullah and other African dialects."[44]

During the twentieth century, Lorenzo Turner, a brilliant linguist, found in his fifteen-year investigation of the Gullah dialect used by Negroes on the Georgia-South Carolina sea coast that the language patterns of the blacks were African in nature. African equivalents were substituted for such English words as "tooth," "pregnancy," "alcohol," "partridge," "sweet potato," and countless others. The pronunciation of many English words and the word order of sentences were often African. Like many Africans, the Gullahs frequently employed groups of words to form nouns, verbs, adverbs, and adjectives. Thus, they used *day clean* for "dawn," *a-beat-on-iron* for "mechanic," and *to sweet mouth* for "flatter." As late as the 1940s the Gullah blacks all had African personal names and used more than 4000 words from the languages of more than twenty-one African tribes.[45]

In most areas of the South traces of African languages disappeared after two or three generations. As long as fresh Africans were imported during the eighteenth century, however, some African linguistic patterns were retained by blacks even when they spoke English. The end of the African slave trade in the last quarter of the eighteenth and early years of the nineteenth century ended the African-English patois in the quarters—after 1830 in most places.

Other African cultural forms were somewhat more resistant to change than language patterns, especially if they did not diverge greatly from English forms. While most of the nineteenth-century slaves were born in the United States, they maintained contact with Africa in various ways. A number had relatives who had been born in Africa and told them stories of their homeland. Samuel Hall, Charles Ball, and Jacob Stroyer learned much of African customs and languages from their African-born relatives.

44. William P. Harrison, *The Gospel Among the Slaves* (Nashville, 1893), 306.

45. Lorenzo D. Turner, *Africanisms in the Gullah Dialect* (Chicago, 1949).

Others sometimes saw freshly imported Africans in the South in the 1840s and 50s.[46]

Clearly one of the general means by which Africans resisted bondage was by retaining their link with their past. Rather than accept the slaveholder's view of his place in society, the African tried to hold onto the African cultural determinants of his status. Charles Ball, who saw many African-born slaves on his plantation, reported many attempts of this nature. Mohammedan slaves continued to pray to Allah, and other Africans tried to keep alive memories of their religions and customs. One slave who had been a priest supported by his tribe in Africa did everything the overseer required him to do but according to African custom refused to help his wife in any way. Like other Africans, this slave believed that the spirit of an African who died in the United States returned to Africa. When his son died, the former priest buried a small canoe, bow and arrows, meal, a paddle, and a lock of his hair with the body to aid the child's spirit on its journey to Africa. Maintaining their native concept of beauty, many of the Africans never lost their revulsion for white skin and longed for revenge on the whites for their enslavement. African-born slaves sometimes sang their tribal songs and performed tribal dances for the amusement of their masters and fellow slaves. The result of such practices was the survival of many African cultural forms in the South throughout the antebellum period.[47]

One of the African forms most resistant to European culture was the folk tale. An overwhelming majority of the tales of Southern slaves retained the structure and motif of their African

46. Jacob Stroyer, *My Life in the South* (Salem, 1890), 9-20; Charles Ball, *Slavery in the United States: A Narrative of the Life and Adventures of Charles Ball* (Lewiston, Pa., 1836), 1-13; John Brown, *Slave Life in Georgia* (London, 1855), 171-200; Austin Steward, *Twenty-two Years a Slave, and Forty Years a Freeman* (Rochester, N.Y., 1861), 32-51; Douglass, *Bondage*, 76, 90-91.

47. Stroyer, *My Life*, 44-49; Ball, *Adventures*, 1-13, 112-56, 168-205, 245-58; Robert Sutcliff, *Travels in Some Parts of North America. . . .* (York, Eng., 1811), 204; Basil Hall, *Travels in North America. . . .* (3 vols., Philadelphia, 1829), II, 184; "Reminiscences of Charles Hardee," 158-76.

prototypes. Anthropologists, Africanists, and folklorists have found so many parallels and identical tales among Africans and Southern slaves that there can be no doubt that many Southern black folk tales were African in origin. In fact, African scholars have traced many of the slave's folk tales directly to Ghana, Senegal, and Mauritius, and the lore of such African peoples as the Ewe, Wolof, Hausa, Temne, Ashanti, and Ibo.[48]

While many of these tales were brought over to the South, the African element appears most clearly in the animal tales. Among Southern slaves such African animals as lions, elephants, and monkeys were retained in folk tales which often included songs and gestures. One Louisiana tale, "Néléphant avec Baleine," is almost identical to a Senegalese story recorded in 1828 describing how the rabbit outwitted the elephant and the whale. The most notable of the African tales imported with few changes are those of the tortoise and the hare and the tar-baby story.[49] The Ewe story of "Why the Hare Runs Away," for instance, contains the basic element of the tar-baby tale. When the hare tricked the other animals and stole their water they set a trap for him by making an "image" and covering it with bird lime:

> The hare came. . . . He approached the image. . . . The hare saluted the image. The image said nothing.
>
> "Take care," said the hare, "or I will give you a slap."

48. Daniel J. Crowley, "Negro Folklore: An Africanist's View," *Texas Quarterly* V (Autumn 1962), 65-71; A. B. Ellis, "Evolution in Folklore: Some West African Prototypes of the Uncle Remus Stories," *Popular Science Monthly* XLVIII (Nov. 1895), 93-104; A. J. Gerber, "Uncle Remus Traced to the Old World," *Journal of American Folklore* VI (Oct.-Dec. 1963), 245-77; William D. Pierson, "An African Background for American Negro Folktales," *Journal of American Folklore* LXXXIV (April-June 1971), 204-14; D. J. M. Muffett, "Uncle Remus Was a HausaMan?" *Southern Folklore Quarterly* XXXIX (June 1975), 151-66.

49. Alcée Fortier, *Louisiana Folk-Tales* (Boston, 1895); Elizabeth Pringle, *Chronicles of Chicora Wood* (Boston, 1940), 53-55; J. Marion Sims, *The Story of My Life* (New York, 1884), 69-70; Le Conte, *Autobiography*, 28-30; Ravenel, "Recollections," 750; Cobb, *Mississippi*, 175-76; for commentaries from informants themselves about the African origin of the slave tales, see A. M. F. Christensen, *Afro-American Folk Lore; Told Round Cabin Fires on the Sea Islands of South Carolina* (Boston, 1892).

He gave a slap, and his right hand remained fixed in the bird-lime. He slapped with his left hand, and that remained fixed also.

"Oh! oh!," cried he, "let us kick with our feet."

He kicked with his feet. The feet remained fixed, and the hare could not get away. . . .[50]

Another good example of the transfer of African forms is the spiritual. Although European words were used in plantation songs, many of them contained African elements. After reviewing a collection of slave songs published in 1867, anthropologist John F. Szwed concluded: "The church songs and spirituals of the Negroes in the Southern United States closely resemble West African song style, particularly in their strong call-and-response patterns."[51] An earlier student not only compared the slave songs with African ones, she compared her notes with recent arrivals from the continent in the 1890s, and talked to former slaves. She wrote:

During my childhood my observations were centered upon a few very old negroes who came directly from Africa, and upon many others whose parents were African born, and I early came to the conclusion, based upon negro authority, that the greater part of their music, their methods, their scale, their type of thought, their dancing, their patting of feet, their clapping of hands, their grimaces and pantomime, and their gross superstitions came straight from Africa.[52]

According to one old former slave, when she attended antebellum religious services:

I'd jump up dar and den and holler and shout and sing and pat, and dey would all cotch de words and I'd sing it to some old

50. A. B. Ellis, *The Ewe-Speaking Peoples of the Slave Coast of West Africa* (Netherlands, 1966 [1890]), 276-77.

51. John F. Szwed, "Musical Adaptation Among Afro-Americans," *Journal of American Folklore* LXXII (April-June 1969), 115; see also, Alan Lomax, "The Homogeneity of African-Afro-American Musical Style," in John F. Szwed and Norman Whitten, eds., *Afro-American Anthropology* (New York, 1970), 181-201.

52. Jeanette R. Murphy, "The Survival of African Music in America," *Popular Science Monthly* LV (Sept. 1899), 660-61.

shout song I'd heard 'em sing from Africa, and dey'd all take it up and keep at it, and keep a-addin' to it, and den it would be a spiritual.[53]

On rare occasions, African words were retained in the slave songs. The writer Lafcadio Hearn transcribed one of these he heard in 1880 from an old African-born slave in New Orleans which contained the Congolese (Fiot) word "Ouendai" or "ouendé," meaning "to go, to continue, to go on."

Ouendé ouendé, macaya!
Mo pas barrassé, *macaya!*
Ouendé ouendé, macaya!
Mo bois bon divin, *macaya!*
Ouendé ouendé, macaya!
Mo mangé bon poulet, *macaya!*
Ouendé ouendé, macaya!
Mo pas barrassé, *macaya!*
Ouendé ouendé, macaya!
Macaya![54]

The significance of the continuing debate over African survivals in black music is not whether African or European patterns predominate or whether the environment of the plantation was the primary determinant of its character. The very existence of the debate is important in any discussion of acculturation for it proves that there is at least a reasonable possibility that there were some survivals of African forms in slave culture. The sophisticated research of ethno-musicologists, anthropologists, and folklorists, coupled with the evidence in a large number of primary sources, suggests that African culture was much more re-

53. Murphy, "Survival," 662.
54. Henry E. Krehbiel, *Afro-American Folksong* (New York, 1914), 39-40. Hearn's translation:

Go on! go on! *eat enormously!*
I ain't one bit ashamed—*eat outrageously*
Go on! go on! eat prodigiously!
I drink good wine!—*eat ferociously!*
Go on! go on! eat unceasingly!
I eat good chicken—gorging myself!
Go on! go on! etc.

sistant to the bludgeon that was slavery than historians have hitherto suspected.[55] Sometimes retention was facilitated by the adoption of a hands-off policy by planters with African-born slaves. For example, a Florida planter recalled in 1829 that

> About twenty-five years ago, I settled a plantation on St. Johns river, in Florida, with about fifty new African negroes, many of whom I brought from the coast of Africa myself. They were mostly fine young men and women, and nearly in equal numbers. I never interfered with their connubial concerns, nor domestic affairs, but let them regulate these after their own manner. I taught them nothing but what was useful. . . . I encouraged as much as possible dancing, merriment and dress, . . . I never allowed them to visit for fear of bad example, but encouraged the decent neighboring people to participate in their weekly festivity. . . .[56]

In many areas, of course, the master tried to prevent the retention of those African cultural forms which he felt were dangerous to his existence. However much scholars may argue about slave music, it is obvious that the slaveholders recognized its revolutionary potential. Clerics rushed forward to teach the psalms to the slaves in an effort to stamp out "heathen" survivals, and masters tried to restrict the slaves' musical activities to prevent the articulation of discontent. Somewhat more sagacious than their Latin American counterparts, Southern planters tried to prevent the slaves from using musical instruments to signal slave uprisings. South Carolinians, recalling that during the Stono rebellion of 1739 the rebels had used a drum to signal other blacks to join them in killing whites, prohibited slaves from beating drums. Similarly, the Georgia slave code provided, since it was "absolutely necessary to the safety of this province, that slaves be prohibited from using and carrying mischievous and

55. For an excellent illustration of the problems involved in the search for African survivals see Melville J. Herskovits, *The Myth of the Negro Past* (Boston, 1958), and E. Franklin Frazier, *The Negro in the United States* (New York, 1949).

56. Z. Kingsley, *A Treatise on the Patriarchal, Or Co-operative System of Society as It Exists . . . Under the Name of Slavery* (n.p., 1829), 14.

dangerous weapons, or using and keeping drums, horns, or other loud instruments, which may call together or give sign or notice to one another of their wicked designs and intentions. . . ."[57]

In spite of all the restrictions, the slaves were able to draw upon their African heritage to build a strong musical tradition. There is overwhelming evidence of the survival of African song and dance forms in the United States in the nineteenth century. The heyday of African cultural influence on Negro slaves, however, was during the eighteenth century. American clergymen and English missionaries were especially horrified at the "idolatrous dances and revels" of the slaves.[58] Alexander Hewatt described the general pattern when he wrote in 1779 that in Georgia and South Carolina

> the Negroes of that country, a few only excepted, are to this day as great strangers to Christianity, and as much under the influence of Pagan darkness, idolatry and superstition, as they were at their first arrival from Africa. . . . Holidays there are days of idleness, riot, wantonness and excess: in which the slaves assemble together in alarming crowds, for the purposes of dancing, feasting, and merriment.[59]

There were probably more African survivals in the music and dances in Louisiana than in any other area. Apparently Louisianians encouraged this, for in 1817 the City Council of New Orleans set aside a special place for the slaves to dance. Louisiana slaves certainly took advantage of this opportunity and often performed African dances.[60] While in New Orleans in 1808, Christian Schultz found

57. William A. Hotchkiss, comp., *A Codification of the Statute Law of Georgia, Including the English Statutes in Force . . .* (Savannah, 1845), 813; Howell M. Henry, *The Police Control of the Slave in South Carolina* (Emory, Va., 1914), 150.

58. Frank J. Klingberg, *An Appraisal of the Negro in Colonial South Carolina: A Study of Americanization* (Washington, D.C., 1941), 12-18; S. C. Bolton, "South Carolina and the Reverend Francis Le Jau: Southern Society and the Conscience of an Anglican Missionary," *Historical Magazine of the Protestant Episcopal Church* XL (March 1971), 74.

59. Hewatt, *Account*, II, 100, 103.

60. Timothy Flint, *Recollections of the Last Ten Years . . .* (New York, 1968 [1826]), 140; Henry C. Knight, *Letters from the South and West* (Bos-

> . . . twenty different dancing groups of the wretched Africans, collected together to perform their *worship* after the manner of their country. They have their own national music, consisting for the most part of a long kind of narrow drum of various sizes, from two to eight feet in length, three or four of which make a band. The principal dancers or leaders are dressed in a variety of wild and savage fashions, always ornamented with a number of tails of the smaller wild animals. . . . These amusements continue until sunset, when one or two of the city patrole show themselves with their cutlasses, and the crowds immediately disperse.[61]

The best description of the African dances in New Orleans appears in the diary of Benjamin Latrobe, the famous architect. On February 21, 1819, Latrobe saw about 500 slaves assembled in a square, dancing in groups around old men beating cylindrical drums, stringed instruments, and calabashes. The men and women danced in separate groups while singing a response to their leaders. In one group

> A man sung [*sic*] an uncouth song to the dancing which I suppose was in some African language, for it was not French, & the women screamed a detestable burthen on one single note. The allowed amusements of Sunday have, it seems, perpetuated here those of Africa. . . . [62]

Contrary to the pattern elsewhere, many African customs prevailed in Louisiana right down to the eve of the Civil War. Helene Allain reported that she saw performances in the 1850s

---

ton, 1824), 127; Georges J. Joyaux, "Forest's Voyage aux Etats-Unis de l'Amerique en 1831," *Louisiana Historical Quarterly* XXXIX (Oct. 1956), 457-72.

61. Christian Schultz, *Travels on an Inland Voyage* . . . (2 vols., New York, 1810), II, 197; for earlier views, see: Pierre C. Laussat, *Mémoire sur ma vie pendant les annees 1803 et suivantes . . . à la Louisiane* (Pau, 1831), 395; Fortescue Cuming, *Sketches of a Tour to the Western Country* (Pittsburgh, 1810), 333-36; Le Page du Pratz, *Histoire de la Louisiane* . . . (2 vols., Paris, 1758), I, 352.

62. Benjamin Latrobe, *Impressions Respecting New Orleans: Diary and Sketches, 1818-1820* (New York, 1950), 46-51.

almost identical to those described by Schultz and Latrobe in New Orlèans.[63] More than thirty years later, Lafcadio Hearn, a new arrival in New Orleans, wrote of the former slaves:

> Yes, I have seen them dance; but they danced the Congo and sang a purely African song to the accompaniment of a drygoods box beaten with sticks or bones and a drum made by stretching a skin over a flour barrel. That sort of accompaniment and that sort of music you know all about; it is precisely similar to what a score of travellers have described. There are no harmonies—only a furious contretemps. As for the dance—in which the women do not take their feet off the ground—it is as lascivious as is possible. The men dance very differently, like savages, leaping in the air. . . .[64]

As persistent as African customs were in New Orleans, they were not restricted to the Crescent City. They were also prevalent on the plantations in Mississippi and Louisiana. For example, Isaac Holmes reported in 1821:

> In Louisiana, and the state of Mississippi, the slaves have Sunday for a day of recreation, and upon many plantations they dance for several hours during the afternoon. . . . The general movement is in what they call the Congo dance; but their music often consists of nothing more than an excavated piece of wood . . . one end of which is a piece of parchment which covers the hollow part on which they beat; this, and the singing or vociferation of those who are dancing, and of those who surround the dancers, constitute the whole of their harmony.[65]

African dances and songs were also recorded in many other areas of the antebellum South. A North Carolina overseer recalled that the Africans he supervised in 1800 "would begin to sing their native songs" when their work ended. In 1805 a South

63. Helene Allain, *Souvenirs d'Amérique et de France* (Paris, 1883), 171-72; see also: James R. Creecy, *Scenes in the South* (Philadelphia, 1860), 20-21, and William Wells Brown, *My Southern Home* (Boston, 1880), 121-24.

64. Quoted in Krehbiel, *Folksong*, 38.

65. Isaac Holmes, *An Account of the United States of America* . . . (London, 1823), 332; see also: Theodore Pavie, *Souvenirs Atlantiques* . . . (2 vols., Paris, 1833), II, 319-20.

Carolina tutor observed a group of "native Africans . . . [who] gave us a specimen of the sports & amusements with which the benighted & uncivilized children of nature divert themselves. . . . Clapping their hands was their music and distorting their frames into the most unnatural figures and emiting the most hideous noises in their dancing. . . ." A Florida planter reported that his fifty slaves continued their native dances for several years after he brought them from Africa around 1804.[66]

In a number of instances, the slaves used musical instruments similar to those used in Africa. Drums, for example, were often made of a hollowed-out piece of wood with an animal skin stretched over it. While the decorative arts degenerated in the South, the slaves continued to carve figures on top of their stringed instruments, as was the traditional practice in Africa. A number of instruments used by the slaves were clearly African in origin. In the latter half of the eighteenth century, Virginia slaves played a three-stringed banjo-like instrument and a "qua-qua" or drum which resembled the African "molo" (banjo) and the Yoruba drum, the "gudugudu." Fortunately, Benjamin Latrobe made several sketches of the instruments used by the slaves in New Orleans. Two of them are African drums while the others are very similar to the gourd rattles and mandolins found in many African tribes.[67]

There were, of course, several other distinctly African features of the slave's culture. Throughout much of the antebellum period, for instance, blacks modelled their mats, rugs, walking canes, and baskets on African patterns. They sometimes built thatched roofs for their cabins as they had done in Africa. Slaves generally retained their taste for such African foods as peanuts, benne (sesame seeds), yams, rice, and sorghum. The social structure of the quarters also reflected African influences: the most revered slaves were native Africans and aged blacks. Joseph Cobb

66. John S. Bassett, *Slavery in the State of North Carolina* (Baltimore, 1899), 93; Dena J. Epstein, "African Music in British and French America," *Music Quarterly* LIX (Jan. 1973), 85-86; Kingsley, *Treatise*, 14.

67. Basil Davidson, *The African Genius* (Boston, 1969), 167; Latrobe, *Impressions*, 50; Smyth, "Travels," 85; Thomas Jefferson, *Notes on the State of Virginia* (Boston, 1832), 147.

Figure 12
African Drum
from Virginia,
c. 1753

acknowledged this when he reported that the Africans on one Georgia plantation "were treated with marked respect by all the other negroes for miles and miles around." Often the oldest blacks constituted a council of elders who were called upon to settle disputes in the quarters. The slaves also retained the African's worship of nature. Blacks in South Carolina, for example, believed that each spring or fountain of water was inhabited by a guardian spirit, "Cymbee."[68]

The strength and longevity of conjurism and voodooism among the blacks illustrate clearly the African element in their culture. In regard to the conjurer, W. E. B. Du Bois concluded that in spite of slavery

> some traces were retained of the former group life, and the chief remaining institution was the priest or medicine man. He

68. Cobb, *Mississippi,* 173; Ravenel, "Recollections," 775-77; "Reminiscences of Charles Hardee," 165-66; Pringle, *Chronicles,* 53-54; Montgomery, "Survivors," 611-23.

> early appeared on the plantation and found his function as the healer of the sick, the interpreter of the unknown, the comforter of the sorrowing, the supernatural avenger of wrong and the one who rudely, but picturesquely, expressed the longing, disappointment and resentment of a stolen and oppressed people.[69]

In the United States, many African religious rites were fused into one—voodoo. From the whole panoply of African deities, the slaves chose the snake god of the Whydah, Fom, and Ewe. Symbolic of the umbilical cord and the rainbow, the snake embodied the dynamic, changing quality of life. In Africa it was sometimes the god of fertility and the determiner of good and ill fortune. Only by worshipping the god could one invoke his protective spirit. There were many worshippers of the snake god Damballa among both slaves and whites in nineteenth-century Louisiana. The voodoo priests and priestesses, claiming the ability to make masters kind, to harm enemies, to insure love, and to heal the sick, had many devotees and frequently led the allegedly wild orgies of the snake worshippers in their ceremonies on the shores of New Orleans' Lake Pontchartrain throughout the nineteenth century. Although elements of Catholicism were sometimes grafted onto the ancient rites, the basic ingredients of voodoo worship were traceable directly to the African snake cults.[70]

The funeral rite was an African custom much more widespread than voodoo. Because of labor requirements on the plantation, a deceased slave was often buried at night with the rites being held weeks later. The similarity to African practices is unmistakable. For example, Mrs. Telfair Hodgson reported that on her father's Georgia plantation in the 1850s:

69. W. E. B. Du Bois, "The Religion of the American Negro," *New World* IX (Dec. 1900), 618.

70. Lyle Saxon, *Fabulous New Orleans* (New York, 1928), 233-46, 309-22; Werner A. Wegner, "Negro Slavery in New Orleans" (M.A. thesis, Tulane University, 1935), 83-85; Napier Bartlett, *Stories of the Crescent City* (New Orleans, 1869), 100-102; New Orleans *Times*, Oct. 27, 1875; Zora Neale Hurston, "Hoodoo in America," *Journal of American Folk-Lore* XLIV (Oct.-Dec. 1931), 317-417.

Figures 13, 14
Slave Musical Instruments and African Prototypes

a

b

c

d

e

f

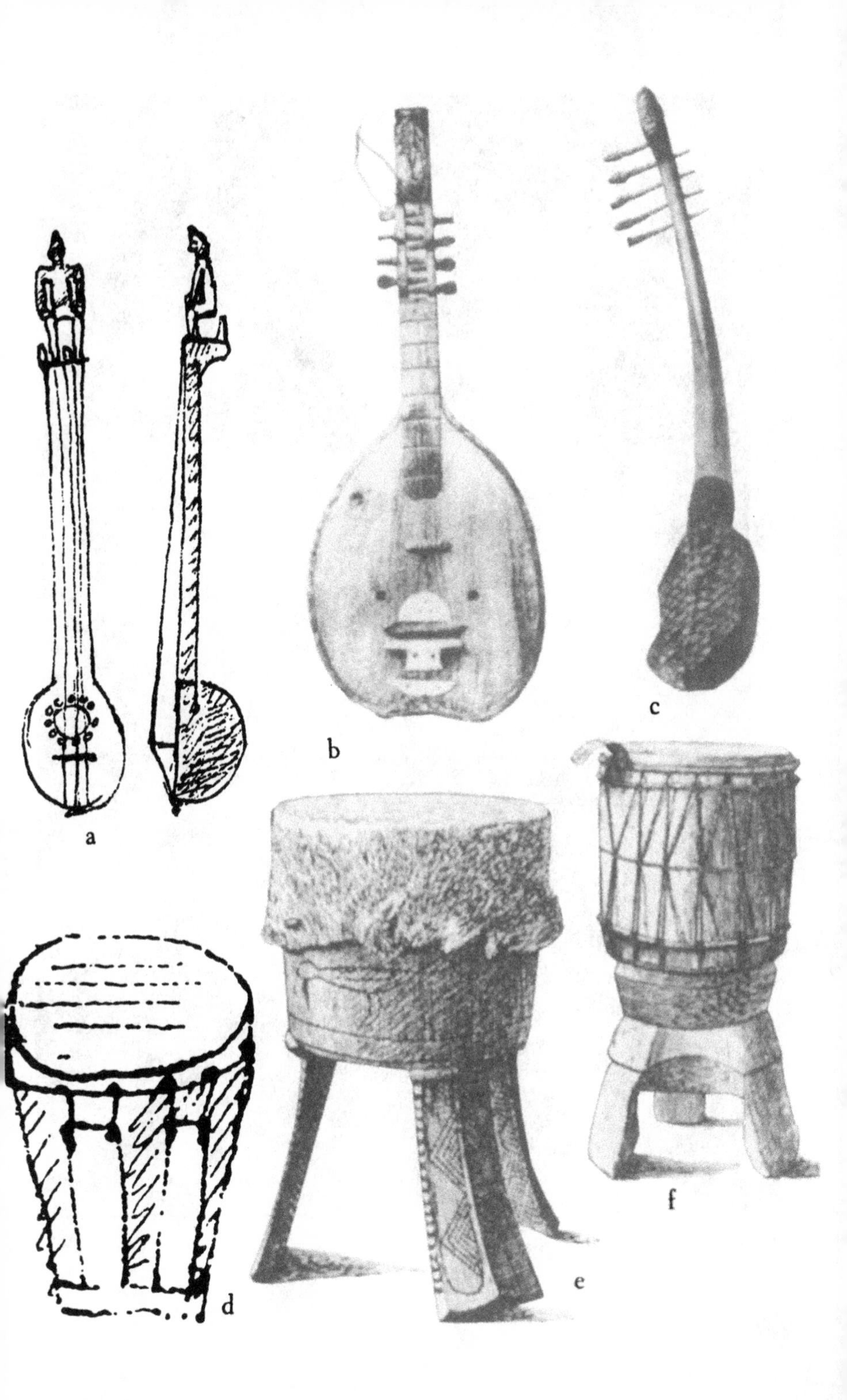
a
b
c
d
e
f

Figure 15. Midnight Slave Funeral

Figure 16
Graveyard of Slaves and Their Descendants at Sunbury, Georgia

> Negro graves were always decorated with the last article used by the departed, and broken pitchers and broken bits of colored glass were considered even more appropriate than the white shells from the beach nearby. Sometimes they carved rude wooden figures like images of idols, and sometimes a patchwork quilt was laid upon the grave.[71]

Not only did Southern slaves decorate graves like their African ancestors, they also retained the practice of celebrating the journey of the deceased to his "home" by dancing, singing, and drinking. According to the traveler Henry Knight, in the Southwest, "When a slave dies, the master gives the rest day, of their [slaves] own choosing, to celebrate the funeral. This, perhaps a month after the corpse is interred, is a jovial day with them; they sing and dance and drink the dead to his new home, which some believe to be in old Guinea."[72]

Even when they were able to maintain some contact with

71. Torian, "Ante-Bellum and War Memories," 352.
72. Knight, *Letters*, 77, 352.

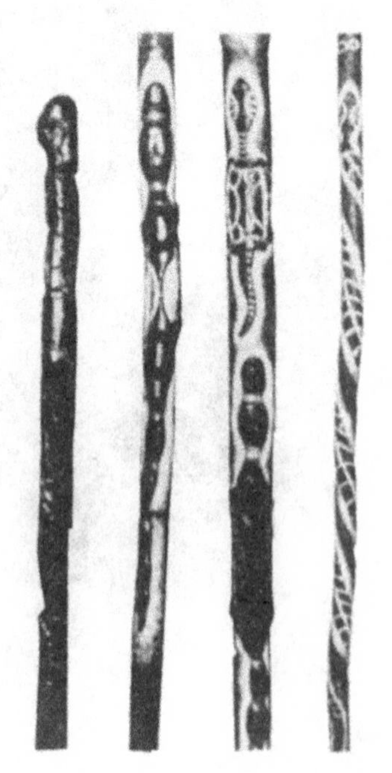

Figure 17
Carvings from the Georgia Coastal Area

their native culture, Africans could rarely escape the psychic shock of bondage. American slavery was so much more cruel than anything they had known in their native lands that some developed suicidal tendencies. Whether they became suicidal or not, however, most African slaves would have agreed with the poetic lament of Olaudah Equiano:

> Well may I say my life has been
> One scene of sorrow and of pain;
> From early days I griefs have known,
> And as I grew my griefs have grown.
>
> Dangers were always in my path,
> And fear of wrath and sometimes death;
> While pale dejection in me reign'd
> I often wept, my grief constrain'd.
>
> When taken from my native land,
> By an unjust and cruel band,

How did uncommon dread prevail!
My sighs no more I could conceal.[73]

In all probability most blacks imported into the American colonies in the seventeenth and early part of the eighteenth century received the same shock as Olaudah Equiano. It is possible, however, to place too much emphasis on this in analyzing the development of the slave's personality. Certainly after the end of the trade in America in the latter half of the eighteenth and early part of the nineteenth century its importance as an explanation of slave personality declines: probably less than 1 million native-born Africans had been brought to the United States before 1807. Since an overwhelming percentage of nineteenth-century Southern slaves were native Americans, they never underwent this kind of shock and were in a position to construct psychological defenses against total dependency on their masters.

All things considered, the few Africans enslaved in seventeenth- and eighteenth-century America appear to have survived their traumatic experiences without becoming abjectly docile, infantile, or submissive. The Africans retained enough manhood to rebel because the Southern plantation was not a rationally organized institution designed to crush every manifestation of individual will or for systematic extermination. The mandatory requirements of the master—labor and obedience—were familiar to the Africans at least in the form of their former occupations and the obeisance they paid to chiefs and elders. Whatever the impact of slavery on their behavior and attitudes, it did not force them to concentrate all of their psychic energy on survival. Once they acquired the language of their master, the Africans learned that their labors, and therefore their lives, were of considerable value. As a result, they were assured of the bare minimum of food, shelter, and clothing. Although provisions were often inadequate and led to many complaints from slaves, they survived.

The most remarkable aspect of the whole process of enslavement is the extent to which the American-born slaves were able to retain their ancestors' culture. While the continuation of the

73. Vassa, *Narrative*, 290.

African slave trade in the nineteenth century to Latin America permitted slaves there to maintain, to a certain degree, the purity of African cultural forms, the discontinuation of the trade to United States severely limited the contacts American slaves had with Africans and led to much adulteration of African cultural forms. Even so, and in spite of his disadvantages when compared with his Latin American counterpart, the American slave was able to retain many African cultural elements and an emotional contact with his motherland. This contact, however tenuous, enabled the slave to link European and African forms to create a distinctive culture, and to contribute to his master's culture.

2

The Americanization of the Slave and the Africanization of the South

Southern whites cannot walk, talk, sing, conceive of laws or justice, think of sex, love, the family or freedom without responding to the presence of the Negroes.

Ralph Ellison

Much of the debate about American slavery has centered on the question of the extent of the acculturation of the African, how and when he became Americanized. Though few scholars have realized it, the Americanization of the African in the South was a process similar in many ways to the acculturation of slaves in other places where bondsmen, black and white, influenced and were influenced by their enslavers. The key determinants in the acculturation of bondsmen historically have been the length of their servitude, the parallels between their culture and that of their masters, the role of the masters' governmental and religious leaders in protecting, training, and converting the slaves to their faith, and the treatment and labor of the bondsmen. Ignoring most of these factors, historians have been confused about the manner in which the African slave in the South became an American and contributed to his master's culture. One way of clearing up some of the confusion is to compare the acculturation of the Southern bondsmen with that of Africans in Latin America and Europeans and American whites enslaved in Africa.

From the eighth to the nineteenth century hundreds of thousands of Europeans were enslaved by Arabs, Turks, and West

Africans. European servitude to the Moslems began when Arabs from North Africa launched their campaign to conquer the Iberian peninsular in 711. After the expulsion of the Arabs from the Iberian peninsular in the fifteenth century, Moslems frequently raided the coasts of Spain, Portugal, Italy, Greece, France, England, Ireland, and Iceland and the islands of Sicily, Sardinia, Corsica, and Cyprus, sacked their towns and carried their inhabitants back to North Africa, where they were enslaved because they were "infidels." Most of the white slaves were Spaniards, Portuguese, and Italians captured during the centuries-long religious wars waged by the Moslems and the Christians in all the lands bordering on the Mediterranean Sea. Thousands more Europeans and Americans, shipwrecked on the North and West African coasts or captured by Arab privateers at sea, were also enslaved. Estimates of the number of whites enslaved range between 500,000 and one million. But since Christians and Moslems representing many nations frequently exchanged slaves, captured and recaptured each other's territory, and carried on a brisk business in ransoms, it is difficult to determine the total number of white slaves in Africa at any given place or time. The best figures we have are for Algiers, where during the sixteenth and seventeenth centuries there were between 25,000 and 40,000 white slaves. Whatever the number of whites enslaved, the primary reason historians are able to document their story was the Arab practice of ransoming Christian bondsmen. Fortunately for scholars, those whites who recovered their freedom often wrote narratives, letters and petitions, and gave interviews and depositions describing their enslavement.[1]

Terrified by their Arab captors (and fearing they would be eaten by them), whites who were shipwrecked on the North African coast initially suffered greatly from hunger and thirst.

1. Stephen Clissold, *The Barbary Slaves* (London, 1977), 1-38; Stanley Lane-Poole, *The Barbary Corsairs* (New York, 1901), 195-225, 235-73; H. G. Barnby, *The Prisoners of Algiers* (London, 1966), 1-57. It should be noted that the Europeans enslaved thousands of Moslems in the same fashion as the Christians were enslaved.

When they had to march through the desert to the camps of nomadic Bedouin tribesmen, many of the white slaves died as they struggled to adapt quickly to a strange diet consisting of boiled rice, roasted snails and locusts, and the milk, blood, entrails, and dung of camels, or became so thirsty they had to drink their own urine or that of camels. Stripped of their clothes and shoes, exposed for long periods of time to the burning sun and with their feet bleeding from walking over the rocks and sand, the whites were customarily called "fonta" (bad), and often spat upon, stoned, beaten, and killed by the Arabs during the first weeks of their captivity. After a few weeks in the desert, the captives turned into dehydrated, dysentery-racked, emaciated walking skeletons. The toll the desert and harsh treatment exacted is revealed clearly in the case of the American ship captain James Riley. The three months Riley spent as a slave of Bedouin tribesmen in the Sahara in 1815 caused his weight to fall from 240 to 90 pounds. Occasionally the captives were so hungry they developed cannibalistic tendencies.[2]

The whites shipwrecked off the West African coast usually were treated less brutally by their black captors than were whites captured by the Arabs. Though often suffering more mental anguish because of the strange color and culture of their black masters, the whites found themselves in a less forbidding environment than the Sahara desert. The relatively mild treatment of white bondsmen in West Africa was due primarily to the abundance of food, the nature of West African slavery, and the infrequent contacts the blacks had with Caucasians. In fact, the Caucasians were enslaved as much to satisfy the African's curiosity about their strange white skin as for their labor. Robert Adams, an American sailor enslaved for several months in Tim-

2. James Riley, *Loss of the American Brig Commerce* (London, 1817), 57-160, 334-35; Viletta Laranda, *Interesting Narrative of the Captivity and Sufferings of Miss Viletta Laranda* (New York, 1830), 6-22; Eliza Bradley, *An Authentic Narrative of the Shipwreck and Sufferings of Mrs. Eliza Bradley* (Boston, 1821), 13-48; M. De Brisson, *An Account of the Shipwreck and Captivity of M. De Brisson* (London, 1789), 10-59; *Voyages to the Coast of Africa, by Messrs. Saugnier and Brisson* (London, 1792), 1-27.

buctoo in 1810, recalled that he was treated kindly and was such an object of curiosity that he was kept as a slave in the king's palace to entertain him and his guests.[3]

Whites captured on the high seas by Arab privateers suffered a far different fate from Robert Adams's. The first shock for the European sailors and passengers came with the pursuit, roar of cannons, and armed sailors from the corsairs boarding their ship, looting it, and beating and stripping them of most of their clothing. Transferred to the privateer, the whites were frequently locked in its small hold, where they suffered from the stifling heat and the attack of vermin. Given one meal every 24 hours and one daily ration of putrid water during their one- to four-week journey to the North African coast, the whites were apprehensive upon reaching the port and frightened by the people who thronged around them when they landed. After condemnation as slaves by a local Admiralty Court, the bare-footed, half-naked captives were marched repeatedly through the city and exhibited at the slave auctions. Forced to run to and fro to demonstrate their stamina while being auctioned, the captives were compelled to let potential purchasers inspect them, while women were taken into private compartments, where they were stripped naked, fondled, and sometimes examined to determine their virginity. After being auctioned off to the highest bidder, poor and unskilled captives were confined in large semi-dark prisons or bagnios, shackled, given a small ration of bread, beans, olives, and vegetable soup, and forced to sleep on stone floors. By the eighteenth century the bagnios often contained taverns and chapels and had Christian corporals, who maintained order and assigned work.[4]

3. Robert Adams, *The Narrative of Robert Adams, a Sailor Who Was Wrecked on the Western Coast of Africa in the Year 1810* (London, 1816), 21-24. For an account of the life of white slaves in East Africa, see Robert Drury, *Madagascar; or, Robert Drury's Journal, During Fifteen Years' Captivity on That Island* (London, 1890).

4. Joshua Gee, *Narrative of Joshua Gee of Boston Mass., While He Was Captive in Algeria of the Barbary Pirates, 1680-1687* (Hartford, Conn., 1943), 7-22; Howell Price, *A Genuine Account of the Life and Transactions of the Howell ap David Price, Gentleman of Wales* (London, 1752), 1-21; Clissold,

Feeling outraged, ashamed, and guilty, the white slaves began immediately after their capture praying that they would soon be ransomed or rescued. During the early months of their captivity the whites became more religious. Whenever possible they bribed their captors (often with promises of a larger ransom) to let them retain their Bibles. Though forced to fight camels and dogs for food and water, the whites delighted in conversing with fellow Christians. Mostly, however, the white slaves prayed for deliverance; they repeated a few Bible verses constantly: "He made them also to be pitied of all those that carried them captives." "And I will deliver thee out of the hand of the wicked, and I will redeem thee out of the hand of the terrible."[5]

The initial shock of enslavement changed to deep depression under the constant insults of and whippings from the Arabs, the necessity to steal food and to give deference to their captors. As days stretched into months and his fellow slaves died (to be buried unceremoniously) or were branded and bastinadoed (beaten on the feet), the white slave almost went insane. The captives found it difficult to sleep and were plagued with horrifying nightmares about their harsh treatment. Suicide weighed heavily on their minds. Occasionally, while in "the fierce paroxysms of frantic despair," the captives took their own lives. The companionship of fellow Christians was a key element in sustaining the spirit of the white slave. But as his comrades were sold or killed, the white captive gave up any ideas of trying to escape and became more resigned to his fate. M. De Brisson, enslaved in 1785, wrote that after all of his ship mates died: "I was now the only slave in this clan; not a soul was left to sympathize with me in my misfortunes. My situation became every day more deplorable; yet I resolved to steel myself to the sense of it." A Welshman, David Price, recalled that a short time after his enslavement he tried to convince himself there was little differ-

---

Barbary Slaves, 31-68; Barnby, *Prisoners*, 1-57; Filippo Pananti, *Narrative of a Residence in Algiers* (London, 1818), 31-68; John Foss, *A Journal of the Captivity and Sufferings of John Foss* (Newburyport, Mass., 1798), 4-18.

5. Laranda, *Narrative*, 8-17; Bradley, *Narrative*, 22, 32, 37, 41-42, 47-50, 54-60; Gee, *Narrative*, 16-17, 25-27; Psalms, 106:46; Jeremiah, 15:21.

Figure 18. Landing of White Slaves

ence between freedom and slavery: "What is it to me . . . whether I am esteemed a Slave, or a Freeman? The Freeman being as much a Slave to his Business, as myself; I am no more a Slave to mine, than he is."[6]

The white slaves tried desperately to get to port cities in an effort to facilitate their redemption. In Tangiers, Algiers, Tunis, and Tripoli they often found consuls, merchants, ambassadors, and clerics from their country and Jewish merchants who contacted their families, governments, or co-religionists and arranged the payment of their ransoms. The port cities were also attractive because there were more white slaves in them than in the countryside as well as a more plentiful supply of food and water. Consequently, those whites captured by Arab privateers considered themselves more fortunate than those who spent much of their captivity in the desert.[7]

Ordinarily, white slaves labored as domestic servants, stevedores, porters, sailors, shepherds, and in stone quarries, fields, and gardens. They constructed buildings, cleaned sewers, and until the seventeenth century rowed the dreaded Arab galleys. Christian slaves on the galleys, often chained to their oars, were repeatedly flogged and usually fed inadequately. For most of the period under review, white slaves also served as soldiers, secretaries, clerks, and civil servants. Skilled slaves hired their time of their masters and often earned enough money to purchase their freedom. The treatment of the slaves varied considerably. Those serving on galleys, on public works or as bondsmen of the Sultan of Morocco or the nomadic Bedouin tribes in the desert fared

6. De Brisson, *Account*, 77; Price, *Account*, 22; see also: Bradley, *Narrative*, 37, 48-50; Riley, *Loss*, 82, 90, 106-7; Laranda, *Narrative*, 8-18; G. S. F. Pfeiffer, *The Voyages and Five Years' Captivity in Algiers, of Doctor G. S. F. Pfeiffer* (Harrisburg, Pa., 1836), 96, 116; De Brisson, *Account*, 33-44, 59-70, 80.

7. Bradley, *Narrative*, 65-66; Riley, *Loss*, 110-60, 301-30; Clissold, *Barbary Slaves*, 102-48; *Gentleman's Magazine* XVIII (1748), 413, 440, 482, 530, XIX (1749), 3, 142, 561. Catholics were among the most active groups redeeming Christian slaves: in 1198 the Order of the Most Holy Trinity for the Ransom of Captives was founded and around 1218 the Order of Our Lady of Mercy was organized primarily for the purpose of ransoming the captives in North Africa.

worst and had the highest mortality rates. Sometimes the white slaves were yoked to ploughs and worked under brutal overseers and drivers. The slaves were, however, freed of labor on Fridays, and many of them ended their work three hours before sunset. White slaves in supervisory positions, such as the corporals in the bagnios, obtained the best food, clothing, and lodging by informing on their fellows and extorting favors from them. Domestic servants of wealthy masters frequently performed little work and received money from them. Pious Moslems usually observed the injunction of the Koran to treat slaves with kindness. But regardless of the kindness of their owners, Christian bondsmen were deferential to all Arabs, frequently prostrating themselves before or kissing the feet of their masters, and moving off streets and paths when Moslems passed by. The white slave who even brushed against an Arab might be summarily beaten or killed because he was considered unclean.[8]

The greatest variety in treatment prevailed in the case of women and children. Among the Bedouins neither sex nor age relieved the captives of cruelty. It was different, however, in Arab port cities. White women who were not ransomed were added to the harems of their masters. Initially, in expectation of higher ransoms for the women or looking forward to adding them to their harems, Arab masters exacted little labor from white females. Later, those not added to harems were imprisoned or put to regular work (sewing, milking, washing, sweeping, etc.). Youthful captives were taken into Arab households, taught Islamic doctrines, and assigned as playmates for their young masters. As the girls matured they joined harems, while many of the boys were brutally sodomized and often became homosexual concubines.[9]

Regardless of the tasks they performed, the white slaves in North Africa were almost always subject to insult, arbitrary pun-

8. Pfeiffer, *Voyages*, 84-88, 95-158; Gee, *Narrative*, 16-19, 23-24; Clissold, *Barbary Slaves*, 41-68; Thomas Pellow, *The Adventures of Thomas Pellow* (London, 1890), 68-71; Foss, *Journal*, 18-25, 28-30; Pananti, *Narrative*, 88-93. For an overview of Arab slavery, see Allan G. B. Fisher and Humphrey J. Fisher, *Slavery and Muslim Society in Africa* (Garden City, N.Y., 1970).

9. Clissold, *Barbary Slaves*, 8, 40-43, 90, 121-22; Pellow, *Adventures*, 53-68.

Figure 19
Sultan
of Morocco,
c. 1670

ishment, and pressures to convert to Islam. Writing from Morocco in 1748, a British captive described the typical experience of many Christians enslaved by the Arabs. The crew and passengers were captured after their ship sank off the Moroccan coast in 1746 and "many were murdered, and the major part of us, after the difficulty of saving our lives, were stript naked, and since sent to the emperor of *Moroco,* who has been pleased to use us much worse than any of his slaves (which he has of several other nations) obliging us to keep at hard labour, whilst the christians aforesaid were unemployed; wherefore 28 of our countrymen turned *Moors,* not being able to undergo the fatigues which we have undergone. . . ."[10]

Like the twenty-eight Englishmen, between 50 and 75 per

10. *Gentleman's Magazine* XIX (1749), 3.

Figure 20. Punishment of White Slaves

cent of the Christian slaves converted to Islam, some with great rapidity. When the religious wars between the Moslems and the Christians were at their height, the Arabs went to great lengths to convert their captives. Since Arabs frowned on marriage to Christians, they tried to convert white women quickly in order to add them to their harems. An overwhelming majority of the captives who converted to Islam did so relatively soon after their capture because they were subjected to such cruel punishment to make them declare: "There is no God but God, and Mohamet is his prophet."[11] Thomas Pellow, who was enslaved in Morocco for twenty-three years, reported that soon after his capture in 1715 his master began trying to force him to become a Moslem. Then eleven years old, Pellow initially refused to convert on the offer of a horse. Consequently,

> [my master] committed me prisoner to one of his own rooms, keeping me there several months in irons, and every day most severely bastinading me, and furiously screaming in the Moorish language "Shehed, Shehed! Cunmoora, Cunmoora!" in English, "Turn Moor! turn Moor!" by holding up your finger. . . . [My refusal made] my accursed master more and more enraged, and my . . . tortures were now exceedingly increased, burning my flesh off my bones by fire; which the tyrant did, by frequent repetitions, after a most cruel manner; insomuch, that through my so very acute pains, I was at last constrained to submit. . . .[12]

Most of the captives were not as strong as Pellow; they quickly converted to Islam, and in the case of men had their heads shaved, were circumcised, assumed Moslem names, and then received a sumptuous meal to celebrate their conversion. The older more pious Christians often refused, however, to commit apostasy. They maintained their faith for many years, especially

11. Pfeiffer, *Voyages*, 151-58; De Brisson, *Account*, 54, 71; Clissold, *Barbary Slaves*, 86-101; Joseph Pitts, *Account of the Religion and Manners of the Mahommetans* (Exeter, 1704), 13-14. Since they were adherents of a proselytizing religion similar to Islam, Europeans also used force to compel captured Arabs to convert to Christianity.

12. Pellow, *Adventures*, 54-55.

when they had Moslem masters who made half-hearted attempts to convert them, when they lived in port cities where the Arabs allowed the Christians to build and staff a few chapels, or as long as they believed they would be rescued from their captivity. The more tolerant Arab masters allowed the white slaves to retain their Bibles, attend the chapels, and to celebrate the Christian holy days. These practices, along with the refusal of most masters systematically to teach the Christian slaves Arabic before trying to convert them, weakened the initial impact of conversion on the white slaves. With the exception of whites enslaved when they were very young, the Christians received little or no instruction in Islamic doctrine before or after their conversion. The consequence was that a majority of the converts were nominal Moslems, conforming publicly to Islamic practice while continuing for years to hold their Christian beliefs and to pray secretly to their God. Threatened with excommunication and eternal damnation of his soul by the Church, and a death sentence from the Inquisition if redeemed, the Christian apostate lived on the horns of a dilemma. If caught repeating Christian dogma by his Arab masters, he was executed for recanting his Moslem faith. When he did not remember enough Christian doctrines to prove he had not left the fold he faced the same fate upon his redemption. The narrow choices open to the Christian converts to Islam led many of them to become sincere practicing Moslems. Some joined Moslem religious orders and became renowned Islamic scholars. Many of the white slaves learned enough about Islam to see the ways it paralleled Christian doctrine and gradually grafted Moslem ideas and practices onto Christian ones as they mastered Arabic.[13]

Conversion to Islam led either to freedom or to a lightening of the burdens on the white slave. Described as renegades by their fellow captives, the Islamic whites often formed part of the crews, piloted, and commanded the Arab privateers which captured the Christians. Sometimes the renegades led the Arab slave

13. See note 11 above; William Okeley, *Eben-Ezer; or, a Small Monument of Great Mercy* (London, 1675), 24-25, 28-30.

raids on the European coast. Both the renegades and those captives who remained Christians participated in the process of acculturation. They taught the Arabs European technological skills and languages. After five to seven years of captivity the white slaves learned to like Arab food and customs and began speaking a patois made up of Arabic and their native language.[14]

The acculturation of the white captives, despite numerous European survivals in their culture, symbolized the mark bondage had made on them. Within a few years after their capture, the world the white bondsmen had known began to recede from their minds, and the degradation of slavery forced them to adopt new behavioral patterns. In the bagnios and slave quarters, strength and guile replaced rank and wealth as the keys to status and survival. Many of the captives became addicted to drink and theft. Though pious Moslems were prohibited from imbibing alcoholic beverages, they encouraged alcoholism among the Christians because Arabs felt the Europeans would be unhappy and sickly without alcohol (especially brandy, which they gave licenses to the Christians to make). As a consequence, most of the taverns in Arab port cities were located in the bagnios. The white slaves' frequently noted addiction to theft was a result of the inadequate food they received and Arab toleration of their dishonesty. In effect, Christian thievery was a self-fiulfilling prophecy: the Arabs constantly told them they were inferior and naturally dishonest. Whether or not they were alcoholics or thieves, many of the white slaves became callous and identified with their masters. Occasionally, old slaves made fun of new captives, the strong exploited the weak, and many informed on their fellows to curry favor with their masters.[15] A Frenchman reported, for instance, that the aged Christian slaves who worked in the bagnios during his captivity in the eighteenth century

14. Riley, *Loss*, 86-87, 113; De Brisson, *Account*, 10; Bradley, *Narrative*, 45-46, 51-52; Pfeiffer, *Voyages*, 76, 84-88, 95-101, 143, 226; Price, *Account*, 36; Laranda, *Narrative*, 22; Clissold, *Barbary Slaves*, 86-101.

15. Pfeiffer, *Voyages*, 84-85, 88-95, 226; Clissold, *Barbary Slaves*, 52-68, 86-101; Pananti, *Narrative*, 68-69, 94-95; Okeley, *Eben-Ezer*, 21.

were "the slaves of the other slaves who, driven by oppression almost to madness, wreak their vengeance on the old men, spitting in their faces, striking them, or pelting them with stones."[16]

Mass escapes and rebellions among the white slaves were rare. Unarmed, ignorant of the geography of Africa, and unable to converse with his fellows, who spoke a multitude of European languages, the white captive found it difficult to act in concert with other Christians. Indeed, it was not uncommon for Christian slaves representing different nationalities and denominations to engage in bloody brawls in the bagnios and streets. Rather than joining in mass-escape attempts, often the white slave accepted his lot while hoping to be rescued or ransomed. The few sporadic mass-escape attempts usually ended in failure, punishment, and death. Still, there were many captives who resisted individually and in concert. Undoubtedly the most notable of the rebels was the famous Spanish novelist Miguel de Cervantes, who often conspired with fellow slaves and tried to escape several times from Algiers after his enslavement in 1575. The future author of *Don Quixote* was ransomed in 1580.[17]

The thousands of Christian slaves who neither escaped nor were ransomed lived out their lives as islamized whites, eventually forgetting much of their native language and culture. Their children would know little but Arab civilization. Sometimes, even a few years of slavery led whites to adopt many features of their captors' culture.[18] Robert Adams, the American sailor shipwrecked in 1810, was a slave both of the West Africans in the city of Timbuctoo and of the Arabs. Three years and seven months after his shipwreck, Adams was ransomed by a Mr. Dupuis, who wrote that the American freedman had been so thoroughly acculturated by his successive masters that

16. P. J. Dumont, *Histoire de l'esclavage en Afrique* (Paris, 1819), 11.

17. De Brisson, *Account*, 83-85; Pfeiffer, *Voyages*, 85-95; Gee, *Narrative*, 21-22; Price, *Account*, 32; Clissold, *Barbary Slaves*, 69-85; Pellow, *Adventures*, 154-75, 231-312; Foss, *Journal*, 25.

18. John Newton, *The Life of the Rev. John Newton* (New York, 1840); 49-62; Pellow, *Adventures*, 34; Drury, *Madagascar*, 79-80, 167-72, 192, 197-98, 210, 229-33, 293, 302-13.

> The appearance, features and dress of this man upon his arrival . . . so perfectly resembled those of an Arab . . . that I had difficulty at first in believing him to be a Christian. When I spoke to him in English, he answered me in a mixture of Arabic and broken English, and sometimes in Arabic only. At this early period I could not help remarking that his pronunciation of Arabic resembled that of a Negro. . . . Like most other Christians after a long captivity and severe treatment among the Arabs, he appeared upon his first arrival, exceedingly stupid and insensible; . . . the only strong feeling which he expressed respecting . . . [Timbuctoo] was that of dread, with which some of the Negroes had inspired him, who, he said, were sorcerers, and possessed the power of destroying their enemies by witchcraft.[19]

Occasionally, white captives were so thoroughly acculturated they refused to be ransomed or found it impossible to readjust to European society after living among the Arabs and West Africans.[20]

The degree of islamization of the white captives depended on the length of their enslavement, treatment while in bondage, age, association with other slaves from their country, and the proselytizing zeal of their masters. An impressive number of the white captives were able to resist the absorption of Arabic culture because their enslavement was so short. They were among the fortunate whites who were ransomed.

African slaves brought to the Americas could not look forward to being ransomed. Though they behaved like the ransomed white slaves during the first years of their captivity, an overwhelming majority of the Africans enslaved in the Americas had to make the kinds of adjustments the white slaves for life did in Africa: learning their captors' language, adopting much of their

19. Adams, *Narrative*, xxiii-xxv.

20. Clissold, *Barbary Slaves*, 88; William Ray, *Horrors of Slavery: or, the American Tars in Tripoli* (Troy, N.Y., 1808), 111, 114, 158-59; Judah Paddock, *A Narrative of the Shipwreck of the Ship Oswego* (New York, 1818), 105, 107, 300-301.

Figure 21. Ransom of White Slaves

culture, and accepting their God. As was the case with the white slave in Africa, the rate of acculturation of the African in the Americas varied with time, place, and numerous other factors. The relative homogeneity of Arabic culture in North Africa was not, however, duplicated in the Americas. Consequently, the pace of acculturation of the Africans was different in various parts of the New World. There was an especially marked difference between Latin America and the United States.

Compared with his Latin American brother, the Southern slave retained relatively few Africanisms in his music, language, dances, and religion. Two factors largely account for the faster rate of and more complete acculturation of Southern slaves. First, the African slave trade ended earlier in the United States than in much of Latin America. Second, Southern churches were far more interested and successful in providing religious instruction for slaves than was the Latin American Catholic Church. Overwhelmingly Protestant, democratic, and evangelical, Southern churches enjoyed many advantages over the autocratic, formalistic, politicized Latin American Catholic Church in their attempt to convert the slaves to Christianity.

The Catholic Church, like many other colonial institutions in Latin America, was weak, under-manned, and overburdened. The Church was an instrument of conquest, colonization, and governance in colonial Latin America. Subject to the supervision of the State, it often served as a bureau of the royal government: the Church created and managed schools, hospitals, and asylums; it pushed back the frontier and pacified the Indians, censored books, and administered justice. Unable to build churches, establish parish boundaries, embark on missionary activity, choose its own leaders, criticize local officials, collect tithes, or instruct slaves without the approval of the Crown, the Latin American Church was constantly embroiled in bitter, energy-sapping controversies with royal officials, the Pope, and Spanish and Portuguese bishops over patronage, doctrine, and governance.[21] Even

21. E. Bradford Burns, *A History of Brazil* (New York, 1900), 27-54, 158; Clarence H. Haring, *The Spanish Empire in America* (New York, 1947), 166-93; J. Lloyd Meacham, *Church and State In Latin America* (Chapel Hill,

with the best of intentions, the Church's relation with the state severely restricted its contact with and impact on blacks.

By royal decree and philosophical commitment, the major focus of the Latin American Catholic Church's missionary activity and interest in promoting social welfare was the Indian. Beginning with De Las Casas's successful plea for the humane treatment of Indians and the substitution of black bondsmen for red ones, the Catholic Church was preoccupied with freeing those Indians who had been enslaved, and christianizing them. Consistently supported by Spanish and Portuguese monarchs, the Latin American clergy translated Indian languages, wrote incomparable descriptions of Indian culture, fought against white encroachment of Indian lands and barbaric exploitation of their labor.[22]

Never did the Catholic Church anywhere in Latin America manifest the same apostolic fervor, offer the same protection, or devote the same resources to blacks as it did to Indians. At the same time the clergymen were trying to prevent the exploitation of Indians, they were joining the crews of Portuguese and Spanish slave ships bound for Africa. Not only did the priests bless the enterprises, they also baptized the slaves on the shores of Africa in a Latin ceremony understood by neither the whites nor the blacks. While the newly imported Africans were to receive regular, systematic religious instruction after they arrived in the colonies, there is little evidence that they did once the Atlantic slave trade reached sizable proportions. As long as the slave population was relatively small, the Church achieved some success in interceding with planters, guaranteeing the humane treatment of slaves and their religious instruction.[23] But as the capitalistic

---

1966), 3-37; Richard E. Greenleaf, ed., *The Roman Catholic Church in Colonial Latin America* (New York, 1971), 1-31.

22. *Greater America: Essays in Honor of Herbert Eugene Bolton* (Los Angeles, 1945), 125-97; William F. Sharp, *Slavery on the Spanish Frontier: The Columbian Choco, 1680-1810* (Norman, Okla., 1976), 98-110; Haring, *Spanish Empire*, 171-74, 182-88; Burns, *Brazil*, 27-37; 53-54; Greenleaf, *Catholic Church*, 13, 21, 31; Frederic B. Pike, ed., *The Conflict Between Church and State in Latin America* (New York, 1964), 90-97.

23. Herbert S. Klein, *Slavery in the Americas: A Comparative Study of*

exploitation of sugar, coffee, and the mine expanded on the base of a large slave population, the balance of power shifted to the master. The more the slaveholders complained about the interference of priests, or expressed their fear that religious instruction would lead slaves to feel first that they were equal to whites and later encourage them to rebel, the more the Spanish and Portuguese monarchs turned a deaf ear to the Church. By the nineteenth century, Catholic humanism had lost its battle with colonial materialism.

Long before the nineteenth century, however, the centralized, monolithic structure that was the Catholic Church had itself succumbed to materialism. A privileged, wealthy, corporate institution, the Catholic Church was too interested in the economic success of Latin American planters to interfere with their absolute control of bondsmen. The Catholic Church was one of the planter's major bankers, holding a large number of the mortgages on slaves and plantations. Then, too, through bequests and purchases, the Catholic Church became the owner of thousands of slaves.

Rather than increasing its interest in the plight of the bondsmen, the Church capitulated to planter demands and ideology from the eighteenth century on. Consequently, nineteenth-century Latin American slaves were as likely to hear priests urging them to obey their masters, be submissive, and to accept earthly tribulations in expectation of Heavenly rewards as were Virginia bondsmen.[24] The priests preached to the slave humility, orderliness, and resignation. A Brazilian priest, arguing that "confession is the antidote to slave insurrections," taught the

---

Virginia and Cuba (Chicago, 1967), 87-105; Frederick P. Bowser, *The African Slave in Colonial Peru, 1524-1650* (Stanford, 1974), 233-37.

24. Robert Conrad, *The Destruction of Brazilian Slavery, 1850-1888* (Los Angeles, 1972), 13, 75-76, 112-13; John V. Lombardi, *The Decline and Abolition of Negro Slavery in Venezuela, 1820-1854* (Westport, Conn., 1971), 98, 110; *Greater America*, 312; Sharp, *Colombian Choco*, 131; Greenleaf, *Catholic Church*, 24, 79, 177-94; Haring, *Spanish Empire*, 173, 176-78; Bowser, *Slave in Peru*, 233, 235; Gwendolyn Midlo Hall, *Social Control in Slave Plantation Societies: A Comparison of St. Dominique and Cuba* (Baltimore, 1971), 40-50.

slaves that their masters were "their fathers to whom they owed love, respect and obedience."[25]

While Southern and Latin American slaves heard some of the same kinds of sermons, blacks in Latin America did not have as much contact with the clergy as did bondsmen in the South. Historically understaffed, the Latin American Catholic Church generally did not have enough priests to permit regular clerical visitations to the plantations, the teaching of the Church's liturgy to the bondsman, or the performance of the sacraments for slaves. Cuba presents a perfect illustration of the problem the Church faced. In 1860 there were only 779 clergymen in Cuba to serve the religious needs of 1,199,429 inhabitants, or one clergyman for every 1539 inhabitants. Even if the white population had been excluded from the clergy's charges, there were too few priests, outside of the urban centers, to give much pastoral care to bondsmen. Cuba's clergymen were concentrated in the cities, with 401, or 51 per cent, of them in Havana. While in Havana there was one clergyman for every 80 slaves, the other 378 clergymen had to serve the 343,950 slaves in the other provinces or an average of one clergyman for every 907 slaves.[26]

The materialistic concerns of the Catholic Church further alienated the priest from the slaves. In order to enjoy the most essential Church rites, the penniless slave or his master had to pay the priest. Between the 1820s and the 1860s, for instance, the charge for baptisms varied between 75 cents and one dollar in Cuba. During the same period, the cost of a burial ranged between $5 and $7.50.[27]

The greatest barrier to the acculturation of the bondsman and the amelioration of slavery was that the low quality of the Latin

25. Quoted in Stanley Stein, *Vassouras: A Brazilian Coffee County, 1850-1900* (Cambridge, Mass., 1957), 138-39.

26. Burns, *Brazil*, 158; Meacham, *Church and State*, 279-80; Greenleaf, *Catholic Church*, 1-10; Sharp, *Colombian Choco*, 130-31; Kenneth F. Kiple, *Blacks in Colonial Cuba, 1774-1899* (Gainesville, Fla., 1976), 63; Franklin W. Knight, *Slave Society in Cuba During the Nineteenth-Century* (Madison, 1970), 107-8.

27. Bowser, *Slave in Peru*, 242; Sharp, *Colombian Choco*, 131; Kiple, *Colonial Cuba*, 43; Knight, *Slave Society*, 110.

American clergy undermined the Church's prestige. Few European clergymen viewed service in Latin America as anything less than exile from Spain or Portugal. And, for many of them, this was literally the case; having broken their vows or disgraced themselves at home, they were banished to the colonies to do penance. Chronically short of native-born clergy, Latin American colonists complained about the worldly living, fraud, breaches of conduct and doctrine, and rampant immorality of their priests. Violations of the vows of celibacy had become so common among Latin American priests by the nineteenth century that many observers argued that celibacy was the exception rather than the rule among the clergy.[28] A visitor to Brazil in the 1830s asserted, perhaps with some exaggeration, that "The present clergy of Brazil are more debased and immoral than any other class of men."[29] The historian Clarence Haring was less hyperbolic, but he concluded of the nineteenth-century Brazilian clergy: "most of the rank and file led rather scandalous lives. Clerical celibacy scarcely existed."[30] The low prestige of the clergy largely nullified attempts of the Catholic Church to minister to the needs of the slaves.

While the Catholic Church's success in evangelizing the slaves, serving their religious needs, and protecting them against the brutal treatment of their masters varied according to place, time, the occupation of bondsmen, and the religious sentiments of slaveholders in Latin America, the Church lost ground to the Protestants in the South in all of these areas in the nineteenth century. When nineteenth-century Latin American slaves had contact with the Church it was likely to be perfunctory and irregular. Outside the major urban centers, rare was the slave who had contact with a priest between his baptism and his burial. Oc-

28. Haring, *Spanish Empire,* 175, 191-93; Burns, *Brazil,* 29; Meacham, *Church and State,* 267-70; Greenleaf, *Catholic Church,* 11-12, 76; Thomas E. Skidmore, *Black into White: Race and Nationality in Brazilian Thought* (New York, 1974), 3-4.

29. Quoted in Meacham, *Church and State,* 270.

30. Clarence H. Haring, *Empire in Brazil* (Cambridge, Mass., 1958) 114; see also John W. Blassingame, "Bibliographical Essay: Foreign Writers View Cuban Slavery," *Journal of Negro History* LVII (Oct. 1972), 415-24.

casionally the priests even refused to bury blacks because they were "heathens." Because of the weaknesses of the Catholic Church and continual accretions to their numbers from the Fatherland, Latin American slaves became nominal Catholics while largely retaining their African religious beliefs, language, and culture. Consequently, the Latin Americanization of the slave was nowhere comparable to the Americanization of the bondsman in the South.[31] The comparative disadvantage or advantage of the Southern slave in this regard significantly affected his "adjustment" to bondage, his contribution to American culture, and the evolution of the peculiar institution.

It is impossible to make exact comparisons between the role of the church in the lives of black slaves in Latin America and in the South. The Catholic Church was established in most Latin American countries more than a hundred years before most Protestant churches were organized in the American South. The hierarchical structure of the Catholic Church was not duplicated in Southern Protestant churches. None of the Protestant denominations were ever as wealthy as the Latin American Catholic Church nor as directly responsible for providing such social services as education and health care. Unlike Catholic clerics, Southern Protestant ministers could rarely call upon the State to enforce religious pronouncements. Monasteries and convents were never as ubiquitous in the American South as they were in Latin America. Differentials in crops, the slave trade, demographic trends, slave tasks, and the rates of urbanization and capitalistic growth all affected church activities among the bondsmen.

Despite the differences between them, the Protestant and Catholic churches responded in remarkably similar ways in demonstrating humanitarian concern for blacks. None of the churches in slaveholding areas in the Americas, however, interceded fre-

31. Sharp, *Colombian Choco*, 130-31; Warren Dean, *Rio Claro: A Brazilian Plantation System, 1820-1920* (Stanford, 1976), 81-82; Knight, *Slave Society*, 106-13; Hall, *Social Control*, 50-51; Colin A. Palmer, *Slaves of the White God: Blacks in Mexico, 1570-1650* (Cambridge, Mass., 1976), 145-66. The best brief description of the large number of African survivals in Latin America appears in Albert J. Raboteau, *Slave Religion* (New York, 1978), 16-42, 87-92.

quently to prevent the barbarous treatment of slaves. Regularly insisting on the duty of slaves to obey their masters, the churches only sporadically supported abolition and emancipation. Their interest in providing religious instruction to the blacks was always second to ministering to the needs of whites. Christianization was rarely completed. Nowhere in the Americas did the churches approach the slave and consistently try to fulfill the prophecy of Esaias: "The spirit of the Lord is upon me, because he hath anointed me to preach the gospel to the poor; he hath sent me to heal the broken-hearted, to preach deliverance to the captives, and recovering of sight to the blind, to set at liberty them that are bruised."

One of the legacies Southern churches inherited from the Reformation was the duty to proselytize heathens, heretics, and infidels in order to establish hegemony over more souls than the Roman Catholic Church. Responding to the demands of English monarchs, the founders of Southern colonies recognized as one of their duties the propagation of the faith among the unsaved. The introduction of African slaves in the Southern colonies in the seventeenth century led to the incorporation of laws regarding their christianization into the charters establishing the colonies. Indeed, royal instructions called for the christianization of the slaves. Because of the paucity of ministers little was done until the eighteenth century, when the Society for the Propagation of the Gospel in Foreign Parts, Bray's Associates, and the Society for Promoting Christian Knowledge sent a few missionaries to the colonies between 1702 and 1785. Having justified the enslavement of blacks because they were "infidels," and "heathens," colonial masters feared that christianization would automatically lead to emancipation of the slaves. Consequently, colonial masters denied religious instruction to their bondsmen throughout the eighteenth century. Although several colonial legislatures passed laws between 1664 and 1712 denying that conversion changed a slave's status and the Bishop of London published a letter in 1727 to the same effect, opposition to converting the slaves did not cease. Because of the low state of religion among whites, the established Anglican Church could do little, despite the repeated urgings of its bishops, to overcome the opposition of the slaveholders. Such dissenting sects as the Quakers, Methodists, Baptists, and Lutherans actively evangelized the slaves with indifferent results until the Great Awakening of the 1740s. The Anglican Church, responding to the threat of the dissenters, expanded its efforts by establishing schools in Charleston, South Carolina, and Williamsburg, Virginia, to teach young slaves to read. Even so, at the time of the American Revolution few slaves had had any contact with white ministers, and an overwhelming majority of them still believed in the religions of their African fathers.[32]

Because creation stories, Supreme Beings, spirits, priest-healers, and elaborate moral and ethical systems were central in African religions, the native Africans enslaved in America found it relatively easy to understand similar features in Christianity. Many Africans were initially attracted to Christianity because they believed the "life after death" concept the white ministers emphasized meant that they would eventually join their ancestors in Africa. For others, the attraction of Christianity was that it appeared " 'that white people could make the book *talk*' " when they read the Bible.[33] A Baptist missionary to the Yoruba described some of the congruencies between Christianity and African religions in an 1853 report: "Besides their knowledge of the one only God, the Yoruba have words to express sin, guilt, sacri-

32. Marcus W. Jernegan, *Laboring and Dependent Classes in Colonial America, 1607-1783* (Chicago, 1931), 24-44; Klein, *Slavery*, 105-26; Susan M. Fickling, *Slave Conversion in South Carolina, 1830-1860* (Columbia, S.C., 1924), 9-11; Nelson W. Rightmeyer, *The Anglican Church in Delaware* (Philadelphia, 1947), 88, 138-39, 160-62; Marshall D. Haywood, *Lives of the Bishops of North Carolina* (Raleigh, 1910), 19-20; Robert S. Cope, *Carry Me Back: Slavery and Servitude in Seventeenth-Century Virginia* (Pikeville, Ky., 1973), 106-12; William S. Plumer, *Thoughts on the Religious Instruction of the Negroes of This Country* (Savannah, 1848), 3-11.

33. Harry V. Richardson, *Dark Salvation* (Garden City, N.Y., 1976), 14-19; John S. M'biti, *African Religions and Philosophy* (New York, 1969), 15-16, 29-57, 207-68; John S. M'biti, *Concepts of God in Africa* (New York, 1970), 327-36; *Literary and Evangelical Magazine* X (1827), 22-25; *African Repository* XVI, (1840), 107-8, 233-36, XVII (1841), 123, XXXVII (1861), 108-12; William P. Harrison, *The Gospel Among the Slaves* (Nashville, 1893), 365, 371-72.

fice, intercession, repentance, faith, pardon, adoption, &c, &c. Hence they very easily understand what the preacher means. . . . They believe . . . there is a heaven and a hell, and some very soon learn to desire the great salvation when they hear the gospel."[34]

Like the Christians, the few Islamic slaves brought to the South were a people of the book. They could read and write Arabic. Clinging tenaciously to their faith, they were sometimes still pleading with their masters to obtain copies of the Koran for them forty years after their initial enslavement. When trying to convert Islamic slaves, whites sometimes read them English translations of the Koran until they had mastered the language and then replaced the Koran with the Bible. While remembering the tenets of Islam, the slaves adopted Christian forms and beliefs because many of them were almost identical to the teachings of Mohamet.[35] For example, the Reverend Charles C. Jones reported in 1842 that the "Mohammedan Africans remaining of the old stock of importations, although accustomed to hear the Gospel preached, have been known to accommodate Christianity to Mohammedanism. 'God,' say they, 'is *Allah*, and Jesus Christ is *Mohammed*—the religion is the *same*, but different countries have different *names*.' "[36]

Though most traditional African religions did not share as many common features with Christianity as did Islam, there were enough congruencies to allow the Africans to recognize and accept some Christian tenets and practices from the outset.

34. *Proceedings of the Southern Baptist Convention, . . . 1853* (Richmond, 1853), 49; see also Robin Horton, "On the Rationality of Conversion," *Africa* XLV (1975), 219-35.

35. "The Autobiography of Omar ibn Said, Slave in North Carolina in 1831," *American Historical Review* XXX (1925), 787-95; Theodore Dwight, "Condition and Character of Negroes in Africa," *Methodist Review* XLVI (1864), 77-90; Douglas Grant, *The Fortunate Slave* (London, 1968); John W. Blassingame, ed., *Slave Testimony: Two Centuries of Letters, Speeches, Interviews, and Autobiographies* (Baton Rouge, 1977), 470-74, 682-86; William B. Poe, "Negro Life in Two Generations," *Outlook* LXXV (1903), 493-98.

36. Charles C. Jones, *The Religious Instruction of the Negroes* (Savannah, 1842), 125.

The small crosses carried by their masters the Africans perceived as "charms" to ward off evil spirits; Jesus was a healer like the priests the slaves had known in their native land; the Bible was a series of stories not unlike some of the lore of their own people, and many Biblical characters communed with God, saw visions, and prophesied the future reminiscent in many ways of the actions of their priests when in trances. These African congruencies the slaves emphasized when they adopted Christianity.[37] Olaudah Equiano, an Ibo, stressed the similarities between some of the Old Testament customs of the Jews and those of his own people:

> Like the Israelites in their primitive state, our government was conducted by our chiefs or judges, our wise men and elders; and the head of a family with us enjoyed a similar authority over his household, with that which is ascribed to Abraham and the other patriarchs. The law of retaliation obtained almost universally with us as with them: and even their religion appeared to have shed upon us a ray of its glory, . . . for we had our circumcision . . . we had also our sacrifices and burnt-offerings, our washings and purifications, and on the same occasions as they did.[38]

A number of slaves adopted Christianity because its animistic features were similar to the African's belief that spirits dwelled in such objects as trees and rivers.[39] One Southerner recalled a native African woman in South Carolina who successfully fused the beliefs of her homeland with Christianity:

> She had forgotten the name of her tribe; even the names of her parents had slipped from her memory; but the river which she had been taught to worship in her infancy had worn deep channels in that treacherous memory. This deep, abiding superstition made it comparatively easy for her to transfer her idolatry

37. Jones, *Religious Instruction*, 125-28; Raboteau, *Slave Religion*, 3-92.

38. Olaudah Equiano, *The Life of Olaudah Equiano, or Gustavus Vassa, the African* (2 vols. Boston, 1837), I, 27; see also Robin Horton, "African Conversion," *Africa* XLI (April 1971), 85-108.

39. Henry W. Ravenel, "Recollections of Southern Plantation Life," *Yale Review* XXV (June 1936), 775-77.

> to some stream in her new home. By consequence she became a Baptist, or rather an immersionist; for she was Baptist no further than the waters of the Great Pedee conveyed her.[40]

While the Africans were trying to master the intricacies of Christianity, the churches were confronting questions about their enslavement in America. Most eighteenth-century Southern churches, with the notable exception of the Quakers, raised few questions about the morality of holding slaves. The egalitarian doctrines of the American Revolution and the Great Awakening created, however, a sizable abolition party in Southern churches which lasted in some states for more than thirty years. In 1789, for example, the Virginia Baptist General Committee, denouncing slavery as a "horrid evil" and "violent deprivation of the rights of nature," called for its abolition. Kentucky Baptists followed suit, organized local associations of Baptist churches committed to emancipation, and several Baptist clergymen preached against slavery from the 1790s to 1820. During the same period several Kentucky Presbyterians declared slavery a "moral evil" and worked to promote emancipation. In 1809 the Baltimore Conference of the Methodist Church forbade the buying and selling of slaves by its members; throughout the antebellum period the Conference forbade its ministers to hold slaves.[41]

Between 1822 and 1828 two antislavery elders presided over the Arkansas District of the Methodist Church, and one of them, Jesse Haile, actively campaigned against the peculiar institution. One eyewitness to the campaign reported that Haile "had a most inveterate hatred to African slavery and he felt in duty bound to preach against the institution on all occasions. . . . The Presiding Elder never held a Quarterly Meeting that he did not fire

40. *Southern Magazine* XVII (1875), 498-502.

41. J. H. Spencer, *A History of Kentucky Baptists* (2 vols., Cincinnati, 1886), I, 182-97, 484; Walter B. Posey, *The Presbyterian Church in the Old Southwest, 1788-1838* (Richmond, 1952), 74-76; James Edward Armstrong, *History of the Old Baltimore Conference* (Baltimore, 1907), 166, 199, 267-86; H. Shelton Smith, *In His Image, But . . . Racism in Southern Religion, 1780-1910* (Durham, 1972), 23-73; Stephen B. Weeks, *Southern Quakers and Slavery* (Baltimore, 1896), 198-223; Lester B. Scherer, *Slavery and the Churches in Early America, 1619-1819* (Grand Rapids, Mich., 1975), 126-41.

into the peculiar institution . . . there was constant friction." Arkansas slaveholders generally rejected Haile's message. But he convinced one of them, the Reverend Thomas Tennant, that, as Tennant later wrote, "all the world knows—that slavery is wrong! morally, religiously, politically wrong!"[42]

Although the ministers led in the formation of hundreds of abolition societies in the upper South states of Maryland, Tennessee, Kentucky, North Carolina, and Delaware between 1790 and 1829, emancipationist sentiment among Southern clergymen began to erode in the early decades of the nineteenth century. A courageous remnant refused, however, to abandon their ideals. In pulpit and press these ministers continued to denounce slavery well into the 1840s.[43] The Reverend John Paxton, writing to his Virginia congregation in 1833, contended that the "morality of slavery must be judged of by comparing it with the moral law, that eternal and immutable law of right and wrong; and this law appears to me to condemn it. . . . Slavery is a violation of the law of love and therefore sinful." The Reverend Robert J. Breckinridge of Kentucky argued in 1833 that slavery was "a system which is utterly indefensible on every correct human principle, and utterly abhorrent from every law of God." A rapacious institution, "cruel and unjust to its victims," and condemned by God, Breckinridge asserted, could not be justified: "The man who cannot see that involuntary domestic slavery, as it exists among us, is founded upon the principle of taking by force that which is another's, has simply no moral sense. And he who presumes that God will approve, and reward habitual injustice and wrong, is ignorant alike of God, and of his own heart. . . . Nature, and reason, and religion unite in their hostility to this system of folly

42. Walter N. Vernon, *Methodism in Arkansas, 1816-1976* (Little Rock, 1976), 39-40.

43. *Christian Intelligencer and Southern Methodist* II (May 1846), 20-21, 27-28 (Jan. 1847), 27-29; Harrison A. Trexler, *Slavery in Missouri, 1804-1865* (Baltimore, 1914), 218-33; George W. Purefoy, *A History of the Sandy Creek Baptist Association* (New York, 1859), 220; Willie G. Todd, "The Slavery Issue and the Organization of a Southern Baptist Convention," (Ph.D. diss., University of North Carolina, 1964), 61.

and crime."[44] Publishing a 64-page appeal for the gradual abolition of slavery in 1835, a committee of Kentucky Presbyterians contended that slavery "is, manifestly, a violation of the laws of God, as revealed by the light of nature as well as the light of Revelation."[45]

The pronouncements of antebellum ministers profoundly affected the way masters thought about and treated their slaves. Until the 1820s many planters, convinced of the immorality of bondage, joined with clergymen in seeking its abolition. Caught up in the egalitarian fervor of the American Revolution and the religious fervor of Baptist and Methodist revivals in the eighteenth century, many masters began manumitting their slaves. In Maryland, for instance, masters manumitted thousands of slaves, primarily as a result of a series of Methodist revivals in the state. Throughout the antebellum period, many planters followed the lead of the Marylanders.[46]

For much of the nineteenth century, religious planters agreed with Thomas Jefferson's 1814 lament that the continued enslavement of blacks was leading to a "condition of moral and political reprobation" of the South.[47] Admissions that slavery was a sin

44. John D. Paxton, *Letters on Slavery* (Lexington, Ky., 1833), 65-71; *African Repository* IX (1834), 326-27.

45. *African Repository,* XII (1836), 92-93, 218-21; Posey, *Presbyterian Church,* 75-79.

46. D. Nelson to J. P. Willston (June 20, 1842), *National Anti-Slavery Standard,* Aug. 25, 1842; Luther Brown to Gamaliel Bailey (n.d.), *ibid.,* 11 May 1842; "Letters from the South," *ibid.,* May 27, 1841; R. S. Stewart to John L. Carey (Aug. 30, 1845), *ibid.,* Oct. 16, 1845; J. W. to Z. Eastman (April 1852), *ibid.,* May 13, 1852; Frank P. Blair, Jr., to C. W. Waite (Sept. 6, 1858), *ibid.,* Oct. 2, 1858; "Letter of Chief Justice Green to the American Tract Society," *ibid.,* May 8, 1858; "A Trip into Virginia," *ibid.,* May 7, 1858; David Dean to W. L. Garrison (Nov. 26, 1857), *ibid.,* Dec. 11, 1857; *African Repository* XI (1835), 144-46, 256; *The Colonizationist and Journal of Freedom* I (1833), 151-54; *Maryland Colonization Journal,* n.s. IV (1847), 91-102.

47. Jefferson to Edward Coles (Aug. 25, 1814), *Pennsylvania Freeman* April 18, 1839; Jonesboro (Tenn.) *Emancipator* I (1820), 2, 4; Shelbyville (Ky.) *Abolition Intelligencer* I (1822), 50-54, 100-1, 150-53; Baltimore *Genius of Universal Emancipation* I (1821-22), 109-11, 123, 140-42, 166, II (1822-23), 11-13, 85, 115-16, III (1823-24), 33, 168.

appeared regularly in planter memoirs, wills, books, and letters and essays published in contemporary newspapers and magazines.[48] James Kirk, a large South Carolina planter, confessed in 1826 that he had "scruples of conscience about slavery." A few years later a planter in the same state complained of "the womanish qualms of conscience which we so often witness among many of our own citizens, as to the justice and morality of keeping men in bondage." The Southern clergyman John Dixon Long argued that one of the major evils of slavery was "the *guilt* contracted, and the remorse endured by those who hold, breed, and sell slaves for the market."[49] Writing to the *Christian Reflector* in 1839, a Southerner asserted that as a result of reading a New York newspaper and a "conversation with a friend, who had formally been guilty of the sin of slaveholding, . . . I was brought to see my guilt, to forsake my sins, and turn my feet into the 'narrow path.' I liberated my slaves."[50]

Even when slaveholders did not manumit their bondsmen, they often lamented their continued connection with an evil, immoral, and sinful institution. Kentucky slaveholder and irrepressible abolitionist Cassius M. Clay wrote to the New York *Tribune* in 1843 that slavery was "the greatest evil that ever cursed a nation. . . . It is utterly subversive of the Christian

48. Bertram W. Korn, *Jews and Negro Slavery in the Old South, 1789-1865* (Elkins Park, Pa., 1961), 31, 63; Harold B. Hancock, ed., "William Yate's Letter of 1837," *Delaware History* XLV (1971), 213; John Dixon Long, *Pictures of Slavery in Church and State* (Philadelphia, 1857), 38; William W. Freehling, *Prelude to Civil War: The Nullification Controversy in South Carolina, 1816-1836* (New York, 1966), 66-81; Martin Boyd Coyner, "John Hartwell Cocke of Bremo: Agriculture and Slavery in the Ante-Bellum South" (Ph.D. diss., University of Virginia, 1961), 312-13; Paxton, *Letters*, 65-71; Beverly Mumford, *Virginia's Attitude Toward Slavery and Secession* (New York, 1909), 98, 101; Madeline H. Rice, *Catholic Opinion in the Slavery Controversy* (New York, 1944), 132-34; Frederick Law Olmsted, *A Journey in the Seaboard Slave States* (New York, 1856), 527; [Nathaniel Ware], *Notes on Political Economy, As Applicable to the United States, by a Southern Planter* (New York, 1844), 200.

49. Freehling, *Prelude*, 68, 79; Long, *Pictures*, 167.

50. A Penitent Slaveholder to Editor, *Christian Reflector, Pennsylvania Freeman*, April 4, 1839.

religion."[51] A large Florida slaveholder agreed, writing in 1845 of her conviction that slavery was "one of the most abominable institutions that the wickedness of man ever invented. I can see no justice in one mortal appropriating the labor of another to their sole use and benefit."[52]

There is overwhelmingly convincing evidence that a substantial number of Southern slaveholders never rested easy with their black species of property. While guilt was neither the South's biggest nor smallest crop, it grew to sizable proportions among women allied to slaveholding families. Louisianian Kate Stone spoke for many of her sisters when she asserted that her first recollection of slavery was "of pity for the Negroes and desire to help them. . . . Always I felt the moral guilt of it, felt how impossible it must be for an owner of slaves to win his way to heaven."[53] Virginia's Anne Meade Page held similar ideas.

A devout Christian and enthusiastic supporter of African colonization, Anne Page gave religious instruction to her slaves, taught some of them to read, tried to manage the blacks without flogging them, often prayed with her bondsmen, and worked diligently to manumit them. Writing in 1823, Anne Page stated her creed when she asked the Lord to take away the "selfishness" of slaveholders, "knowing that we must give an account of our stewardship." Considering the evils of slavery, she wrote that "they cannot be seen by human powers. They form a part of those hidden things of darkness, which are linked by a chain

51. Quoted in *National Anti-Slavery Standard,* Dec. 14, 1843.

52. G. S. to Brother Lee (n.d.), *National Anti-Slavery Standard,* May 22, 1845.

53. John Q. Anderson, *Brockenburn: The Journal of Kate Stone* (Baton Rouge, 1955), 6-8; Anne F. Scott, *The Southern Lady* (Chicago, 1970), 48-50; Mrs. George P. Coleman, ed., *Virginia Silhouettes: Contemporary Letters Concerning Negro Slavery in the State of Virginia* (Richmond, 1934), 11-14; Margaret Weber, "Reminiscences," Elmina Foster, "Reminiscences of Childhood," Letitia D. Miller, "Some Recollections," Southern Historical Collection, University of North Carolina; Peter R. Opper, "The Mind of the White Participant in the African Colonization Movement, 1816-1840" (Ph.D. diss., University of North Carolina, 1972), 259-66; Charles Wesley Andrews, *Memoir of Mrs. Anne R. Page* (Philadelphia, 1844), 25-52.

which reaches into the dominion of Satan, not only here on earth, but into his more complete dominion in the realms of deepest hell!" After acknowledging her desire to free her slaves, Anne Page fervently prayed: "Oh my Father, from the distressing task of regulating the conduct of my fellow-creatures in bondage, I turn and rest my weary soul on thy parental bosom. . . . My soul hath felt the awful weight of sin, so as to despair in agony—so as to desire that I had never had being. Oh God! then—then I felt the importance of a mediator, not only to *intercede* but to *suffer* under the burden of my guilt."[54]

Reduced in wealth after her husband's death in 1826, Anne Page manumitted a group of slaves and sent them to Liberia in 1832. About this time she declared: "The Bible . . . commands all 'to do unto others as they would that others should do unto them.' This had made me see that slavery is not a state wherein we can obey the law of love, and blessed be God, many others see it as well as myself."[55] By the time Anne Page died in 1838, she had sent thirty-three of her slaves to the land of their fathers.

At the beginning of the nineteenth century probably a majority of Southern planters accepted slavery as a necessary evil bequeathed to them by their fathers. Reeling from the attacks of abolitionists after 1830, the planters launched a massive propaganda campaign to convince whites at home and abroad that slavery was a positive good. Led by the brilliant South Carolinian John C. Calhoun, the Southern propagandists quickly began to attack the churches. Arguing that slavery was a political institution, the propagandists insisted first that it was outside the sphere of church interest. As antislavery Northern clergymen pushed their Southern co-religionists to acknowledge slavery as a sin and to excommunicate slaveholders, planters began forbidding ministers to talk to their slaves. Accused of being abolitionists, Southern clergymen launched a campaign in the 1830s to convince the planters that they held orthodox views about the peculiar institution. Practically every state convention of Southern churches

54. Andrews, *Page*, 25-28.
55. Andrews, *Page*, 52.

held during this period ended with a blistering attack on fanatical abolitionists bent on inciting insurrection.[56]

Southern emancipationists learned some painful lessons in the nineteenth century. They saw the number of slaveholding preachers, bishops, and elders increase. Occasionally, churches as corporate bodies even purchased slaves. As the peculiar institution expanded, more and more ministers were connected through family ties to planters. After 1830 the rising tide of threats against and mob attacks on antislavery ministers made the clergy more cautious. The more outspoken critics abandoned their Southern pulpits for Northern ones.[57] Putting distance between themselves and Northern abolitionists, Southern churches increasingly espoused the 1836 doctrine of the Hopewell Presbytery: "Slavery is a political institution, with which the church has nothing to do, except to inculcate the duties of Master and Slave, and to use lawful, spiritual means to have all, both bond and free, to become one in Christ by faith."[58] By the 1840s, the propagandists had largely succeeded in silencing the churches. Torn between their eighteenth-century abolition heritage and their desire to remain as viable institutions in nineteenth-century Southern society, the churches carefully avoided any action which might be interpreted as an attack on slavery. Calls for emancipation were muted. Clerical leaders muzzled antislavery ministers or chased them out of the South.

The loud silence of Southern churches on slavery did not satisfy the propagandists. They demanded that clergymen defend the institution. Those ministers who were slaveholders or who were closely identified with slaveholding families quickly answered the call. Even so, the ministerial trail from abolition to defense of slavery was a tortuous one. The belief in the sinfulness of slaveholding was too deeply engrained in the Southern clergy for them to abandon it quickly. In the 1830s and 1840s

56. Laurence L. Brown, *The Episcopal Church in Texas, 1838-1874* (Austin, 1963), 28, 96-97; Posey, *Presbyterians*, 89-90; Vernon, *Methodism*, 85.
57. *African Repository* XI (1835), 370, XII (1836), 38, 216-18.
58. *African Repository* XII (1836), 218.

Southern ministers conceded that slavery in the abstract was a sin, but that as practiced in the South it was not. During this same period, Southern clergymen became almost frenetic in their support of African colonization (as a substitute for emancipation), frequently preaching sermons in favor of the enterprise and regularly passing resolutions supporting the American Colonization Society.[59] Finally, in the 1850s Southern clergymen capitulated almost completely to the propagandists. Led by the hierarchical denominations, the ministers not only denied that slavery in the abstract was immoral, they also insisted it was a divine institution which was a blessing to both master and slave.[60]

The movement of the clergy toward support of slavery was accompanied by increasing concern over the treatment and education of the bondsmen. The clergy urged slaveholders to treat their bondsmen humanely. A multitude of sermons, pastoral letters, essays in newspapers and magazines, reports and resolutions of ecclesiastical bodies, and books between 1740 and 1860 dealt with the temporal needs of the slaves of Christian masters. The major campaign of the clergy was, however, to convince nineteenth-century masters to give religious instruction to their slaves. Pointing to a long list of Bible verses, white ministers argued that Christianity would make the slaves easier to manage because obedience would be inner-directed rather than based on the whip. Christian blacks would work harder than non-Christian ones. For his own salvation and his profits, the planter had a responsibility to give religious instruction to his slaves.[61]

59. *African Repository* VIII (1832), 86-89, IX (1833), 94-95, (1834), 321-32, X (1834), 29, XIII (1837), 38, 96-97.

60. Thornton Stringfellow, *A Brief Examination of Scripture Testimony on the Institution of Slavery* (Richmond, 1841); *Southern Christian Advocate*, Feb. 2, 1861; William S. Jenkins, *Pro-Slavery Thought in the Old South* (Chapel Hill, 1935); *Southern Presbyterian Review* IV (1850), 105-41, VII (1854), 266-83.

61. *Evangelical and Literary Magazine* IV (1821), 309-14, V (1822), 67-71, 642-45; Charles C. Jones, *The Religious Instruction of the Negroes* (Princeton, 1832); Fickling, *Slave Conversion*, 10-18; *Journal, Protestant Episcopal Church, Alabama, 1847*, 12; Nathaniel Bowen, *A Pastoral Letter, on the Religious Instruction of the Slaves . . . .* (Charleston, 1835); Posey, *Presbyterian Church*, 83-84; *Journal, P. E. Church, Virginia, 1841*, 12-14;

Acceptance of the legitimacy of slavery severely limited the humanitarianism of the white minister. In the same sermon where a minister called upon masters to treat their slaves with kindness, he often read earnestly from Proverbs: "A servant will not be corrected by words; for though he understands, he will not answer." The Reverend William G. Brownlow revealed the contradictions in the humanism of many Southern clergymen when he told slaveholders bluntly in 1857: "The Scriptures look to the correction of servants, and really enjoin it, as they do in the case of children. We esteem it the duty of Christian masters to feed and clothe well, and in the case of disobedience to *whip well.*"[62]

Because of their intimate relations with the planters, few of the ministers took active steps to ameliorate the conditions under which blacks lived. On occasion, however, they had planters investigated or expelled from their churches because of their cruel treatment of slaves.[63] On March 5, 1823, for example, a church in Clinton, Louisiana, considered the case "of Bro. Edds for abuse of his slave which was proven against him and he was excommunicated." Sometimes the ministers went even further and adopted policies designed to prevent cruel treatment. When whites established churches, they sometimes followed the lead of the covenanters of South Carolina's Salem Baptist church in 1812: "We promise if we should be the possessors of negroes or other slaves . . . that we will not treat them with cruelty or

---

D. Y. Riddle, "African Slavery—Its Duties and Responsibilities," *Southern Baptist Review* II (1856), 697-708; *African Repository,* XI (1835), 140-44, 268, 333-34, 371, XII (1836), 70, 319-20; *Southern Presbyterian Review* I (1847), 63-102; Richmond (Va.) *Religious Herald,* Sept. 11, Oct. 30, Dec. 18, 1845, Jan. 15, April 9, June 25, Sept. 3, Dec. 3, 1846.

62. William G. Brownlow, *A Sermon on Slavery* (Knoxville, Tenn., 1857), 17.

63. Daniel W. Harrison, "Virginia Baptists and the Negro in the Early Republic," *Virginia Magazine of History and Biography* LXXX (1972), 60-69; Gaston H. Wamble, "Negroes and Missouri Protestant Churches Before and After the Civil War," *Missouri Historical Review* LXI (1967), 321-47; Robert O. Fife, "Alexander Campbell and the Christian Church in the Slavery Controversy" (Ph.D. diss., Indiana University, 1960), 120-21; Raboteau, *Slave Religion,* 181-82.

unmercifully use them in any respect." The Dover Baptist Association of Virginia, arguing in 1813 that some masters "exercise an unreasonable authority" over their slaves, urged the churches to monitor the treatment of blacks and to deal with masters who abused them as they would "offenders in other crimes." In 1819 the Mississippi Baptist Association sent out a circular letter reminding its members to be "just in their treatment" of slaves. The same sentiment appeared in numerous pastoral letters, sermons, and essays in Southern religious periodicals.[64]

While trying to restrain the cruelty of masters, white ministers were attempting to make the slaves submissive.[65] Many slaves testified that the white ministers, dedicated to preserving slavery, tried to promote good behavior, contentment, industry, and humility in the quarters and to discourage stealing, lying, and rebelliousness. Indeed, the Bible verses the white ministers quoted frequently admonished slaves to be orderly and dependable workers devoted to their owners' interests, to be satisfied with their station in life, to accept their stripes patiently, and to view their faithful service to earthly masters as a service to God.[66] The

64. Annie H. Mallard, "Religious Work of South Carolina Baptists Among the Slaves from 1781 to 1830" (M.A. thesis, University of South Carolina, 1946), 22-23, 78, 81; Harrison, "Virginia Baptists," 64; Mississippi Baptist Association, *Minutes* (1819), 22. See also: Savannah River Baptist Association of South Carolina, *Minutes* (1807), 6; Thomas S. Clay, *Detail of a Plan for the Moral Improvement of Negroes on Plantations* (n.p., 1833), 11-23; *Southern Presbyterian Review* VII (1854), 266-83; E. T. Baird, "The Religious Instruction of Our Colored Population," *Southern Presbyterian Review,* XII (1859), 345-61; *Southern Episcopalian* V (1858), 482-91.

65. Lewis M. Purifoy, "The Methodist Episcopal Church, South, and Slavery, 1844-1865" (Ph.D. diss., University of North Carolina, 1965), 121-25; Stiles B. Lines, "Slaves and Churchmen: The Work of the Episcopal Church Among Southern Negroes, 1830-1860" (Ph.D. diss., Columbia University, 1960), 160-86; Jones, *Religious Instruction of the Negroes,* 206-19; Donald G. Mathews, *Slavery and Methodism* (Princeton, 1965), 78-79; Lunsford Lane, *The Narrative of Lunsford Lane* (Boston, 1848), 20-21; William Wells Brown, *Narrative of William W. Brown, a Fugitive Slave* (Boston, 1847), 83-84; Peter Randolph, *Sketches of Slave Life* (Boston, 1855), 62; Henry Box Brown, *Narrative of Henry Box Brown* (Boston, 1851), 45; W. H. Robinson, *From Log Cabin to the Pulpit* (Eau Claire, Wis., 1913), 74-79; William Webb, *The History of William Webb* (Detroit, 1873), 8-14.

66. Matthew 24: 45-51, 25: 14-30; Luke 12: 42-48; First Corinthians, 7:

Reverend Alexander Glennie, for example, taught South Carolina slaves to look upon their "daily tasks as 'the will of God.'" The central message of his sermon, however, was Glennie's assertion that "by disobedience, you not only offend your earthly master, but you sin against God." In some of the sermons, the master was practically transmogrified into God's earthly representative. Thomas Bacon of Maryland gave a typical early exegesis in the 1740s when he informed the slaves:

> Poor creatures! you little consider, when you are idle and neglectful of your master's business,—when you *steal*, and *waste*, and *hurt* any of their substance—when you are *saucy* and *impudent*—when you are telling them lies, and deceiving them . . . [that] what faults you are guilty of towards your masters and mistresses, are faults done against God himself, who hath set your masters and mistresses over you in His own stead, and expects that you will do for them just as you would do for Him. And pray do not think that I want to deceive you when I tell you that your *masters* and *mistresses* are GOD'S OVERSEERS, and that, if you are faulty towards them, God himself will punish you severely for it in the next world, unless you repent of it, and strive to make amends by your *faithfulness* and *diligence* for the time to come; for God himself hath declared the same. . . .[67]

White ministers often taught the slaves that they did not deserve freedom, that it was God's will that they were enslaved, that the devil was creating those desires for liberty in their breasts, and that runaways would be expelled from the church. Then followed the slave beatitudes: blessed *are* the patient, blessed *are* the faithful, blessed *are* the cheerful, blessed *are* the submissive,

---

20-22; Ephesians, 6: 5-8; Colossians, 3: 22-25; Titus, 2: 9-14; First Peter 2: 18-25; *Gospel Messenger and Southern Episcopal Register* VII (1830), 5-11; William Troy, *Hair-Breadth Escapes From Slavery to Freedom* (Manchester, Eng., 1861), 30.

67. Alexander Glennie, *Sermons Preached on Plantations to Congregations of Negroes* (Charleston, 1844), 23, 24; William Chambers, *American Slavery and Colour* (London, 1857), 143-44; Thomas Bacon, *Four Sermons* (London, 1753), 30-31.

blessed *are* the hardworking, and above all, blessed *are* the obedient.[68]

Although white ministers often waxed lyrical about the restraining power religion exercised over the slaves when they spoke to the planters, they quickly learned that Biblical injunctions to obedience were unpopular with black congregations. For instance, one Georgia minister reported that when he "insisted upon fidelity and obedience as christian virtues in servants and . . . condemned the practice of *running away*, one half of my audience deliberately rose up and walked off . . . some solemnly declared . . . 'that it was not the Gospel'; others, 'that I preached to please the masters'; others, 'that they did not care if they ever heard me preach again.' "[69] Continued stress on obedience discouraged slaves from going to church, caused them to shift their allegiance to other denominations, or led to complete rejection of Christianity.[70]

Because of the resistance of the bondsmen, the extant published sermons prepared especially for slaves downplayed obedience while covering a great variety of other topics. Most of them dwelt on sin, the necessity of prayer and Christian rebirth, the life and teachings of Christ, and the mercy of God. The slaves frequently heard proscriptions against worldly living, slander, malice, adultery, drunkenness, impenitence, dancing, and murder. The Biblical stories of the creation, judgment day, the resurrection, and miracles were among the staples of the sermon. The white ministers contemplated with the slaves death, sickness, and sorrow. The Books of the Bible from which white ministers most often chose the texts of their sermons were Psalms,

68. Levi Branham, *My Life and Travels* (Dalton, Ga., 1929), 44; Peter Bruner, *A Slave's Adventures Toward Freedom* (Oxford, O., 1918?), 22.

69. *Tenth Annual Report of the Association for the Religious Instruction of the Negroes in Liberty County, Georgia* (Savannah, 1845), 24. See also: Paxton, *Letters*, 131-32; Henry Bibb, *Narrative of the Life and Adventures of Henry Bibb, an American Slave* (New York, 1849), 24.

70. George P. Rawick, ed., *The American Slave: A Composite Autobiography* (31 vols., Westport, Conn., 1972-77), XII, pt. 1:20, 25, 190, 195, 258, 294-96, 323, pt. 2:53, 94, 325, XIII, pt. 3:49, 152, 188-89, 201, 219.

John, Matthew, Luke, Ephesians, Proverbs, Timothy, Romans, Philemon, and Acts.[71]

It is difficult to determine whether the published sermons accurately reflect what the slaves were taught. Apparently, however, white ministers laid great stress on the admonitions in First Corinthians: "Let every man abide in the same calling wherein he was called. Art thou called servant? Care not for it. . . ." The ministers put much more emphasis on obedience when teaching black children than when preaching to adults. The special catechisms prepared for slaves included explicit injunctions to obedience:

> QUES. What command has God given to Servants concerning the obedience to their Masters?
>
> ANS. 'Servants be obedient to them that are your Masters, according to the flesh.'—Eph. 6:5
>
> QUES. If the servant professes to be a Christian, ought he not to *set an example* to all the other Servants of love and obedience to his Master?
>
> ANS. Yes.
>
> QUES. And if his Master is a Christian, ought he not especially love and obey him?
>
> ANS. Yes.—I Tim. 6:1-2
>
> QUES. Is it right for the Servant to run away; or is it right to harbor a *runaway*?
>
> ANS. No.[72]

Although injunctions to obedience occupied less than 5 per cent of the space in most catechisms, they were skillfully inserted in the places where they would have the maximum impact. The favorite devices were to conjoin masters, mistresses,

71. Glennie, *Sermons;* T. T. Castleman, *Plain Sermons for Servants* (Philadelphia, 1851); A[ndrew] F. Dickson, *Plantation Sermons* (Philadelphia, 1856).

72. Charles C. Jones, *A Catechism for Colored Persons* (Charleston, 1834), 93-94.

overseers, and drivers with either parents, ministers, or civil authorities to whom a child was to submit.[73] The "Plantation Catechism" published in 1859 in the *Southern Episcopalian* illustrates the technique:

> Q. What is the fifth commandment?
>
> A. Honour thy father and thy mother, that thy days may be long in the land which the Lord thy God giveth thee.
>
> Q. What does this commandment require you to do?
>
> A. This commandment requires me to respect and to obey my father and mother, my master and mistress, and everybody else that has authority over me.[74]

In preaching to adults white ministers muted their calls for slave obedience. Such calls were more often implicit than explicit in their sermons. Generally the ministers tried to expose the slaves to the major tenets of Christianity. The duty of servants to obey their masters was, the ministers contended, simply one of these tenets. For example, when a committee of South Carolina's Episcopal Church asked ministers what they taught slaves in 1843, it learned that

> In preaching, the same great subjects seem to have been inculcated, which are insisted on in white congregations, viz. Our fall in Adam, and our redemption in Christ—the sinfulness and lost state of man, and the glorious privileges to which the Gospel admits him; the necessity of repentance, faith, and holy obedience. To these subjects are added, as occasion may allow, the peculiar duties arising out of the condition of servants in relation to their owners, fellow-servants and families. . . . The daily service is frequently explained. The nature of the sacraments is often dwelt upon, their binding nature and great importance and benefits inculcated, and the bearers warned against superstitious notions of their efficacy. . . . The Ten Command-

73. *Southern Episcopalian* I (1854), 5-8, VI (1859), 369-75; Protestant Episcopal Church, South Carolina, *A Cathechism, To Be Used by Teachers in the Religious Instruction of Persons of Color* (Charleston, 1837), 63-67; *Instruction from the Book of Common Prayer, for Plantations by a Clergyman* (Charleston, 1854), 21.

74. *Southern Episcopalian* VI (1859), 369-75.

> ments are also often explained and enforced, especially the 3rd, 6th, 7th, 8th, 9th and 10th.[75]

The testimony of former slaves interviewed in the 1930s supports the declarations of the antebellum white clergy. For instance, only 15 per cent of the Georgia slaves who had heard antebellum whites preach recalled admonitions to obedience.[76]

Whatever the message in the special services for bondsmen, the slave was often spared the long, frequently dull sermons to which his master listened. Manuals on the religious instruction of slaves urged ministers to adopt a plain style in preaching, to keep the sermons brief, and to use simple, direct language with vivid and varied illustrations. Repetition of key points and an animated, stirring style was thought best suited to the slaves.[77] One minister insisted that the first thing to do when instructing slaves was: "To study to make the instructions given both pleasant and profitable to the instructed. The whole carcass of modern technical theology—its metaphics—its subtle distinctions—its mystical dogmas—its sectarian polemics—its technical phrases, &c. &c. —should be cast away by him who goes to this simple and ignorant people as a Christian teacher."[78] White ministers emphasized oral instruction, memorization, interrogatories, and singing in their efforts to christianize the slaves. Slaves memorized the Lord's Prayer, the Ten Commandments, and many aspects of the denomination's liturgy. Ministers, bishops, and masters often questioned the slaves to make sure they understood what had been taught.[79]

The most attractive thing many slaves found in going to

75. *Journal, P. E. Church, South Carolina,* 1843, 38-39.

76. Rawick, ed., *American Slave,* XII, pt. 1:20, 25, 190, 195, 258, 294-96, 323, pt. 2:53, 94, 325, XIII, pt. 3:49, 152, 188-89, 201, 219.

77. Dickson, *Plantation Sermons,* vii-xii; Fickling, *Slave Conversion,* 20-21; Plumer, *Thoughts,* 23-28; *Southern Presbyterian Review* VIII (1855), 1-17.

78. Plumer, *Thoughts,* 25.

79. Fickling, *Slave Conversion,* 20-21; *Journal, P. E. Church, Virginia,* 1841, 36, 1843, 50; *Journal, P. E. Church, South Carolina,* 1839, 22, 25, 1840, 19-20, 1856, 72; *Gospel Messenger and Southern Christian Register* I (1824), 286-87; *Minutes, Welsh Neck Baptist Association . . . 1858* (Columbia, S.C., 1858), 5-6.

church was the opportunity it gave them to sing. Consequently, *Watts Hymnal* was the key book in every minister's library. Writing from Virginia in 1755, the Reverend Samuel Davies observed that "the negroes above all the human species that I have ever known, have an ear for music, and a kind of ecstatic delight in psalmody; and there are no books they learn so soon, or take so much pleasure in, as those used in that heavenly part of divine worship." Ministers would continue to find the frequent singing of hymns the most attractive part of their-services for slaves. Almost one hundred years after Davies's reflections, South Carolina clergymen wrote: "In all cases, it has been found advisable to sing three or more times, as these people are peculiarly susceptible to the influence of music. The psalms and hymns, it is believed, being associated with the music, and often sung by them, have more influence over their minds than prayers, lessons or sermons."[80]

The kind of religious instruction a slave received depended largely on the religious persuasion of his master. Even so, the slaves forced the planters to adopt a rough form of ecumenicalism in evangelizing in the quarters. Because of the desires of the bondsmen, occasionally an Episcopalian invited a Baptist or Methodist to preach to his slaves. Generally, however, masters tried to convert the slaves to their faith. But when it came time to join a church, slaves exercised their own choice, demonstrating their autonomy. Slaves catechized by Episcopalians or Roman Catholics persisted in joining Baptists and Methodists. Indeed, the long-standing lament of Episcopalians was that they sowed and tilled the black vineyards while the Methodists and Baptists reaped the fruits of their labors. The predilections of the slaves forced the more formalistic churches to imitate the Baptists and Methodists in preaching style and occasionally to resort to total immersion when baptizing the blacks. Sometimes in spite of the ministers, the slaves would "get happy" and make the church rock with their singing and shouting.[81]

80. Plumer, *Thoughts*, 12; *Journal, P. E. Church, South Carolina, 1843*, 38.

81. *Journal, P. E. Church, Georgia, 1860*, 36; *Journal, P. E. Church, South*

Blacks also chose denominations on the basis of the degree of autonomy they could exercise and the amount of discrimination they encountered from their white co-religionists and tutors. At this point, however, the master interposed his authority. Terrified of separate black religious services, masters insisted that Southern whites preach to the slaves and banned or sharply curtailed the activities of black preachers because of the prominent roles they played in insurrections. Most states required a few whites to attend religious services for slaves even when conducted by white preachers. In the governance of the denominations to which they belonged, slaves generally had no voice; when separate slave congregations were founded, they were represented at association and state meetings by white delegates. Despite all of the restrictions, however, blacks insisted on exercising some autonomy over their lives. Consequently, most denominations had black class leaders, catechists, watchmen, and exhorters.[82]

Remarkably, in spite of the well-nigh universal sentiment against slave preachers, the clerical leaders of the nineteenth-century Southern black church were trained by white ministers. Many of the postwar Southern black bishops and ministers had either been converted or ordained by antebellum white denominations. Bishops J. A. Beebe, Isaac J. Lane, Henry McNeal Turner, Lucius H. Holsey, and other nineteenth-century black clergymen testified that they were among the "brands plucked from the burning" by white ministers.[83]

Carolina, 1849, 37, *1850*, 57, *1852*, 44; Brown, *Episcopal Church in Texas*, 63.

82. *Journal, P. E. Church, South Carolina, 1852*, 47; *Journal, P. E. Church, Louisiana, 1857*, 50-51; Plumer, *Thoughts*, 13; Fickling, *Slave Conversion*, 22-23; Vernon, *Methodism in Arkansas*, 87; Spencer, *Kentucky Baptists*, I, 722, II, 653-58; *Journal, P. E. Church, Virginia, 1860*, 64-69; Edward E. Joiner, *A History of Florida Baptists* (Jacksonville, 1972), 47; Alfred M. Pierce, *A History of Methodism in Georgia* (Atlanta, 1956), 132-35; Charles B. Williams, *A History of the Baptists in North Carolina* (Raleigh, 1901), 161-62; Harrison, *Gospel*, 364-94.

83. Pierce, *Methodism in Georgia*, 132-35; Spencer, *Kentucky Baptists*, II, 653-58; Williams, *Baptists in North Carolina*, 161-62; Harrison, *Gospel*, 364-94.

Sponsored and supervised by associations of white churches, black ministers sometimes traveled the circuits with Baptist and Methodist clergymen and helped them conduct services for blacks and whites. A few black ministers belonging to slaveholding clergymen served as assistant pastors for their owners. Among Baptists and Methodists, who often interacted on virtually equal terms with slaves and who had few educational requirements for the ministry, an especially well-trained black noted for his piety, conservatism, obsequiousness, and preaching skill was occasionally permitted to preach to white congregations. The rough egalitarianism of the Southern frontier, the ecumenicalism growing out of the paucity of ministers, the sincerely held belief in the brotherhood of all in Christ, and the drama inherent in a unique show, all contributed to the acceptance of black preachers by whites. Since many of the whites had prayed, been converted, and baptized with their slaves, and others had shouted with them at camp meetings and been converted by them, they saw no great contradiction in listening to sermons from the bondsmen. Then, too, many whites had regularly attended plantation services and were accustomed to hearing slaves preach or had developed a preference for them. Whites accepted slave ministers in their congregations because the blacks were remarkably well trained (some of them read Greek, Latin, and Hebrew) or famous for their oratorical skills. The black preachers in white pulpits compromised; they either ignored the evils of slavery, preached submission to their brothers in bonds, or defended the peculiar institution.[84]

Like slaves throughout the Americas, Southern blacks were engaged in an unequal struggle with whites for religious instruction. A frontier area in many respects, the low population density and low rate of urbanization in the South placed limits on the number of church buildings and clergymen in the region. While

84. Patrick C. Kennicott, "Negro Anti-Slavery Speakers in America," (Ph.D. diss., Florida State University, 1967), 21-26; James B. Sellers, *Slavery in Alabama* (University, Ala., 1950), 307-8; J. C. Ballagh, *A History of Slavery in Virginia* (Baltimore, 1902), 110-13; *African Repository* XXIII (1847), 46-48, XXIV (1848), 151-52, XXV (1849), 28, XXVI (1850), 118-19, XXVII (1851), 2-4.

these limits clearly restricted the religious instruction Southern blacks received, their opportunities were considerably better than those of Latin American blacks. In 1850 there was one white clergyman for every 1143 inhabitants in the South, and one clergyman for every 385 slaves. By 1860, the slave's access to religious instruction had improved. The 11,716 clergymen and 22,587 churches meant that there was one clergyman for every 1044 inhabitants and one church for every 541 inhabitants. Excluding the whites, there was one clergyman for every 337 slaves and one church for every 174 slaves. Though the ratio of inhabitants to clergymen in the South was considerably lower than Cuba's 1539 inhabitants per clergyman, in the American context, the Southern slave did not receive the same kind of regular pastoral care as did most antebellum whites.[85]

An overwhelming majority of the slaves throughout the antebellum period attended church with their masters. Then, after the regular services ended, the ministers held special services for the slaves. Occasionally, the Sunday afternoon sermons were supplemented by an evening prayer meeting during the week. Pious planters and their wives also taught the slaves and acted as their sponsors for church membership or served as godparents of children being baptized.[86]

Since a sizable number of plantation slaves did not attend regular church services, many white ministers began in the 1820s to go to the plantations to preach to the blacks. By the 1840s most ministers included plantation preaching as a part of their

85. Appendix III, tables 1 and 2. Though there are no comparable statistics for Latin America, it should be noted that in 1850 and 1860 there were nearly two church seats for every slave. Catholic Louisiana was the exception among Southern states; in 1850 Louisiana had only one clergyman for every 2260 inhabitants.

86. *Journals* of the annual conventions of the Protestant Episcopal Church in Alabama, Florida, Georgia, North Carolina, Louisiana, Mississippi, South Carolina, and Virginia, 1839-1860; A. F. Dickson, "Our Problem," *Southern Presbyterian Review* X (1857), 451-63; Richmond (Va.) *Religious Herald* Oct. 30, 1845; Alex[ander] Glennie, "The Religious Instruction of Negroes," *Southern Episcopalian* III (1856), 198-99; Rawick, ed., *American Slave,* II, pt. 1: 43, 131, pt. 2: 81, 179, XII, pt. 1: 175-76, 257, pt. 2: 69, 340, XIII, pt. 3: 105, 168, pt. 4: 148.

pastoral duties. Although as a general rule regular ministers could not visit the plantations often, some of them were remarkably conscientious. The Episcopal rector of Wacamaw, South Carolina, Alexander Glennie, for instance, annually held between 114 and 167 services for the 6000 slaves on the plantations in his parish between 1841 and 1850. Most often, however, a minister visited ten or twelve plantations contiguous to his church on an average of four or five times annually. Many planters made special arrangements for the minister's visits, sometimes giving slaves time off from their work as an inducement for them to attend religious services voluntarily. The regular visitations of bishops to confirm candidates were a special boon to the slaves of Episcopal masters, for work usually ceased in the area.[87]

Encouraged by the ministers, pious planters began building chapels on their plantations for the slaves. Often, a group of planters would build a chapel for the use of slaves from several plantations. Though never equaling the number of churches built for whites, plantation chapels dotted the Southern countryside in the 1850s and planters often paid itinerant missionaries and pious laymen to preach to their slaves. In Wacamaw, South Carolina, for example, there were fifteen plantation chapels in 1860.[88]

Beginning in the 1820s, white ministers complained repeatedly that they could not minister adequately to the needs of blacks on widely scattered plantations and called upon their denominations to appoint special missionaries to the plantations. In the 1830s Southern planters began petitioning church leaders for missionaries for their slaves and occasionally established

87. *Journals* of the annual conventions of the Protestant Episcopal Church in Alabama, Florida, Georgia, North Carolina, Louisiana, Mississippi, South Carolina, and Virginia, 1839-1860.

88. *Journals* of the annual conventions of the Protestant Episcopal Church in Alabama, Florida, Georgia, North Carolina, Louisiana, Mississippi, South Carolina, and Virginia, 1839-1860; *Southern Christian Advocate,* May 23, 1861; Paul Trapier, "Efforts of Christians for the Spiritual Benefit of Slaves," *Southern Episcopalian* I (1854), 119-23; Rawick, ed., *American Slave,* XIII, pt. 3:19, pt. 4:129, 225; *Charleston Gospel Messenger and Protestant Episcopal Register* XXI (1845), 342-43.

county-wide associations to support missions. Methodists, Presbyterians, and Episcopalians responded in the 1830s by launching large-scale, systematically organized, state-wide slave missions.[89] Thereafter, the reports of missionaries to the slaves became a regular feature at the annual conventions of most Southern denominations.[90]

Although pastoral care was severely limited, it appears that many of the slave members had almost as much access to most of the sacraments of the church as did whites. Denominational statistics on baptisms, weddings, funerals, and confirmations show that the clergy readily performed these rites between 1830 and 1860. For example, while blacks represented between 19.1 and 23.2 per cent of the communicants in the Episcopal church during the period 1851 to 1860, they accounted for between 17.4 and 19.3 per cent of the funeral sermons preached; 26.4 to 28.2 per cent of the Sunday School scholars; 18.3 to 21.9 per cent of the confirmations; and 40.3 to 48 per cent of the baptisms in those states reporting such statistics.[91] The rules of most denominations required ministers to perform rites for all members, and associations regularly passed resolutions reminding ministers of their responsibilities to the slaves.[92] While the size of congregations, the availability of ministers, and the moods of masters all affected the slave's access to the sacraments, his opportunities certainly increased as the nineteenth century progressed.

The Methodists were by far the most active in evangelizing the slaves, devoting far more money and manpower to the enterprise than any other denomination. The investment paid off;

89. Posey, *Presbyterian Church,* 84-85; Fickling, *Slave Conversion,* 12-46; Jones, *Religious Instruction* (1832); Pierce, *Methodism in Georgia,* 135-40; *Southern Episcopalian,* I (1854), 91-92, 355-56, 494-97; *Southern Christian Advocate,* Nov. 19, 1852, Jan. 3, 10, March 14, 1861; Richmond (Va.) *Religious Herald,* March 21, 1846.

90. *Journals* of the annual conventions of the Protestant Episcopal Church in Alabama, Florida, Georgia, North Carolina, Louisiana, Mississippi, South Carolina, and Virginia, 1839-1860.

91. See Appendix III, tables 6-12; Rawick, ed., *American Slave,* II, pt. 1: 300, XII, pt. 1:66, 79, 208, 244, pt. 2:95, 286, 296, XIII, pt. 3:17, 125, 182, 252, pt. 4:70, 118.

92. Plumer, *Thoughts,* 13-15.

there was, after establishing the missions, a substantial increase in the number of black Methodists. Between 1786 and 1829 the number of black members rose steadily from 1890 to 62,814. The establishment of the missions led to a dramatic upsurge in black membership: in 1840 there were 94,532 black Methodists; twenty years later the number had risen to 207,423. Counting the 65,887 slaves served by missionaries and the 180,000 black Sunday School scholars, at least 453,310 slaves received regular religious instruction from the Methodists in 1860.[93]

Unlike the Methodists, Southern Baptists devoted relatively little money and manpower to special missions to the slaves. At the same time, the Baptists were apparently more successful than the Methodists in attracting slave members. But because Baptists failed to compile records of black members by state or region it is difficult to determine the total number of black Baptists. The manuscript records of local churches, the published statistics of a few intra-state associations, and contemporary estimates do, however, suggest some trends. Blacks represented about 45 per cent of the Baptists in South Carolina in 1830 and the Southern Baptist Convention estimated there were 150,000 black members of Southern Baptist churches as early as 1846. Substantial numbers of slaves appeared in the reports of those Baptist associations which began in the 1830s to report their black members. Virginia's Dover, Rappahannock, Middle District, and Salem Union Associations, Georgia's Sunbury and Georgia associations, North Carolina's Chowan Association, and South Carolina's Welsh Neck, Bethel, and Charleston Associations regularly reported that between 40 and 80 per cent of their members were black between 1840 and 1860. Scattered reports from other states indicate that in 1860 blacks constituted between 30 and 40 per cent of the total number of Baptists in the South. Consequently, the 1860 estimate of the Southern Baptist Convention that there were 150,000 slave members seems too low. There were probably 400,000 black Baptists in the South in 1860 and another 200,000 blacks attending Baptist Sunday Schools.[94]

93. Appendix III, tables 3-5.

94. Appendix III, tables 13-16; Fickling, *Slave Conversion;* James A. Delke,

Thousands of slaves belonged to the smaller Southern denominations: Presbyterians, Episcopalians, Church of Christ, Lutherans, Quakers, and others. Since none of these denominations consistently made racial distinctions in their reports of membership, the number of slaves exposed to their religious teachings can only be ascertained by examining the records of local churches and informed contemporary estimates. Robert Fife's study of congregations of the Church of Christ revealed that generally from 20 to 40 per cent of their members were black. In 1854 the Reverend Paul Trapier, after examining denominational reports, asserted that there were 7000 black Presbyterians, and 20,000 black members of smaller denominations in the South.[95]

Reliable statistics on the total slave membership in Southern churches are extremely difficult to compile because so few denominations reported them. Some clues are furnished, however, by scholars who have examined the manuscript records of local churches and by rare statistical abstracts of state and regional associations of various denominations. For instance, Susan Fickling found that by 1860 one-fifth or 82,000 of South Carolina's 402,406 blacks were members of the Methodist, Episcopalian, Baptist, or Presbyterian churches. In his examination of the conversion of slaves, Clarence Bruner discovered that "in 1860 approximately one fourth of the slaves above eighteen years of age were members of the church [*c.* 530,000] as compared with one third of the whites within the same age limits."[96] Including

---

History of the North Carolina Chowan Baptist Association, 1806-1881 (Raleigh, 1882), 86; Mallard, "South Carolina Baptists," 82-88; Jesse H. Campbell, *Georgia Baptists: Historical and Biographical* (Richmond, 1847), 286-88; Billy Walker Jones, *History of Ebeneezer Missionary Baptist Association of Georgia, 1814-1964* (Macon, Ga., 1965), 62; Richmond (Va.) *Religious Herald* Nov. 28, 1839, Nov. 26, 1840, Sept. 9, 16, 1841, Oct. 17, 1844, Nov. 6, Dec. 18, 1845, July 30, Sept. 10, Dec. 24, 1846; Raboteau, *Slave Religion*, 176.

95. Paul Trapier, "Efforts of Christians for the Spiritual Benefit of Slaves," *Southern Episcopalian* I (June 1854), 119-23; Fife, "Alexander Campbell," 104-13.

96. Clarence V. Bruner, *An Abstract of the Religious Instruction of the Slaves in the Antebellum South* (Nashville, 1933), 5; Fickling, *Slave Conversion*, 39-40.

black Sunday School scholars and catechumens, there were probably 1,000,000 slaves under the regular tutelage of Southern churches in 1860.

The number of blacks who received religious instruction in antebellum white churches is significant because the church was the only institution other than the plantation which played a major role in acculturating the slave. Just as the school was the major institution for "Americanizing" nineteenth- and twentieth-century European immigrants, the church was the single most important institution for the "Americanization" of the bondsman. Masters in general were not interested in systematically teaching their slaves all of the intricacies of American morals, manners, language, and customs. Ministers were; they could not fulfill Christ's injunction to preach the word if the slaves could not understand English.

In their sermons and Sunday School classes, white ministers taught not only moral precepts to the slaves, they also taught them their masters' language. Southern clergymen learned quickly that one of the greatest barriers to their instructing Africans in the seventeenth and eighteenth centuries was the inability of the adult slaves to understand spoken English. The language barrier and the adherence of the Africans to their previous religious beliefs forced the clergymen to focus on slave children. The continuation of Africanisms in nineteenth-century black speech led most denominations bent on evangelizing the slaves to devote a disproportionate share of their resources to Sunday Schools for blacks. Because of the lessons they learned in the churches, Biblical language would resonate in nineteenth-century black speech and writing. This was, perhaps, the Southern church's greatest legacy to the slave.

Historically, West African peoples have been adept at borrowing cultural elements from their conquerors and victims and fusing them with their own. Similarly, Africans have traditionally been among the world's leading linguists, learning a staggering number of dialects and languages of other peoples with whom they traded, fought, or interacted. Though European languages lacked the symmetry of African ones, in the eighteenth century the slaves began mastering their essentials and in the nineteenth gave an African tint to them. The most obvious way the slave influenced the evolution of language in the South was by forcing whites to adopt African words when trying to communicate with blacks. Among the words of such African peoples as the Mandingo, Hausa, and Ibo incorporated into English were the following: cooter (turtle), cola, okra, goober and pinder (peanut), yam, gumbo, mumbo-jumbo, juju, buckra (white man), banjo, bamboula, hoodoo, okay, and tote.[97]

Perhaps the greatest contribution of the slaves to the formation of Southernisms was the host of new idiomatic expressions, based on a combination of African forms, Biblical lore, and archaic Anglicanisms. Through his close association with indentured servants and his master's children, the slave gave the Southern white his drawl, African intonation of words, and elision of syllables. Expressive, picturesque, allegorical, and figurative, the slave's language remained singular in spite of the linguistic loans he made to his master. Because he learned so much of his language from white ministers, the slave's speech was sprinkled with Biblical allusions. Since language is one of the unalienable cultural possessions, the slaves and their descendants (like European immigrants) also retained African equivalents and forms in their conversation and oratory.[98] A former slaveholder, Edward A. Pollard, writing in 1871, asserted that the blacks' use of language was "extraordinary" and reflected "a kind of genius." Analyzing Southern black oratory, Pollard continued by observing:

97. Anne W. Whitney, "Negro American Dialects," *Independent* LIII (Aug. 22, 1901), 1979-81; Melvin A. Butler, "African Linguistic Remnants in the Speech of Black Louisianians," *Black Experience: A Southern University Journal* LV (June 1969), 45-52; John Bennett, "Gullah: A Negro Patois," *South Atlantic Quarterly* VIII (1909), 39-52; David Dalby, "The African Element in American English," in Thomas Kochman, ed., *Rappin' and Stylin' Out: Communication in Urban Black America* (Urbana, 1972), 179-86.

98. William C. Elam, "Lingo in Literature," *Lippincott's Magazine* LV (Feb. 1895), 286-88; John V. Lloyd, "The Language of the Kentucky Negro," *Dialect Notes* II (1901), 179-84; "Word-Shadows," *Atlantic Monthly* LXVII (Jan. 1891), 143-44; John Bennett, "Gullah: A Negro Patois," *South Atlantic Quarterly* VII (1908), 332-47.

> The forte of the negro orator is decidedly the pathetic; he is most effective in the low tones. In his melancholic cast of speech, he has the habit of sometimes chanting or half-singing his words—what his race very characteristically knows as "moaning"; and it has occasionally the most weird and touching effect. . . . "Speaking in parables," as he calls it, is his favorite rhetorical pastime. There is a great fondness for Biblical illustrations. . . . His strong imagination leads him to personify nearly every object of his discourse, and this produces a vividness and reality that are his peculiar virtues as an orator.[99]

The idiomatic expressions of the quarters filtered up to the big house with amazing rapidity. Because the slave found such a close congruence between African proverbs and those in the Bible, he was able to pass on to his master many African expressions.

Antebellum Southerners frequently noted the Africanization of their children by the slaves. For example, a group of ministers declared in 1847 that "Our children catch the very dialect of our servants, and lisp all their perversions of the English tongue, long before they learn to speak it correctly." Viewing the close interaction of African slaves with white children, Southern leaders encouraged the christianization of the bondsmen in an effort to halt the Africanization of the South. It was mandatory to educate the slaves, the Charleston *Southern Evangelical Messenger* wrote in 1820, because

> They are of necessity the constant attendants upon children in their early years. From them they mostly learn to talk; from them their minds receive their first impressions; and from them a *taint* is often acquired which remains through the whole of their succeeding lives. Superstition takes complete possession of a benighted mind, and hence the ready credit which is given to tales of witchcraft, of departed spirits and of supernatural appearances, with which servants terrify the young committed to their care, and impressions are made, which no after efforts of the understanding are able entirely to eradicate. This evil may

99. Edward A. Pollard, "The Romance of the Negro," *American Missionary* XV (Nov. 1871), 241-48.

> be remedied by giving to slaves as much instruction as will enable them to speak the English language without corruption, and to supply that vacancy of mind which is now haunted by the terrors of superstition.[100]

So few slaveholders followed the *Messenger*'s advice that their children incorporated many African cultural elements into their behavior, attitudes, and language. Nineteenth-century Southern whites, for instance, often resorted to slave doctors and conjurors. When whites worshipped with slaves, they sometimes adopted the blacks' religious customs. In a typical case, the South Carolina missionary George W. Moore reported that while preaching on the Baring plantation, "I have often seen Mrs. Baring, when the negroes were singing, catch the motion of their bodies and do just as they did."[101]

Southern whites not only adapted their language and religion to that of the slaves but also adapted agricultural practices, sexual attitudes, rhythm of life, architecture, food and social relations to African patterns. During the colonial period, for instance, the slaves planted rice according to African practice. The African tradition of cooperative work led some masters to adopt gang labor, which the slaves accompanied by rhythmic music. Other masters adopted the African tradition of the task system, thus giving the slaves a portion of each day to labor for themselves. Coming from a tropical zone, Africans had learned that one had to work at a relatively slow pace in order to survive the heat. They refused to speed up to the frenetic pace of their European masters, and in the process slowed down the tempo of Southern life. From their slaves and the Indians, Southern whites first learned of the daily bath and by the nineteenth century had adopted many aspects of the practice. The Southern white's materia medica received infusions from Africans skilled in curing various diseases. African traditional crafts also contributed to the development of the economy and material culture of the South such items as baskets woven on African patterns and colonial

100. *Southern Presbyterian Review*, I (June 1847), 90; *Southern Evangelical Messenger*, II (April 29, 1820), 32.
101. Harrison, *Gospel*, 202.

Figures 22, 23. African's House in South Carolina, *c.* 1890

slave houses with thatched roofs. The slaves began at an early date to force their masters to adapt to African tastes in food. Since the early slaves found it difficult to eat European dishes without adding African spices, they also used them to prepare savory stews and rice dishes for their owners quite unlike the lightly seasoned English dishes they had known. The bondsmen took Indian maize and turned it into hoe cakes, mush, and dumplings akin to African Fufu and Kenkey. Spoon bread, a soft pudding-like dish made from corn meal, grew out of this mélange and appeared on the master's table. The evolution of forms of social relations among Southern whites owed much to Africa. First, as Earle Thorpe has shown, Southern whites developed healthier attitudes toward sex as a result of their interaction with slaves. Second, though European individualism retained its primacy among Southern whites, in imitation of slaves, the white man's circle of friends expanded. Whatever the impact on whites, memories of Africa's formalized friendship groupings and societies led to their partial replication in the quarters with blacks often referring to non-relatives as "cousins" and "brothers."[102]

The acculturation of the African slave in the South proceeded in ways similar to that of bondsmen in other parts of the world. At the same time, Southern blacks were more thoroughly acculturated than the white slaves in Africa or bondsmen in Latin America primarily because of the activities of white churches in the South. While the Protestant mission to the blacks led to their Americanization by 1860, there remained many African remnants in their culture. As masters adopted many of these remnants, and slaves borrowed beliefs and practices from owners, black and white culture became more homogeneous. The interpenetration of white culture in the quarters did not, however, prevent the evolution of a distinctive culture in the slave community.

102. William R. Bascom, "Acculturation Among the Gullah Negroes," *American Anthropologist* n.s. XLIII (Jan.-March 1941), 43-50; "Negro Dialect," *Nation* I (Dec. 14, 1865), 744-45; Earl Thorpe, *Eros and Freedom in Southern Life and Thought* (Durham, 1967); Eugene D. Genovese, *Roll, Jordan, Roll* (New York, 1974), 542-43, 547; Peter Wood, *Black Majority: Negroes in Colonial South Carolina* (New York, 1974), 59-62; Todd L. Savitt, *Medicine and Slavery* (Urbana, 1978), 174, 179.

3

Culture

The irony of the situation is that in folk-lore, folk-song, folk-dance, and popular music the things recognized as characteristically and uniquely American are products of the despised slave minority. . . . What accounts for it in the past and promises great momentum to it in the future is the simple fact of the intensification of the emotional side of life by persecution and suffering. . . . This is the Negro's compensation for his hard lot and generation-long sacrifice.

Alain Locke

Antebellum black slaves created several unique cultural forms which lightened their burden of oppression, promoted group solidarity, provided ways for verbalizing aggression, sustaining hope, building self-esteem, and often represented areas of life largely free from the control of whites. However oppressive or dehumanizing the plantation was, the struggle for survival was not severe enough to crush all of the slave's creative instincts. Among the elements of slave culture were: an emotional religion, folk songs and tales, dances, and superstitions. Much of the slave's culture—language, customs, beliefs, and ceremonies—set him apart from his master. His thoughts, values, ideals, and behavior were all greatly influenced by these processes. The more his cultural forms differed from those of his master and the more they were immune from the control of whites, the more the slave gained in personal autonomy and positive self-concepts.

The social organization of the quarters was the slave's primary environment which gave him his ethical rules and fostered cooperation, mutual assistance, and black solidarity. The work experiences which most often brought the slave in contact with whites represented his secondary environment and was far less important in determining his personality than his primary environment. The slave's culture or social heritage and way of life determined the norms of conduct, defined roles and behavioral patterns, and provided a network of individual and group relationships and values which molded personality in the quarters. The socialization process, shared expectations, ideals, and enclosed status system of the slave's culture promoted group identification and a positive self-concept. His culture was reflected in socialization, family patterns, religion, and recreation. Recreational activities led to cooperation, social cohesion, tighter communal bonds, and brought all classes of slaves together in common pursuits.[1]

The few periods of recreation the slave enjoyed and his religious beliefs gave him some hours of joy and a degree of hope amid his sufferings. Since his recreation was less supervised than his labor, these hours were especially important to him. Leisure time and religious activities broke the monotony of daily toil and permitted the slave to play roles other than that of the helpless dependent driven to his tasks. During his leisure hours the slave could take out his anger toward whites in physical contests with other slaves or seek relief in religious devotion by turning to One more powerful than his earthly master. Religious and recreational activities and the differences between the slave's and the master's customs prevented his total identification with the slaveholder's interests and gave him some respite from constant toil.[2]

While some slaves had to use their "leisure" time (usually Saturday afternoons) to perform their personal chores—washing clothes, cleaning cabins, or working on garden plots—Sunday was almost universally a day of rest. The more pious planters also freed the slaves from labor on religious holidays. The largest

1. Milton M. Gordon, *Assimilation in American Life* (New York, 1964), 19-39 and Leslie A. White, *The Science of Culture* (New York, 1949), 121-89, discuss the nature of culture.

2. Practically all secondary accounts of slavery discuss what could be generally described as slave "culture," but give little solid information on life in the quarters. See: Charles S. Sydnor, *Slavery in Mississippi* (New York, 1933), 55-66; Joe G. Taylor, *Negro Slavery in Louisiana* (Baton Rouge, 1963), 125-52; J. Winston Coleman, *Slavery Times in Kentucky* (Chapel Hill, 1940), 67-80.

and most important holidays were the end of labor on the corps before harvesting and Christmas. During these periods, which lasted from four to six days, the restrictions on interplantation visiting were dropped and the planters prepared sumptuous feasts for their slaves. Whole hogs, sheep, or beeves were cooked and the slaves ate peach cobbler and apple dumplings, and frequently got drunk. Often the festival seasons included dances and athletic contests.[3]

The planters generally had little concern about the recreational activities in the quarters. They did not, however, want their slaves carousing all over the county and wearing themselves out before the day's labor commenced. Consequently, some planters locked the doors of the cabins at night and instituted the patrol system to keep slaves in the quarters after dark. In the face of the resourcefulness of the slaves, their efforts were frequently to no avail. One of the blacks' pastimes was tying vines across trails to trip the horses of the patrollers. The bolder ones fought the patrollers when they were caught at parties without passes. William Webb wrote that when his overseer started locking the cabins at 9 p.m. the slaves crawled out of the chimneys to keep their evening rendezvous.[4]

3. Carl D. Arfwedson, *The United States and Canada in 1832, 1833 and 1834* (2 vols., London, 1834), I, 334; Philip V. Fithian, *Journal and Letters of Philip Vickers Fithian, 1773-1774* (Williamsburg, 1943), 52-83, 121-28, 265; Charles Lanman, *Haw-He-Noo: Or the Records of a Tourist* (Philadelphia, 1850), 139-41; Jacob Stroyer, *My Life in the South* (Salem, 1890), 44-49; Louis Hughes, *Thirty Years a Slave* (Milwaukee, 1897), 13-22, 39-58; Frederick Douglass, *My Bondage and My Freedom* (New York, 1968 [1855]), 251-56; Allen Parker, *Recollections of Slavery Times* (Worcester, Mass., 1895), 40-53.

4. Robert Anderson, *From Slavery to Affluence* (Hemingford, Neb., 1927), 29-38; Henry Clay Bruce, *The New Man; Twenty-nine Years a Slave. Twenty-nine Years a Free Man* (York, Pa., 1895), 67-72, 96-106; William Grimes, *Life of William Grimes, the Runaway Slave, Brought Down to the Present Time* (New Haven, 1855), 36-48; William Green, *Narrative of Events in the Life of William Green* (Springfield, O., 1853), 8-9; Solomon Northup, *Twelve Years a Slave* (London, 1853), 191-222; Austin Steward, *Twenty-two Years a Slave, and Forty Years a Freeman* (Rochester, N.Y., 1861), 32-51; William Webb, *The History of William Webb* (Detroit, 1873), 8-12.

Many slaves did not have to use these stratagems. Their masters did not try to restrict their recreational activities as long as they did not interfere with the plantation routine. According to Robert Anderson, "The slaves on a plantation could get together almost any time they felt like it, for little social affairs, so long as it did not interfere with the work on the plantation. During the slack times the people from one plantation could visit one another, by getting permission and sometimes they would slip away and make visits anyway." Similarly, Elijah Marrs said his master "allowed us generally to do as we pleased after his own work was done, and we enjoyed the privilege granted to us."[5]

Slaves spent their Sundays fishing, hunting, wrestling, running races, strumming the banjo, singing, dancing, playing marbles, recounting tales, fiddling, drinking whiskey, gambling, or simply visiting and conversing with friends. With or without their master's permission, they often organized dances and parties to which all of the slaves in the neighborhood were invited.

The social leaders at many of these affairs were the house slaves to whom the field slaves looked "as a pattern of politeness and gentility."[6] At one of the balls, Austin Steward recalled that the domestic servants came dressed in their masters' cast-off clothing and brought some of their owners' silverware, table cloths, wine, and food for the guests who were dancing to the tunes played by a slave fiddler. Anderson reported that his overseer once even permitted the slaves to use his master's house for a dance when the master and his family went visiting.

Apparently the European reels, minuets, and schottisches were too sedate and formalized for the slave. In the quarters the dance was more often a test of physical endurance, a means of winning praise and expressing the slave's inner feelings. Often openly

5. Anderson, *From Slavery,* 31; Elijah P. Marrs, *Life and History* (Louisville, 1885), 11; see also: Orland K. Armstrong, ed., *Old Massa's People: The Old Slaves Tell Their Story* (Indianapolis, 1931), 134-39; Ronnie C. Tyler and Lawrence R. Murphy, eds., *The Slave Narratives of Texas* (Austin, 1974), 70-79.

6. Steward, *Twenty-two Years,* 32.

lascivious, the dances involved wild gyrations to a furious rhythm.[7] According to a former slave,

> These dances were individual dances, consisting of shuffling of the feet, swinging of the arms and shoulders in a peculiar rhythm of time developed into what is known today as the Double Shuffle, Heel and Toe, Buck and Wing, Juba, etc. The slaves became proficient in such dances, and could play a tune with their feet, dancing largely to an inward music, a music that was felt, but not heard.[8]

The unrestrained exhibitions gave the slave some escape, some temporary relaxation from toil, and refreshed his spirit.

In addition to these activities, several other customs prevented the slaves from identifying with the ideals of their masters. Because of their belief in fortune tellers, witches, magic, signs, and conjurers, many of the slaves constructed a psychological defense against total dependence on and submission to their masters. Whatever his power, the master was a puny man compared with the supernatural. Often the most powerful and significant individual on the plantation was the conjurer.

The conjurers gained their control over the slaves in various ways. Shrewd men, they generally were industrious enough to avoid punishment. They then told the slaves they were not punished because they had cast a spell on their masters. Claiming the ability to make masters kind, prevent floggings and separations, cause and prevent pain and suffering, ensure love and happiness, the conjurers were often very successful in gaining adherents. Frequently they were able to do this because they used their knowledge of the medicinal value of roots and herbs to cure certain illnesses.

7. Fithian, *Journal*, 83; Nicholas Cresswell, *The Journal of Nicholas Cresswell, 1774-1777* (New York, 1924), 18-19, 30; James K. Paulding, *Letters from the South . . .* (New York, 1817), 119; Lanman, *Haw-He-Noo*, 144-45; Francis and Theresa Pulzsky, *White, Red and Black* (3 vols., London, 1853), III, 13; John Finch, *Travels in the United States of America and Canada* (London, 1833), 237.

8. Anderson, *From Slavery*, 30-31.

William Webb, who became a conjurer after observing a skillful practitioner at work, explained how he obtained complete sway over the slaves on one plantation in Kentucky. Observing that the slaves were disgruntled over their master's cruel treatment, Webb visited the quarters secretly, prayed for better treatment for the slaves, and then had the slaves collect various roots, put them in bags, march around the cabins several times, and point the bags toward the master's house every morning. When the master started treating his slaves better (because he had a dream in which they wreaked vengeance on him), the slaves were completely in Webb's power: they regaled him with sumptuous meals nightly, and the women were especially attentive.[9]

Faith in the conjurer was so strong that slaves often appealed to him to prevent floggings. M. F. Jamison declared that the conjurer on his plantation claimed that he "could prevent the white folks from mistreating you, hence those of us who could believe in such would visit him and have him 'fix' us." In many instances, the conjurer had more control over the slaves than the master had. Henry Clay Bruce felt that conjurers were so successful that the slaves had a mortal fear of them and "believed and feared them almost beyond their masters."[10]

Sometimes the charms the slaves obtained from the conjurers bolstered their courage and caused them to defy their masters. For example, after the powders and roots a conjurer gave to Henry Bibb appeared to prevent him from receiving a flogging, Bibb then had, he wrote,

> great faith in conjuration and witch-craft. I was led to believe that I could do almost as I pleased without being flogged. . . .

9. Henry Bibb, *Narrative of the Life and Adventures of Henry Bibb, an American Slave* (New York, 1849), 24-32; William Wells Brown, *Narrative of William W. Brown, a Fugitive Slave* (Boston, 1847), 90-96; A. M. Bacon, "Conjuring and Conjure Doctors," *Southern Workman* XXIV (Nov. 1895), 193-94, (Dec. 1895), 209-11; Thaddeus Norris, "Negro Superstitions," *Lippincott's Magazine* VI (July 1870), 90-95; Armstrong, *Old Massa's People*, 245-54; Tyler and Murphy, *Slave Narratives*, 83-91.

10. Monroe F. Jamison, *Autobiography and Work of Bishop M. F. Jamison, D.D.* (Nashville, 1912), 34; Bruce, *New Man*, 54.

Figure 24. The Fiddler

Figures 25, 26. Dance

> [after going off the plantation without permission] my master declared that he would punish me for going off; but I did not believe that he could do it, while I had this root and dust; and as he approached me, I commenced talking saucy to him.[11]

The black nurses who cared for the planters' children probably did as much to ensure the success of the conjurer as any one else. Because of the tales they heard from their nurses and black childhood playmates, many antebellum whites were convinced of the conjurer's power. William Wells Brown reported that the conjurer on his plantation, one-eyed, ugly Dinkie, terrified everyone in the neighborhood. His usual accouterments certainly must have contributed to this: "He wore a snake's skin around his neck, carried a petrified frog in one pocket, and a dried lizard in the other."[12] Dinkie never worked, never received a flogging, and was never stopped by the patrollers. When the planter sold Dinkie, the slave trader brought him back immediately. A new overseer once threatened to whip the conjurer for not going to the fields; Dinkie either frightened or talked him out of it, for he returned to his old carefree ways, and the overseer never bothered him during his tenure on the plantation. Even some of the most refined white ladies visited Dinkie's cabin to have their fortunes told or to obtain love potions. In light of his privileged status and the ritual deference he received from whites, there is little wonder that the slaves stood in "mortal fear" of the conjurer's power.[13]

While their customs sometimes allowed the slaves to exercise power over their masters, they also served as a means of social control in the quarters. The identity of a thief in the quarters, for example, was ascertained by various means. If the accused man could not hold a Bible or a sieve on a string without its turning, he was obviously the culprit. Another method was related to the slaves' beliefs about death. They believed that if one stole something from a fellow slave, lied about it, and then drank

11. Bibb, *Adventures,* 26-27.
12. William Wells Brown, *My Southern Home* (Boston, 1880), 71.
13. Hughes, *Thirty Years,* 13-22; Stroyer, *My Life,* 50-76.

a bottle of water filled with dust from the grave of a recently departed slave, he would die. Most thieves, not wanting to take the risk, preferred to confess when confronted rather than drink from the bottle.

Although research on the subject is limited, it is clear when one examines nineteenth-century sources that the slaves brought many of their signs, omens, and proverbs directly from Africa. The transference is especially true of proverbs, because they did not have to be altered in the same way as omens and signs to fit American flora and fauna. Like other African peoples, the slaves used proverbs to teach the young and as commentaries on life. The African element appears in about 30 per cent of the slave proverbs. For example, to indicate that things often look better from a distance, the slave said, "Distant stovewood am [is] good stovewood," while his Ewe ancestors in Ghana said, "Distant firewood is good firewood." Slave signs and omens focused primarily on the weather and death. At the same time, there was a preoccupation with predicting such plantation calamities as whippings, sales, and family separations. The slaves believed, for instance, that if you "dream of your master or mistress counting money, and if you don't want any body on the place to be sold, don't tell your dream until after sun-up,—no one will be sold. . . ."[14]

Among the most important distinctive cultural forms in the quarters were folk songs and tales. It must be acknowledged at the outset that there are innumerable problems involved in using folk tales and songs to delineate the slave's world view. The major problem in attempting to analyze these elements of the culture is that all too many of the eyewitness accounts were recorded long after slavery ended. While undoubtedly many of the tales and songs recorded in the nineteenth century reflected

14. A. B. Ellis, *The Ewe-Speaking Peoples of the Slave Coast of West Africa* (London, 1890), 265; Alan Dundes, ed., *Mother Wit from the Laughing Barrel* (Englewood Cliffs, N.J., 1973), 249; *Southern Workman* XXIII (March 1894), 46-47; see also: J. Mason Brewer, ed., *American Negro Folklore* (Chicago, 1968), 287-35; *Southern Workman* XXVIII (July 1898), 145-46.

the slave experience, they had, in effect, been corrupted by freedom. Even when authentic antebellum sources are used, they are limited because they generally represented only what blacks wanted white folks to hear. When this fact is added to the unfamiliarity of many of the whites with the slaves' language patterns and their general ignorance of music and folklore, the complexities of the problem are manifest. Then, too, many of the profane tales and secular songs were ignored by most witnesses. While some of these problems are insurmountable, others can be eliminated by a strict application of the rules of evidence. This is especially true in regard to slave music. Only evidence from witnesses who actually heard this music before and during the Civil War has been relied upon in this analysis.[15]

The secular songs told of the slave's loves, work, floggings, and expressed his moods and the reality of his oppression. On a number of occasions he sang of the proud defiance of the runaway, the courage of the black rebels, the stupidity of the patrollers, the heartlessness of the slave traders, and the kindness and cruelty of masters.[16] Comments on the latter are especially informative. Nicholas Cresswell declared in 1774 that in the songs of slaves of Maryland, "they generally relate the usage they have received from their Masters and Mistresses in a very satirical stile and manner." William Faux wrote from Charleston in 1819 of the songs of the slaves: "Some were plaintive love songs. The verse

15. Many essays on the subject, while often informative, are marred by their heavy reliance on songs written and recorded after the Civil War or those popularized and commercialized by such groups as the Fisk Jubilee Singers and the New Orleans University Singers. See Sterling Stuckey, "The Black Ethos in Slavery," *Massachusetts Review* IX (Summer 1968), 417-37; David McD. Simms, "The Negro Spiritual: Origin and Themes," *Journal of Negro Education* XXXV (Winter 1966), 35-41; John Lovell, "The Social Implications of the Negro Spiritual," *Journal of Negro Education* XVIII (Oct. 1939), 634-43.

16. George W. Cable, "Creole Slave Songs," *Century Magazine* XXXI (April 1886), 807-28; William C. Bryant, *Letters of a Traveller* (London, 1850), 85-86; Paulding, *Letters*, 126-27; Henry B. Whipple, *Bishop Whipple's Southern Diary* (Minneapolis, 1937), 33-34; Benjamin W. Griffith, "Longer Version of 'Guinea Negro Song' from a Georgia Frontier Songster," *Southern Folklore Quarterly* XXVIII (June 1964), 117.

was their own, and abounding either in praise or satire intended for kind and unkind masters."[17]

On a number of occasions the slaves sang sarcastically of the actions of their masters. The Reverend John Long wrote that Maryland slaves sometimes sang:

William Rino sold Henry Silvers;
Hilo! Hilo!
Sold him to de Gorgy trader;
Hilo! Hilo!
His wife she cried, and children bawled,
Hilo! Hilo!
Sold him to de Gorgy trader;
Hilo! Hilo![18]

Frederick Douglass recorded one song indicative of the slave's sense of the planter's oppression:

We raise de wheat,
Dey gib us de corn;
We bake de bread,
Dey gib us de cruss;
We sif de meal,
Dey gib us de huss;
We peal de meat,
Dey gib us de skin
And dat's de way
Dey takes us in.[19]

Because of their sense of oppression, the blacks occasionally made folk heroes of the rebellious slaves. In the "Dirge of St. Mâlo," Louisiana slaves sang:

Alas! young men, come make lament
For poor St. Mâlo in distress!
They chased, they hunted him with dogs,
They fired at him with a gun,

17. Cresswell, *Journal*, 17-19; William Faux, *Memorable Days in America* (London, 1823), 77-78.

18. John Dixon Long, *Pictures of Slavery in Church and State* (Philadelphia, 1857), 197-98.

19. Douglass, *Bondage*, 253.

They dragged him up into the town.
Before those grand Cabildo men
They charged that he had made a plot
To cut the throats of all the whites.
They asked him who his comrades were;
Poor St. Mâlo said not a word![20]

A majority of the secular songs recounted the slave's loves and foibles or served as rhythmic accompaniments to labor.[21] Corn-shucking probably produced more secular songs than any other kind of work. In order to finish the work of removing the husks from his corn, a planter would invite all of the slaves in the neighborhood to gather one night at his barn. The slaves received whiskey and a big meal in payment for their labor.[22] Looking forward to the food and fun (and probably trying to "con" the planter), the slaves marched to the barn singing:

All dem puty gals will be dar,
  Shuck dat corn before you eat,
Dey will fix it fer us rare,
  Shuck dat corn before you eat,
I know dat supper will be big,
  Shuck dat corn before you eat,
I think I smell a fine roast pig,
  Shuck dat corn before you eat.
I hope dey'll have some whisky dar,
  Shuck dat corn before you eat.
I think I'll fill my pockets full,
  Shuck that corn before you eat.[23]

20. Cable, "Creole," 815.

21. Charles Lyell, *Travels in North America, Canada, and Nova Scotia* (2 vols., London, 1855), I, 181; Thomas Low Nichols, *Forty Years of American Life, 1821-1861* (New York, 1937), 357; Timothy Flint, *Recollections of the Last Ten Years* (New York, 1968), 139; Thomas W. Higginson, "Negro Spirituals," *Atlantic Monthly* XIX (June 1867), 692-93; Brown, *Southern Home,* 96.

22. Lanman, *Haw-He-Noo,* 141-44; Garnett Andrews, *Reminiscences of an Old Georgia Lawyer* (Atlanta, 1870), 10-12.

23. Brown, *Southern Home,* 92-93.

The corn-shucking was a combination of labor and recreation. The slaves enjoyed the evening away from the quarters, meeting friends and sweethearts, drinking the cider or hard liquor, eating cakes and pies, telling tall stories and singing hilarious songs. While shucking the corn they sometimes passed the time by singing this ditty:

> Massa an' Missus hab gone far away,
> Gone on dey honeymoon a long time to stay,
> An' while dey's gone on dat little spree,
> I'se gwine down to Charles-Town a purty gal to see.[24]

The most impressive of the work songs that have survived are those created by black steamboat men, deck hands, and rowers. Basically call-and-response chants, the boat songs spanned a wide spectrum, often including a number of the shout songs heard in the religious meetings. Most observers, however, noted their rhythmic and improvisational quality. William Grayson recalled that he was often serenaded on his travels on South Carolina's rivers:

> The singers were the Negro oarsmen. One served as chief performer, the rest as chorus. The songs were partly traditionary, partly improvised. They were simple and inartificial consisting of one line only and the chorus. The singer worked into his rude strain any incident that came his way relating to the place of destination, the passengers on board, the wife or sweetheart at home, his work or amusements by field or flood. There was sometimes a playful humour about them; sometimes compliments were introduced to the master or mistress more hearty than polished. The voices were generally good, the tunes pleasing and various, sometimes gay, sometimes plaintive.[25]

24. Coleman, *Kentucky*, 75.

25. "The Autobiography of William John Grayson," *South Carolina Historical and Genealogical Magazine* XLIX (Jan. 1948), 24-25; See also: Charles Lyell, *A Second Visit to the United States* (2 vols., New York, 1849), I, 244-45; Jay B. Hubbell, "Negro Boatmen's Songs," *Southern Folklore Quarterly* XVIII (Dec. 1954), 244-45; Charles C. Jones, Jr., "Negro Boat Song," C. C. Jones Collection, University of Georgia; George P. Rawick, ed., *The American Slave: A Composite Autobiography* (31 vols., Westport, Conn., 1972-77) (Supplement), IX, 1373-75.

Abounding in rough satire, alluding to sweethearts, masters, and dreams, the boat songs were lusty and sometimes plaintive tunes improvised by the slaves to keep time with their oars.[26] While rowing their master to town, the slaves would set the stroke by singing:

> Sing, fellows, for our own true loves.
> My lottery prize! Zoè, my belle!
> She's like a wild young doe, she knows
> The way to jump and dance so well!
>
> Black diamonds are her bright, black eyes.
> Her teeth and lilies are alike.
> Sing, fellows, for my true love, and
> The water with the long oar strike.
>
> See! see! the town! Hurrah! hurrah!
> Master returns in pleasant mood.
> He's going to treat his boys all 'round,
> Hurrah hurrah for master good![27]

If the master were not aboard, the song might be more melancholy:

> Going away to Georgia, ho, heave, O!
> Massa sell poor negro, ho, heave, O!
> Leave poor wife and children, ho, heave, O! &c. &c.

Boatmen of a more religious bent sang "Michael Row the Boat Ashore":

> Michael boat a music boat,
> Gabriel blow de trumpet horn.
> O you mind your boastin' talk.
> Boastin' talk will sink your soul.

26. John Lambert, *Travels Through Canada and the United States of North America in the Years 1806, 1807 and 1808* (2 vols., London, 1814), II, 253-54; Whipple, *Diary*, 13, 33-34; Paulding, *Letters*, 126-27; Catherine Stewart, *New Homes in the West* (Nashville, 1843), 150; Arfwedson, *United States*, I, 378; Sarah H. Torian, ed., "Ante-Bellum and War Memories of Mrs. Telfair Hodgson," *Georgia Historical Quarterly* XXVII (Dec. 1943), 350-56; Fredrika Bremer, *The Homes of the New World* (2 vols., New York, 1853), I, 385.

27. Cable, "Creole," 822.

Brudder, lend a helpin' hand.
Sister help for trim dat boat.[28]

At their dances the slaves sang merrier tunes often noted more for their rhythmic qualities than for their lyrics. The following was characteristic of many of these tunes:

Harper's creek and roaring ribber,
Thar, my dear, we'll live forebber,
Den we'll go to de Ingin Nation,
All I want in dis creation,
Is a pretty little wife and big plantation.[29]

Frequently the songs were composed during the dance:

I love my darlin', dat I do;
Don't you love Miss Susy, too?

Once the beat was established, a few lines would be repeated over and over:

Sally's in de garden siftin' sand,
And all she want is a honey man.
De reason why I wouldn't marry,
Because she was my cousin
O, row de boat ashore, hey, hey,
Sally's in de garden siftin' sand.[30]

Master satirists, slaves made fun of themselves, their masters, and antebellum politicians. The most popular of their secular songs was "Run, Nigger, Run," in which the slaves boasted of running faster than or outsmarting whites, and described their confrontations with the patrollers:

Run nigger, run, de pat'roller' ketch yo'
Run nigger, run, it's almos' day.
Dat nigger run, dat nigger flew,
Dat nigger tore his shirt in two.
Dat nigger, he sed don't ketch me,

28. Paulding, *Letters*, 127; William F. Allen *et al.*, eds., *Slave Songs of the United States* (New York, 1867), 23.
29. Northup, *Twelve Years*, 167-68.
30. Parker, *Recollections*, 66-67.

But git dat nigger b'hind de tree.
Dat nigger cried, dat nigger lied,
Dat nigger shook his old fat side,
Run, nigger, run, it's almos' day.[31]

In the fields, at corn-shuckings, and dances, politicians became the butt of the slave's humor:

Polk and Clay went to war,
Polk came back with a broken jaw.[32]

The slaveholders and their hypocrisy were major subjects of satire. The slaves, for example, frequently sang "My Old Mistress Promised Me":

My old missus promise me
  Shoo a la a day,
When she die she set me free
  Shoo a la a day.
She live so long her head git bald,
  Shoo a la a day.
She give up de idea of dyin' a-tall,
  Shoo a la a day.[33]

The African's use of metaphor, indirection, insult, irony, and praise in songs of work, love, war, and celebration was replicated in the secular songs in the quarters. Drawing on their African musical heritage, Southern slaves had created by 1850 music that would later be popularized as "the blues." Relying heavily on circumlocution, metaphor, and innuendo, the slaves often referred to fear, infidelity, love, hard times, work, slave coffles, conjura-

31. Rawick, *American Slave* (Supplement), VII, 646; for variants, see: Rawick, *American Slave* IV, pt. 2:52, V, pt. 4:105, 152, VII, pt. 1:65, pt. 2: 162, VIII, pt. 1:15, X, pt. 5:25, 268, pt. 6:367, XIII, pt. 3:214; (Supplement), I, 33, V, 227-28, 279-80, VII, 743; *Southern Workman* XXIV (Feb. 1895), 31; John W. Blassingame, ed., *Slave Testimony* (Baton Rouge, 1977), 656-57; Armstrong, *Old Massa's People*, 149; Charles L. Perdue *et al.*, eds., *Weevils in the Wheat: Interviews with Virginia Ex-Slaves* (Charlottesville, 1976), 310, 326.

32. Rawick, *American Slave*, VI, 193.

33. Rawick, *American Slave*, V, pt. 3:126; variants appear in Rawick, *American Slave*, IX, pt. 3:175, XI, pt. 7:211.

tion, food, drinking, sex, and freedom in their songs.[34] When away from whites, however, the slaves frequently dropped the metaphors. Freedom was a major motif in party songs:

> Rabbit in de briar patch,
> Squirrel in de tree,
> Wish I could go huntin',
> But I ain't free.
>
> Rooster's in de henhouse,
> Hen's in de patch,
> Love to go shootin',
> But I ain't free.

The slaves also sang during their dances of the way slaveholders appropriated the finest food, clothing, and furnishings while leaving little to the bondsman:

> Massa sleeps in de feather bed,
> Nigger sleeps on de floor;
> When we'uns gits to Heaven,
> Dey'll be no slaves no mo'.[35]

The secular songs reflected the rhythm of plantation work. Marching to the fields the slaves sang:

> This ain't Christmas mornin', just a long summer day,
> Hurry up, yellow boy and don't run 'way,
> Grass in the cotton and weeds in the corn,
> Get in the field, 'cause it soon be morn.

But as the sun grew hotter, the slaves began a series of "field hollers," those short outbursts of song, often in a call-and-response pattern, expressive of their feelings about their condition in life and their work. They bragged about deceiving their masters:

34. Francis M. Deng, ed., *The Dinka and Their Songs* (Oxford, Eng., 1973), 78-95; Lawrence Levine, *Black Culture and Black Consciousness* (New York, 1977), 7-10; Rawick, *American Slave*, IV, pt. 2:154, 194, 235, VI, 280, VII, 53, 98-99, 254, 264, 274, VIII, pt. 2:109-110, 195, XI pt. 7:208-9 (Missouri), 336-37, XII, pt. 1:166, XVI (Kentucky), 102; (Supplement), VII, 582-83; Blassingame, *Slave Testimony*, 705-6; Perdue, *Weevils*, 39, 42, 106, 131, 212, 223.

35. Rawick, *American Slave*, IV, pt. 2:89, 233, V, pt. 4:172.

Fool my Massa seben years.
Gwiner fool him seben mo'.
Hey diddle, de diddle, de diddle, de do'.

The "eye servant" who pretended to labor conscientiously appeared frequently:

You may call me Raggedy Pat
'Cause I wear this raggedy hat,
And you may think I'm a workin'
But I ain't.

Central to the slave's attitude toward work was how his master treated him:

Don't mind working from Sun to Sun,
Iffen you give me my dinner—
When the dinner time comes!

Bondsmen complained that though the sugar was sweet, "de plantation's sour," because the slave had to "jump and run every hour." Even when the slave contemplated love, his master's work raised barriers to fulfillment:

Sat'day night and Sunday too
Young gals on my mind,
Monday mornin' way 'fore day
Ole marster got me gwine.

At the end of the day as the slaves reflected on the work they had done, they would shout:

O—he, I's gwine home,
And cuss de old overseer.[36]

Many of the themes and motifs later incorporated into the blues appeared in the tunes slaves sang at cakewalks, dances, and parties. At cakewalks the slaves sang:

36. Rawick, *American Slave*, IV, pt. 2:16, 96, 99, 167, V, pt. 3:215, VI, 168, 387, VII, 296, VIII, pt. 2:335; Armstrong, *Old Massa's People*, 89, 220; Perdue, *Weevils*, 39, 309-10.

Step light, ladies, de cake is all dough,
Neber min' de weather so de wind dont blo.[37]

Often the men sang of their love of alcoholic beverages.[38]

In their love songs the slaves referred by indirection to sex. Like the blues singers of a later era, the slaves used such metaphors as pushing, rocking, blowing, cooking, shaking, riding, beating, and rolling to refer to sexual intercourse.[39] Often the singers interspersed sexual allusions with nonsense rhymes:

You, by word, now all we go,
In fact we spoke both high and low,
In the house and out of doors,
Ebening in the baby's nose.
When I was young an' in my prime,
I'se a courtin' courtin' them gals,
Most all de time.
Now I'm old and you will see,
I'm not as young as I used to be.

Now when the elephant moves aroun'
The music begins to play,
Oh, the boys aroun' dat monkey's cage
I'd better keep away.
Rock, the cradle, John,
Rock, the cradle, John,
Many a man is rockin' another man's son
When he thinks he's rockin' his own.

The slaves also commented more directly on women who were so free with love they became pregnant before marriage:

One mornin' in May,
I spies a beautiful dandy,
A-rakin' way of de hay.
I asks her to marry,
She say, scornful, "No."

37. Rawick, *American Slave* (Supplement), VI, 47.
38. Rawick, *American Slave* (Supplement), IX, 1589-90, VIII, 932-33.
39. Rawick, *American Slave*, IV, pt. 2:280, XI, pt. 7:208, XVI (Kentucky), 63; (Supplement), V, 349; see Levine, *Black Culture*, 242-45, for a discussion of double meanings in the blues.

But befo' six months roll by
Her apron strings wouldn't tie.
She wrote me a letter,
She marry me then,
I say, no, no, my gal, not I.

Like the bluesmen, the slaves sang of their disappointments in courtship and spurned love:

Farewell, farewell, sweet Mary;
I'm ruined forever
By lovin' of you;
Your parents don't like me,
That I do know
I am not worthy to enter your do.[40]

Closely allied with the secular songs was the practice of "patting juba." When slaves had no musical instruments they achieved a high degree of rhythmic complexity by clapping their hands. Solomon Northup, an accomplished slave musician, observed that in juba the clapping involved "striking the hands on the knees, then striking the hands together, then striking the right shoulder with one hand, the left with the other—all the while keeping time with the feet, and singing. . . ."[41] Often the rhythmic patterns used in juba were little short of amazing. After viewing a performance in Georgia in 1841, a traveler from Rhode Island observed that, while the slaves were patting juba, it was "really astonishing to witness the rapidity of their motions, their accurate time, and the precision of their music and dance. I have never seen it equalled in my life."[42] The South Carolina poet Sidney Lanier declared that in juba the slaves often used "quite complex successions of rhythm, not hesitating to syncopate, to change the rhythmic accent for a moment, or to indulge in other highly-specialized variations of the current rhythmus."[43]

40. Rawick, *American Slave,* IV, pt. 2:285, VIII, pt. 2:114, XI, 160-61.
41. Northup, *Twelve Years,* 219.
42. Lewis Paine, *Six Years in a Georgia Prison* (New York, 1851), 180.
43. Sidney Lanier, *The Science of English Verse* (New York, 1880), 186-87.

The slaves also used a great variety of musical instruments. Most of these were either made by the slaves themselves or given to them by their masters. The musical instruments they used included fiddles, clarinets, fifes, tambourines, triangles, flutes, castanets, and banjos. The favorites were the banjo, fiddle, and the drum (often made from hollowed-out logs). The effect of castanets was obtained by beating two hollowed-out sticks together or on the floor. Individually or in bands these musicians performed both for the slaves and the master.[44]

Secular music played an especially large role in the life of plantation blacks. The songs expressed their feelings and desires, gave them solace, and lightened their daily burdens. Those slaves who had some special musical skills won the praise of blacks and whites, achieved a degree of self-esteem, and could relieve themselves of sorrow. Solomon Northup recalled:

> Alas! had it not been for my beloved violin, I scarcely can conceive how I could have endured the long years of bondage. . . . It was my companion—the friend of my bosom—triumphing loudly when I was joyful, and uttering its soft melodious consolations when I was sad. Often, at midnight, when sleep had fled affrighted from the cabin, and my soul was disturbed and troubled with the contemplation of my fate, it would sing me a song of peace.[45]

The mass of slaves, of course, played no instrument. Their solace came from singing. Robert Anderson asserted that the "steady rhythm of the marching songs carried many a slave across the tobacco and hemp fields ahead of a slave driving overseer, when their tired muscles refused to budge for any other stimulant than

44. Bryant, *Letters*, 86-87; Thomas Ashe, *Travels in America* . . . (New York, 1811), 100; Paulding, *Letters*, 118; Whipple, *Diary*, 50-51; Helen T. Catterall, ed., *Judicial Cases Concerning American Slavery and the Negro* (5 vols., Washington, D.C., 1926-37), I, 365-67; Northup, *Twelve Years*, 216-17; Ronald Killion and Charles Waller, eds., *Slavery Time When I Was Chillun down on Marster's Plantation: Interviews with Georgia Slaves* (Savannah, 1973), 11, 24-25, 40, 82, 110, 142; Blassingame, *Slave Testimony*, 644, 652; Armstrong, *Old Massa's People*, 139-42; Perdue, *Weevils*, 82, 113, 265, 316.

45. Northup, *Twelve Years*, 216-17.

that of the rhythm of song, while the weird and mysterious music of the religious ceremonies moved old and young alike in a frenzy of religious fervor."[46]

Folk tales are in many respects easier to analyze than spirituals or secular songs even though the systematic collection of them is more recent. Most folklorists tried in various ways to ascertain the provenience of the tales they recorded. Consequently, there is some assurance that slaves actually told these tales around their cabin fires.[47] There was probably less distortion of the folk tales in the transition from slavery to freedom than of the songs. If, as John Mason Brewer has observed, "folk materials offer a true and unbiased picture of the ways in which a given people . . . think and act," they represent valuable materials for the historian.[48] While there are few explicit references to slavery, the patterns and symbolism of the tales often tell us much about the slave's world view.

Primarily a means of entertainment, the tales also represented the distillation of folk wisdom and were used as an instructional device to teach young slaves how to survive. A projection of the slave's personal experience, dreams, and hopes, the folk tales allowed him to express hostility to his master, to poke fun at himself, and to delineate the workings of the plantation system. At the same time, by viewing himself as an object, verbalizing his dreams and hostilities, the slave was able to preserve one more area which whites could not control. While holding on to the reality of his existence, the slave gave full play to his wish fulfillment in the tales, especially in those involving animals. Identifying with the frightened and helpless creatures, so similar in their relations to the larger animals to the relationship of the slave to

46. Anderson, *From Slavery*, 26.

47. William Owens, "Folklore of the Southern Negroes," *Lippincott's Magazine* XV (Dec. 1877), 748-55; Walter F. Peterson, ed., "Slavery in the 1850's: The Recollections of an Alabama Unionist," *Alabama Historical Quarterly* XXX (Fall and Winter 1968), 219-27; R. Q. Mallard, *Plantation Life Before Emancipation* (New Orleans, 1892), 62-73; Charles W. Hutson, "My Reminiscences" 25, 52, and George W. Polk, "Some Reflections and Reminiscences," 16, Southern Historical Collection, University of North Carolina.

48. John M. Brewer, *Worser Days and Better Times* (Chicago, 1965), 21.

the master, the slave storytellers showed how the weak could survive. Especially in the Brer Rabbit tales, the hero, whether trickster or braggart, always defeated the larger animals through cunning. On occasion the weaker animals (slaves?) injured or killed the stronger ones (masters?). Although it is obviously possible to read too much into these tales, the slave's fascination with weakness overcoming strength cannot be discounted.[49]

Sometimes there are direct references to masters and overseers in these tales. If the slave had suffered at the hands of either, he might thus make them the verbal target of his revenge. A former slaveholder recalled hearing one tale during his childhood in which the slave obviously expressed his hope that some misfortune would befall the overseer:

> Once der was a ole man dat was a conjeror, an' his wife was a witch; an' dey had a son, an' dey larnt him to be a conjeror too; an' every night dey used to get out of deir skins an' go ride deir neighbors. Well, one night de conjeror tetch his son wid his staff an' say, "Horum scarum" (dat mean, "It's pas' de hour o' midnight"). "Come, git up; let's go ride the overseer an' his oldes' son; I had a spite 'gin 'em dis long time." So dey goes to de overseer's house, an' give de sign an' slip t'rough de keyhole. Den dey unbar de door on de inside an' take out de overseer an' his son, widout deir knowin' it; an' de conjeror tetch de overseer wid his switch an' he turns to a bull, an' tetch de overseer's son an' he turns to a bull-yerlin'. Den de conjeror mounts de bull, an' de boy he mounts de bull-yerlin', an' sets off a long way over de creek to blight a man's wheat what de conjeror had a spite again. . . . An' de same minit de overseer was alseep in his bed at home, an' his son was in his bed. An' in de mornin' dey feel very tired, an' know dat de witches been ridin' 'em, but dey never find out what witches it was.[50]

49. Langston Hughes and Arna Bontemps, eds., *The Book of Negro Folklore* (New York, 1966); Richard Dorson, *American Negro Folktales* (Greenwich, Conn., 1967); Bruce Jackson, ed., *The Negro and His Folklore* (London, 1967); Joel Chandler Harris, *The Complete Tales of Uncle Remus* (Boston, 1955); Zora Neale Hurston, *Mules and Men* (London, 1935); Alcée Fortier, *Louisiana Folk-Tales* (Boston, 1895), 1-39; Levine, *Black Culture*, 81-135.

50. Norris, "Negro Superstitions," 95.

The most explicit and realistic portrayal of slavery appears in the John or Jack series. John frequently makes fools of whites, pretends to be more ignorant and humble than he is, dissembles, longs for freedom, runs away, is threatened and beaten, and often defies his master and expresses a desire for revenge for his sufferings.[51] In one tale John prays "for God to come git him [master] and take him to Hell right away because Massa is evil." On another occasion Efram prays: "I'm tired staying here and taking these beatings. . . . kill all the white folks and leave all the niggers."[52] Obviously, John was, as Zora Neale Hurston observed, "the wish fulfillment hero of the race."[53] But he also symbolized the discontent of the slaves, the range of actions open to them, a compendium of survival techniques, and a way of bolstering self-esteem.

The existence and content of the folk tales and secular songs can be interpreted in many ways. In the first place, the mere existence of these cultural forms is proof that the rigors of bondage did not crush the slave's creative energies. Through these means the slave could view himself as an object, hold on to fantasies about his status, engender hope and patience, and at least use rebellious language when contemplating his lot in life. The therapeutic value of this should not be dismissed lightly. Not only did these cultural forms give the slave an area of life independent of his master's control, they also were important psychological devices for repressing anger and projecting aggressions in ways that contributed to mental health, involved little physical threat, and provided some form of recreation. By objectifying the conditions of his life in the folk tales, the slave was in a better position to cope with them. The depersonalization of these con-

51. J. Mason Brewer, "Juneteenth," *Publications of the Texas Folklore Society* X (1932), 9-54; Hughes, *Book*, 61-101; Fred O. Weldon, Jr., "Negro Folklore Heroes," *Publications of the Texas Folklore Society* XXIX (1959), 178-82; John Q. Anderson, "Old John and the Master," *Southern Folklore Quarterly* XXV (Sept. 1961), 195-97; Fortier, *Louisiana*, 7-13, 62-69, 89; J. Mason Brewer, "John Tales," *Publications of the Texas Folklore Society* XXI (1946), 81-104; Perdue, *Weevils*, 34, 98-99, 312-13.

52. Dorson, *Folktales*, 124-65; Hurston, *Mules*, 96-122, 144.

53. Hurston, *Mules*, 305.

ditions did not, however, distort the slave's sense of the brutal realities of his life.

The slave found some hope of escape from the brutalities of his daily life in conventional religion. The Protestant mission to the slaves had exposed thousands of bondsmen to Christian doctrines by 1860. Though the white missionary's humanitarianism was often limited by his support of slavery, though he preached too frequently about obedience to suit the blacks, he succeeded in teaching the slaves the rudiments of Christianity. The slaves acquired many of their religious ideas at the camp meetings they attended with their masters. They, of course, enjoyed the conviviality of these great social gatherings and often sold whiskey and food to both black and white communicants. Many of the slaves, viewing the business opportunities such gatherings provided, cared nothing at all about salvation. William Webb acted the typical businessman at one camp meeting when he made $42 selling ginger cakes and whiskey.

Many of the slaves imitated their master's shouting at both the camp meetings and at their own religious services. Slave preachers often could virtually reproduce the emotional sermons delivered by the white ministers they heard. Frequently attended by all of the blacks in the neighborhood, the slaves' services were similar in many ways to those of their masters: they served as meeting places for friends and sweethearts, furnished avenues for exercising responsibility and leadership, and opportunities for socializing, releasing pent-up emotions, or simply getting drunk.[54]

Most slaves, repelled by the brand of religion their masters taught, the racial inequalities in white churches, and the limita-

54. Henry Box Brown, *Narrative of Henry Box Brown* (Boston, 1851), 28, 45; Moses Roper, *A Narrative of the Adventures and Escape of Moses Roper from American Slavery* (London, 1840), 62-63; John Thompson, *The Life of John Thompson, a Fugitive Slave* (Worcester, Mass., 1856), 13-19; Peter Randolph, *Sketches of Slave Life* (Boston, 1855), 61-62; W. H. Robinson, *From Log Cabin to the Pulpit* (Eau Claire, Wis., 1913), 74-79; Lucius H. Holsey, *Autobiography, Sermons, Addresses, and Essays* (Atlanta, 1898), 254; Richard Allen, *The Life, Experience, and Gospel Labors of the Rt. Rev. Richard Allen* (Philadelphia, 1887), 7; Lunsford Lane, *The Narrative of Lunsford Lane* (Boston, 1848), 20-21; Tyler and Murphy, *Slave Narratives*, 81-83; Armstrong, *Old Massa's People*, 221-34.

tions on the bondsmen's autonomy, formulated new ideas and practices in the quarters. The true shepherd of the black flock was the slave preacher. Often one of few slaves who could read, the black preacher was usually highly intelligent, resourceful, and noted for his powerful imagination and memory. Because of his traits of character and remarkable personality, he was able to unify the blacks, console the sick, weak, and fearful, uplift and inspire them. Suffering with his flock, he understood their tribulations and was accepted as a counsellor and arbiter in the quarters. In his sermons the slaves often saw the invisible hand of God working for their earthly freedom and retribution against whites.[55] Whatever the content of the sermons, the slaves preferred a black preacher. One white missionary to the slaves observed that when a black man was "in the pulpit there is a wonderful sympathy between the speaker and the audience."[56]

The black preacher had special oratorical skills and was master of the vivid phrase, folk poetry, and picturesque words. Described by many white observers as "rude eloquence" and "genuine oratory," the sermons of black preachers excited the emotions. They were orations in which "Exposition was not attempted. Description, exhortation, appeal formed the warp and woof. The whole being expressive of . . . all negro experiences, trials, comforts, and assurances."[57] The sermon of the black preacher was a singular performance. Marked by call and response, his allusions to earthly trials and heavenly rewards were punctuated with groans and gestures designed to engage the audience's attention.[58]

Since the black preacher was himself enslaved, he had to make

55. Nancy B. Woolridge, "The Slave Preacher—Portrait of a Leader," *Journal of Negro Education* XIV (Winter 1945), 28-37; Hughes, *Thirty Years*, 53-54; Charles A. Raymond, "The Religious Life of the Negro Slave," *Harper's Magazine* XXVII (Sept. 1863), 479-85; (Oct. 1863), 676-82; (Nov. 1863), 816-25; G. W. S. "Negro Sermons," *Good Words* VIII (March 1, 1867), 186-88; Armstrong, *Old Massa's People*, 224-34; Albert J. Raboteau, *Slave Religion* (New York, 1978), 231-43, 291-97.

56. Raymond, "Religious Life," 485.

57. Raymond, "Religious Life," 679.

58. William S. Gordon, *Recollections of the Old Quarter* (Lynchburg, Va., 1902), 109-10; Rawick, *American Slave*, XVI (Kentucky), 36-38; *Southern Workman* XXIV (April 1895), 59-61.

some painful compromises in order to minister to the needs of his fellows. Trained by the white clergy, continually under suspicion of plotting insurrection, and often under the surveillance of whites, black ministers frequently joined their masters in preaching obedience and submissiveness to the slaves. On some Sundays the slaves attended white churches and heard virtually the same sermon from white and black preachers.[59] Lewis Favor, for example, recalled that on Sundays in Georgia the slaves "sat in the back of the church as the white minister preached and directed the following text at them: 'Don't steal your master's chickens or his eggs and your backs won't be whipped.' In the afternoon of this same day when the colored minister was allowed to preach the slaves heard this text: 'Obey your masters and mistresses and your back won't be whipped.' "[60] Whether preaching from the pulpit or on the plantations, the black minister's sermon was often an "authorized" one, approved either by the white clergy or the master before it was delivered.

Many black ministers preached obedience to the slaves because when they did not they were flogged. Others did so because the whites rewarded them with money, relief from labor, or manumission. A small minority, reading the Bible literally, apparently sincerely believed that obeying their masters was one of the ways slaves would get to Heaven. For the most part, however, the black ministers knew they were giving conservative advice on how to avoid the lash in this world. Sometimes obsequious to a fault, a few black preachers so valued the rewards and the marks of respect they received from whites they occasionally voluntarily advised the slaves to be content with their lot in life. After Alabama and Mississippi Presbyterians manumitted the Reverend Harrison W. Ellis and sent him as a missionary to Liberia, for instance, he sent back a letter in 1850 proclaiming his "unadulterated friendship and gratitude to the white man of the South," and advising Alabama slaves that "the path of duty is always the path of safety, and all those who wish to be lovely

59. Rawick, *American Slave*, XII, pt. 2:15-16, XIII, pt. 4:129, 201; Armstrong, *Old Massa's People*, 226-28.

60. Rawick, *American Slave*, XII, pt. 1:323.

must learn to be good. As long as it appears to be the will of the Lord, make yourselves, and all around you as contented and happy as possible where you are."[61] Tennessee slaves heard similar admonitions from the slave Baptist preacher George Bentley.[62]

The advice of such ministers as Ellis and George Bentley, along with fears of collaborationists among fellow communicants, forced the slaves to adopt protective measures in their churches. The discipline of the slave church enjoined secrecy on the communicants about affairs in the quarters and religious societies. The Reverend Charles C. Jones asserted in 1842 that slave "members of the same church are sacredly bound by their religion not to reveal each other's sins, for that would be backbiting and injuring the brotherhood." Similarly, a South Carolina missionary reported that when the slaves organized their own religious societies, "It was a rule among the members of these societies, rigidly enforced, never to divulge the secret of stealing; to do so brought dire punishment upon the informer."[63]

The slave's religious principles were colored by his own longings for freedom and based on half-understood sermons in white churches or passages from the Old Testament describing the struggles of the Jews, beautiful pictures of a future life, enchantment and fear, and condemnation of sin. The heaviest emphasis in the slaves' religion was on change in their earthly situation and divine retribution for the cruelty of their masters.[64] According to Charles Ball, "The idea of a revolution in the conditions of the whites and blacks is the cornerstone of the religion of the latter."[65] Dwelling on such ideas in their meetings, afterwards the faces of the slaves shone with "a happy light—their very countenance showed that it had been 'good for them to be

61. *African Repository* XXVII (Jan. 1851), 4.

62. *African Repository,* XXXV (Aug. 1859), 255-56; see also, Rawick, *American Slave,* VII (Oklahoma), 78; (Supplement), IV, 555.

63. Charles C. Jones, *The Religious Instruction of the Negroes in the United States* (Savannah, 1842), 126; William P. Harrison, *The Gospel Among the Slaves* (Nashville, 1893), 167.

64. Charles Ball, *Slavery in the United States: A Narrative of the Life and Adventures of Charles Ball* (Lewiston, Pa., 1836), 190.

65. Hughes, *Thirty Years,* 54.

there.' " Frequently the praise meetings started on Saturday or Sunday evenings and lasted far into the night.

A syncretism of African and conventional religious beliefs, the praise meeting in the quarters was unique in the United States. While whites might be carried away by religious frenzy at occasional "Awakenings," slaves had an even more intense emotional involvement with their God every week. In contrast to most white churches, a meeting in the quarters was the scene of perpetual motion and constant singing. Robert Anderson recalled that in meetings on his plantation there was much singing and "While singing these songs, the singers and the entire congregation kept time to the music by the swaying of their bodies, or by the patting of the foot or hand. Practically all of their songs were accompanied by a motion of some kind."[66] A black plantation preacher testified to the uniqueness of the religion in the quarters when he asserted:

> The way in which we worshipped is almost indescribable. The singing was accompanied by a certain ecstasy of motion, clapping of hands, tossing of heads, which would continue without cessation about half an hour; one would lead off in a kind of recitative style, others joining in the chorus. The old house partook of the ecstasy; it rang with their jubilant shouts, and shook in all its joints.[67]

Besides voodoo ceremonies along the Gulf Coast, the best example of the syncretism of African and conventional religious patterns appears in the "ring shout." H. G. Spaulding gave an excellent description of the "shout" on the Sea Islands in 1863:

> After the praise meeting is over, there usually follows the very singular and impressive performance of the "Shout," or religious dance of the negroes. Three or four, standing still, clapping their hands and beating time with their feet, commence singing in unison one of the peculiar shout melodies, while the others walk round in a ring, in single file, joining also in the

66. Anderson, *From Slavery*, 24-25.

67. James L. Smith, *Autobiography of James L. Smith* (Norwich, Conn., 1881), 27.

Figure 27. Invisible Church

song. Soon those in the ring leave off their singing, the others keeping it up the while with increased vigor, and strike into the shout step, observing most accurate time with the music. This step is something halfway between a shuffle and a dance, as difficult for an uninitiated person to describe as to imitate. At the end of each stanza of the song the dancers stop short with a slight stamp on the last note, and then, putting the other foot forward, proceed through the next verse. . . . The shout is a simple outburst and manifestation of religious fervor—a "rejoicing in the Lord"—making a "joyful noise unto the God of their salvation."[68]

Shouting, singing, and preaching, the slaves released all of their despair and expressed their desires for freedom. Their expression of the latter was restricted because discreet whites occasionally attended their meetings. Henry Clay Bruce recalled that one old slave preacher once forgot about the white man who

68. H. G. Spaulding, "Under the Palmetto," *Continental Monthly* IV (Aug. 1863), 196-97.

Figure 28. A Joyful Noise

was present at the meeting and in his enthusiasm prayed: "Free indeed, free from death, free from hell, free from work, free from white folks, free from everything."[69] Although the preacher was upbraided by the white man later, he had expressed the sentiments of most of his fellows.

The sentiments of the slave often appear in the spirituals. Songs of sorrow and hope, of agony and joy, of resignation and rebellion, the spirituals were the unique creations of the black slaves. Since, however, the spirituals were derivations from Biblical lore and served as a means of intra-group expression in a hostile environment, they naturally contain few explicit references to slavery. As a consequence of the similarities of themes in the black spirituals and white hymns, a number of scholars contend that the slaves borrowed their songs from whites. While it would be almost as logical to argue the opposite, it must be admitted that the songs the slaves heard in white churches did have a limited influence on the spirituals. For the most part, however, the white hymns were too cold and static to allow for the full expression of the slave's religious sentiments. After listening to the singing of former slaves in South Carolina during the Civil War, Thomas Wentworth Higginson wrote:

> As they learned all their songs by ear, they often strayed into wholly new versions, which sometimes became popular, and entirely banished the others. . . . they sang, reluctantly, even on Sundays, the long and short metres of the hymnbooks, always gladly yielding to the more potent excitement of their own "spirituals." By these they could sing themselves, as had their fathers before them, out of the contemplation of their own low estate, into the sublime scenery of the Apocalypse.[70]

Even when slaves did model their songs on those of whites, they changed them radically. South Carolina slaves, for example, added the following verse to "Blow Your Trumpet Gabriel":

69. Bruce, *New Man,* 73.
70. Higginson, "Spirituals," 693-94.

O, Satan is a liar, and he conjure too,
And, if you don't mind, he'll conjure you,
So blow your trumpet Gabriel. . . .[71]

The emphases, words, phrases, structure, and call-and-response pattern of the spirituals differ so strikingly from the songs of whites, that one must look outside the white church to discover their origin.[72] According to a number of antebellum white observers, the spiritual was the unique creation of black slaves.[73] In 1842, for instance, Charles C. Jones of Georgia noted the slaves' "extravagant and non-sensical chants, and catches and hallelujah songs of their own composing. . . ."[74] An Alabamian, Ella Christian, gave even clearer evidence on this: "When Baptist Negroes attended the church of their masters . . . they used hymn books, but in their own meetings they often made up their own words and tunes. They said their songs had more religion than those in the books."[75]

The spiritual, reflecting the day-to-day experience of the slave, his troubles, and his hopes of release from bondage, was indeed more vibrant and expressive than those songs that came from books. "The songs of the slave," Frederick Douglass wrote, "rep-

71. Higginson, "Spirituals," 690.

72. Dena J. Epstein, "Slave Music in the United States Before 1860: A Survey of Sources," *Music Library Association Notes* XX (Spring 1963), 195-212, (Summer 1963), 377-90; H. H. Procter, "The Theology of the Songs of the Southern Slave," *Southern Workman* (Dec. 1907), 652-56; Whipple, *Diary*, 36; Francis Hall, *Travels in Canada and the United States in 1816 and 1817* (London, 1818), 358-59; Myrtil Lon Candler, "Reminiscences of Life in Georgia During the 1850's and 1860's," *Georgia Historical Quarterly* XXXIII (June 1949), 110-23; Levine, *Black Culture*, 3-80; Dena J. Epstein, *Sinful Tunes and Spirituals: Black Folk Music to the Civil War* (Urbana, 1977); Lazarus Ekwueme, "African-Music Retentions in the New World," *The Black Perspective in Music* II (Fall 1974), 128-40.

73. On the origins of the spirituals, see: Lucy McKim, "Songs of the Port Royal Contrabands," *Dwight's Journal of Music* XXI (Nov. 8, 1862), 254-55; John Mason Brown, "Songs of the Slave," *Lippincott's Magazine* II (Dec. 1868), 617-23; "Songs of the Blacks," *Dwight's Journal of Music* IX (Nov. 15, 1856), 51-52; J. M. McKim, "Negro Songs," *Dwight's Journal of Music* XVI (Aug. 9, 1862), 148-49; Bremer, *Homes*, I, 352, 369-71, 393-94.

74. Jones, *Religious Instruction*, 266.

75. James B. Sellers, *Slavery in Alabama* (University, Ala., 1950), 300.

resent the sorrows of his heart."[76] Whatever their station in life, few white men had shared those sorrows. As a result, the hymns heard in the white churches did not have the same inspiration as the spiritual. One recorder of spirituals, for example, contended that they

> were composed in the fields, in the kitchen, at the loom, in the cabin at night, and were inspired by some sad or awe-inspiring event. The death of a beloved one, even one of the master's family, the hardness of a master or his cruelty, the selling of friends or relatives, and heart-rending separations, a camp-meeting, a great revival, the sadness and loneliness of old age, unusual phenomena such as the bursting of a comet,—any of these might be sources of inspiration.[77]

Often combining secular and sacred themes, narrating personal experiences, and uplifting the disconsolate, the spirituals frequently served as accompaniments to labor or dealt with the prosaic details of life. They served, for instance, as a secret means of communication. Whenever the slaves on one plantation had decided to gather secretly for a dance, prayer meeting, or the clandestine barbecue of a stolen pig, they might let other slaves know of the event by singing:

> I take my text in Matthew, and by Revelation,
> I know you by your garment.
> Dere's a meeting here tonight.
> Dere's a meeting here tonight.[78]

If a slave spotted the master or overseer coming to check on the workers while they were taking an "unauthorized rest," he sang:

> Sister, carry de news on,
> Master's in de field;
> Sister, carry de news on,
> Master's in de field.[79]

76. Frederick Douglass, *Narrative of the Life of Frederick Douglass* (Cambridge, Mass., 1960), 38.
77. A. E. Perkins, "Negro Spirituals from the Far South," *Journal of American Folklore* XXXV (July-Sept. 1922), 223.
78. Allen, *Slave Songs*, 9.
79. Perkins, "Spirituals," 229.

The relationship of the spirituals to the slave's actual experiences emerges from a careful study of themes. For example, one of the most striking characteristics of the spirituals was the frequent reference to meeting fathers, mothers, relatives, and friends in Heaven. Although possibly related to ancestor worship in Africa, songs of this nature probably grew out of the slaves' longing to be reunited with loved ones torn away from them by cruel masters. According to Jacob Stroyer, when slaves were sold those remaining on the plantations sang "little hymns that they had been accustomed to for the consolation of those that were going away, such as

> When we all meet in Heaven,
> There is no parting there;
> When we all meet in Heaven,
> There is no parting more.[80]

Often the real world of the slave and his reaction to it appeared even more explicitly in the spirituals. In the song "No more rain fall for wet you" the slaves described their condition in graphic terms:

> No more rain fall for wet you, Hallelujah,
> No more sun shine for burn you,
> Dere's no hard trials
> Dere's no whips a-crackin'
> No evil-doers in de kingdom
> All is gladness in de kingdom.[81]

The slaves sought some hope, some solace for their suffering in the spirituals. Toiling from day to day, they sang to lighten their burdens:

> Breddren, don' get weary, breddren don' get weary,
> Breddren don' get weary. Fo' de work is mos' done.
> Keep yo' lamp trim an' a burnin',
> Keep yo' lamp trim an' a burnin',

80. Stroyer, *My Life*, 41.
81. Allen, *Slave Songs*, 46.

Keep yo' lamp trim an' a burnin',
Fo' de work is mos' done.[82]

When there were no whites around, the slaves dropped symbols and expressed their dissatisfaction and longings in unmistakably clear words. In "Hail Mary," for example, the slaves look forward to the coming of a "valiant soldier" to help them bear their cross until they will be

Done wid driber's dribin', Done wid driber's dribin',
Done wid driber's dribin', Roll, Jordan roll.
Done wid massa's hollerin',
Don wid missus scoldin'.[83]

While William Wells Brown was working for a slave trader, he often heard the slaves singing these words as they were carried to New Orleans:

See these poor souls from Africa
Transported to America;
We are stolen, and sold in Georgia,
Will you go along with me?
We are stolen, and sold in Georgia,
Come sound the jubilee!

See wives and husbands sold apart,
Their children's screams will break my heart;—
There's a better day a coming,
Will you go along with me?
There's a better day a coming,
Go sound the jubilee![84]

There were frequent references to freedom and deliverance in the spirituals. Certainly in some cases this must have meant temporal freedom:

O my Lord delivered Daniel
O why not deliver me too?

82. Mary Dickson Arrowood and T. F. Hamilton, "Nine Negro Spirituals, 1850-61, from Lower South Carolina," *Journal of American Folklore* XLI (Oct.-Dec. 1928), 582.
83. Allen, *Slave Songs*, 45.
84. W. W. Brown, *Narrative*, 51.

There is considerable evidence that many of the spirituals refer to the actual longings of the slaves for earthly freedom. Frederick Douglass, for example, recalled that when he and a group of slaves were preparing to escape to the North they sang spirituals:

> A keen observer might have detected in our singing of
>
> "O Canaan, sweet Canaan,
> I am bound for the land of Canaan,"
>
> Something more than a hope of reaching heaven. We meant to reach the *north*—and the north was our Canaan
>
> "I thought I heard them say,
> There were lions in the way,
> I don't expect to stay
> Much longer here.
> Run to Jesus—shun the danger—
> I don't expect to stay
> Much longer here"
>
> Was a favorite air, and had a double meaning. . . . in the lips of *our* company, it simply meant, a speedy pilgrimage toward a free state, and deliverance, from all the evils and dangers of slavery.[85]

The double meanings are most clearly apparent in the stress on deliverance and escape in the spirituals. The escape motif appears in hundreds of songs: the slaves are always sailing, walking, riding, rowing, climbing, and crossing over into Canaan. They "have no time for stay at home," for they are "Bound to go," to "Trabel on, trabel on."[86] In some cases the desire to escape is spelled out even more explicitly:

> Member walk and never tire.
> Member walk Jordan long road.
> You go home to Wappoo.
> I go to seek my fortune.

Another slave on the road to Jubilee, sang

85. Douglass, *Bondage*, 278-79.
86. Allen, *Slave Songs*, 22, 25, 31.

I been to Jerusalem.
Patrol aroun' me,
Tank God he no ketch me.[87]

Generally, the slave's longing for freedom was hidden behind Biblical symbols. This was not, however, always the case. On one occasion near Georgetown, South Carolina, a group of slaves forgot to hide their desires and were imprisoned for singing:

And it won't be long, And it won't be long,
And it won't be long, Poor sinner suffer here.
We'll soon be free
De Lord will call us home.

. . . .

We'll fight for liberty
When de Lord will call us home.[88]

Other slaves echoed the desires of their South Carolina brethren. For instance, they often sang the following lines:

Working all day,
And part of the night,
And up before the morning light.

Chorus: When will Jehovah hear our cry,
And free the sons of Africa?[89]

Many of the spirituals spoke so directly of the slave's longing for freedom that he could only sing them in secret. Certainly a slave had to be far away from whites when he sang:

I'se gwine on er journey, tell yo',
I hyar yo' better go 'long;
I'se gwine fer de kingdom, tell yo',
I hyar yo' better go 'long.
O blow, blow, Ole Massa, blow de cotton horn,
Ole Jim'll neber wuck no mo' in de cotton an' de corn.[90]

87. Allen, *Slave Songs*, 50, 35.
88. Allen, *Slave Songs*, 93-94.
89. Long, *Pictures*, 198.
90. *Journal of American Folklore* X (July-Sept. 1897), 216.

The same was true of the words that Missouri slaves sometimes sang as they contemplated their bondage:

> O, gracious Lord! When shall it be,
> That we poor souls shall all be free;
> Lord, break them slavery powers–
> Will you go along with me?
> Lord break them slavery powers,
> Go sound the jubilee!
>
> Dear Lord, dear Lord, when slavery'll cease,
> Then we poor souls will have our peace;–
> There's a better day a coming.
> Will you go along with me?
> There's a better day a coming,
> Go sound the jubilee![91]

Whether the slaves stated their desires or intentions explicitly or obliquely, planters often felt they were singing about temporal freedom. One former slave told Lydia Maria Child of white reaction to the song "Better days are coming" around the time of Nat Turner's revolt. The whites, the slave said, "wouldn't let us sing that. They thought we were going to *rise* because we sung 'better days are coming.' " The words of the apparently innocuous song were:

> A few more beatings of the wind and rain,
> Ere the winter will be over–
> Glory, Hallelujah!
> Some friends has gone before me,–
> I must try to go and meet them–
> Glory, Hallelujah!
> A few more risings and settings of the sun,
> Ere the winter will be over–
> Glory, Hallelujah!
> There's a better day a coming–
> There's a better day a coming–
> Oh, Glory, Hallelujah![92]

91. W. W. Brown, *Narrative*, 51-52.
92. Maria Chapman, ed., *The Liberty Bell* (Boston, 1839), 42-43.

In spite of the discontent with their earthly lot revealed in the slaves' sorrow songs, the desire for revenge on whites is hidden by symbolism—probably behind the frequent portrayals of a wrathful God, or Moses besieging evil lands (the South?) and smiting sinners (masters?) to force them "to let my people go."

As other-worldly as they often appear, the spirituals served as much more than opiates and escapist fantasies. They affirmed the slave's personal autonomy and recognized the reality of his earthly suffering. While looking beyond the dismal present to a brighter future, the spiritual enabled blacks to transcend degradation and to find the emotional security to endure pain.

The strong sense of family and community solidarity is indicated by frequent references in the spirituals to relatives and friends by name. Because the church served as the major social center in the quarters, there are numerous references to "going to the meeting." Often the slaves were so filled with the Holy Ghost (the Spirit) that they could forget their oppression in an outburst of shouting and singing. Their joyful noises to the Lord indicated that they valued the ideals of personal honor, godly living, strict morality, integrity, perseverance, faith, freedom, and family life.[93]

While the spirituals reveal the slave's attitude toward his condition in life, they are, like most sacred songs, primarily reflections of his religious concepts. A content analysis of the spirituals in William F. Allen's *Slave Songs of the United States* (1867) reveals several distinctive features. Presenting the living drama of the whole Bible, blacks found an especial appeal in passages from Revelation, Matthew, John, Genesis, Exodus, and Isaiah. Rejecting literal interpretations of these passages, the slaves altered them, appropriating those symbols corresponding closely with their own situation.[94]

93. Jeremiah A. Wright, "The Treatment of Biblical Passages in Negro Spirituals" (M.A. thesis, Howard University, 1969), 123-77.

94. W. P. Darby, *Bearing Arms in the Twenty-Seventh Massachusetts Regiment of Volunteer Infantry During the Civil War, 1861-1865* (Boston, 1883), 217; A. R. Small, *The Sixteenth Maine Regiment in the War of the*

In an overwhelming majority of the songs the slaves sang of their search for God in the wilderness, rocks, storms, and valleys in order to obtain relief from the pain, weariness, and troubles of the world, or patience to bear them. For the slave, Satan was a personal Devil, a snake in the grass pulling him toward Hell. Yet he was always optimistic; he was most poetic in depicting the road to Heaven as a way of escaping from his dismal existence on earth. Through the spirituals, the slave sought redemption from sin and communion with God. The God of the spirituals was visible in nature, present in the consciousness of man, omnipotent and omnipresent; He revealed himself directly to men, and was the Father who would help the slaves in their tribulations.

The slave's faith in his God was deep and abiding. He was no abstraction, but a Being who took an interest in the lowly slave and interceded in his behalf. He was the God of freedom to whom slaves prayed for deliverance from bondage. They poured out their troubles to Him and saw visions of Him. He was the great Comforter. Isaac Mason found in times of affliction "that by turning my heart toward God, He would take care of me and provide for my wants."[95] Slavery weighed heavily on William Grimes, he wrote, "yet, under the consolation of religion, my fortitude never left me." God's personal assurance of freedom buoyed up the sagging spirits of many slaves. William Webb prayed for deliverance from a cruel master and asserted that he "found that when I called on God in my trials he sent comfort to my heart, and told me the time would come, when I would be free in this world."[96]

Rebellion, 1861-1865 (Portland, Me., 1886), 113-14; Henry E. Valentine, *Story of Co. 7, 23d Massachusetts Volunteers in the War for the Union, 1861-1865* (Boston, 1896), 28; John W. Hanson, *Historical Sketch of the Old Sixth Regiment of Massachusetts Volunteers, During Its Three Campaigns in 1861, 1862, 1863 and 1864* (Boston, 1866), 165-67; Frederic Denison, *Shot and Shell: Third Rhode Island Heavy Artillery Regiment, in the Rebellion, 1861-1865* (Providence, 1879), 62, 135-36, 208-9.

95. Green, *Events*, 3-4; Webb, *History*, 4-8; Isaac Mason, *Life of Isaac Mason as a Slave* (Worcester, Mass., 1893), 24-27.

96. Mason, *Slave*, 27; Grimes, *Life*, 34; Webb, *History*, 7.

Religious faith often conquered the slave's fear of his master. The more pious slaves persisted in attending religious services contrary to the order of their masters and in spite of floggings. In this test of wills the slave asserted that his master could inflict pain on his body, but he could not harm his soul. After administering a few floggings, most masters gave up and allowed the slave to go to church when he pleased. Clearly, religion was more powerful than the master, engendering more love and fear in the slave than he could. William Webb's reaction to conversion was similar to that of many slaves: "As soon as I felt in my heart, that God was the Divine Being that I must call on in all my troubles, I heard a voice speak to me, and from that time I lost all fear of men on this earth."[97]

Religious services and recreational activities provided the slave with welcome respites from incessant labor. They not only gave him joy and companionship, they also permitted him to gain some status in the quarters and gave him some hope. By engaging in religious activities, the slave could, for a while, shift his mind from his hopeless *immediate* condition to the bright *future* awaiting him. In his daily tribulations, he could turn either to the conjurer or to God for succor.

Having a distinctive culture helped the slaves to develop a strong sense of group solidarity. They united to protect themselves from the most oppressive features of slavery and to preserve their self-esteem. Despite their weakness as isolated individuals, they found some protection in the group from their masters. The code of the group, for example, called for support for those slaves who broke plantation rules. The most important aspect of this group identification was that slaves were not solely dependent on the white man's cultural frames of reference for their ideals and values. As long as the plantation black had cultural norms and ideals, ways of verbalizing aggression, and roles in his life largely free from his master's control, he could preserve some personal autonomy, and resist infantilization, total identification

97. Webb, *History*, 5.

with planters, and internalization of unflattering stereotypes calling for abject servility. A communalism born of oppression led to an emphasis on mutual cooperation, joyful camaraderie, humor, respect for elders, and an undisguised zest for life. The slave's culture bolstered his self-esteem, courage, and confidence and served as his defense against personal degradation.

4

The Slave Family

O, where has mother gone, papa?
What makes you look so sad?
Why sit you here alone, papa?
Has anyone made you mad?
O, tell me, dear papa.
Has master punished you again?
Shall I go bring the salt, papa,
To rub your back and cure the pain?

W. H. Robinson

The Southern plantation was unique in the New World because it permitted the development of a monogamous slave family. In sharp contrast to the South, the general imbalance in the sex ratio among Latin American slaves severely restricted the development of monogamous mating arrangements. For example, in 1860 there were 156 males for every 100 female slaves in Cuba. The German traveler Alexander von Humboldt found that there was only one female to every four male slaves on most Cuban sugar estates, and in the San Juan de los Remedios region there was only one female to every 19 males. One Cuban plantation that Humboldt visited had 700 males and no female slaves. According to the Cuban Census of 1857, there were 164 males for every 100 females between the ages of 12 and 60. In the countryside the situation was even worse; there were 191 males for every 100 females between the ages of 12 and 60. The imbalance in the sex ratio among Latin American slaves was partly a result of the planter's initial lack of interest in reproducing the slave population and his preference for importing more males than females from Africa. For instance, in the Brazilian coffee-growing county of Vassouras, Stanley Stein found that between 1820 and

1880 70 per cent of the African-born slaves were males. Robert Conrad's analysis of ship manifests in the 1830s and 1840s showed that four out of every five Africans imported into Brazil were males. Whatever the cause, the great disparity in the sex ratio restricted the development of monogamous family patterns among Latin American slaves.[1]

The physical basis for the monogamous slave family appears clearly in the sex ratio among slaves in the Southern states. The number of females to every 100 male slaves in the United States was 95.1 in 1820, 98.3 in 1830, 99.5 in 1840, 99.9 in 1850, and 99.3 in 1860. When the sex ratio is broken down by ages, there were 99.8 and 99.1 females for every 100 male slaves over 15 years of age in 1850 and 1860 respectively. The excess of male over female slaves was very slight in the South in comparison with the disparity in Latin America. For example, in 1860 only one Southern state, Missouri, had as many as 109 male to every 100 female slaves. Actually, the sex ratio among slaves was more nearly equal in most Southern states than among whites. In 1860, in the Southern states, there were 106 white males for every 100 white females; in six states there were more than 110 white males for every 100 white females.[2]

1. Philip D. Curtin, "Epidemiology and the Slave Trade," *Political Science Quarterly* LXXXIII (June 1968), 190-216; Stanley J. Stein, *Vassouras: A Brazilian Coffee County: 1850-1900* (Cambridge, Mass., 1957); Alexander von Humboldt, *Personal Narratives of Travels to the Equinoctial Regions of the New Continent, During the Years 1799-1804* (7 vols., London, 1829), VII, 276-79; Alexander von Humboldt, *The Island of Cuba* (New York, 1856), 189, 203-16, 249; Carl Degler, *Neither Black nor White* (New York, 1971), 36-39; Franklin W. Knight, *Slave Society in Cuba During the Nineteenth Century* (Madison, 1970), 79.

2. *Eighth Census of the United States*, I, 594-95; *Compendium of the Seventh Census* (Washington, D.C., 1854), 87, 91. For earlier surveys of the slave family, see: Bobby F. Jones, "A Cultural Middle Passage: Slave Marriage and Family in the Ante-Bellum South" (Ph.D. diss., University of North Carolina, 1965); Orville W. Taylor, *Negro Slavery in Arkansas* (Durham, 1958), 189-202; J. Winston Coleman, *Slavery Times in Kentucky* (Chapel Hill, 1940), 57-61; E. Franklin Frazier, *The Negro Family in the United States* (Chicago, 1948); E. Franklin Frazier, "The Negro Slave Family," *Journal of Negro History* XV (April 1930), 198-259; Herbert Gutman, *The Black Family in Slavery and Freedom, 1750-1925* (New York, 1976).

Since childhood is the most crucial era in the development of personality, and parents play so large a role in determining behavioral patterns, attitudes, ideals, and values, the slave family must be analyzed in order to understand slave life. The family, while it had no legal existence in slavery, was in actuality one of the most important survival mechanisms for the slave. In his family he found companionship, love, sexual gratification, sympathetic understanding of his sufferings; he learned how to avoid punishment, to cooperate with other blacks, and to maintain his self-esteem. However frequently the family was broken, it was primarily responsible for the slave's ability to survive on the plantation without becoming totally dependent on and submissive to his master. The important thing was not that the family was not recognized legally or that masters frequently encouraged monogamous mating arrangements in the quarters only when it was convenient to do so, but rather that some form of family life did exist among slaves.

While the form of family life in the quarters differed radically from that among free Negroes and whites, this does not mean that it failed to perform many of the traditional functions of the family—the rearing of children being one of the most important of these functions. Since slave parents were primarily responsible for training their children, they could cushion the shock of bondage for them, help them to understand their situation, teach them values different from those their masters tried to instil in them, and give them a referent for self-esteem other than the master.

If he was lucky, the slave belonged to a master who tried to foster the development of strong family ties in the quarters. Although the slaveholders sometimes encouraged monogamous mating arrangements because of their religious views, they generally did so to make it easier to discipline their slaves. A black man, they reasoned, who loved his wife and his children was less likely to be rebellious or to run away than would a "single" slave. The simple threat of being separated from his family was generally sufficient to subdue the most rebellious "married" slave. Besides,

Figure 29. Home

there was less likelihood of fights between slaves when monogamous mating arrangements existed.[3]

A number of planters attempted to promote sexual morality in the quarters, punished slaves for licentiousness and adultery, and recognized the male as the head of the family. On William J. Minor's plantations, slaves had to give a month's notice before their "marriage" or "divorce."[4] One planter asserted in 1836 that

3. William Wells Brown, *Narrative of William W. Brown, a Fugitive Slave* (Boston, 1847), 21-26, 80-90; James Watkins, *Narrative of the Life of James Watkins* (Bolton, Eng., 1852), 18-21; I. E. Lowery, *Life on the Old Plantation in Ante-Bellum Days: Or a Story Based on Facts* (Columbia, S.C., 1911), 42; William O'Neal, *Life and History of William O'Neal* (St. Louis, 1896), 33-41; James L. Smith, *Autobiography of James L. Smith* (Norwich, Conn., 1881), 1-9.

4. J. Carlyle Sitterson, "The William J. Minor Plantations: a Study in Ante-Bellum Absentee Ownership," *Journal of Southern History* IX (Feb. 1943), 59-74; L. Tibbetts to "Sister," Jan. 23, 1853, John C. Tibbetts Cor-

he particularly enjoined upon his slaves, "the observance of their marriage contracts. In no instance do I suffer any of them to violate these ties; except where I would consider myself justified in doing so."[5] Hugh Davis of Alabama also sought to promote morality on his plantation. He informed his overseer that "all violations of the right of husband and wife and such other immorality will meet with chastisement[.] From 10 to 50 stripes is the general measure of punishment for stated offenses according to their grade."[6]

Most planters were far less successful or interested in promoting morality in the quarters than Hugh Davis. The typical experience was related by a Mississippi planter: "As to their habits of amalgamation and intercourse, I know of no means whereby to regulate them, or to restrain them; I attempted it for many years by preaching virtue and decency, encouraging marriages, and by punishing, with some severity, departures from marital obligations; but it was all in vain."[7] It is obvious that most slaveholders did not care about the sexual customs of their slaves as long as there was no bickering and fighting. As a result, planters were generally more interested in encouraging monogamy because it was conducive to discipline than because of any interest in encouraging morality in the quarters. According to one planter, "the general rule of the plantation recognized the relation of man and wife and compelled not virtue perhaps, but monogamy."[8] Many of the plantations were so large that it was impossible for masters to supervise both the labor and the sex life of their slaves. Sexual morality, often imperfectly taught (or violated by whites

---

respondence; Jan. 4, 1862, Priscilla Bond Diary, Memoranda Book No. 9, Alexandre DeClouet Papers, Louisiana State University Archives; Philip H. Jones, "Reminiscences of Days Before and After the Civil War," Southern Historical Collection, University of North Carolina; Mathilda Houston, *Hesperos* (2 vols., London, 1850), II, 157-59.

5. *Southern Agriculturalist* IX (Dec. 1836), 626.

6. Weymouth T. Jordan, "The Management Rules of an Alabama Black Belt Plantation, 1848-1862," *Agricultural History* XVIII (Jan. 1944), 64.

7. *DeBow's Review* X (June 1851), 623.

8. John W. DuBose, "Recollections of the Plantations," *Alabama Historical Quarterly* I (Spring 1930), 66.

with impunity), drifted down through a heavy veil of ignorance to the quarters. Consequently, for many slaves, sex was a natural urge frequently fulfilled in casual liaisons. William Wells Brown's mother, for example, had seven children fathered by seven different men, black and white.[9]

The white man's lust for black women was one of the most serious impediments to the development of morality. The white man's pursuit of black women frequently destroyed any possibility that comely black girls could remain chaste for long. Few slave parents could protect their pretty daughters from the sexual advances of white men. This was particularly true when the slaves belonged to a white bachelor or lived near white bachelors. Lucius Holsey's white father, for instance, never married but instead chose successive lovers from among the female slaves on his plantation.[10]

The black autobiographers testified that many white men considered every slave cabin as a house of ill-fame. Often through "gifts," but usually through force, white overseers and planters obtained the sexual favors of black women. Generally speaking, the women were literally forced to offer themselves "willingly" and receive a trinket for their compliance rather than a flogging for their refusal and resistance. Frederick Douglass declared that the "slave woman is at the mercy of the fathers, sons or brothers of her master."[11] Many of the black autobiographers recounted stories of slave women being forced to submit to white men: Henry Bibb's master forced one slave girl to be his son's concu-

9. Brown, *Narrative,* 1-15; William Grimes, *Life of William Grimes, the Runaway Slave, Brought Down to the Present Time* (New Haven, 1855), 5-14.

10. Grimes, *Life,* 5-14; Annie L. Burton, *Memories of Childhood's Slavery Days* (Boston, 1909), 3-9; Harriet Martineau, *Retrospect of Western Travel* (3 vols., London, 1838), II, 146-48; Thomas Anburey, *Travels Through the Interior Parts of America* (London, 1789), 385; John Davis, *Travels in the United States of America 1798 to 1802* (2 vols., Boston, 1910), I, 70, II, 141; Robert Sutcliff, *Travels in Some Parts of North America in the Years 1804, 1805 and 1806* (York, Eng., 1811), 53, 101; Victor Tixier, *Travels on the Osage Prairies* (Norman, Okla., 1940), 97.

11. Frederick Douglass, *My Bondage and My Freedom* (New York, 1968 [1855]), 60.

bine; M. F. Jamison's overseer raped a pretty slave girl; and Solomon Northup's owner forced one slave, "Patsey," to be his sexual partner. Slave traders frequently engaged in the same kind of practices. Moses Roper, who once helped a slave trader, declared that the traders often had intercourse with the most beautiful black women they purchased. When Henry Bibb and his wife were sold to a trader in Louisville, Kentucky, the trader forced Bibb's wife to become a prostitute.[12]

A number of white men sought more than fleeting relationships with black women. Frequently they purchased comely black women for their concubines. In many cases the master loved his black concubine and treated her as his wife. Jacob Stroyer declared that the white groom on his master's plantation shared his cabin with his black lover and their two daughters. (One of the girls married a white man after the Civil War.) Two of the black autobiographers, Jermain Loguen and John Mercer Langston, lived in such households. Langston's father was a wealthy Virginia planter, Ralph Quarles, who wanted to abolish slavery. Ostracized by his neighbors because of his abolitionist views, Quarles restricted himself almost solely to the company of his slaves. He took Langston's mother, Lucy, as his concubine, made her mistress of his household, and had four children by her. Eventually he freed her and the children. Langston declared that his father treated him "tenderly and affectionately." Early each morning he would rise and tutor his children, and when the boys reached a certain age, he sent them to school in Ohio. Upon the marriage of his daughter to a slave, Quarles purchased and freed her husband and gave them a plantation and some slaves. At his death in 1834, Quarles freed some of his slaves and willed all of his property to his three sons.[13]

12. Henry Bibb, *Narrative of the Life and Adventures of Henry Bibb, an American Slave* (New York, 1849), 98-99, 112-16; Moses Roper, *A Narrative of the Adventures and Escape of Moses Roper from American Slavery* (London, 1840), 24, 63-66; Bethany Veney, *The Narrative of Bethany Veney, a Slave Woman* (Worcester, Mass., 1889), 26.

13. Israel Campbell, *An Autobiography* (Philadelphia, 1861), 228-35; John Mercer Langston, *From the Virginia Plantation to the National Capital* (Hartford, 1894), 1-36; Jermain Wesley Loguen, *The Rev. J. W. Loguen, as a*

Miscegenation often led to complications in the South. Sometimes, white men loved their black concubines more than they did their white wives. Consequently, the white women sued for, and obtained, divorce. Henry Watson asserted that the wife of a Natchez, Mississippi, slave trader divorced him because of his concubine. White women were frequently infuriated by their husbands' infidelities in the quarters and took revenge on the black women involved. When Moses Roper was born, for example, his mistress tried to kill him when she discovered that her husband was Roper's father. To prevent this, the man sold Roper and his mother.

On innumerable occasions white women also had assignations with black slaves. The evidence from Virginia divorce petitions is conclusive on this point: a Norfolk white man asserted in 1835 that his wife had "lived for the last six or seven years and continues to live in open adultery with a negro man. . . ." A Nansemond County white man declared in 1840 that his wife had given birth to a mulatto child and that she had "recently been engaged in illicit intercourse with a negro man at my own house and on my own bed." In many cases the sexual relations between Negro men and white women went undetected because the children resulting from such unions were light enough to pass for white. For example, one Virginian testified that when his white wife gave birth to a mulatto he "did not at first doubt [it] to be his, notwithstanding its darkness of color, and its unusual appearance." One white woman in eighteenth-century Virginia who had a mulatto child convinced her husband that the child was dark because someone had cast a spell on her. (He believed the story for eighteen years.)[14]

Regardless of the actions of the planters, the courtship pattern in the quarters differed, in many respects, from that of whites. An imperfect understanding of the unnatural puritanical code of their masters freed blacks from the insuperable guilt complexes

---

Slave and as a Freedman (Syracuse, N.Y., 1859), 19-37; Jacob Stroyer, *My Life in the South* (Salem, 1890), 30-37.

14. James H. Johnston, *Race Relations in Virginia and Miscegenation in the South, 1776-1860* (Amherst, Mass., 1970), 253-56.

that enslaved nineteenth-century white Americans in regard to sex. Besides, they argued, they could gain nothing from observing this part of the American creed when whites considered them outside the rest of it. Consequently, freed from social restraints, young slave men pursued their black paramours with a reckless abandon which was often the envy of their white masters.

Viewing the courting of their young masters, the slaves imitated their language and then transformed the American ritual by adding elements from African courtship and betrothal practices. Traditionally, Africans resorted to metaphor, indirection, story-telling, poems, songs, riddles, and symbolic language in their courtship and betrothal rituals. During courtship among the Ewe, for example,

> Whether the girl is interested or not, tradition and good form demand that at first she simulate indifference and even dislike. . . . A youth must not only be witty and ready to flatter the girl effusively, he must also be ready to answer and counter any questions she may ask. Girls are never willing to succumb without testing the ability of the youth as a person well versed in wooing tactics. . . . Some girls say they try to be impossible only to pull the legs of youths they find to be inexperienced. Others say they would be considered cheap if they gave in readily, but they also consider that should they become too difficult their suitors might leave them and look for other girls, so that although they are neither easy with their virtue nor give straight answers to proposals, they can do their best to make it known to a youth that they are not altogether averse to him. This is usually done by polite prevarications and tricky evasions. Both words and actions are needed during the period of wooing.[15]

15. G. K. Nukunya, *Kinship and Marriage Among the Anlo Ewe* (London, 1969), 79-80; see also: John W. Blassingame, ed., *Slave Testimony* (Baton Rouge, 1977), 643; Heli Chatelain, "Folklore in an African's Life," *Southern Workman* XXV (Aug. 1896), 164-66; Marie-André du Sacre-Cœur, *The House Stands Firm: Family Life in West Africa* (Milwaukee, 1962), 74-75; George P. Rawick, ed., *The American Slave: A Composite Autobiography* (31 vols., Westport, Conn., 1972-77), XIII, pt. 4:124; Orland Kay Armstrong, ed., *Old Massa's People: The Old Slaves Tell Their Story* (Indianapolis, 1931), 153-57, 159-63; Ronnie C. Tyler and Lawrence R. Murphy, eds., *The Slave*

The combination of African and American elements led to the evolution of unique courtship practices in the slave quarters.

Courtship in the quarters was based on a highly formalized ritual involving the propounding of a series of questions to determine one's availability as a sexual partner. A verbal duel, the ritual varied slightly from state to state and was taught to the young by old men and women. The slaves believed that in order to win a mate, a young man or woman had to "know how to talk."[16] The courtship ritual consisted of riddles, poetic boasting, sexual innuendos, figurative speech, circumlocution, and was a test of wit. A major preoccupation in the ritual was the asking of metaphorical questions to determine whether a young man or woman was free to go courting and whether an individual would be accepted as a suitor. In a characteristic wooing of a maiden, the following conversation ensued:

> HE. My dear kin' miss, has you any objections to me drawing my cher to yer side, and revolvin' de wheel of my conversation around de axle of your understanding?
>
> SHE. I has no objection to a gentleman addressin' me in a proper manner, kin' sir.
>
> HE. My dear miss, de worl' is a howlin' wilderness full of devourin' animals, and you has got to walk through hit. Has you made up yer min' to walk through hit by yerself, or wid some bol' wahyer?[17]

Narratives of Texas (Austin, 1974), 75; Charles L. Perdue *et al.*, *Weevils in the Wheat: Interviews with Virginia Ex-Slaves* (Charlottesville, 1976), 96; R. C. Abraham, *The Tiv People* (Lagos, 1933), 211; Ulli Beier, ed., *Yoruba Poetry* (Cambridge, Eng., 1970), 24, 67-72, 122-23; Francis M. Deng, ed., *The Dinka and Their Songs* (Oxford, Eng., 1973), 20-22, 43-46, 79-83.

16. "Old Time Courtship," *Southern Workman* XXIV (Jan. 1895), 14-15; "Courtship," *ibid.*, XXIV (May 1895), 78; "Courtship Customs," *ibid.*, XXV (Jan. 1896), 15-16; "Courtship in Old Virginia," *ibid.*, XXV (Feb. 1896), 38; Daniel Webster Davis, "Echoes from a Plantation Party," *ibid.*, *XXVIII* (Feb. 1899), 54-59; Rawick, *American Slave*, V, pt. 4:49-50, VI (Alabama), 307; (Supplement), IV, 630-31.

17. Unless otherwise indicated, all quotes are from material gathered by the Hampton Folklore Society and published in the articles in the *Southern Workman* cited in note 16.

For the most part, the young man initiated the courting. As in many courtship rituals, flattery was a constant; young men wasted little time demonstrating how they regarded the young women. Interjected with flattery was almost always a question about the young woman's availability as a partner: "Kin' lady, since I have been trav' lin up hill, vally an mountain, I nebber seed a lady dat suit my fancy mo' so den you does. Now is you a towel dat had been spun, or a towel dat had been woven. (Answer—if spun, single.)"

Having found a towel that was spun, the young man would begin boasting of his prowess and proclaiming, through poetic allusions, his love for her: "I love you, kind Miss, harder dan a mule can kick up de hill backwards." The poetry of love resonated through the quarters. Similar in structure to African ones, the poetic effusions of young slaves were promises and pledges. Young men spent a great deal of time creating or memorizing the poems in an effort to win the maidens of their choice. Seeking to widen the province of his pleasures, a young man would ask a young woman:

> If you was passin' by
> And seed me hangin' high
> Would you cut me down and lie
> Or would you let me hang there an die?

If a young lady seemed to doubt the young man's professions of interest and sincerity, he might say:

> O, when I first saw you lovely face,
> Laugh at me if you will,
> My heart jumped clean out of its place.
> I could not keep it still.

While men were clearly the initiators during courtship in the quarters, women controlled, by their answers to the questions propounded by the men, the pace, the length, and determined the success or failure of the wooing. Initially, the woman's reactions might vary from indifference to slight interest. Thus, she challenged the young man to arouse her interest, to earn her love. A young man's initial queries might elicit a *promise* of a response as soon as he proved "dat it is not for er form and er fashion dat you put de question." Further claims of sincerity might lead the young lady to respond: "I has knowed many a gentleman to talk wid wise words and flatterin' looks, and at de same time he may have a deceivin' heart." While this was the general pattern, the young slave girl did not hesitate when she met a man who was attractive to her. Instead, she answered the man's questions unambiguously in ways to indicate her desire for him. In the courtship ritual she became the initiator. To a simple greeting a young lady might respond: "Honorable mister, at dis time presen' my ears is a waitin' an' a listenin' to hear from your sweet little lips some words. Thirty years I's been looking to de eas' an' lookin' to de wes' to see some one to suit my fancies mo' so dan you has." Sometimes young women initiated the ritual by trying to determine if the young men preferred them. Attempting to fathom a suitor's intentions, a young lady might say: " 'Suppose you was walkin' by de side o' de river an dere was three ladies in a boat, an' dat boat was overturned, which lady would you save, a tall lady or a short lady or a middle-sized lady?' " If the young man asserted that he would save a lady corresponding in height to his questioner, it signified he was interested in her.

The young slaves did much of their courting at plantation parties on Saturday and Sunday nights, at molasses stews (similar to taffy pullings), watermelon feasts, corn-shuckings, and dances. A favorite pastime at the parties was ring games enabling young men to kiss the ladies.[18] Daniel Webster Davis gave a clear portrait of plantation parties when he wrote:

> The party would start off with a general greeting and conversation. Telling tales, some of them calculated to "freeze the young blood, and cause each particular hair to stand on end like quills upon the fretful porcupine," was a common mode of entertaining. Next would come the guessing of riddles propounded by the more erudite portion of the company or "pulling handkerchiefs" for kisses. "Fruit in the Basket," "Walking

18. Rawick, *American Slave,* II, pt. 1:171, 222, 302, 304, pt. 2:89, XII, pt. 1:81, 163, 170, pt. 2:6, 151, 216, 348.

> the Lonesome Road," "I'm in the Well," and "Fishing," were devices for getting a kiss from some fair one. In the play "I'm in the Well," a gentleman would make the startling announcement that he was in the well. Some sympathizing friend would ask, "How many feet deep?" and it is surprising how many feet a fellow could get in the well, if some pretty girl asked the question. He would then be asked, "Who will you have to pull you out?" He would answer, "Miss so and so," and the lady mentioned would be expected to kiss him as many times as he was feet deep in the well. This was certainly a most pleasant way to be rescued from drowning. By this effort the lady would get into the well herself and have to be rescued in like manner.

The cakewalk was a perennial at such parties. So was the singing of those secular songs which were the precursors of the blues. Lusty songs about courting and love, they were filled with metaphoric references to sexual intercourse.

The slaves' attitude toward sex and procreation was an amalgam of European and African beliefs. Determined largely by extended kinship networks and religious obligations, the sexual attitudes of traditional African societies differed greatly from those current in Europe and antebellum America. Premarital sex among some African peoples was institutionalized soon after the onset of puberty and among others accepted as a normal part of the courtship process. Some African peoples, however, such as the Hausa and Nupe of Nigeria, required premarital virginity. Africans viewed sex as fundamental to procreation, and procreation as a religious duty to ensure the continuation of the family line established by one's ancestors. Barrenness was a calamity in Africa.[19] While providing socially sanctioned forms for engaging

19. Felix Bryk, *Dark Rapture: The Sex-Life of the African Negro* (New York, 1975), 74-98, 127-43; E. Franklin Frazier, "Negro, Sex Life of the African and American," *The Encyclopedia of Sexual Behavior* (New York, 1961), 769-75; Arthur Phillips, ed., *Survey of African Marriage and Family Life* (London, 1953); Daryll Forde and A. R. Radcliffe-Brown, eds., *African Systems of Kinship and Marriage* (London, 1950), 46-85, 252-84; K. A. Busia, *Report on a Social Survey of Sekondi-Takoradi* (London, 1950), 30-33; A. W. Cardinall, *The Natives of the Northern Territories of the Gold Coast* (London, 1920), 75-81; Abraham, *The Tiv People*, 149-50; M. J. Field, *Social Organization of the Gá People* (London, 1940), 37-44; Daryll Forde,

in premarital sex, African societies generally forbade extramarital sex, punishing adulterers with heavy fines, divorce, slavery, and sometimes death.[20]

Because Africans so highly valued children, they could neither conceive of the European concept of celibacy nor, like the European, regard sexual intercourse as dirty, evil, or sinful. Puberty rites in West Africa, for instance, were either preceded or followed by training of the young in their sexual responsibilities. Some societies concluded puberty rites of young girls with defloration.[21]

As he was gradually transformed into an Afro-American, the Southern slave lost the African religious significance of sex and procreation. What he retained was the belief that sex was a natural act largely unconnected with sin. The christianization of the slave, however, brought ambivalence toward sex to the quarters in the nineteenth century. White ministers, for example, repeatedly railed against the continuation of the African tradition of polygamy in the quarters. They called upon the slaves to adopt Christian monogamy and to cleave to one mate throughout their lives. In numerous sermons and catechisms prepared especially for the slaves the ministers stressed Biblical prohibitions against premarital sexual intercourse, adultery, fornication, and the separation of mates. Typical of the lessons thousands of slaves learned was the section in the 1837 catechism published by South Carolina Episcopalians, where young blacks memorized such passages as "Thou shalt not commit adultery. . . . Our

---

Paula Brown, and Robert G. Armstrong, *Peoples of the Niger-Benue Confluence* (London, 1955), 42-44, 60-61, 67-68; Gladywn M. Childs, *Kinship & Character of the Ovimbundu* (London, 1969), 111-18.

20. Robert F. Gray and P. H. Gulliver, eds., *The Family Estate in Africa* (London, 1964), 97, 102-3; Meyer Fortes, *Kinship and the Social Order* (London, 1969), 146, 155-57; A. B. Ellis, *The Ewe-Speaking Peoples of the Slave Coast of West Africa* (London, 1890), 199-207; Adrian C. Edwards, *The Ovimbundu Under Two Sovereignties* (London, 1962), 115, 122.

21. G. T. Basden, *Among the Ibos of Nigeria* (Philadelphia 1921), 75; C. M. N. White, *Tradition and Change in Luvale Marriage* (London, 1962), 2-8, 11.

Saviour saith, He who looketh on a woman, to lust after her, hath committed adultery with her already in his heart. . . . St. Paul saith, Fornication and all uncleanness, let it not be once named among you, as becometh saints; neither filthiness, nor foolish talking, nor jesting, which are not convenient. . . . St. Paul saith, Let every man have his own wife, and every woman her own husband." The catechumens also learned they should avoid "impure thoughts," "lewd and filthy words," that fornication was "a great sin," a disgrace, "a sin against God," leading to "falsehoods, and jealousies, and murders, and loss of health." God would punish adulterers in "everlasting Hell" or, like the people of Sodom and Gomorrah, destroy them.[22]

Although the link between sin and sex was not as pervasive among slaves as among whites, it was an inevitable concomitant of the christianization of the blacks. Christian slaves often taught their children, for instance, that "shame" and premarital sex were the same. The children of such slaves learned little about sex except Christian injunctions against it before marriage. Minnie Folkes, a former Virginia slave, typified the impact of such practices when she recalled: "I married when I wuz 14 years old. So help me God, I didn't know what marriage meant. . . . I slept in bed—he on his side an' I on mine fer three months an dis ain't no lie . . . he never got close to me 'cause my muma sed 'Don't let nobody bother yo' principle'; 'cause dat wuz all yo' had. I 'bey my muma, an' tol' him so, and I said to go an' ask muma an ef she sed he could get close to me hit waz alright." A South Carolina slave, Harry Macmillan, asserted in 1863, that, though many slave women engaged in premarital sexual intercourse, "They regard it as a disgrace and the laws of the Church are against it." When unmarried women became pregnant, Macmillan testified, "they are thought less of among their companions,

22. Protestant Episcopal Church, South Carolina, *A Catechism, To Be Used by Teachers in the Religious Instruction of Persons of Color* (Charleston, 1837); see also: *Southern Episcopalian*, I (1854), 5-8, VI (1859), 369-75; Charles C. Jones, *A Catechism for Colored Persons* (Charleston, 1834); *Instruction from the Book of Common Prayer, for Plantations by a Clergyman* (Charleston, 1854).

unless they get a husband and before the child is born, and if they cannot the shame grows until they do get a husband."[23]

Sexual conquest became a highly respected avenue to status in the quarters. The slave caroused with black damsels on his own plantation and slipped away, with or without a pass, to other estates until he was smitten by love. He persistently pursued the one of his choice often over a long period of courtship. He flattered her, exaggerated his prowess, and tried to demonstrate his ambition and especially his ability to provide for her. If he won her affections, he often had to obtain the consent of her parents. This was almost always required in the few cases where slave men married free women. In some cases the slaves were engaged for as much as a year before their union was consummated. In the interim, the prospective husband prepared a cabin and furniture for his family, and the prospective wife collected utensils she would need to establish a household.[24]

Love is no small matter for any man; for a slave it represented one of the major crises in his life. Many slaves vowed early in life never to marry and face separation from loved ones. If they had to marry, the slave men were practically unanimous in their desire to marry women from another plantation. They did not want to marry a woman from their own and be forced to watch as she was beaten, insulted, raped, overworked, or starved without being able to protect her. John Anderson declared that when he was contemplating marriage: "I did not want to marry a girl belonging to my own place, because I knew I could not bear to see her ill-treated."[25] Henry Bibb felt the same way. He contended: "If my wife must be exposed to the insults and licentious passions of wicked slavedrivers and overseers; if she must bear the stripes of the lash laid on by an unmerciful tyrant; if this is to be done with impunity, which is frequently done by slave-

23. Perdue, *Weevils*, 95-96; Blassingame, *Slave Testimony*, 382; Gutman, *Black Family*, 60-86; Todd L. Savitt, *Medicine and Slavery* (Urbana, 1978), 128.

24. Brown, *Narrative*, 88-90; Solomon Northup, *Twelve Years a Slave* (London, 1853), 191-222; Stroyer, *My Life*, 15-20.

25. John Anderson, *The Story of the Life of John Anderson, a Fugitive Slave* (London, 1863), 129.

holders and their abettors, Heaven forbid that I should be compelled to witness the sight."[26] Most of the slaves tried every stratagem to avoid being placed in this position. Moses Grandy summed up the general view when he wrote: "no colored man wishes to live at the house where his wife lives, for he has to endure the continual misery of seeing her flogged and abused, without daring to say a word in her defence."[27]

Unfortunately for most slaves, the master had the final word in regard to their marriage partners. Most slaveholders, feeling that the children their male slaves had by women belonging to other planters was so much seed spewed on the ground, insisted that they marry women on their own estates. Such a practice placed all of the slave's interests under the control of the master and gave the slave fewer excuses to leave the estate. Some masters brought both of the prospective mates together and inquired if they understood the seriousness of their undertaking. If they belonged to different masters it was often more difficult for them to obtain the consent of either one. But, if both the lovers persistently spurned prospective partners on their own plantations, the planters, by mutual agreement, might resolve the controversy. Wealthy masters frequently purchased the female slave and thereby won the loyalty of the male. If the matter could not be resolved by the planters, the love might be consummated in spite of their objections. The marriage ceremony in most cases consisted of the slaves' simply getting the master's permission and moving into a cabin together. The masters of domestic servants either had the local white minister or the black plantation preacher perform the marriage ceremony and then gave a sumptuous feast in their own parlors to the slave guests. Afterwards, the slaves had long dances in the quarters in honor of the couple.[28]

26. Bibb, *Adventures*, 42.

27. Moses Grandy, *Narrative of the Life of Moses Grandy* (London, 1843), 25.

28. John Brown, *Slave Life in Georgia* (London, 1855), 31-44; Lunsford Lane, *The Narrative of Lunsford Lane* (Boston, 1848), 9-16; Thomas Jones, *The Experiences of Thomas Jones, Who Was a Slave for Forty-three Years* (Boston, 1850), 29-36; W. H. Robinson, *From Log Cabin to the Pulpit* (Eau

One aspect of slave nuptials confused their descendants and later historians. On many plantations masters and slaves developed a humorous test to determine who would exercise the most authority in a union. As part of the post-nuptial revelries, the couple was required to jump over a broom stick. The partner jumping over first, highest, or without falling was recognized by the wedding party as the one who would "wear the pants" or rule the family. Tempie Herndon, over a hundred years old when interviewed in the 1930s, had a vivid recollection of the pre- and post-nuptial revelries when she married:

> When I growed up I married Exter Durham. . . . We had a big weddin'. We was married on de front porch of de Big House. Marse George killed a shoat and Mis' Betsy had Georgianna, de cook, to bake a big weddin' cake all iced up white as snow with a bride and groom standin' in de middle holdin' hands. . . . I had on a white dress, white shoes, and long white gloves dat come to my elbow, and Mis' Betsy done made me a weddin' veil out of a white net window curtain. When she played de weddin' march on de piano, me and Exter marched down de walk and up on de porch to de altar Mis' Betsy done fixed. Dat de prettiest altar I ever seed. Back 'against de rose vine dat was full of red roses, Mis' Betsy done put tables filled with flowers and white candles. She done spread down a bed sheet, a sure 'nough linen sheet, for us to stand on, and dey was a white pillow to kneel down on. . . . Uncle Edmond Kirby married us. He was de nigger preacher dat preached at de plantation church. After Uncle Edmond said de last words over me and Exter, Marse George got to have his little fun. He say, "Come on, Exter, you and Tempie got to jump over de broom stick backwards. You got to do dat to see which one gwine be boss of your household." Everybody come stand round to watch. Marse George hold de broom about a foot high off de floor. De one dat jump over it backwards, and never touch handle, gwine boss de house. If both of dem jump over without touchin' it, dey won't gwine be no bossin', dey just

---

Claire, Wis., 1913), 152-63; Charles Sealsfield, *The Americans as They Are* (London, 1828), 133; Tixier, *Travels*, 47; Amelia Murray, *Letters from the United States, Cuba and Canada* (New York, 1856), 224, 351.

> gwine be congenial. I jumped first, and you ought to seed me. I sailed right over dat broom stick same as a cricket. But when Exter jump he done had a big dram and his feets was so big and clumsy dat dey got all tangled up in dat broom and he fell headlong. Marse George he laugh and laugh, and told Exter he gwine be bossed 'twell he scared to speak lessen I told him to speak.[29]

Looking back on bondage from the 1930s, blacks who had been children watching such ceremonies often conflated the wedding ritual and the post-nuptial jumping of the broom. Either they had not seen or had forgotten the wedding ceremony. Often children were misled because their parents used the metaphor "jumping the broom" when discussing weddings of any sort. Consequently, when asked by the WPA interviewers how slaves got married, the informants reported that the bondsmen literally jumped over the broom. Historians did not closely examine what the slaves told the WPA interviewers and were misled about the character of wedding ceremonies in the quarters. Significantly, black informants who had been adults in 1860, who were interviewed before the 1930s or who wrote nineteenth-century autobiographies rarely mentioned jumping the broom stick except *after* a more formal ceremony.[30]

Presbyterians, Methodists, Baptists, and Episcopalians all devoted a great deal of attention to the wedding ceremony in the quarters.[31] Concerned about the impact of sexual immorality on

29. Norman R. Yetman, ed., *Voices from Slavery* (New York, 1970), 164; see also: Rawick, *American Slave,* V, pt. 5:329-30; Ronald Killion and Charles Waller, eds., *Slavery Time When I Was Chillun down on Marster's Plantation: Interviews with Georgia Slaves* (Savannah, 1973), 45-46.

30. Gutman, *Black Family,* 275-81; George Rawick, *From Sunup to Sundown* (Westport, Conn., 1972), 86-87; Eugene Genovese, *Roll, Jordan, Roll* (New York, 1974), 475; Armstrong, *Old Massa's People,* 166; Perdue, *Weevils,* 36, 134, 245; Blassingame, *Slave Testimony,* 23, 262, 525, 591-92, 639; James Redpath, *The Roving Editor: Or, Talks with Slaves in the Southern States* (New York, 1859), 40, 66, 164-65, 173, 313-14.

31. For the spirited but largely undocumented debate over the role of whites in shaping the slave family, see Frazier, *The Negro Family* and Gutman, *The Black Family.* Donald Mathews, *Religion in the Old South* (Chicago, 1977), presents a good brief analysis of the Southern churches' concern with the slave family.

both blacks and whites, the clergymen earnestly worked to guarantee that slaves were united in Christian ceremonies. The Georgia clergy had one of the longest traditions in this regard, for when the Board of Trustees governing the colony authorized the introduction of slavery in 1749, it ordered that Christian ceremonies be employed when slaves married and made ministers responsible for this task. The pronouncements of Southern associations, synods, presbyteries, and conferences on slave weddings constitute a monotonous refrain in their annual proceedings after 1840. First, many of the denominations required their ministers and missionaries to perform slave weddings.[32] The resolution of the Presbytery of Lexington, Kentucky, was typical: "That our coloured people be taught the sacredness and perpetuity of the marriage relation; and it is further recommended that proper efforts should be made to have the rites of matrimony celebrated, in all cases among them, with due solemnity and in accordance with the word of God."[33] Second, most Southern ministers also repeatedly urged masters to promote morality in the quarters by requiring slaves to be married by regularly ordained ministers and to observe the obligations of marriage. Between 1830 and 1860 many denominations required all slave members to take their marriage vows in the church.[34] While it is relatively easy to document the desire of the white clergy to have ministers perform slave weddings, it is difficult to determine with

32. Charles C. Jones, *Suggestions on the Religious Instruction of the Negroes in the Southern States* (Philadelphia, 1847), 47-48; Henry T. Malone, *The Episcopal Church in Georgia, 1733-1957* (Atlanta, 1960), 29; Charles F. Deems, ed., *Annals of Southern Methodism for 1855* (Nashville, 1856), 223; James B. Sellers, *Slavery in Alabama* (University, Ala., 1950), 322-23.

33. Jones, *Suggestions,* 48.

34. Jones, *Suggestions,* 23; *Southern Literary Messenger* X (1844), 329-39; Charles C. Jones, *The Religious Instruction of the Negroes. A Sermon, Delivered Before Associations of Planters in Liberty and McIntosh Counties, Georgia* (Princeton, 1832), 7; *Southern Episcopalian* V (1858), 487; *Southern Presbyterian Review* VIII (1854), 275; *Seventh Annual Report of the Association for the Religious Instruction of the Negroes in Liberty County, Ga.* (Savannah, 1842), 4-5; Lewis M. Purifoy, "Methodist Episcopal Church, South, and Slavery, 1844-1865" (Ph.D. diss., University of North Carolina, 1965), 172-73; *Journal, Protestant Episcopal Church of South Carolina, 1839* (Charleston, 1839), 29.

any certainty how many slave weddings the ministers actually performed. Planter letters and journals, the diaries and autobiographies of ministers, the manuscript records of specific churches and slave interviews do, however, contain frequent notations of white clergymen performing slave weddings.[35]

"Even in the observance of 'Holy Matrimony,' the slaves seem to have been more scrupulous than their masters," an abolitionist wrote incredulously when reviewing a Southern church publication in 1854.[36] Abolition doubts notwithstanding, thousands of slaves were married in Southern churches between 1800 and 1860. For example, out of a total of 1228 marriages performed in Episcopal churches in South Carolina, Alabama, North Carolina, Georgia, Louisiana, Mississippi, and Virginia in 1860, at least 469, or 38.1 per cent, were slave weddings. At many times between 1830 and 1860 more slaves were married in the Episcopal churches in some states than were whites. Between 1841 and 1860 Episcopal ministers performed 3225 weddings in South Carolina; 1705, or 52 per cent, of these were slave marriages. In practically every state for which statistics exist for the years 1841 to 1860, slaves accounted for a larger percentage of the marriages than they did of the members of the Episcopal church. While Alabama slaves, for instance, accounted for between 14.5 and 32.9 per cent of the marriages performed in the Episcopal

35. R. Q. Mallard, *Plantation Life Before Emancipation* (Richmond, 1892), 49; Alfred M. Pierce, *A History of Methodism in Georgia* (Atlanta, 1956), 132; William H. Milburn, *Ten Years of Preacher Life: Chapters from an Autobiography* (New York, 1859), 337-38; Joseph D. Cushman, Jr., *A Goodly Heritage: The Episcopal Church in Florida, 1821-1892* (Gainesville, Fla., 1965), 36; *Journal, P. E. Church, Virginia, 1844* (Richmond, 1844), 58; "The Slave Wedding," *Maryland Colonization Journal* VI (July 1851), 31-32; "Letter from a Mississippi Slaveholder," *National Anti-Slavery Standard,* Sept. 9, 1854; H. B. B. to the Editor, *ibid.*, Oct. 4, 1849; Rawick, *American Slave,* II, pt. 1:300, VI (Alabama), 307, pt. 5:57, pt. 1:79, 244, pt. 2:95, 296, XIII, pt. 3:125, pt. 4:70, 118; (Supplement), II, 73-74, III, 251, 273, IV, 396, 442, XI, 136; Henry W. Ravenel, "Recollections of Southern Plantation Life," *Yale Review* XXV (Summer 1936) 756; Stiles B. Lines, "Slaves and Churchmen: The Work of the Episcopal Church Among Southern Negroes, 1830-1860" (Ph.D. diss., Columbia University, 1960), 228-29.

36. J. W. Simmons to the editor (n.d.), *National Anti-Slavery Standard,* Aug. 19, 1854.

Church between 1848 and 1860, they never represented more than 7.9 per cent of the total membership. Scattered and irregular reports of other denominations indicate that a sizable number of slaves were married in Southern churches.[37]

White churches continued to exercise moral oversight over the slaves after their weddings. Frequently investigating charges of adultery and fornication, the churches tried to promote the development of Christian moral precepts in the quarters. Consequently, they often excommunicated or publicly criticized slaves for abandoning their mates, having premarital pregnancies, and engaging in extramarital sex. Since an overwhelming majority of the cases were brought to the attention of the church by the slave members, the increase in the charges of moral lapses between 1830 and 1860 represented the spread of Christian moral precepts in the quarters.[38]

One of the first great issues confronting Southern churches with black members was the impact of the forcible separation of mates upon a slave union. When a slave whose mate had been sold wanted to have a wedding or continue in fellowship with the church after taking a new mate, the clergy had to reconsider the meaning of marriage. Southern churches struggled with this issue throughout the antebellum period. Strict constructionists, reading Biblical injunctions literally, argued that the forcible separation of mates did not dissolve a slave union. North Caro-

37. See Appendix III, tables 10 and 11, for statistics on marriages and communicants.

38. Mary W. Highsaw, "A History of Zion Community in Maury County, 1806-1860," *Tennessee Historical Quarterly* V (June 1946), 111-40; William H. Gehrke, "Negro Slavery Among the Germans in North Carolina," *North Carolina Historical Review* XIV (Oct. 1937), 304-24; Leah Townsend, *South Carolina Baptists, 1670-1805* (Florence, S.C., 1935), 241, 259; Walter Brownlow Posey, *The Presbyterian Church in the Old Southwest, 1778-1838* (Richmond, 1952), 88; *Journal, P. E. Church, South Carolina, 1848* (Charleston, 1848), 48; Jones, "Cultural Middle Passage," 156-57; John D. Long, *Pictures of Slavery in Church and State* (Philadelphia, 1857), 85-86; Annie H. Mallard, "Religious Work of South Carolina Baptists Among the Slaves from 1781 to 1830" (M.A. thesis, University of South Carolina, 1946), 34, 67-75; Robert O. Fife, "Alexander Campbell and the Christian Church in the Slavery Controversy" (Ph.D. diss., Indiana University, 1960), 115-20; Albert J. Raboteau, *Slave Religion* (New York, 1978), 184-85.

lina's Broad River Baptist Association typified the strict constructionists in its 1820 answer to a query from one of its churches: " 'How shall a church proceed with a member in slavery whose companion was taken away out of the country and sold, and the member left has married another?' Answer, 'Agreeably to the Scriptures, the church could not hold such an one in fellowship.' " Recognizing the practical hardships involved in the strict constructionist's position, many ministers contended that a forcible separation was tantamount to the death of one's mate or equivalent to divorce by the state (since permitted by its laws) and allowed remarriage. Whatever the positions adopted, Southern churches never rested easy with "double marriages" among slaves. It appeared to many clergymen that masters were forcing their slaves into polygamy by separating mates.[39]

In spite of the fact that some men had two wives simultaneously, there was a great deal of respect for the monogamous family. Whether the result of religious teachings, the requirements of the master, or the deep affection between mates, many slaves had only one partner. Henry Box Brown, for instance, refused his master's order to take another mate after his wife was sold because he felt marriage "was a sacred institution binding upon me." Affection was apparently the most important factor which kept partners together. This emerges most clearly in the lamentations and resentments which pervade the autobiographies over the separation of family members. Frequently when their mates were sold, slaves ran away in an effort to find them. The fear of causing disaffection forced planters to recognize the strength of the monogamous family; they frequently sold a slave in the neighborhood of his mate when they moved their slaves farther South. Because they were denied all the protection which the law afforded, slaves had an almost mythological respect for legal marriage. Henry Bibb believed that "there are no class of people in the United States who so highly appreciate the legality of marriage as those persons who have been held and treated as

39. John R. Logan, *Sketches, Historical and Biographical, of the Broad River and King's Mountain Baptist Associations, from 1800 to 1882* (Shelby, N.C., 1887), 38.

property."[40] In no class of American autobiographies is more stress laid upon the importance of stable family life than in the autobiographies of former slaves.

After marriage, the slave faced almost insurmountable odds in his efforts to build a strong stable family. First, and most important of all, his authority was restricted by his master. Any decision of his regarding his family could be countermanded by his master. The master determined when both he and his wife would go to work, when or whether his wife cooked his meals, and was often the final arbiter in family disputes. In enforcing discipline, some masters whipped both man and wife when they had loud arguments or fights. Some planters punished males by refusing to let them visit their mates when they lived on other plantations. In any event, these slaves could only visit their mates with their master's permission. When the slave lived on the same plantation with his mate, he could rarely escape frequent demonstrations of his powerlessness. The master, and not the slave, furnished the cabin, clothes, and the minimal food for his wife and children. Under such a regime slave fathers often had little or no authority.[41]

The most serious impediment to the man's acquisition of status in his family was his inability to protect his wife from the sexual advances of whites and the physical abuse of his master. Instead, according to Austin Steward, slave husbands had to "submit without a murmur" when their wives were flogged.[42] Sometimes, in spite of the odds, the men tried to protect their mates. W. H. Robinson's father once told him that he "lay in the woods eleven months for trying to prevent your mother from being whipped."[43] The black male frequently could do little to protect his wife from the sexual advances of whites. Most whites, however, realized that a liaison with a slave's wife could be dangerous. Occasionally, slaves killed white men for such acts. Gen-

40. Henry Box Brown, *Narrative of Henry Box Brown* (Boston, 1851), 57; Bibb, *Adventures*, 152.

41. Douglass, *Bondage*, 51.

42. Austin Steward, *Twenty-two Years a Slave, and Forty Years a Freeman* (Rochester, N.Y., 1861), 18.

43. Robinson, *Pulpit*, 25.

Figure 30. The Lonely Hearth

erally, however, the women had no choice but to submit to the sexual advances of white men.[44] Henry Bibb wrote that "a poor slave's wife can never be . . . true to her husband contrary to the will of her master. She can neither be pure nor virtuous, contrary to the will of her master. She dare not refuse to be reduced to a state of adultery at the will of her master. . . ."[45]

By all odds, the most brutal aspect of slavery was the separation of families. This was a haunting fear which made all of the slave's days miserable. In spite of the fact that probably a majority of the planters tried to prevent family separations in order to maintain plantation discipline, practically all of the black autobiographers were touched by the tragedy. Death occurred too frequently in the master's house, creditors were too relentless in collecting their debts, the planter's reserves ran out too often,

44. Northup, *Twelve Years*, 176-90, 223-62; Loguen, *Freedman*, 19-25, 38-52; Henry Watson, *Narrative of Henry Watson, a Fugitive Slave* (Boston, 1848), 5-17; Bibb, *Adventures*, 112-18.

45. Bibb, *Adventures*, 191-92.

and the master longed too much for expensive items for the slave to escape the clutches of the slave trader. Nothing demonstrated his powerlessness as much as the slave's inability to prevent the forcible sale of his wife and children.[46]

Slaves received the greatest protection for their families from white churches and ministers. Occasionally, the churches testified "against the inhumane and unfeeling practice" of separating slave families and censured or excommunicated guilty masters. By the 1840s ministers and laymen had begun suggesting the passage of laws prohibiting the separation of slave families.[47] The Reverend William H. Milburn, for example, contended in 1859 that the "first and most imperative demand which justice makes of the people of the southern States is the passage of laws forbidding the separation of man and wife, of parents and children. Such rending asunder of the holiest bonds of our nature should not be allowed, cannot without incurring the dread anathema of a Christian civilization and the righteous indignation of God."[48]

Most clergymen appealed not to the law but to the conscience of masters to ensure the inviolability of slave marriages. The Reverend Charles C. Jones stated bluntly in an 1848 sermon that masters "should *not separate, nor allow the separation of husband and wife, unless for causes lawful before God.*" Since marriage was a "divine institution" a master was not to "separate husband and wife either by sale or purchase. On the contrary, he should consider the parties as *united for life,* and so far as Providence puts it in his power, he should endeavour to keep them together and their children around them." South Carolina Presbyterians went further. In 1854 the Charleston Presbytery called upon its

46. Charles Ball, *Slavery in the United States: A Narrative of the Life and Adventures of Charles Ball* (Lewiston, Pa., 1836), 15-22, 258-300; Elkanah Watson, *Men and Times of the Revolution* (New York, 1857), 69; Henry B. Whipple, *Bishop Whipple's Southern Diary* (Minneapolis, 1937), 69, 88-89; John O'Connor, *Wanderings of a Vagabond* (New York, 1873), 110.

47. Posey, *Presbyterian Church,* 76-77; R. Fuller to Elon Galusha [1840] *National Anti-Slavery Standard,* Nov. 12, 1840; Purifoy, "Methodist Episcopal Church, South," 172-73; *Maryland Colonization Journal* VI (Aug. 1852), 238; Raboteau, *Slave Religion,* 183-85.

48. Milburn, *Ten Years,* 350; *Southern Presbyterian Review* VIII (1854), 276.

ministers and church courts to protect slaves "by enforcing on *Masters* themselves, the obligation to adhere more rigidly to the Saviour's command, and refrain from separating their married servants, except in cases of criminal offence which would justly subject the offending party to a legal sentence involving separation." Similarly, in 1859 a committee of the South Carolina Episcopal Church asserted that "every Christian master should so regulate the sale or disposal of a married slave, as not to infringe the Divine injunction forbidding the separation of husband and wife."[49] Though the convention delegates never voted on the resolutions, the Committee had expressed the sentiments of a majority of nineteenth-century Southern ministers.[50] Biblical injunctions were not, however, efficacious restraints on masters bent on maximizing profits and minimizing losses when selling slaves.

The best objective evidence available concerning the separation of mates by planters appears in the marriage certificates of former slaves preserved by the Union army and the Freedmen's Bureau in Tennessee (Dyer, Gibson, Wilson, and Shelby counties), Louisiana (Concordia Parish), and Mississippi (Adams County) from 1864 to 1866. Although these records contain the best material available on the actions of masters in regard to the slave family, they must be used with caution. In the first place, the number of unbroken unions may be exaggerated: those blacks who had retained the strongest sense of family would be most likely to come to the posts to be married. Second, multiple separations by masters were apparently understated (often old slaves simply noted how they were separated from their *last* mate). Third, it was sometimes impossible to determine from the army records whether a childless couple had been united in slavery. Despite their shortcomings, the marriage certificates con-

49. *Thirteenth Annual Report of the Association for the Religious Instruction of the Negroes, in Liberty County, Georgia* (Savannah, 1848), 16-17; *Southern Presbyterian Review* VIII (1854), 17; *Journal*, P. E. *Church of South Carolina*, 1859 (Charleston, 1859), 34-35.

50. *Southern Presbyterian Review* IX (1856), 359, XII (1859), 358-59; *Southern Episcopalian* V (1858), 487; Purifoy, "Methodist Episcopal Church, South," 172-73.

tain revealing data on 2888 slave unions in three states; 1225 in Mississippi, 1123 in Tennessee, and 540 in Louisiana.[51]

The most difficult problem involved in analyzing the slave family is defining the term "unbroken." Since the most important characteristics of the slave union which differentiated it from legal marriage was the right the master had to separate mates, this factor must be isolated, and separations caused by death, war-related activities, and personal choice treated as unions "unbroken by masters." Through this technique, we can arrive at an approximation of the role of masters in dissolving slave families. This is not to argue, of course, that casual separations and high mortality rates did not lead to instability in these families. In fact, the dissolution of 1557, or 53.7 per cent, of the unions was directly attributable to these causes. However intimately related they are to family instability, neither of these factors involved the deliberate intervention of the master for the purpose of separating mates.

It seems logical to treat couples separated by war and death as unbroken unions, since many of them had cohabited together for decades before impersonal forces caused their dissolution. If the 1153 couples separated by death are dropped from the total, 66 per cent of the remaining unions were dissolved by masters in Mississippi, 50 per cent in Louisiana, and 43 per cent in Tennessee. This, however, would seem unfair, because it penalizes the planters for events over which they had little control. The issue here is not family stability (which involves an analysis of a number of complex factors) but the extent to which masters deliberately separated their "married" slaves. It is obvious, when all of the factors contributing to dissolution are added together, that

51. Unbound "Marriage Certificates," Bureau of Refugees, Freedmen and Abandoned Lands, Record Group 105, National Archives; Appendix III, table 17. Herbert Gutman, *Black Family,* 145-51 utilized a different source on slave marriages, "Bound Volumes of Marriage Registers, 1864-1865," for Warren and Adams counties Mississippi and analyzed his data in a different fashion than employed in the following pages. According to Gutman, 42 per cent of the slave families in Mississippi were broken and masters dissolved 17 per cent of them.

the slave family was an extremely precarious institution. Even so, the high mortality rate among slaves was apparently more important in this than any other single factor. In a strict sociological sense, only 394, or 13.6 per cent, of the unions were unbroken.

The callous attitudes frequently held by planters toward slave unions are revealed clearly in the statistics: 937, or 32.4 per cent, of the unions were dissolved by masters. An overwhelming majority of the couples were separated before they reached their sixth anniversary. The heartlessness of the planters is revealed more clearly in their separation of slaves who had lived together for decades. Several instances of this appeared in Louisiana: Hosea Bidell was separated from his mate of twenty-five years; Valentine Miner from his after thirty years; and, in the most horrifying case of them all, Lucy Robinson was separated from her mate after living with him for forty-three years. Although such separations made the slave family one of the most unstable institutions imaginable, it should be emphasized that there were numerous unions which lasted for several decades. Those enduring for twenty or thirty years were not uncommon, and a few recorded in Tennessee lasted for more than forty years. If only the actions of masters are considered, 67.6 per cent of the slave unions were unbroken. In other words, in spite of their callous attitudes, masters did not separate a majority of the slave couples.

Initially, familial roles in the quarters were determined by African concepts. Women in most traditional West African societies were subordinate to men. In their proverbs the Africans emphasized woman's inferiority. "Woman never reigns," say the Ibo. At the same time, Africans recognized woman's independence. "Woman has no chief," the Tonga declare. While a man ruled his household, he had to listen to his mate: "If you want peace, give ear to your wives' proposals," advise the Fan. Africans required children to respect their parents (especially the father) and the young to pay deference to the elders. Proverbs reinforced societal rules: "He who goes to the father need not go to the mother. The young cannot teach the elders tradition. Children sing the song which they hear from their father and mother. Even though you may be taller than your father you still are not his equal."[52]

By the 1830s, the traditional African family the blacks remembered had been transformed. Still, white churches reinforced in the quarters family patterns inherited from Africa. Episcopalians, for example, by requiring that all children have godparents before being baptized, strengthened the extended family in the quarters. While building on African traditions of marital fidelity and respect for elders, white churches gave wide currency to Biblical pronouncements against adultery and fornication, urging the submission of wives to husbands and children to parents and elders in the quarters. As slaves, however, black men could no longer exercise the same power over their families as they had in Africa. Instead, they struggled to gain and retain status. The transformation of African familial roles led to the creation of America's first democratic family in the quarters, where men and women shared authority and responsibility.

Many slaves were lucky enough to have masters who refused to intercede in family affairs. In order to relieve themselves of responsibility, many planters gave slave parents complete control of their children. Some masters did not punish slave children but instead asked their parents to do so. On Charles Ball's plantation the overseer did nothing to undermine the authority black males had in their families even when they beat their wives.[53] On large plantations and in cities the slaves were so rarely under the constant surveillance of their masters that there the black male faced no obstacle (other than his mate) in exercising au-

52. Ellis, *The Ewe-Speaking Peoples*, 259-68; Harold Courlander, ed., *A Treasury of African Folklore* (New York, 1975), 35, 37, 66, 117; H. A. S. Johnston, *A Selection of Hausa Stories* (Oxford, Eng., 1966), 105-9; Arthur G. Leonard, *The Lower Niger and Its Tribes* (London, 1906), 75; A. B. Ellis, *The Yoruba-Speaking Peoples of the Slave Coast of West Africa* (London, 1894), 225, 237-40; Richard S. Fletcher, *Hausa Sayings & Folk-Lore* (New York, 1912), 9-34; Merlin Ennis, *Umbundu* (Boston, 1962), 313; Alta Jablow, ed., *An Anthology of West African Folklore* (London, 1961), 127; *African Repository* XXXI (Aug. 1855), 246-47.

53. J. Brown, *Slave Life*, 62-68; J. Anderson, *Story*, 8-20; Northup, *Twelve Years*, 176-90.

thority in his family. While living in Baltimore, for instance, Noah Davis declared that he had "the entire control" of his family.[54]

There were several avenues open to the slave in his effort to gain status in his family. Whenever possible, men added delicacies to their family's monotonous fare of corn meal, fat pork, and molasses by hunting and fishing. If the planter permitted the family to cultivate a garden plot or to raise hogs, the husband led his wife in this family undertaking. The husband could also demonstrate his importance in the family unit by making furniture for the cabin or building partitions between cabins which contained more than one family. The slave who did such things for his family gained not only the approbation of his wife, but he also gained status in the quarters.[55] According to William Green, in the view of the slaves when one tried to provide for his family in this manner: "the man who does this is a great man amongst them."[56] Sometimes, by extra work, slave men earned enough money to buy sugar and coffee for the family or to surprise their wives with scarves or dresses. Often, when masters did not provide adequate clothing for their slaves, black men bought clothes for their children and wives.

Masters, not the black men, determined how much care and attention slave women received when they were pregnant and the treatment that infants received. During her pregnancy a slave wife usually continued her back-breaking labor until a few weeks before her child was born. Solicitous of the health of the new child, the slave owners generally freed the mother of labor for a few days and often for weeks to nurse the infant. If he were especially interested in rearing slave children (and most masters were), he established a definite routine for nursing the child. The mother either carried the infant to the field with her or returned to the cabin at intervals during the day to nurse it.

54. Noah Davis, *A Narrative of the Life of Rev. Noah Davis, a Colored Man* (Baltimore, 1859), n.p.

55. Ball, *Slavery*, 168-205; Grandy, *Narrative*, 52-64.

56. William Green, *Narrative of Events in the Life of William Green* (Springfield, O., 1853), 9.

Figure 31. A Father's Love

The routine of the plantation prevented the lavishing of care upon the infant. In this regard, Frederick Douglass, who did not remember seeing his mother until he was seven years old, asserted: "The domestic hearth, with its holy lessons and precious endearments, is abolished in the case of a slave-mother and her children."[57] On many plantations women did not have enough time to prepare breakfast in the morning and were generally too

57. Douglas, *Bondage*, 48.

tired to make much of a meal or to give much attention to their children after a long day's labor. Booker T. Washington's experience was typical: "My mother . . . had little time to give to the training of her children during the day. She snatched a few moments for our care in the early morning before her work began, and at night after the day's work was done."[58] At a very early stage the child was placed in the plantation nursery under the care of old women or placed in the hands of his elder siblings. In either case, he was neglected. Fed irregularly or improperly, young black children suffered from a variety of ills. Treated by densely ignorant mothers or little more enlightened planters, they died in droves.[59]

If he survived infancy, the slave child partook, in bountiful measure for a while, of many of the joys of childhood. One important reason for this was the large size of most slave families. Some of the black autobiographers enjoyed the exquisite pleasure of being the youngest child. Sibling rivalry was apparently minimal. Slave parents, in spite of their own sufferings, lavished love on their children. Fathers regaled their children with fascinating stories and songs and won their affection with little gifts. These were all the more important if the father lived on another plantation. The two weekly visits of the father then took on all the aspects of minor celebrations. They were truly this for Elizabeth Keckley, for her father was only allowed to visit his family at Easter and Christmas time. Grandparents, as for all children, loomed large in the life of the slave child. Grandmothers frequently prepared little tidbits for the children, and grandfathers often told them stories about their lives in Africa.[60]

Memories of Africa were important in the development of self-awareness in slave children. In the seventeenth and eighteenth

58. Booker T. Washington, *Up From Slavery* (Boston, 1928), 4.

59. John Thompson, *The Life of John Thompson, a Fugitive Slave* (Worcester, Mass., 1856), 13-19; J. Smith, *Autobiography*, 33; Allen Parker, *Recollections of Slavery Times* (Worcester, Mass., 1895), 32-40; Yetman, *Voices*, 64, 71, 104, 168, 264; Armstrong, *Old Massa's People*, 64-66, 68-70, 181-83.

60. Yetman, *Voices*, 45, 50, 104-5, 140-41, 192, 228; Armstrong, *Old Massa's People*, 44-47, 52, 93, 141.

Figure 32. The Auction

centuries, the slaves drew on these memories for their naming practices. Consequently, until the nineteenth century, African cognomens were prominent in any list of slaves. From around 1750 to the 1830s masters steadily encroached on slave naming practices, and by the latter date the bondsmen's cognomens had been anglicized and they exercised less autonomy in this area. Reviewing his enslavement in South Carolina, Lorenzo Ezell recalled in the 1930s: "In dem days cullud people just like mules and hosses. Dey didn't have no last name." Slaves struggled to gain those elemental marks of identity, a first and a last name. While most nineteenth-century slave children were named by their parents, many were named by their masters and mistresses. However much a slave valued his first name, masters placed a low valuation on it. For example, David Holmes testified in 1853 on how fragile was the link between a slave's name, his kinship network, and his identity: "Slaves never have any name. I'm called David, now; I used to be called Tom, sometimes; but I'm not, I'm Jack. It didn't much matter what name I was called by. If master was looking at one of us, and call us, Tom, or Jack, or anything else, whoever he looked at was forced to answer." While answering to one name when called by his master, the slave used his actual name in conversations in the quarters and adopted it officially when he was freed. Before emancipation, the slave had to go beyond naming practices to maintain his self-esteem and identity.[61]

Mothers tried in many ways to bolster the self-esteem of their children. The lessons began early as the women crooned lullabies to their infants. Commenting on the white child born "rich and free" in "ole massa's big fine house," a black mother sang:

> To a cabin in woodland drear
> You've come a mammy's heart to cheer,
> In this ole slave cabin,
> Your hands my heart strings grabbin,
> Jes lay your head upon my bres,
> An snuggle close an res an res,
> My little colored chile.
>
> Yo daddy ploughs ole massa's corn,
> Yo mammy does the cooking,
> She'll give dinner to her hungry chile
> When nobody is a lookin'
> Don't be ashamed my chile, I beg,
> Ca[u]se you was hatched from a buzzard's egg;
> My little colored chile.[62]

The love and affection blacks received in infancy and early childhood initially determined how much self-esteem and sense of security they would have as young adults.

Another important factor in the evolution of self-consciousness in the quarters was the extent and character of the young slave's interaction with whites, especially children. Often assigned as playmates to their young masters, black children played in pro-

61. Yetman, *Voices*, 112; Blassingame, *Slave Testimony*, 297; Armstrong, *Old Massa's People*, 58-62; Gutman, *Black Family*, 185-201; Redpath, *Roving Editor*, 56.

62. Rawick, *American Slave*, VI, 195, VII, 35; Armstrong, *Old Massa's People*, 58.

miscuous equality with white children. Together they roamed the plantation or went hunting, fishing, berry picking, or raiding watermelon and potato patches. Indeed, at first, bondage weighed lightly on the shoulders of the black child.[63] Lunsford Lane, in reflecting on his childhood on a North Carolina plantation, wrote: "I knew no difference between myself and the white children, nor did they seem to know any in turn. Sometime my master would come out and give a biscuit to me and another to one of his white boys; but I did not perceive the difference between us."[64]

The pleasures of early childhood and the equality of playmates which transcended color sometimes obscured the young slave's vision of bondage. During this period many of the young blacks had no idea they were slaves. J. Vance Lewis wrote that on a Louisiana plantation during his early childhood: "As a barefoot boy my stay upon the farm had been pleasant. I played among the wild flowers and wandered, in high glee, over hill and hollow, enchanted with the beauty of nature, and knew not that I was a slave, and son of a slave." Sam Aleckson, though in less lyrical terms, declared the same thing. Until he was ten years old, he asserted, "it had never dawned on me that my condition was not as good as that of any boy in the country." Frederick Douglass reported that during his childhood, "it was a long time before I knew myself to be a *slave*." This was true, he said, because "the first seven or eight years of the slave-boy's life are about as full of sweet content as those of the most favored and petted *white* children of the slaveholder . . . freed from all restraint, the slave-boy can be, in his life and conduct, a genuine boy, doing whatever his boyish nature suggests. . . ."[65]

63. R. Anderson, *From Slavery*, 3-8; Stroyer, *My Life*, 15-20; Lucy Ann Delaney, *From the Darkness Cometh the Light: Or Struggles for Freedom* (St. Louis, n.d.), 13; Thomas L. Johnson, *Twenty-eight Years a Slave: Or the Story of My Life in Three Continents* (London, 1909), 2; Yetman, *Voices*, 200; Blassingame, *Slave Testimony*, 130, 132, 465, 512, 632, 641, 710; Armstrong, *Old Massa's People*, 69, 73-78; Tyler and Murphy, *Slave Narratives*, 24, 87; Perdue, *Weevils*, 84.

64. Lane, *Narrative*, 6.

65. J. Vance Lewis, *Out of the Ditch* (Houston, 1910), 8; Sam Aleckson,

The planters frequently contributed directly to the idyllic existence of the young slaves. Many of the black autobiographers were the favorites of their masters, who, in a number of cases, were their fathers. In such an event, the child would be fondled, taken on horseback rides, or rewarded with numerous gifts and acts of kindness. William Grimes recalled that his master "was very fond of me, and always treated me kindly." Other slaves declared that their masters were indulgent and often gave them sweets and sometimes protected them from parental wrath. Amanda Smith's childhood was typical of this experience. She declared: "I was a good deal spoiled for a little darkey. If I wanted a piece of bread, and it was not buttered, and sugared on both sides, I wouldn't have it; and when mother would get out of patience with me, and go for a switch, I would run to my old mistress and wrap myself up in her apron, and I was safe. And oh! how I loved her for that."[66]

Most of the slaves, of course, did not have such idyllic childhoods. While J. Vance Lewis recalled that his master's son "was as true a friend as I ever had," the memories of many slaves were clouded with tales of brutal treatment from their little white playmates who were often spurred on by their masters. Others were cuffed about by the planters and flogged for daring to visit the plantation house. Thomas Jones summed up the experience of many slaves when he declared: "I was born a slave. . . . I was made to feel, in my boyhood's first experience, that I was inferior and degraded, and that I must pass through life in a dependent and suffering condition."[67]

Those who were lucky enough to avoid Jones's experience in early childhood knew what he felt by the time they reached their teens. Many began working irregularly at light tasks before they were ten. After that age they usually started working in the fields. Such labor was the first, and irreparable, break in the

---

Before the War and After the Union (Boston, 1929), 113; Douglass, *Bondage,* 38, 40-41; Armstrong, *Old Massa's People,* 58, 67-68, 78-80.

66. Grimes, *Life,* 8; Amanda Smith, *An Autobiography* (Chicago, 1893), 22.

67. Lewis, *Ditch,* 9; Jones, *Experiences,* 5.

childhood equality in black-white relations. Lunsford Lane's reaction illustrates the impact of this change:

> When I began to work, I discovered the difference between myself and my master's white children. They began to order me about, and were told to do so by my master and mistress. . . . Indeed all things now made me *feel,* what I had before known only in words, that *I was a slave.* Deep was this feeling, and it preyed upon my heart like a never dying worm. I saw no prospect that my condition would ever be changed.[68]

Most black children learned vicariously what slavery was long before this point. They were often terrified by the violent punishment meted out to the black men around them. The beginning of Jermain Loguen's sense of insecurity and brutal awareness of what he was, for example, occurred when he saw a vicious white planter murder a slave and was cautioned to silence by his mother. The shock of seeing their parents flogged was an early reminder to many black children of what slavery was.[69] When young William Wells Brown saw his mother flogged for being late going to the fields, he recalled that "the cold chills ran over me, and I wept aloud."[70] The flogging Charles Ball's mother received when he was four years old still retained its "painful vividness" to him forty-seven years later.

In the face of all of the restrictions, slave parents made every effort humanly possible to shield their children from abuse and teach them how to survive in bondage. One of the most important lessons for the child was learning to hold his tongue around white folks. This was especially true on those plantations where the masters tried to get the children to spy on their parents.[71] Sam Aleckson pointed out that as a child he "was taught to say nothing" about the conversations in the quarters. Frequently mothers had to be severe with their children to prevent them

68. Lane, *Narrative,* 7-8; see also: Yetman, *Voices,* 40, 72, 124, 191-92, 264, 288, 316, 322; Armstrong, *Old Massa's People,* 80-81, 86-97; Tyler and Murphy, *Slave Narratives,* 50, 53, 56-57, 59-61.

69. Loguen, *Freedman,* 38-52, 109-22; Watson, *Narrative,* 5-17; Thompson, *Life,* 13-19; Douglass, *Bondage,* 91.

70. W. W. Brown, *Narrative,* 16.

71. Grandy, *Narrative,* 7-18; Ball, *Slavery,* 74-94; Stroyer, *My Life,* 9-14.

from breaking this important rule. Elijah P. Marrs, for example, declared: "Mothers were necessarily compelled to be severe on their children to keep them from talking too much. Many a poor mother has been whipped nearly to death on account of their children telling white children things. . . ."[72]

Many of the slave parents tried to inculcate a sense of morality in their children. The children were taught to be honest and to lead Christian lives.[73] The Reverend Lucius Holsey gave his "intensely religious" mother credit for the moral lessons he had learned as a boy. Henry Box Brown's mother taught him "not to steal, and not to lie, and to behave myself in other respects." Strict and pious parents not only taught religious principles to their children, they also taught them not to rebel against their masters. William Webb asserted that his mother "taught me there was a Supreme Being, that would take care of me in all my trials; she taught me not to rebel against the men that were treating me like some dumb brute, making me work and refusing to let me learn."[74] Learning to accept personal abuse and the punishment of loved ones passively was one of the most difficult lessons for the slave child. Young Austin Steward indicated this when he recounted how he felt upon observing a white man flogging his sister:

> The God of heaven only knows the conflict of feeling I then endured; He alone witnessed the tumult of my heart, at this outrage of manhood and kindred affection. God knows that my will was good enough to have wrung his neck; or to have drained from his heartless system its last drop of blood! And yet I was obliged to turn a deaf ear to her cries for assistance, which to this day ring in my ears. Strong and athletic as I was, no hand of mine could be raised in her defence, but at the peril of both our lives.[75]

72. Aleckson, *Union*, 67; Elijah P. Marrs, *Life and History* (Louisville, 1855), 11.
73. Aleckson, *Union*, 17-21; Davis, *Colored Man*, 9-17; Stroyer, *My Life*, 24-29; Veney, *Woman*, 7-13.
74. H. B. Brown, *Narrative*, 16; William Webb, *The History of William Webb* (Detroit, 1873), 3.
75. Steward, *Twenty-two Years*, 97.

The lessons the slave child learned about conformity were complex and contradictory. Recognizing the overwhelming power of the whites, parents taught children obedience as a means of avoiding pain, suffering, and death. At the same time, they did not teach unconditional submission. Instead, children were often taught to fight their masters and overseers to protect their relatives. For instance, W. H. Robinson's father once told him: "I want you to die in defense of your mother. . . ."[76] On many occasions the children saw their parents disobey and sometimes fight their master. Listening to stories of runaways and seeing slaves interact in the quarters, the slave child had many models of behavior. In fact, he saw his parents playing two con-

76. Robinson, *Pulpit,* 25.

Figures 33, 34, 35. Going South
(Figure 34 Courtesy Chicago Historical Society)

tradictory roles. In the quarters, for example, where he saw his parents most often, his father acted like a man, castigating whites for their mistreatment of him, being a leader, protector, and provider. On the few occasions when the child saw him at work the father was obedient and submissive to his master. Sometimes children internalized both the true personality traits and the contradictory behavioral patterns of their parents. Since, however, their parents' submission was on a shallow level of convenience directed toward avoiding pain, it was less important as a model of behavior than the personality traits they exhibited in the quarters.

When a young slave received his first flogging he was usually so angry that he either wanted to run away or to seek revenge. His parents, upon learning this, tried to dissuade him, advised him of ways to avoid future punishment, or attempted to raise his hopes.[77] After receiving his first flogging, for example, Jacob Stroyer vowed to fight the next time he was attacked. His father argued against such action, saying: " 'the best thing for us to do is to pray much over it, for I believe that the time will come when this boy with the rest of the children will be free, though we may not live to see it.' " His father's comments on freedom, according to Stroyer, "were of great comfort to me, and my heart swelled with the hope of the future, which made every moment seem an hour to me."[78]

The degree to which slaves were able to give their children hope in the midst of adversity is reflected in the attitudes the black autobiographers held toward their parents. Fathers were loved and respected because of their physical strength, courage, and compassion. Austin Steward described his father as "a kind, affectionate husband and a fond, indulgent parent." James Watkins admired his father because he was "a clever, Shrewd man." James Mars stood in awe of his father, who "was a man of considerable muscular strength, and was not easily frightened into obedience." Although they were not always perfect male models,

77. J. H. Banks, *A Narrative of Events of the Life of J. H. Banks* (Liverpool, 1861), 20.
78. Stroyer, *My Life*, 23.

most slave fathers had the respect of their children. Viewing the little things that they did to make life more pleasant for their children, Charles Ball asserted: "Poor as the slave is, and dependent at all times upon the arbitrary will of his master, or yet more fickle caprice of the overseer, his children look up to him in his little cabin, as their protector and supporter."[79]

Slave mothers, were, of course, held in even greater esteem by their children. Frequently small children fought overseers who were flogging their mothers. Even when they had an opportunity to escape from bondage, many slaves refused to leave their mothers. As a young slave, William Wells Brown did not run away because he "could not bear the idea" of leaving his mother. He felt that he, "after she had undergone and suffered so much for me would be proving recreant to the duty which I owed to her."[80]

The love the slaves had for their parents reveals clearly the importance of the family. Although it was weak, although it was frequently broken, the slave family provided an important buffer, a refuge from the rigors of slavery. While the slave father could rarely protect the members of his family from abuse, he could often gain their love and respect in other ways. In his family, the slave not only learned how to avoid the blows of the master, but also drew on the love and sympathy of its members to raise his spirits. The family was, in short, an important survival mechanism.

79. Steward, *Twenty-two Years,* 126; Watkins, *Narrative,* 7; James Mars, *Life of James Mars, a Slave Born and Sold in Connecticut* (Hartford, 1864), 3; Ball, *Slavery,* 211.

80. W. W. Brown, *Narrative,* 31-32.

5

Runaways and Rebels

O, that I were free! . . . O, why was I born a man, of whom to make a brute! I am left in the hottest hell of unending slavery. O, God, save me! God deliver me! Let me be free! Is there any God? Why am I a slave? I will run away. I will not stand it. Get caught, or get clear, I'll try it. . . . I have only one life to lose. I had as well be killed running as die standing.

Frederick Douglass

There is overwhelming evidence, in the primary sources, of the Negro's resistance to his bondage and of his undying love for freedom.[1] The yearning for freedom came with the first realization of the finality, of the fact, of slavery. Lunsford Lane claimed that his first realization that he was a chattel, a thing for the use of others, caused him deep anxiety: "I saw no prospect that my condition would ever be changed. Yet I used to plan in my mind from day to day, and from night to night, how I might be free."[2] Several factors combined to keep the flame of freedom burning: a free Negro kidnapped into slavery explained to his fellows the blessings of liberty; anti-slavery whites, conversing with slaves, dwelt on the boon denied to them; an old African told speechless young boys about the wonders of his native land; and, above all, each escape of a fellow sufferer produced prayers of success,

1. William Green, *Narrative of Events in the Life of William Green* (Springfield, O., 1853), 9-14; Lunsford Lane, *The Narrative of Lunsford Lane* (Boston, 1848), 7-8; Elijah P. Marrs, *Life and History* (Louisville, 1885), 11-16; Austin Steward, *Twenty-two Years a Slave, and Forty Years a Freeman* (Rochester, N.Y., 1861), 76-78, 106-15; Jacob Stroyer, *My Life in the South* (Salem, 1890), 24-29; Louis Hughes, *Thirty Years a Slave* (Milwaukee, 1897), 98-114.

2. Lane, *Narrative*, 8.

fed the rumor mill, fired dreams, and raised the level of curiosity about freedom throughout the quarters.

In spite of all the floggings, there were hopes and dreams.[3] When William Webb talked to the overworked, underfed, and frequently flogged slaves on one plantation he discovered that they still yearned for freedom: "They said they had been thinking they would be free, for a long time, and praying that they would live to see it. . . ."[4] Josiah Henson asserted that "From my earliest recollection freedom had been the object of my ambition, a constant motive to exertion, an ever-present stimulus to gain and to save."[5] Frederick Douglass recalled that as a child, he was "strongly impressed with the idea of being a free man some day."[6]

The slave's constant prayer, his all-consuming hope, was for liberty. Fathers opened family religious observances with prayers for freedom which held out the slender thread of hope to their children. Jacob Stroyer's father, for example, disturbed over the cruel punishment of his son, knelt one night and prayed: "Lord, hasten the time when these children shall be their own free men and women." The prayer raised Jacob's spirits, and he wrote that at that time "my faith in father's prayer made me think that the Lord would answer him at the farthest in two or three weeks." W. H. Robinson recalled that all of the slaves "prayed for the dawn and light of a better day . . . many looked long and eagerly for freedom but died without the sight."[7]

Anything might fan the fires of freedom higher. The overseer's lash, the master's celebration of the Fourth of July, a heated political campaign, the whites' disparagement of abolitionists, a painful reminder of the invidious distinctions between blacks and whites, or a sermon might cause the slave to dream

3. Moses Roper, *A Narrative of the Adventures and Escape of Moses Roper from American Slavery* (London, 1840), 10.

4. William Webb, *The History of William Webb* (Detroit, 1873), 26.

5. Josiah Henson, *The Life of Josiah Henson* (Boston, 1849), 25.

6. Frederick Douglass, *My Bondage and My Freedom* (New York, 1968 [1855]), 91.

7. Stroyer, *My Life*, 24; W. H. Robinson, *From Log Cabin to the Pulpit* (Eau Claire, Wis., 1913), 50.

about freedom. According to William Webb, a few literate slaves followed the John C. Frémont presidential campaign in 1856 and told others that his election would mean their freedom. When Frémont lost, the slaves were disappointed, but still hopeful. At one meeting they discussed how they could obtain freedom, and "some would speak about rebelling and killing, and some would speak, and say 'wait for the next four years.'" Austin Steward declared that a "superbly grand" militia training session made such an impression on him that "it became very hard for me to content myself to labor as I had done. I was completely intoxicated with a military spirit, and sighed for liberty to go out 'on the line' and fight the British . . . besides, I was sick and tired of being a slave, and felt ready to do almost anything to get where I could act and feel like a free man."[8]

The slave understood clearly what freedom was.[9] He only had to feel the scars on his back, recall the anguished cry of his wife and child as they were torn away from him, or to look at the leisure time, delicious and abundant food, and dry house of his master to know, and to know concretely, what liberty meant. Louis Hughes wrote that the slaves often discussed freedom:

> Though freedom was yearned for by some because the treatment was bad, others, who knew it was a curse to be held a slave—they longed to stand out in true manhood—allowed to express their opinions as were white men. Others still desired freedom, thinking they could then reclaim a wife, husband, or children. The mother would again see her child. All these promptings of the heart made them yearn for freedom.[10]

Solomon Northup contended that even the most ignorant slaves understood the meaning of freedom:

> They understand the privileges and exemptions that belong to it—that it would bestow upon them the enjoyment of domestic

8. Webb, *History,* 13; Steward, *Twenty-two Years,* 77-78.
9. Solomon Northup, *Twelve Years a Slave* (London, 1853), 260; Henson, *Life,* 10-31; Hughes, *Thirty Years,* 75-79; John Brown, *Slave Life in Georgia* (London, 1855), 31-44; Webb, *History,* 13-19.
10. Hughes, *Thirty Years,* 79.

> happiness. They do not fail to observe the difference between their own condition and the meanest white man's, and to realize the injustice of laws which place it within his power not only to appropriate the profits of their industry, but to subject them to unmerited and unprovoked punishment, without remedy, or the right to resist, or to remonstrate.[11]

The more slaves knew of freedom, the more desirous they were of obtaining it. The continuing conversations about freedom in the quarters shaped Elijah P. Marr's desire for freedom: "I had heard so much about freedom, and of colored people running off and going to Canada, that my mind was busy with this subject even in my young days." The more slaves knew about freedom, Austin Steward averred, "the more we desired it, and the less willing we were to remain in bondage."[12]

It is impossible to measure exactly the extent of the slave's dissatisfaction with his lot. The best objective evidence we have on this appears in Helen T. Catterall's five-volume *Judicial Cases Concerning American Slavery and the Negro*. Restricted to cases which reached colonial or State Supreme Courts between 1640 and 1865, the evidence in Catterall represents only a small part of slave discontent. According to these records, 591 slaves sued for their freedom, 561 ran away from their masters, and 533 assaulted, robbed, poisoned, and murdered whites, burned their masters' dwellings, and committed suicide. Hundreds more fought whites in self-defense, and were guilty of insubordination.[13] The cases reveal that slaves were often unruly, refused to learn trades, killed livestock, and burned plantation buildings in retaliation for mistreatment. Marion J. Russell's survey of the

11. Northup, *Twelve Years*, 260.
12. Marrs, *History*, 12; Steward, *Twenty-two Years*, 107.
13. Helen Catterall, ed., *Judicial Cases Concerning American Slavery and the Negro* (5 vols., Washington, D.C. 1926-37); see also: William T. Harris, *Remarks Made During a Tour Through the United States of America in the Years 1817, 1818, and 1819* (London, 1821), 57, 67; Harriet Martineau, *Retrospect of Western Travel* (3 vols., London, 1838), II, 97-101, 145-47; Alexander Mackay, *The Western World* (3 vols., Philadelphia, 1849), I, 287.

Supreme Court records revealed several types of discontent and insubordination.[14]

As the Supreme Court records indicate, the slave's desire for freedom was eventually translated into action. An especially painful flogging or an unusually severe work load frequently led the slave to make a momentous decision: he had had enough, he would run away. Although his immediate purpose might be to escape the overseer's lash or to obtain a temporary respite from incessant labor, the black faced almost insuperable odds. As he plunged into nearby woods or swamps, the overseer, gun in hand, was close on his heels. Almost immediately, or certainly in a few days, he would hear the hounds as they picked up the scent of his tracks. Reaching the woods unscathed, he had to fight off the pangs of hunger as well as bloodthirsty wild cats, wolves, and white men. Avid hunters, his master and overseer might know the woods as well, or better, than he did. Besides, any white man might stumble inadvertently onto his hideout. Capture would probably mean cancellation of all passes, inability to travel to the next plantation to see his wife or family, being sold down South, imprisonment in the stocks, being handcuffed to heavy logs at night and to another slave during the day, or having a cow bell hung around his neck or a tall instrument with several prongs covered with little bells attached to his head. At the very least he could look forward to being strung up and flogged severely—and excruciating pain.

The ubiquitous runaway defied all the odds. Sometimes he stayed away until his anger or that of his master subsided. Cold and hungry, he frequently returned after a few days, took his flogging, and went back to work. More often than not, he was caught while trying to see his wife or to get the food the sympathetic slaves left for him. On other occasions, however, the runaway eluded his pursuers for weeks, months, or even years, safe in his bailiwick near the plantation. Peter Randolph's brother, for instance, ran away and stayed in the woods seven months while

14. Marion Russell, "American Slave Discontent in Records of the High Courts," *Journal of Negro History* XXXI (Oct. 1946), 411-34; Appendix III, table 18.

Figure 36. Escape

Figure 37. Trailed by Bloodhounds

his mother carried him food. Sold South, William Grimes's sister returned to be near her husband, hid in the woods for years, and bore three children there.[15]

The slave who decided to follow the North Star to freedom faced almost insurmountable obstacles. The most formidable one he had to overcome was the psychological barrier of having to leave a home, friends, and family he loved. Mothers and wives argued passionately against it. Douglass felt that "thousands would escape from slavery . . . but for the strong cords of affection that bind them to their families, relatives and friends." Considering the likelihood of punishment and a harder life in

15. Peter Randolph, *Sketches of Slave Life* (Boston, 1855), 16-19; Hughes, *Thirty Years*, 79-98; Henry Bibb, *Narrative of the Life and Adventures of Henry Bibb, an American Slave* (New York, 1849), 57-93; Orland Kay Armstrong, ed., *Old Massa's People: The Old Slaves Tell Their Story* (Indianapolis, 1931), 270-71; Ronnie C. Tyler and Lawrence Murphy, eds., *The Slave Narratives of Texas* (Austin, 1974), 64-69.

Figure 38. Keeping the Wolves at Bay

case of failure, ridicule from the other slaves, his ignorance of the world and of geography, his penniless condition, his viewing every white man as his enemy, and his memory of his master's tales of the horrible fate which befell fugitives who succeeded in reaching the North, a slave had to think a long time before he took the first step toward permanent freedom. William Green and his friends often talked about escaping to Canada, but he declared that "it requires all the nerve and energy that a poor slave can bring to his support to enable him to make up his mind to leave in this precarious manner." Henry Bibb said that when he left his family enslaved it was "one of the most self-denying acts of my whole life, to take leave of an affectionate wife, who stood before me on my departure, with dear little Frances in her arms, and with tears of sorrow in her eyes as she bid me a long farewell. It required all the moral courage that I was master of to suppress my feelings while taking leave of my little family." On the eve of his escape from bondage, Frederick Douglass expressed what most slaves probably felt upon contemplating escape: "I was making a leap in the dark. . . . I was like one going to war without weapons—ten chances of defeat to one of victory."[16]

The slaves who escaped were extremely resourceful men. Of the fugitive autobiographers, seven escaped from cities and eleven from plantations. Since so many of the fugitives had served in so many capacities as slaves, it is difficult to classify them by occupation. Four had been house slaves all of their lives; seven had been craftsmen all of their lives; six were house servants when they escaped, six were craftsmen; and six were field slaves. Weekends, Christmas holidays, and the months when corn was still standing in the fields were the favorite times for running away. They mailed themselves in boxes, hid, often with the aid of black sailors or sympathetic white captains, in the holds of North-bound ships, disguised their sex, paid poor whites to write passes for them, or, when literate, wrote their own passes; they stowed away on steamboats, pretended to be so loyal and so submissive that their masters took them to the North where they disappeared; or they passed for white. A limited amount of material was needed to begin the journey, but it was often crucial. A warm jacket, some pepper, a gun or knife, and a small cache of food (a couple of ears of corn would suffice) were essential. All the material could be stolen from the master. The bolder slaves took their master's fastest horse and any money they could find.

Slipping away on the weekend or during the Christmas revelries, the fugitive could be far away from his immediate neighborhood by the time he was missed. But just in case his trail had not gotten cold by then, he used a liberal supply of pepper to throw the dogs off his trail. Remaining in the woods at night, he avoided all inhabited areas. His two greatest enemies were the white man and hunger. The latter problem he solved by appropriating ears of corn from the fields or barns, chickens from chicken houses, or, if desperate, he begged for food in the slave quarters or ate garbage. But the white man was, by far, the runaway's most deadly enemy. If the slave was surprised by an ig-

16. Douglass, *Bondage,* 333; Green, *Events,* 15; Bibb, *Adventures,* 46; Douglass, *Bondage,* 422.

Figure 39. Fighting Off Pursuers

norant white man, he flashed any piece of paper with writing on it in front of his face and usually succeeded in deceiving his adversary. When accosted by a white man he could not deceive, he ran. If cornered, he sometimes fought and killed his pursuers.[17]

One of the most objective and revealing sources of information on the character of the fugitive appears in the runaway slave notices in the antebellum Southern newspapers. Unbiased attempts of owners to recover property worth hundreds of dollars, the notices were carefully composed, dispassionate descriptions of the fugitives, indicating their character, clothing, motives, and identifying marks. The notices are, however, somewhat misleading in regard to slaves with exceptional talents. Since such slaves were more valuable, planters were more likely to try to recover them than the common slave. Even so, it is possible to draw some

17. William Craft, *Running a Thousand Miles for Freedom: Or the Escape of William and Ellen Craft from Slavery* (London, 1860), 12-80; John Anderson, *The Story of the Life of John Anderson, a Fugitive Slave* (London, 1863), 8-126; Henson, *Life*, 40-58.

generalizations from the notices about the character of the fugitives. Most of them were young, robust men.[18]

The fugitive slaves first appear in the colonial period when from 5 to 10 per cent of them were natives of Africa and most were young men. In a collection of 134 runaway notices from eighteenth-century newspapers, 76 per cent of the fugitives were under 35, and 89 per cent of them were men. Detailed studies of fugitives in the colonial period indicate that the sample is reliable. In colonial South Carolina 75 per cent of the 2000 eighteenth-century fugitives noted in the newspapers were young males between the ages of 18 and 30. Similarly, 88 per cent of the 1279 runaways listed in eighteenth-century Virginia journals were males. Throughout the eighteenth century, field hands and native-born slaves predominated in the runaway notices. The pattern established in the colonial period continued in the nineteenth century.[19]

Most studies of the notices indicate that there was no uniformity of personality types among the fugitives. For instance, Orville W. Taylor systematically examined notices in Arkansas newspapers and found they showed "among other things, that slaves were as individualistic as white people, despite the regimentation of slavery."[20] The major thing to remember about these notices is that they contained information which would help to distinguish the fugitive from the mass of slaves. Most of the

18. "Eighteenth Century Slaves as Advertised by Their Masters," *Journal of Negro History* I (April 1916), 163-216; Lorenzo J. Greene, "The New England Negro as Seen in Advertisements for Runaway Slaves," *Journal of Negro History* XXIX (April 1944), 125-46; John W. Coleman, *Slavery Times in Kentucky* (Chapel Hill, 1940), 218-44; James B. Sellers, *Slavery in Alabama* (University, Ala., 1950), 277-81; Joe Gray Taylor, *Negro Slavery in Louisiana* (Baton Rouge, 1963), 174-79.

19. See note 18; Daniel Meaders, "South Carolina Fugitives as Viewed Through Local Colonial Newspapers with Emphasis on Runaway Notices, 1732-1801," *Journal of Negro History* LX (April 1975), 288-319; Gerald W. Mullin, *Flight and Rebellion: Slave Resistance in Eighteenth-Century Virginia* (New York, 1972), 98, 103; see also Robert S. Cope, *Carry Me Back: Slavery and Servitude in Seventeenth-Century Virginia* (Pikeville, Ky., 1973), 97-105.

20. Orville W. Taylor, *Negro Slavery in Arkansas* (Durham, 1958), 225.

fugitives had no readily identifiable behavioral patterns which set them apart from their fellows.

Those who were different in character from most slaves fell into two relatively broad categories. One group was composed of what Southerners called Sambo, the slave who allegedly viewed his master as his father and identified with his interest. The other consisted of rebels. The fugitive Sambo often stuttered, whined, laughed, grinned, trembled, was "easily frightened or scared," "rather stupid," "addicted to lying," or had a "sly," "down guilty" look, or "shuffled" and had a "low voice," or "a small impediment in speech when frightened" in the presence of whites.[21]

Such peculiarities of speech as afflicted fugitive slaves are sometimes the best indicators of psychological stress. They have, however, been blown all out of proportion in regard to slaves. Only 19, or 11.6 per cent, of a group of 163 fugitives appearing in three New Orleans newspapers between 1839 and 1860 were said to have had speech defects: five replied quickly, seven spoke very slowly when spoken to by whites, two laughed, and five stuttered. Except for those who laughed, the meaning of these peculiarities is not clear. Much of the hesitation, stuttering, or rapidity in speech may have resulted from the slave's unfamiliarity with European languages, missing teeth, and other physical infirmities. The peculiarities may have had no relation to any extreme anxiety about white people. For example, although the Louisiana fugitive Mose spoke slowly, he had "easy manners, and [was] very shrewd." In any case, almost 90 per cent of the Louisiana fugitives had no speech defects and many spoke "loud and very positive" or were "very forward and talkative."[22]

Apparently many of the behavioral patterns mentioned in the runaway notices were not limited to slaves. In 1854, for instance, the New Orleans *Delta* penned a description of a white man

21. See note 18; New Orleans *Picayune*, July 15, 1857; New Orleans *Daily Delta*, Nov. 16, 1858.

22. New Orleans *Picayune*, June 5, 1839, July 8, Aug. 28, 1840; New Orleans *True Delta*, Feb. 16, Aug. 24, 1854; New Orleans *Daily Delta*, Oct. 16, 1855, Nov. 16, 1858; Ulrich B. Phillips, ed., *Plantation and Frontier, 1649-1863* (2 vols., Cleveland, 1910), I, 79, 87-89, 92.

who had allegedly stolen a slave, which was remarkably similar to the ones masters used when depicting runaway slaves. According to the *Delta,* the white man "speaks slowly, [and] has a sly countenance." When eighteenth-century employers tried to recapture runaway white indentured servants they depicted them in the same way as planters did black fugitives. In eighteenth-century South Carolina newspapers many white indentured servants were described as having speech impediments and a "down look." Samuel Kennerly's employer, for instance, wrote in 1766 that Kennerly was "remarkable for seldom or ever looking in the face of the person when spoken to."[23]

Regardless of his similarity to runaway white indentured servants, the fugitive Sambo was a very complex fellow. Frequently, in the same sentence in which the Sambo traits cited above appeared, the planters observed that the slave was artful, could read and write, and had probably forged a pass, and stolen money, horses, and clothes. A Virginia planter wrote in 1784 that Dick had "a very roguish down look . . . is artful and plausible. . . ." Another Virginia planter in 1793 described Will as "of a black complexion, round shouldered and down look, when spoken to is apt to grin, is an artful sensible fellow, much accustomed to driving a wagon, is good at any kind of plantation business, tolerably ingenious, and I am informed, has a pass. . . ." In the same year, a Maryland planter wrote that his Jem "has a great hesitation in his speech, and when he laughs shows his gums very much, takes snuff, one of his legs is sore; he is very artful and can turn his hand to any thing. . . ."[24]

The fugitive Sambo was a bundle of contradictions. On the one hand, he was the epitome of loyalty and docility, and completely trusted by his master. On the other, in spite of his "loyalty," he ran away. A South Carolina master in 1786 indicated how much of an enigma Sambo was when he observed that one of his fugitive slaves was

23. Meaders, "South Carolina Fugitives," 311; New Orleans *True Delta,* Aug. 24, 1854.

24. *Maryland Gazette,* Aug. 26, 1784; "Eighteenth Century Slaves Advertised," 189, 203.

sensible and artful, speaks quick, and sometimes stutters a little; HE MAY POSSIBLY HAVE A TICKET THAT I GAVE HIM TWO DAYS BEFORE HE WENT AWAY, DATED THE 6TH OF APRIL, MENTIONING HE WAS IN QUEST OF A RUNAWAY, AS I DID NOT MENTION WHEN HE WAS TO RETURN, HE MAY ENDEAVOUR TO PASS BY THAT. . . .[25]

How could a slave so completely gain the confidence of his master that he would be sent out to look for a runaway slave and then become a fugitive himself?

Did Sambo grin and look down all the while he was "artfully" and "ingeniously" planning to escape? Was he only play-acting when he grinned? Did he reveal his true character when he stepped out of the Sambo role or did the master misperceive his character, read too much into his "down look," while being selectively inattentive to his artfulness and roguish behavior? Many of these questions plagued the planters. For example, a Maryland slaveholder wrote in 1755 lamenting the escape of James: "That this Slave should run away and attempt getting his liberty, is very alarming, as he has always been too kindly used, if any Thing, by his Master, and one in whom his Master has put great Confidence, and depended on him to overlook the rest of the Slaves, and he had no Kind of provocation to go off." Other planters were apparently less mystified by the contradiction inherent in an overly simplified perception of Sambo. An Alabama planter obviously suspected that the Sambo role involved a great deal of play-acting. He warned other whites to be wary of a fugitive who was "a smooth tongued fellow and when spoken to used the word 'master' very frequently, particularly when accused of any misdemeanor."[26]

The other character type which appears in the notices is the rebellious slave. The rebellious fugitive was very artful, cunning, a "well set, hardy villain," "of good sense, and much ingenuity," "saucy," "very surly," "very great rogue," "sober and intelligent,"

25. *South Carolina Gazette,* May 1, 1786.

26. "Eighteenth Century Slaves Advertised," 202; Sellers, *Alabama,* 279-80; New Orleans *Picayune,* June 5, 1839, Dec. 16, 1858; New Orleans *Daily Delta,* Oct. 16, 1855.

"bold," "fights like the Devil when arrested," and often stole large sums of money and took along a "nice short shot gun." Many of these fugitives were habitual runaways and quick to try to get revenge when punished.[27] The archetype of the rebellious fugitive was "Sarah," whom a Kentucky planter described in 1822 as

> the biggest devil that ever lived, having poisoned a stud horse and set a stable on fire, also burnt Gen. R. Williams stable and stock yard with seven horses and other property to value of $1500. She was handcuffed and got away at Ruddles Mills on her way down the river, which is the fifth time she escaped when about to be sent out of the country.[28]

Throughout the antebellum period groups of slaves occasionally banded together in attempting to escape. Often this occurred when they were being taken to the deep South to be sold. A group of blacks being transported through Southampton County, Virginia, killed two whites in 1799 in an attempt to escape. Seventy-seven slaves mutinied on a Mississippi River steamer in 1826, killed five white men on board and escaped to Indiana. When slaves lived near swamps, impenetrable forests, or near frontier areas, they often banded together in such mass efforts.[29] After a Spanish decree welcomed English slaves to Florida in 1733, often as many as twenty South Carolina slaves marched in a body to the colony, occasionally killing whites along the way. The most impressive of the South Carolina incidents began at Stono in September 1739, when a group of slaves sacked and burned the armory. Then they began marching toward a Spanish fort in Florida which contained a colony of runaway slaves

27. See note 18; New Orleans *Picayune,* Aug. 5, 1840; Phillips, *Plantation and Frontier,* I, 81-82, 87, 90.

28. Coleman, *Kentucky,* 233.

29. Herbert Aptheker, *American Negro Slave Revolts* (New York, 1943), 218-19, 276-79; Herbert Aptheker, "Maroons Within the Present Limits of the United States," *Journal of Negro History* XXIV (April 1939), 167-84; Herbert Aptheker, "Additional Data on American Maroons," *Journal of Negro History* XXXIII (Oct. 1947), 452-60.

Figure 40. Conspirators

and was manned by a black militia company. Beating a drum as they marched, the slaves attacked all of the plantations along the way, and killed twenty or thirty whites before a militia company killed or captured most of them. A contemporary wrote of the Stono uprising: "Several Negroes joined them, they called out liberty, marched on with colours displayed, and two drums beating."[30]

Few states were immune to organized mass escape attempts.

30. Edward McCrady, "Slavery in the Province of South Carolina," *Annual Report of the American Historical Association for the Year 1895* (Washington, D.C., 1896), 631-73.

Figure 41. Resistance

In July 1845, seventy-five slaves from three Maryland counties armed themselves and began marching toward the Pennsylvania state line. Caught and surrounded by whites near Rockville, Maryland, several of the blacks were killed and thirty-one recaptured. A similar dash for freedom occurred in August 1848 in Kentucky when a white college student led a group of seventy-five slaves toward the Ohio River. Pursued by the slaveholders, the fugitives fought two battles with them, but all were eventually killed or recaptured. Thirty slaves in Missouri emulated the Kentucky fugitives in 1850 when they armed themselves and began marching toward freedom. Later, surrounded by heavily armed whites, the slaves held out for a while and then surrendered.[31]

For the most part, the possibility of a large body of slaves marching undetected to a free state was remote. Realizing this, many runaways built "free" or "maroon" communities in the

31. Aptheker, *Revolts*, 337-43; John Finch, *Travels in the United States of America and Canada* (London, 1833), 241-42; Henry C. Knight, *Letters from the South and West* (Boston, 1824), 29.

swamps and mountains in the South.[32] The character of the maroon settlements and their inhabitants appears in a report from Alabama in 1827. In that year a group of whites reported that:

> A nest of runaway negroes was discovered last week in the fork of the Alabama & Tombecke [Tombigbee] Rivers, by a party from the upper end of Mobile County. . . . The negroes were attacked and after a very severe action they were conquered. Three negroes were shot . . . several were taken prisoner and others escaped. They had two cabins, and were about to build a Fort. . . . Some of these negroes have been runaways several years, and have committed many depredations on the neighbouring plantations. They fought desperately.[33]

The maroon communities represented one of the gravest threats to the planters. In the first place, these communities undermined the master's authority and emboldened other slaves to join them. For example, a group of North Carolina planters complained in December 1830 that their "slaves are become almost uncontrollable. They go and come when and where they please, and if an attempt is made to stop them they immediately fly to the woods and there continue for months and years Committing depredations on our Cattle hogs and Sheep. . . . patrols are of no use on account of the danger they subject themselves to. . . ."[34] Second, and perhaps more important, the maroons often engaged in guerrilla-like activities, plundering and burning plantations, stealing stock, and attacking, robbing, and murdering whites. If they obtained enough arms or allied themselves with poor whites and Indians they could terrorize almost any isolated white community. Sometimes their activities were rationally planned, systematic attacks on the plantations. This

32. Aptheker, *Revolts*, 336; George P. Rawick, ed., *The American Slave: A Composite Autobiography* (31 vols., Westport, Conn., 1972-77), XII, pt. 2: 14-15; Octavia Albert, ed., *The House of Bondage, Or Charlotte Brooks and Other Slaves* (New York, 1891), 86-100; James Redpath, *The Roving Editor: Or, Talks with Slaves in the Southern States* (New York, 1859), 288-95.

33. Aptheker, *Revolts*, 280.

34. Aptheker, *Revolts*, 289; see also: Alan D. Watson, "Impulse Toward Independence: Resistance and Rebellion Among North Carolina Slaves, 1750-1775," *Journal of Negro History* LXIII (Fall 1978), 317-28.

was certainly the case in Accomac County, Virginia, in 1781. A resident of the county declared, "We have had most alarming times this Summer all along shore, from a sett of Barges manned mostly by our own negroes who have run off—These fellows are dangerous to an individual singled out for their vengeance whose property lay exposed—They burnt several houses."[35] On other occasions maroons formed outlaw bands and raided plantations in order to obtain supplies. The Norfolk *Herald* described one of these bands when it announced in 1823 that whites in the county

> have for some time been kept in a state of mind peculiarly harassing and painful, from the too apparent fact that their lives are at the mercy of a band of lurking assassins, against whose fell designs neither the power of the law, nor vigilance, or personal strength and intrepidity, can avail. These desperadoes are runaway negroes (commonly called outlyers) . . . Their first object is to obtain a gun and ammunition, as well to procure game for subsistence as to defend themselves from attack, or accomplish objects of vengeance.[36]

The maroon was a resourceful black man who, having obtained his freedom, challenged any white man to take it away from him. If his hideout was discovered, he was willing to die defending it. For instance, when a group of North Carolina whites attacked a maroon camp in August 1856, the slaves fought back and killed one of them. Then, the "negroes ran off cursing and swearing and telling them to come on, they were ready for them again."[37] On a number of occasions the maroons fought pitched battles with militia in the seventeenth and eighteenth centuries. Later, improvements in roads and communications facilities enabled whites to concentrate large bodies of armed men in the vicinity of the camps and to destroy them. Smaller maroon camps, however, continued to develop in inaccessible swamps in the South, and as long as the slaves did not

35. Aptheker, *Revolts*, 207.
36. Aptheker, *Revolts*, 276.
37. Aptheker, *Revolts*, 346.

attack surrounding plantations they might go undetected for years.[38]

The largest semi-permanent maroon communities grew up in areas where there was international rivalry over borders, or which were near sympathetic Indian tribes. Although some of the tribes like the Choctaw and Chickasaw held blacks in bondage similar to that on Southern white plantations, most of the other tribes either welcomed the blacks as freemen or subjected them to a relatively mild form of slavery. Under the latter group of Indians, blacks performed light labor, owned property, and intermarried with their masters. The closest relations between red and black men developed in Florida when a branch of the Creek tribe, the Seminoles, moved into the Spanish territory. Some of the Seminoles owned black slaves who were almost indistinguishable from free men. These blacks were joined by groups of runaways from South Carolina and Georgia who accepted the Spanish invitation to desert their Protestant masters. By 1836 there were probably about 1,200 maroons living in the Seminole towns. Better acquainted with whites than the Indians were, the maroons and slaves often acted as interpreters for their red masters. By the mid-nineteenth century so many of the Indians and blacks had intermarried that they were almost indistinguishable.[39]

Aided by Indian wars and Spanish and British intrigues on the Georgia-Alabama border of Florida, large numbers of slaves escaped and joined the maroons. A special inducement was held out to runaways when during the War of 1812 the British built a fort on the eastern side of the Appalachicola River for themselves

38. Aptheker, *Revolts,* 171-83, 196-217, 277-89, 342-51; Ulrich B. Phillips, *American Negro Slavery* (Baton Rouge, 1966), 509-10; James McKaye, *The Mastership and Its Fruits* (New York, 1864), 7-12.

39. J. Lutch Wright, "A Note on the First Seminole War as Seen by the Indians, Negroes, and Their British Advisers," *Journal of Southern History* XXXIV (Nov. 1968), 565-75; Kenneth W. Porter, "Negroes and the Seminole War, 1817-1818," *Journal of Negro History* XXXVI (July 1951), 49-80; Wilton M. Krogman, "The Racial Composition of the Seminole Indians of Florida and Oklahoma," *Journal of Negro History* XIX (Oct. 1934), 412-30; Joshua R. Giddings, *The Exiles of Florida* (Columbus, O., 1858).

and their black and red allies. Abandoning the fort in 1816 but leaving behind guns and cannon for their allies, the British inadvertently incited the First Seminole War. Three hundred runaway slaves immediately took over the fort and cultivated land located within fifty miles of it. Led by the maroon Garçon, the runaways attacked a group of sailors from a U.S. gunboat in July and scalped most of them. After a short artillery duel the gunboat was successful in blowing up the fort's magazine, killing most of the blacks. The survivors were recaptured and returned to their owners.

Seeking revenge for their fallen comrades, the Negroes and Indians began drilling in separate units under their officers. In 1817 and 1818 between 400 and 600 runaways joined with the Seminoles in raiding plantations in Georgia, killing the whites and carrying off slaves. On April 16, 1818, Andrew Jackson captured one of the Seminole towns in which the blacks, after their initial retreat, fought valiantly.[40] According to one observer: "They fought desperately, and did not give way until eighty out of three hundred and forty were killed." Unable to follow the survivors into the trackless swamps, Andrew Jackson unilaterally ended what he called "this savage and negro war."[41]

The presence of hundreds of runaway slaves plagued every effort to make a permanent peace with the Seminoles before 1865. The Seminoles were so steadfast in their refusal to agree to the return of the fugitives to their owners that when the U.S. acquired Florida in 1819 plans began almost immediately to remove the Indians to the West. The role of the blacks in the controversy was summarized by an Indian agent in 1821:

> It will be difficult to form a prudent determination, with respect to the maroon negroes, who live among the Indians, on the other side of the little mountains of Latchiova. Their number is said to be upwards of three hundred. They fear being again made slaves, under the American government; and will omit

40. Kenneth W. Porter, "Relations Between Negroes and Indians Within the Present Limits of the United States," *Journal of Negro History* XVII (July 1932), 287-367.

41. Porter, "Relations," 333-34.

nothing to increase or keep alive mistrust among the Indians, whom they in fact govern. If it should become necessary to use force with them, it is to be feared the Indians would take their part.[42]

Fearing that they would be returned to slavery if they ever gathered at a central point to be transported to the West under military supervision, the maroons took a leading part in stirring up resistance to removal among the Seminoles. The immediate cause of the Second Seminole War was intimately related to the problem of the maroons. The war can be traced to the kidnapping and enslavement of the wife of the Seminole chief, Osceola. She was the daughter of a Negro fugitive. As a result of this, in December 1835 the Indians, after being informed by a Negro guide of the route of a company of American soldiers, massacred about 100 of the troops. Negro warriors fought in most of the battles during the next seven years and were so numerous in some of them that on one occasion General Thomas Jesup declared: "This, you may be assured, is a negro, not an Indian war. . . ."[43]

Among the several black warriors, Abraham was the most impressive. After escaping from his Florida master, Abraham became a Seminole slave and interpreter for his master. Later, he won his freedom and married the widow of a chief. Considered one of the most dangerous of the maroon leaders, Abraham was described by one white officer as "the most noted, and for a time an influential man in the [Seminole] nation. He dictated to those of his own color, who to a great degree controlled their masters. They were a most cruel and malignant enemy. For them to surrender would be servitude to the whites; but to retain an open warfare, secured to them plunder, liberty, and importance."[44]

Peace efforts were hindered because planters always rushed in to claim those Negroes who were captured or who surrendered. Between 1835 and 1843 about 500 blacks were returned to their owners in Florida and Georgia. Since the maroons al-

42. Porter, "Relations," 334.

43. Porter, "Relations," 341.

44. Porter, "Relations," 341; for a brief overview of the Seminole wars, see Daniel F. Littlefied, *Africans and Seminoles* (Westport, Conn., 1977), 3-31.

ways renewed hostilities when any of their number were returned to slavery, army officers began pleading with the War Department to treat the blacks as prisoners of war to be removed to the Southwest. General Jesup, for instance, wrote in 1837 that "The negroes rule the Indians and it is important that they should feel themselves secure: if they should become alarmed and hold out, the war will be renewed." Failing in their efforts to prevent the re-enslavement of the maroons, the military officers tried to convince the rapacious planters that it would be better to remove the rebellious blacks to the Southwest rather than add them to their plantation force and possibly incite revolts. One officer tried to demonstrate this by describing the character of the maroons: "The Negroes, from the commencement of the Florida war, have, for their numbers, been the most formidable foe, more blood-thirsty, active, and revengeful than the Indian. . . . Ten resolute negroes, with a knowledge of the country, are sufficient to desolate the frontier, from one extent to the other." The war ended in 1842 only after Zachary Taylor guaranteed the blacks that they would be taken to the Southwest.[45]

In spite of widespread maroon activity and individual resistance among slaves in the South, there have been considerably fewer large-scale slave rebellions in the United States than in Latin America. The explanation for this lies in the differences between conditions in Latin America and in the South. A chronic shortage of military forces and high slave to white population ratio (7 to 1 in the British West Indies, 11 to 1 in Haiti, 20 to 1 in Surinam) severely limited the ability of South American and Caribbean masters to control plantation blacks. Faced with an underdeveloped communication and transportation network, along with the propinquity of plantations to jungles, swamps, and mountains, Latin American masters found it difficult to prevent slaves from rebelling or escaping to the "trackless wilderness." When the slaves did escape to the almost impenetrable forests, they were able to form free communities in relative security. The military forces were so weak in Latin

45. Porter, "Relations," 342, 347.

America that it once took a Cuban army two months to dislodge 700 slaves from a mountain stronghold, while a colonial Mexican army took months to reach the site of a slave revolt in the mining region and then could not defeat the rebels. Although an ignorant slave may not have known in advance that the army was weak, the existence of the slave communities was public knowledge. These communities stood, moreover, as an open invitation for escape and a monument to the weakness of the master class. Besides, blacks had before them the knowledge and tradition of successful slave resistance. Of overriding importance in the apparent greater inclination of Latin American slaves to rebel was the constant importation of Africans and a slave population composed of from 60 per cent to 70 per cent males.[46]

Having the advantage over their Latin American counterparts in practically every respect, Southern planters were able to crush every slave rebellion with relative ease, and, more importantly, to prevent the development of a tradition of successful revolt in the quarters. Unless he were totally blind, a slave could not fail to perceive how hopeless revolt was, given the size and undeniably superior firepower of the whites. In this regard, the few revolts which did occur in the United States are convincing evidence of the indomitability of the Southern slave. After all, he had far less chance of success than his Latin American brother.

There has been so much controversy surrounding the whole question of slave rebellions that one has to apply a very strict definition to the word "revolt." While some scholars conflate conspiracies and revolts, a conspiracy belongs in the general category of "resistance." A revolt is defined in this study as any concerted action by a group of slaves with the settled purpose of and the actual destruction of the lives and property of local whites. In addition, the activities must have been recognized as an insurrection by public officials who called out the armed forces of the

46. Hubert H. S. Aimes, *A History of Slavery in Cuba, 1511 to 1868* (New York, 1967), 89, 160, 264; Stanley Stein, *Vassouras: A Brazilian Coffee County, 1850-1900* (Cambridge, Mass., 1957), 30-130; David M. Davidson, "Negro Slave Control in Colonial Mexico, 1519-1650," *Hispanic American Historical Review* XLVI (Aug. 1966), 235-53.

locale to destroy the rebels. Applying this rigid definition, there were at least nine slave revolts in America between 1691 and 1865. Although most of the large-scale conspiracies occurred in cities, most of the actual rebellions took place in plantation counties.[47]

A few of these revolts must be analyzed in order to understand the full range of the black man's reaction to slavery. In 1712 several Africans formed a plot in New York City to burn the town, to destroy all whites "for some hard usage they apprehended to have received from their masters," and to obtain their freedom. Sealing an oath of secrecy by sucking each other's blood and rubbing powder prepared by a black conjurer on their bodies to make them invincible, the conspirators armed themselves with guns, pistols, swords, daggers, knives, and hatchets. On the night of April 6th, they set fire to several buildings and then murdered or wounded at least sixteen whites who came to put out the blaze. When the alarm was sounded and troops called out, the rebels retreated and were later captured by the militia. At least six of the rebels committed suicide rather than surrender. The twenty-five rebels who were captured and convicted were either burnt alive, hanged, or broken on the wheel.[48]

A larger uprising occurred in Louisiana's St. Charles and St. John the Baptist parishes in 1811. Led by a free Negro, Charles Deslondes, 400 slaves killed two whites and burned several plantations in St. John early in January. Gaining adherents along the Mississippi River, the insurgents formed into units of as many as 500 slaves and began marching the 31 miles to New Orleans. Before they reached the city, U.S. troops attacked and killed 66

47. Thomas W. Higginson, *Black Rebellion* (New York, 1969); Harvey Wish, "American Slave Insurrections Before 1861," *Journal of Negro History* (July 1937), 299-320; William S. Drewry, *Slave Insurrections in Virginia (1830-1865)* (Washington, D.C., 1900); Marion D. deB. Kilson, "Towards Freedom: An Analysis of Slave Revolts in the United States," *Phylon* XXV (Summer 1964), 175-87.

48. Kenneth Scott, "The Slave Insurrection in New York in 1712," *New-York Historical Society Quarterly* XLV (Jan. 1961), 43-74; "Journal of Rev. John Sharpe," *Pennsylvania Magazine of History and Biography* XL (1916), 421.

slaves in open battle. Later, 16 leaders were executed in New Orleans, and their heads were placed on poles on roads leading from the city.[49]

The most destructive of all the slave revolts occurred near Jerusalem, Southampton County, Virginia, in 1831.[50] Fortunately, a white lawyer, Thomas R. Gray, recorded the confession of "the leader of this ferocious band" and "the origin and progress of this dreadful conspiracy." According to Gray, the rebellion "was not instigated by motives of revenge or sudden anger, but the results of long deliberation and a settled purpose of mind." Nat Turner, the arch rebel, was born in October 1800, on the plantation of Benjamin Turner. Nat was a precocious child and so impressed his fellow slaves by his knowledge of things that had happened before his birth that they predicted he would be a prophet. Like many other slaves, Nat was strongly influenced by his father, mother, and his religious grandmother. His parents taught him to read and stressed his uniqueness and great destiny. Of them he said, "my father and mother strengthened me . . . saying in my presence, I was intended for some great purpose. . . ."[51]

Restless, inquisitive, and observant, Nat learned to read quickly and was admitted to religious services in his master's household. Because of his ability to read, the slaves looked up to him and chose young Nat as their leader "when they were going on any roguery, to plan for them." As he grew to manhood, Nat consolidated his leadership over the slaves "by the austerity of my life and manners, which became the subject of remark by white and black—Having soon discovered to be great, I must appear so, and therefore studiously avoided mixing in society, and wrapped myself in mystery, devoting my time to fasting and prayer."[52]

From his prayers, fasts, and revelations from the Lord, Nat

49. Aptheker, *Revolts*, 249-51.
50. F. Roy Johnson, *The Nat Turner Slave Insurrection* (Murfreesboro, N.C., 1966).
51. Johnson, *Turner*, 228-30.
52. Johnson, *Turner*, 231.

Figure 42. Capture

was convinced, he declared, "that I was ordained for some great purpose in the hands of the Almighty." Several things confirmed this for him. Upon reaching manhood he recalled vividly that both whites and blacks during his childhood had often said "that I had too much sense to be raised, and if I was, I would never be of any use to any one as a slave." Apparently Nat's discontent with slavery was inspired by his father, who had managed to escape. When Nat was placed under a new overseer he too ran away but returned to the plantation after remaining in the woods for thirty days. His fellow slaves were dismayed at his voluntary return, "saying if they had my sense they would not serve any master in the world."[53]

Shortly after this Nat had a vision where he saw "white spirits and black spirits engaged in battle, and the sun was darkened—the thunder rolled in the Heavens, and blood flowed in streams—and I heard a voice saying, 'Such is your luck, such you are called to see, and let it come rough or smooth, you must surely bare it.' "[54] Meditating on this and other revelations, seeking religious perfection, Nat had decided in 1828 that he was destined to wreak the vengeance of the Lord on the planters. Choosing four trusted lieutenants, Nat communicated his desire for rebellion to them. After discussing many plans the conspirators decided to strike on July 4, 1831. Because of Nat's illness as a result of anxiety the revolt was postponed.

On August 20th the original conspirators, joined by Will and Jack, barbecued a pig and drank a bottle of brandy. To make sure of the new recruits, Nat queried Will, who declared that "his life was worth no more than others, and his liberty as dear to him. I asked him if he thought to obtain it? He said he would, or lose his life." Now confident of his men, Nat decided to strike first at the home of his master, Joseph Travis, who, he asserted, "was to me a kind master, and placed the greatest confidence in me; in fact, I had no cause to complain of his treatment of me." Nat entered the house of his sleeping master and then opened the door for the other rebels. Armed with a dull light sword, Nat failed in his first attempt to kill his master who was dispatched by Will. Hoping to gather a large black army from the surrounding plantations before an alarm could be raised, the conspirators decided that until they had taken sufficient arms from the whites, "neither age nor sex was to be spared (which was invariably adhered to)."[55]

Parading silently through the night and led in military maneuvers by Nat, the rebels left a trail of ransacked plantations, decapitated bodies and battered heads across Southampton. At

53. Johnson, *Turner*, 232-33.
54. Johnson, *Turner*, 234.
55. Johnson, *Turner*, 235-36.

the Whitehead plantation, Nat caught Margaret Whitehead "and after repeated blows with a sword, I killed her by a blow on the head, with a fence rail." By mid-morning of August 21st the little band had grown to forty men, some of them mounted. Determined "to carry terror and devastation" throughout the county, Nat used his cavalry to lead attacks on plantations and to prevent the escape of whites.[56] After several white families had been massacred and the rebels had increased to sixty men, Nat turned toward the little town of Jerusalem. By this time, however, the alarm had been spread, and the insurgents were confronted by eighteen armed white men.

Nat and his men immediately charged the small band of white men and chased them over a hill, where they were joined by a large number of additional whites. At this point Nat's men panicked and beat a hasty retreat. Still, he did not give up the struggle: "After trying in vain to collect a sufficient force to proceed to Jerusalem, I determined to return, as I was sure they would make back to their old neighborhood, where they would join me, make new recruits, and come down again."[57] His men scattered, Nat at first attempted to recruit more, but the militia prevented this, and he "gave up all hope for the present." He had been in hiding for two months, hoping to escape, when an armed white man captured him. Nat was lodged in jail and executed. More than forty blacks were either executed or murdered as an aftermath of the revolt.

A short, coal-black man, Turner was fearless, honest, temperate, religious, and extremely intelligent. Gray asserted that Turner "for natural intelligence and quickness of apprehension, is surpassed by few men I have ever seen." He knew a great deal about military tactics, and had a "mind capable of attaining anything. . . ."[58] Feeling no remorse for the fifty-five whites killed during the rebellion, Turner calmly contemplated his execution. Gray gave the best characterization of him when he wrote:

56. Johnson, *Turner*, 239.
57. Johnson, *Turner*, 240-41.
58. Johnson, *Turner*, 244.

> He is a complete fanatic, or plays his part most admirably. . . . The calm, deliberate composure with which he spoke of his late deeds and intentions, the expression of his fiend-like face when excited by enthusiasm, still bearing the stains of blood of helpless innocence about him; clothed with rags and covered with chains; yet daring to raise his manacled hands to heaven, with a spirit soaring above the attributes of man; I looked on him and my blood curdled in my veins.[59]

The black rebels and runaways "curdled" the blood of many Southern whites. The ubiquitous runaway was the "bogey man" for young whites, "worrisome property" for his master, and a hero in the quarters. Symbolic of black resistance to slavery, the rebel and the runaway indicate quite clearly that the black slave was often ungovernable.

Although information is limited, it is possible to draw a portrait of the antebellum black rebel leaders. For the most part, they were young, literate, married, charismatic men. Finding sanctions for their bloodletting in the Bible, inspiring the faint-hearted with apocalyptic visions from the Scriptures of God delivering the Israelites from the hands of their oppressors, the leaders convinced the blacks that slavery was contrary to the will of God and that He commanded them to rise. Gabriel Prosser, for example, often met with his co-conspirators and gave "an impassioned exposition of Scripture. . . . The Israelites were glowingly portrayed as a type of successful resistance to tyranny; and it was argued that now, as then, God would stretch forth his arm to save, and would strengthen a hundred to overthrow a thousand."[60] Often the leaders joined with African or native-born conjurors to recruit followers and to convince them that they would be invincible to the white man's bullets.

Generally, the leaders had been privileged slaves of relatively humane masters; they were not only trusted and well treated, they were able to travel about more freely than the average slave. The privileged position of the leaders along with the occasional

59. Johnson, *Turner*, 244-45.
60. Thomas Wentworth Higginson, *Travellers and Outlaws* (Boston, 1889), 18-19.

inspiration of contemporary revolutionary movements at home and abroad made many of the black rebellions a political act. Practically all of the leaders saw their bloodletting as a way of freeing both their intimate friends and unknown fellow sufferers. This "nationalism," or close identification with and loyalty to the larger group, was a prominent feature in many of the revolts.

While it is obvious that running away was a highly personal act constituting a safety valve for slavery by ridding the institution of "deviants" who could not fit in, a conspiracy or rebellion was a threat to the stability and very existence of plantation slavery. The paucity of successful revolts in the South in comparison with Latin America is an indication of the greater vigilance of Southern slaveholders and relative strength and vitality of American slavery. At the same time, the large number of blacks either actively involved in conspiracies and rebellions or in sympathy with them is a clear indication of the willingness of American slaves to fight for their freedom in the face of hopeless odds.[61]

61. Kilson, "Towards Freedom," 175-87; W. K. Moore, "An Abortive Slave Uprising," *Missouri Historical Review* LII (Jan. 1958), 123-26; John M. Lofton, "Denmark Vesey's Call to Arms," *Journal of Negro History* XXXIII (Oct. 1948), 395-417; Jack D. L. Holmes, "The Abortive Slave Revolt at Pointe Coupée, Louisiana, 1795," *Louisiana History* XI (Fall 1970), 341-62; "The Insurrection and Its Hero," *Liberty Bell* (Boston, 1848), 1-28; George R. Lee, "Slavery and Emancipation in Lewis County, Missouri," *Missouri Historical Review* LXV (April 1971), 294-317; Vincent Harding, "Religion and Resistance Among Antebellum Negroes, 1800-1860," in August Meier and Elliott Rudwick, eds., *The Making of Black America* (New York, 1969), 179-97.

6

Plantation Stereotypes and Institutional Roles

Because my mouth
Is wide with laughter
And my throat
Is deep with song,
You do not think
I suffer after
I have held my pain
So long.

Because my mouth
Is wide with laughter,
You do not hear
My inner cry,
Because my feet
Are gay with dancing,
You do not know
I die.

Langston Hughes

Personal relations on the plantation were, as in most institutions, determined by spatial arrangements, the frequency of interaction between high- and low-powered individuals, and how the high-powered individual defined the behavioral norms. In practice, of course, many of the institutionally defined roles were imperfectly played. Before one can examine the *actual* behavior on the plantation, however, the societal images and the planter's expectations of the slave must be compared. In the final analysis, the planter's expectations were more closely related to the slave's actual behavior than publicly held stereotypes. Even so, neither the planter's expectations nor the stereotypes were proscriptive. In other words, the slave did not necessarily act the way white people expected him to behave or the way they perceived him as behaving.

Antebellum Southern novelists, dramatists, and journalists were so influential in the creation and reflection of public attitudes toward slaves that their works must be examined. An investigation of this literature is also mandatory because its impact has been so pervasive that twentieth-century historians have often uncritically accepted the most popular literary stereotype as an accurate description of slave personality. In many instances, historians have been misled by analyzing only one literary stereotype. The accuracy of the literary treatment of the plantation can be determined, however, only when several of the stereotypes of the slave are examined. This is all the more necessary because the legitimacy of each stereotype is tied irrevocably to the legitimacy of all the others.

The portrait of the slave which emerges from antebellum Southern literature is complex and contradictory.[1] The major slave characters were Sambo, Jack, and Nat. The one rarely seen in literature, Jack, worked faithfully as long as he was well treated. Sometimes sullen and uncooperative, he generally refused to be driven beyond the pace he had set for himself. Conscious of his identity with other slaves, he cooperated with them to resist the white man's oppression. Rationally analyzing the white man's overwhelming physical power, Jack either avoided contact with him or was deferential in his presence. Since he did not identify with his master and could not always keep up the

1. Francis P. Gaines, *The Southern Plantation: A Study in the Development and Accuracy of a Tradition* (New York, 1925); Tremaine McDowell, "The Negro in the Southern Novel Prior to 1850," *Journal of English and Germanic Philology* XXV (Oct. 1926), 455-73; Charles E. Burch, "Negro Characters in the Novels of William Gilmore Simms," *Southern Workman* LII (April 1923), 192-95; Jack B. Moore, "Images of the Negro in Early American Short Fiction," *Mississippi Quarterly* XXXII (Winter 1968-69), 47-57; Sterling A. Brown, *The Negro in American Fiction* (Washington, D.C., 1937), 1-47; John H. Nelson, *The Negro Character in American Literature* (Lawrence, Kan., 1926), 23-48, 86-92; Catherine J. Starke, *Black Portraiture in American Fiction* (New York, 1971), 30-45.

façade of deference, he was occasionally flogged for insubordination. Although often proud, stubborn, and conscious of the wrongs he suffered, Jack tried to repress his anger. His patience was, however, not unlimited. He raided his master's larder when he was hungry, ran away when he was tired of working or had been punished, and was sometimes ungovernable. Shrewd and calculating, he used his wits to escape from work or to manipulate his overseer and master.

Nat was the rebel who rivaled Sambo in the universality and continuity of his literary image. Revengeful, bloodthirsty, cunning, treacherous, and savage, Nat was the incorrigible runaway, the poisoner of white men, the ravager of white women who defied all the rules of plantation society. Subdued and punished only when overcome by superior numbers or firepower, Nat retaliated when attacked by whites, led guerrilla activities of maroons against isolated plantations, killed overseers and planters, or burned plantation buildings when he was abused. Like Jack, Nat's customary obedience often hid his true feelings, self-concept, unquenchable thirst for freedom, hatred of whites, discontent, and manhood, until he violently demonstrated these traits.[2]

Sambo, combining in his person Uncle Remus, Jim Crow, and Uncle Tom, was the most pervasive and long lasting of the three literary stereotypes. Indolent, faithful, humorous, loyal, dishonest, superstitious, improvident, and musical, Sambo was inevitably a clown and congenitally docile. Characteristically a house servant, Sambo had so much love and affection for his master that he was almost filio-pietistic; his loyalty was all-consuming and self-immolating. The epitome of devotion, Sambo often fought and died heroically while trying to save his master's life. Yet, Sambo had no thought of freedom; that was an empty boon compared with serving his master.[3]

2. Howard Braverman, "An Unusual Characterization by a Southern Ante-Bellum Writer," *Phylon* XIX (Summer 1958), 171-79; Calvin H. Wiley, *Life in the South: A Companion to Uncle Tom's Cabin* (1852); Bayard R. Hall, *Frank Freeman's Barbershop* (1852).

3. For portraits of Sambo risking his life to save his master see: Hector, Cato, Scipio, Braugh, and Tom in William Gilmore Simms, *The Yemassee*

The Sambo stereotype was so pervasive in antebellum Southern literature that many historians, without further research, argue that it was an accurate description of the dominant slave personality. According to historians of this stripe, the near unanimity of so many white observers of the slave cannot be discounted.[4] While this is obviously true, it does not follow that the Sambo stereotype must be treated uncritically. Instead, it must be viewed in the context of the other slave stereotypes, and from the perspective of psychology and comparative studies of literature.

Any attempt to generalize about individual and group personality traits based on stereotypes must assess the degree to which "outsiders" are able to perceive someone else's behavior correctly. Since so much of one's personality is socially non-perceivable, hidden, or invisible, the way other people describe an individual is not totally reliable as an index of his attitudes and behavior. Consequently, students must be cautious in equating societal images with personality traits. There is too much distortion in people's perception, observation, and interpretation of the behavior of other individuals for historians to rely solely upon their reports. Prior experiences, situational factors, cultural frames of reference, and selective inattention all influence perception of individual behavior.[5] So many of these factors may be operative in society that *sham* characteristics are attributed to a group or individual. According to psychologist Gustav Ichheiser:

> The sham characteristics are those which are attributed to an individual from the point of view of other people. They might, or might not, reflect themselves in his own conception about himself. They can originate entirely through misinterpretations by others without his participation, or he can directly or indirectly share the responsibility for their development through pretending to have the characteristics. The given individual

---

(1835), *The Forayers* (1855), *Mellichampe* (1836), *Southward Ho!* (1854), and *The Partisan* (1835).

4. Stanley Elkins, *Slavery: A Problem in American Institutional and Intellectual Life* (New York, 1963), 86-89.

5. Gustav Ichheiser, *Appearances and Realities* (San Francisco, 1970).

does not possess these sham characteristics but only seems to possess them.[6]

One of the best examples of how external forces and cultural frames of reference lead to the ascription of sham characteristics to a group appears in the changing stereotypes of the Chinese. When California needed laborers in the mid-nineteenth century, the newspapers characterized the Chinese as thrifty, sober, tractable, inoffensive, and law-abiding. Twenty years later, when Californians were competing with Chinese laborers, they began to describe the Chinese as clannish, criminal, debased, servile, deceitful, vicious, filthy, and loathsome.[7]

In light of these observations, scholars cannot accept the Sambo stereotype uncritically. Instead, they must try to examine the roots of this conception of the black slave: First, and most important, was the American attitude toward Negroes or Africans as a race. Most antebellum whites firmly believed that Africans were ignoble savages who were innately barbaric, imitative, passive, cheerful, childish, lazy, cowardly, superstitious, polygamous, submissive, immoral, and stupid.[8] For instance, Dr. Samuel A. Cartwright, a Louisiana physician, wrote that Africans were "endowed with a will so weak, passions so easily subdued, and dispositions so gentle and affectionate" that they had "an instinctive feeling of obedience to the stronger will of the white man." In 1850, "L.S.M." argued that Negroes were naturally "good-tempered, unambitious, unintellectual, incapable of civilization,

6. Ichheiser, *Appearances*, 95.

7. Earl Raab, ed., *American Race Relations Today* (Garden City, N.Y., 1962), 29-57; Otto Klineberg, *The Human Dimension in International Relations* (New York, 1964), 33-48; Sigmund Freud, *Psychopathology of Everyday Life* (New York, 1951), 66-67, 73-76.

8. Milton Cantor, "The Image of the Negro in Colonial Literature," *New England Quarterly* XXXVI (Dec. 1963), 452-77; Matthew Estes, *A Defense of Negro Slavery, as It Exists in the United States* (Montgomery, Ala., 1846), 50-70; Henrietta Tolbert, "A Study of the Inferiority of the Negro in American History" (M.A. thesis, Howard University, 1939), 1-98; L.A., "The Diversity of Origin of the Human Race," *Christian Examiner* XLIX (July 1850), 110-45; "Uncle Tom at Home," *Putnam's Monthly* VIII (July 1856), 1-10; Dr. Cartwright, "On the Caucasians and the African," *DeBow's Review*, XXV (July 1858), 45-56.

and unfit for amalgamation." An anonymous contributor to the *Christian Examiner* contrasted "the submissive, obsequious, imitative negro" to other races.[9]

Most whites felt that the "natural" traits of Negro character were so deeply ingrained that they were immutable. Regardless of climate, condition, or circumstance, the Negro retained his native African characteristics. Julien Virey, a Frenchman whose works were widely read in America, supported this view when he asserted: "All the facts which have been collected, concur to prove how constant and indelible are the natural and moral characteristics of negroes in every climate, notwithstanding a diversity of circumstances, which condemn him to indolence and degradation."[10]

Sambo became a universal figure in antebellum Southern literature partly because he belonged to a subordinate caste. Traditionally, writers in caste and slave societies, representing and identifying with the ruling class and supporting the status quo, have drawn unflattering stereotypes of the lowest caste. David B. Davis, for example, concluded from his study of several slave societies that, almost universally, slaves were described as loyal, faithful, lazy, irresponsible, and untrustworthy. According to Davis, "The white slaves of antiquity and the middle ages were often described in terms that fit the later stereotype of the Negro." Similarly, nineteenth-century Russian writers portrayed the white serfs as callous, shiftless, dishonest, lazy, hypocritical, and stupid.[11]

The greatest confusion in the comparative study of literary stereotypes of slaves has been caused by cursory examinations of

9. Cartwright, "Caucasians," 47-48; L.S.M., "The Diversity of the Races; Its Bearing upon Negro Slavery," *Southern Quarterly Review* XIX (April 1851), 412; L.A., "Diversity," 144.

10. Julien J. Virey, *Natural History of the Negro Race* (Charleston, 1837), 19.

11. David B. Davis, *The Problem of Slavery in Western Culture* (Ithaca, N.Y., 1966), 59; Hannah S. Goldman, "The Tragic Gift: The Serf and Slave Intellectual in Russian and American Fiction," *Phylon* XXIV (Spring 1963), 51-61.

Brazilian and Southern literature. From such examinations it appears at first glance that there was not only a great diversity of types, but no Sambo character in Brazilian literature. In order to place this in true perspective, one must understand that we are comparing the literature of a slaveholding region (the South) produced largely by white pro-slavery advocates with the literature of a nation produced by slaveholders, abolitionists, and black writers. Since Brazilian writers varied so much in character, there was naturally greater diversity in the portrayal of slaves than in the South. When, however, Northern, abolitionist, and black writers are added to Southern writers, the same range of slave characters appear in American as in Brazilian literature. Like their American counterparts and contrary to the allegations of some historians, Brazilian writers often portrayed the slaves as Sambos. Brazilian novelists, poets, and dramatists frequently characterized slaves as indolent, faithful, immoral, submissive, ignorant, happy, patient, docile, irresponsible, promiscuous, loyal, and lazy.[12]

The commitment of Southern writers to drawing unflattering stereotypes of subordinate groups was so great that they even characterized some whites in terms remarkably similar to their picture of Sambo. For example, they portrayed non-slaveholding white Southerners as "poor whites" who were densely ignorant, irresponsible, lawless, lazy, shiftless, dirty, careless, stupid, listless, unambitious, dishonest, and morally degraded.[13] Frances

12. Raymond S. Sayers, *The Negro in Brazilian Literature* (New York, 1956), 73-83, 121-26, 138-39, 145-64, 186-97; Lorenzo D. Turner, *Anti-Slavery Sentiment in American Literature Prior to 1865* (Port Washington, N.Y., 1966); Carl Degler, *Neither Black nor White* (New York, 1971), 12-13; Barry D. Amis, "The Negro in the Columbian Novel," (Ph.D. diss., Michigan State University, 1970), 57-83; Fannin S. Belcher, "The Place of the Negro in the Evolution of the American Theatre, 1767 to 1940" (Ph.D. diss., Yale University, 1945), 1-34; Ruby Z. Madden, "American Anti-Slavery Fiction, 1850-1865" (M.A. thesis, Howard University, 1941), 11-26.

13. Gaines, *Plantation*, 1-17; William R. Taylor, *Cavalier and Yankee* (Garden City, N.Y., 1963), 156-67, 279-94; A. N. J. Den Hollander, "The Tradition of 'Poor Whites'" in William T. Couch, ed., *Culture in the South* (Chapel Hill, 1934), 403-31; Frank Lawrence Owsley, *Plain Folk of the Old*

Kemble typified this attitude when she described the poor whites as "filthy, lazy, ignorant, brutal, proud, penniless savages, without one of the nobler attributes which have been found occasionally allied to the vice of savage nature."[14]

Southern writers were also compelled to portray the slave as Sambo because of their need to disprove the allegations of antislavery novelists. Facing the withering attack of the abolitionists, they had to prove that slavery was not an unmitigated evil. The loyal contented slave was a *sine qua non* in Southern literary propaganda. Whether he existed in fact was irrelevant to the writer. Without Sambo, it was impossible to prove the essential goodness of Southern society.[15]

Another of the important reasons for the pervasiveness of the Sambo stereotype was the desire of whites to relieve themselves of the anxiety of thinking about slaves as men. In this regard, Nat, the actual and potential rebel, stands at the core of white perceptions of the slave. With Nat perennially in the wings, the creation of Sambo was almost mandatory for the Southerner's emotional security. Like a man whistling in the dark to bolster his courage, the white man *had* to portray the slave as Sambo. This public stereotype only partially hid a multitude of private fears, which reached the proportion of mass hysteria at the mere mention of the word "rebellion." Generally, historians have been so intent upon proving that these fears were groundless that they have ignored the relationship between the countless rumors of rebellions and the white man's stereotype of the slave and the slave's actual behavior. If whites really believed that a majority of slaves were Sambos, how could they also believe that these

---

South (Baton Rouge, 1949), 1-22; Clement Eaton, *The Growth of Southern Civilization* (New York, 1963), 150-76; J. E. Cairnes, *The Slave Power* . . . (New York, 1862), 54-79; Paul H. Buck, "The Poor Whites of the Ante-Bellum South," *American Historical Review* XXXI (Oct. 1925), 41-54.

14. Frances Anne Kemble, *Journal of a Residence on a Georgian Plantation in 1838-1839* ([1863] New York, 1961), 182.

15. Jeanette Tandy, "Pro-Slavery Propaganda in American Fiction of the Fifties," *South Atlantic Quarterly* XXI (Jan. 1922), 41-50, (April 1922), 170-78; Jay B. Hubbell, *Southern Life in Fiction* (Athens, Ga., 1960).

pathetically loyal and docile blacks would rise up and cut their throats?

Judging from the ease with which whites conjured up Nat, they apparently felt that the relationship between the planter and the slave was one of continual war requiring eternal vigilance in order for the master to maintain the upper hand. In a sense, this is indicated by the constant changes in the slave codes. If the slave had accepted the Sambo role, there would have been little need to continue changing the codes after the first generation of American-born slaves had grown to adulthood. Slaveholders apparently never believed in Sambos, for they were constantly searching for new ways to guarantee the subordination of slaves. Was this search simply a result of the formulation of new management techniques, or did it reflect slave behavior which contradicted the Sambo stereotype?

From an analysis of the constantly recurring rumors of insurrections, it is obvious that many whites considered black slaves dangerous, insubordinate, bold, evil, restless, turbulent, vengeful, barbarous, and malicious.[16] For example, the Georgia planter John Jacobus Flournoy contended that slaves had "a natural disposition to endless riot" which fitted them "for the work of carnage and insurrection."[17] The white man's fear of the slave was so deep and pervasive that it was sometimes pathological. An epidemic of runaways, a group of whispering slaves, mysterious fires, or almost any suspicious event caused alarm, apprehension, and a deepening state of paranoia among whites.[18] John Dixon

16. Jeremiah B. Jeter, *Recollections of a Long Life* (Richmond, 1891), 173-77; James P. Carson, ed., *Life, Letters and Speeches of James Louis Pettigru* (Washington, D.C., 1920), 367; Hugh A. Garland, *The Life of John Randolph of Roanoke* (2 vols., New York, 1857), I, 293-95; A Southron, "The Insurrection and Its Hero," *The Liberty Bell* (Boston, 1848), 1-28; Edmund Jackson, "Servile Insurrections," *The Liberty Bell* (Boston, 1851), 158-64; Baltimore *Genius of Universal Emancipation* III (1823-24), 107-8, 187.

17. E. Merton Coulter, *John Jacobus Flournoy* (Savannah, 1942), 45, 48.

18. Herbert Aptheker, *American Negro Slave Revolts* (New York, 1943); Thomas W. Higginson, "Nat Turner's Insurrection," *Atlantic Monthly* VIII (Aug. 1861), 173-87; Robert N. Elliott, "The Nat Turner Insurrection as Reported in the North Carolina Press," *North Carolina Historical Review*

Long, a Maryland native, asserted that there were "men in the slave States, who neither fear God nor regard the white man, that act like nerveless women at the very mention of a slave insurrection. Their imaginations take fire, and they see a 'Nat Turner' in every negro boy. . . . there is a vast amount of uneasiness among the white population of the South from fear of the negroes. . . ."[19]

Considering the overwhelming power of the whites, the censorship of news about insurrections, and the general reluctance of men to parade their fears, the constant discussion of Nat among antebellum Southern whites appears at first glance to be remarkable. After all, no white man could possibly be anxious about his safety if a majority of the slaves were thought to be Sambos. Perhaps the Governor of the colony of Virginia gave a clearer insight into the white man's characterization of slaves when in 1723 he urged the legislators to pass more oppressive laws because he was "persuaded you are . . . well acquainted with the cruel dispositions of these creatures. . . ." Arthur Lee agreed with the Governor; in 1767 he declared that slavery, "wherever encouraged, has sooner or later been productive of very dangerous commotions . . . we are like the wretch at the feast; with a drawn sword depending over his head by a Single hair. . . ." Similarly, a South Carolina white wrote that "We regard our negroes as the 'Jacobins' of the country, against whom we should always be on guard. . . ."[20] It is obvious that many whites did not believe the slaves were innately docile. Too many governors received requests for arms and troops from thousands of whites, the U.S. Army marched and countermarched too often, too many panic-stricken whites spent their nights guarding

---

XXXVIII (Jan. 1961), 1-18; Donald B. Kelley, "Harper's Ferry: Prelude to Crisis in Mississippi," *Journal of Mississippi History* XXVII (Nov. 1965), 351-72.

19. John Dixon Long, *Pictures of Slavery in Church and State* (Philadelphia, 1857), 232-33; see also: James Redpath, *The Roving Editor: Or, Talks with Slaves in the Southern States* (New York, 1859), 269-83.

20. Aptheker, *Revolts*, 14, 15; Richard K. MacMaster, ed., "Arthur Lee's Address on Slavery," *Virginia Magazine of History and Biography* LXXX (April 1972), 156-57.

their neighborhoods to believe that most Southern whites equated the Sambo stereotype with the dominant slave personality.

Thinking about Nat kept whites "in a state of mind peculiarly harassing and painful," and "a state of perpetual anxiety and apprehension, than which nothing could be more painful." The stereotype of Nat forced some whites to conclude that to live among black slaves was "really a dreadful situation to be in."[21] The character of the slave was felt to be such that it led to a deep and abiding fear among large numbers of whites. Many of them slept behind barricaded doors with pistols under their pillows. One Louisiana planter recalled that "I have known times here, when there was not a single planter who had a calm night's rest; they then never lay down to sleep without a brace of loaded pistols at their sides."[22]

It is almost impossible to square the white's fear of Nat with the predominance of the Sambo stereotype in plantation literature. Apparently both slave characters were real. The more fear whites had of Nat, the more firmly they tried to believe in Sambo in order to escape paranoia. This psychological repression was augmented by public acts to relieve anxiety. Every effort was made to keep the slaves in awe of the power of whiteness, and ignorant of their own potential power. The congregation of crowds of slaves, their independent movement, possession of arms, and degree of literacy, were all strictly regulated. The rebellious slave was punished swiftly and cruelly to discourage others. The oppressive acts consisted of cropping ears, castrating, hanging, burning, and mutilating. The army, the militia, and the entire white community stood ready to aid any embattled region. In all of these actions, the whites demonstrated that even if slaves did not revolt they were considered rebellious. Consequently, Southern whites restricted their own freedom of speech, censored their

21. Aptheker, *Revolts, passim.*

22. Fredrika Bremer, *The Homes of the New World* (2 vols., New York, 1853), II, 190. For similar expressions see: James H. Johnston, *Race Relations in Virginia* (Amherst, Mass., 1970), 27, 116-21; Kemble, *Journal*, 379; Emily P. Burke, *Reminiscences of Georgia* (Oberlin, 1850), 156-58; James Stirling, *Letters from the Slave States* (London, 1857), 59.

newspapers, interfered with the U.S. mails, and lynched abolitionists to make sure that no one incited the rebellious slaves.[23]

Obviously, Southern leaders manipulated the Sambo and Nat stereotypes to promote their own objectives. After his travels in and observation of the South, for example, Edmund Jackson concluded:

> At one time when it suits the immediate object in view, we hear southern members of Congress eloquently deprecating anything and everything, which, in their distempered imagination, they choose to consider as exciting to insurrection, and to pronounce the utter ruin and depopulation of the South, should any serious conflict occur between the races. And, on the other hand, when the power and prosperity of the South is to be magnified for some sinister purpose, the idea of a successful servile insurrection, or any outbreak at all, among the contented and happy slaves, is scouted as absurd and preposterous to the last degree.

The real or potential rebelliousness of the slave was too explosive a political issue for the leaders to confront it directly. To admit that his constituents were sitting on a volcano was political suicide for any Southern leader. South Carolina legislators explicitly recognized this in 1835 when they declared:

> Let it be admitted that the white inhabitants of the Slaveholding States are amply competent to hold the slaves in secure and pacific subjection. Are we to sit down content because, from our own vigilance and courage the torch of the incendiary or the midnight assassin *may* never be applied? Impossible! No people can live in a state of perpetual excitement and apprehension although real danger may be long deferred. Such a condition of the public mind is destructive of all social happiness and consequently must prove essentially injurious to the prosperity of a community that has the weakness to suffer under a continual panic.[24]

23. Clement Eaton, *Freedom of Thought in the Old South* (New York, 1951), 89-117; Herbert Aptheker, *One Continual Cry: David Walker's Appeal to the Colored Citizens of the World* (New York, 1965), 45-53.

24. Jackson, "Servile Insurrections," 159; Lydia M. Child, comp., *The Patriarchal Institution* (New York, 1860), 44.

The slaveholder apparently sought peace of mind by claiming that unrest among slaves was the result of the hellish designs of outside incendiaries. This was so much a part of writings about insurrections that John Brown's raid on Harpers Ferry in 1859 has all the appearance of a self-fulfilling prophecy. While the slave was considered incapable of initiating a rebellion, most whites felt that all blacks would join in the bloodletting once it started. In other words, Southern whites admitted that, given the personality of the slave, preconditions always existed for black revolt; the abolitionist was simply one of the most feared potential precipitants. Paradoxically, whites also argued that their slaves were the most content and happiest creatures on earth. Apparently both the abolitionist incendiary and the contented slave were stereotypes intended for internal consumption, a mere device for quieting fears and promoting vigilance. Societies, like the Old South, confronted with an internal enemy, have often used the "dangerous outsider," the external threat, as a way of promoting ideological unity and convincing people that the potential native revolutionaries are either quiescent or entirely under control.[25]

Like most men, Southern white men learned to live with their fears. After all, they were more numerous, better organized, armed, educated, and more mobile than slaves. Any actual rebellion could be crushed relatively easily. Through cruelty or kindness a planter might discourage his own slaves from bloodthirsty acts, even if there were an insurrection. In addition to this rational view of the situation, the planter tried to reduce the anxiety produced by the incongruity between the Sambo and Nat stereotypes by pushing Nat deep into his subconscious. However frequently the planters argued that the slaves were docile, they always insisted that whites should keep their powder dry. For example, although South Carolinian Edwin C. Holland asserted that no slave rebellion could succeed, he felt that it was "indispensable to our safety to watch all their motions with a careful and scrutinizing eye . . . to save us from catastrophe which at

25. Jackson, "Servile Insurrections," 158-64; Robert R. Howison, *A History of Virginia* (2 vols., Philadelphia, 1846), II, 439-45.

all times threatens us. . . . Let it never be forgotten that 'our Negroes are truly the *anarchists* and the *domestic enemy;* the common enemy of *civilized society,* and the barbarians who would, If They Could, become the Destroyers of our race.'" Similarly, while J. H. Hammond could write lyrical passages on the contented slave, he felt that in governing blacks "we have to rely more and more on the power of fear. We must, in all our intercourse with them, assert and maintain strict mastery, and impress it on them that they are slaves. . . . We are determined to continue masters, and to do so, we have to draw the rein tighter and tighter day by day, to be assured that we hold them in complete check." Another South Carolina planter placed loyal, contented Sambo in true perspective when he wrote: "Were *fidelity* the only security we enjoyed . . . deplorable indeed would be our situation. The fear of punishment is the principle to which we must and do appeal, to keep them in awe and order."[26]

When these stereotypes held by antebellum whites are compared, some interesting questions about planter psychology and slave behavior emerge. Did the contradictory portraits of Sambo and Nat indicate that Southerners were not entirely sure that the slave's actual personality was indeed the same as the Sambo stereotype? This question lies at the heart of white reaction to Nat Turner's bloody revolt. Admittedly a favored slave, with a kind master, Nat gave no prior indications of his desire for revenge. Did this mean that the wide grins and servile bows represented the impenetrable masks of the black slaves' character? Were they all "Jacobins"? Did they view their masters as good fathers to be loved or as cruel tyrants to be exterminated? If the latter, could more and more oppressive legislation ensure their subordination? Regardless of what was done, would a white

26. Edwin C. Holland, *A Refutation of the Calumnies Circulated Against the Southern & Western States* (Charleston, 1822), 82, 86; W. G. Addington, "Slave Insurrections in Texas," *Journal of Negro History* XXXV (Oct. 1950), 419; William W. Freehling, *Prelude to Civil War: The Nullification Controversy in South Carolina, 1816-1836* (New York, 1966), 66. For similar expressions, see: John Rankin, *Letters on American Slavery* (Newburyport, Ky., 1837), 72-73, 117.

man's family ever be secure from the vengeance of the black slave? These questions haunted the Southern white man, and their very existence raises doubts about the predominance of the Sambo personality on the antebellum plantation. How much stock can be placed in the Sambo stereotype when antebellum Southern whites questioned it as a representation of the typical slave? Their uncertainty was indicated clearly in debates in the Virginia legislature after Nat Turner's revolt. One legislator observed that the widespread fear of revolt was caused by

> the suspicion eternally attached to the slave himself, the suspicion that a Nat Turner might be in every family, that the same bloody deed could be acted over at any time and in any place, that the materials for it were spread through the land and always ready for a like explosion. Nothing but the force of this withering apprehension, nothing but the paralyzing and deadening weight with which it falls upon and prostrates the heart of every man who has helpless dependents to protect, nothing but this could have thrown a brave people into consternation, or could have made any portion of this powerful Commonwealth, for a single instant, to have quailed and trembled.[27]

Any attempt to reconcile the white man's "suspicion that a Nat Turner might be in every family" with the widespread existence of the Sambo stereotype places the historian on the horns of a dilemma. On the one hand, the persistent fear of the slave in the absence of revolts may indicate that there was overwhelming circumstantial evidence and hundreds of individual acts which convinced whites that slaves were ungovernable. On the other, the white man may have been grossly in error when he perceived the slave as rebellious; and if the latter was true, then the antebellum white man is not a good witness, for it follows that he may also have been grossly in error in stereotyping the slave as Sambo. It is possible, however, to deal with these contradictory portraits. For various reasons, often having more to do with whites than blacks, antebellum whites apparently focused on two extreme forms of slave behavior—childlike docility and

27. Eric Foner, ed., *Nat Turner* (Englewood Cliffs, N.J., 1971), 113.

rebellion—in formulating the Nat and Sambo stereotypes. Both stereotypes were probably blown out of proportion to their relationship to the actual behavior of most slaves. In effect, each of the stereotypes is so contrary to the other that the legitimacy of each as a representation of typical slave behavior is limited. Perhaps the only thing that the white man's stereotypes of the slave as Sambo, Jack, and Nat does is to indicate the range of personality types in the quarters.

Without supporting evidence, none of these literary stereotypes can be accepted as indicative of the dominant slave personality. At any rate, few, if any planters depended on literary stereotypes in managing their plantations. Although many of them may have held the Sambo stereotype, they had a different set of expectations for their own slaves. Obviously, if Sambo represented the sum of the master's expectations, the slaveholder could not have survived. Lazy, inefficient, irresponsible, dishonest, childish, stupid Sambo was a guarantee of economic ruin. Whatever the literary stereotypes, the institutionally defined roles and behavior expected of planters, overseers, and slaves were quite clear. The best definition of these roles appears in contracts and numerous essays on plantation management in antebellum journals.[28]

The planter, in these essays, explained the ideal which guided his relationship with slaves and his perception of their personalities gained from years of experience. According to most advisers on slave management, the plantation was somewhat like an army camp: authority descended downward from the master, to the overseer, to the slave driver. The planter was comparable to a general, a ship captain, or an unlimited monarch directing the lives of a large group of people toward one objective: large profits. The first requirement in achieving this objective was to maintain regularity and order in everything. It was the planter's duty to

28. *Southern Agriculturalist* VII (April 1834), 117-83, IX (Feb. 1836), 70-75, IX (Nov. 1836), 580-84; *Southern Cabinet* I (May 1840), 279-80; *Southern Cultivator* X (Aug. 1852), 227-28; *American Farmer* II (March 16, 1821), 402, X (Oct. 17, 1828), 244; *Farmer's Register* II (Sept. 1834), 248-49 (Feb. 1835), 579-80, V (May 1837), 32-33; *DeBow's Review* XV (June 1851), 621-25, XXI (Sept. 1856), 277-79.

calculate how many supplies were required, how large a crop to plant, and how much labor could be performed.

In order to obtain the maximum labor at the cheapest cost, the planter had to construct healthy cabins, provide adequate, wholesome food and proper clothing, permit recreation, and provide medical attention for his slaves. If the slaves adhered to certain moral precepts, rested during the hottest part of the day, spent all of their time on the plantation, marched to the fields, ate, and went to bed at the sound of bugles or bells, and were kept under proper subjection, they would be healthy and industrious. In his relations with slaves, the planter had to maintain strict discipline and require unconditional obedience. He also had to maintain a great degree of social distance between himself and his slaves. In this regard, a Virginia planter asserted: "All conversation with a negro is forbid, except about his work. This is important; he should be kept as far from his master as possible, but with no accompanying *harshness;* he ought to be made to feel that you are his superior, but that you respect his feelings and wants."[29]

Advisers on plantation management insisted that, while being aloof from slaves, planters had to enforce all rules rigidly. Proper discipline, they contended, was maintained by the certainty rather than the severity of punishment for infractions. Closely allied with the certainty of punishment as an inducement to labor was the use of flattery, praise, and rewards. Most planters felt that little could be gained from deriding or threatening slaves.

Since the master had the most power and authority on the plantation, he defined the institutional roles. A representative definition of plantation roles appeared in an article in *DeBow's Review* in 1855:

> The master should never establish any regulation among his slaves until he is fully convinced of its propriety and equity. Being thus convinced, and having issued his orders, implicit obedience should be required and rigidly enforced. Firmness of manner, and promptness to enforce obedience, will save

29. *American Farmer* VII (May 1852), 397.

> much trouble, and be the means of avoiding the necessity for much whipping. The negro should feel that his master is his lawgiver and judge; and yet is his protector and friend, but so far above him, as never to be approached save in the most respectful manner. That where he has just cause, he may, with due deference, approach his master and lay before him his troubles and complaints; but not on false pretexts or trivial occasions. . . .[30]

Placed in the position of a general planning strategy, the planter had to depend on the overseer to carry out the tactics and see to the day-to-day operation of the plantation. Most advisers contended that the overseer was an "indispensable agent" on the plantation. He had to wake the slaves at daylight and drive them to the fields, attend the sick and prevent malingering, supervise the planting, tillage, and harvesting of the crops; and show the slaves how to perform their work, keep a daily record of plantation events, see that the slave's food was properly prepared, and maintain fences and tools in good repair. In managing slaves in such a fashion as to ensure a large quantity and high quality of the money crop, the overseer was required to "push the hands fast," preserve the health and morals of slaves by prohibiting the use of alcohol, interplantation visiting, theft of plantation stock and produce, and trading with whites. He had to supervise and examine the work of each slave, regularly inspect each cabin and person to ensure cleanliness, order, and sobriety, and ring the bell or blow the bugle to signal "lights out" in the quarters and then make sure that each laborer received enough rest to complete his task the next day. Overseers, one planter argued, should

> be accustomed to early rising, and to steady, settled customs and ways. Let them learn regularity in arranging plantation business *in advance,* in order to avoid delay, confusion and loss of work; regularity in settling every one to their work betimes; in closely watching the driver or drivers, urging them on to their duty, and by a vigilant eye over every individual labourer's progress, as the day advances, ascertaining that none of these,

30. *DeBow's Review* XIX (Sept. 1855), 361-62.

Figure 43. The Stake-out

> and of course, that none of the business of the place is getting behind hand.[31]

The overseer had to be especially adept at keeping slaves under proper subjection. Speaking to them only in regard to their work, he was required to keep them under almost constant surveillance. Consequently, he had to remain on the plantation at all times. Most planters enjoined the overseer from maiming, scarring, or disabling their property. Instead, he was to treat slaves with "care & humanity," and punish them in a "humane" fashion free from passion. In addition, the overseer was not to "use abusive language to nor to threaten the negroes, as it makes them unhappy and sometimes induces them to run away." The overseer had to be careful not to become so familiar with slaves that they learned all of his secrets and shortcomings. An Alabama planter wrote: "The overseer must hide all his faults if possible from the negroes —but if not possible then never in any event what ever request or require the Negroes to conceal his faults from the employer— In such case the overseer is unmanned—better to retire at once from a place he can but disgrace, when afraid his hands will tell on him—"[32]

Planters and overseers defined the role of the slave in very explicit terms. The institutionally defined role of the slave required him to identify with his master's interest, to be healthy, clean, humble, honest, sober, cheerful, industrious, even-tempered, patient, respectful, trustworthy, and hard-working. This was the kind of slave the master *wanted:* a laborer who identified so closely with his master's interest that he would repair a broken fence rail without being ordered to do so. Systematic labor, implicit obedience, and unconditional submission (as child to parent or soldier to general) was expected of slaves.

The extent to which slaves acted the way their masters ex-

31. *American Farmer* XI (Oct. 16, 1829), 42.

32. J Carlyle Sitterson, "The William J. Minor Plantations: A Study in Ante-Bellum Absentee Ownership," *Journal of Southern History* IX (Feb. 1943), 63; Weymouth T. Jordan, "The Management Rules of an Alabama Black Belt Plantation, 1848-1862," *Agricultural History* XVIII (Jan. 1944), 57.

pected them to behave can be explained partially by examining "role theory." According to the proponents of this theory, a person's behavior is generally determined by the socially defined roles or the behavioral patterns expected of him in certain situations. A policeman, for instance, behaves differently in his law enforcer, father, husband, and Sunday School teacher roles. Man learns these roles by becoming an object, or learning how several other people define how a husband, father, or policeman should act. This process begins when the child discovers how his parents expect him to behave. A person internalizes the roles (accepts them as a part of himself, as a legitimate, desirable way of behaving) expected of him to the degree that the sanctions and rewards attached to them are great enough.[33] The relationship of this behavior to personality, however, is not a deterministic one. Indeed, several psychologists have pointed out that there is no demonstrable one-to-one relationship between the roles we play and our personality. In fact, Jones, Davis, and Gergen assert that a person only reveals his true self when he fails to play roles. They declared: "The performance of social roles tends to mask information about individual characteristics because the person reveals only that he is responsive to normative requirements."[34]

The plantation, like most large institutions, permitted deviations from the roles it defined. Sociologist Florian Znaniecki noted this characteristic of institutions when he observed that role proscriptions do not mean "that every individual who performs a specific role always has to conform strictly with all the norms which regulate his conduct. For, as a matter of fact, the

33. William F. Knoff, "Role: A Concept Linking Society and Personality," *American Journal of Psychiatry* CXVII (May 1961), 1010-15; Ralph H. Turner, "Role-Taking, Role Standpoint, and Reference Group Behavior," in Edward E. Sampson, ed., *Approaches, Contexts, and Problems of Social Psychology* (Englewood Cliffs, N.J., 1964), 219-31; Reinhard Bendix, "Compliant Behavior and Individual Personality," *American Journal of Sociology* LVIII (Nov. 1952), 290-303; Bruce J. Biddle and Edwin J. Thomas, eds., *Role Theory: Concepts and Research* (New York, 1966), 144-48, 195-200, 282-87, 313-17.

34. Edward E. Jones, Keith E. Davis, and Kenneth Gergen, "Role Playing Variations and Their Informational Value for Person Perception," in Biddle and Thomas, *Role,* 172.

cultural patterns of most roles allow for variations, changes, and even some failures and transgressions."[35] An individual is frequently able to deviate from role expectations because he does not have to play the role continuously; part of his behavior is immune from surveillance. Because there is no continuous social interaction, Robert K. Merton concluded that the lack of observability "allows for role-behavior which is at odds with the expectations of some in the role-set to proceed without undue stress."[36]

Many individuals do not internalize the behavioral patterns of a specific role because in their daily lives they play so many roles and their behavior and attitudes are different for each of them. The behavior of a worker, for example, who is promoted to foreman may become more pro-management. When he is demoted to a worker, he may become more anti-management. The more roles a person plays the less likely is he to internalize the attitudes and behavior of any one of them. Generally, this is facilitated because many roles are peripheral and involve little emotional involvement. Even when there is strong pressure to conform to role expectations, a person has several options other than internalization. He may have a counternorm, or adhere to the values of his subgroup at the same time that he behaves in the accepted pattern.[37]

It is obvious from the writings of the planters that the slaves did not internalize the roles and automatically submit unconditionally to their masters. Consequently, the primary guarantee of obedience was the lash. While accepting the central role of coercive force in maintaining plantation discipline, however, slaveholders recognized its limitations. As a result, they argued that several techniques had to be combined in order to control the slaves. One slaveholder declared that in managing slaves:

35. Florian Znaniecki, *Social Relations and Social Roles* (San Francisco, 1965), 274.

36. Robert K. Merton, "Instability and Articulation in the Role-Set," in Biddle and Thomas, *Role*, 284.

37. Seymour Lieberman, "The Effects of Changes in Roles on the Attitudes of Role Occupants," in Henry Clay Lindgren, ed., *Contemporary Research in Social Psychology* (New York, 1969), 317-31; Daniel Katz and Robert L. Kahn, *The Social Psychology of Organizations* (New York, 1966), 171-206.

"Love and fear, a regard for public opinion, gratitude, shame, the conjugal, parental, and filial feelings, these all must be appealed to and cultivated."[38] Reason and persuasion, slaveholders argued, had to be among the primary instruments of slave management.[39]

Many of the planters asserted that the frequent punishment of slaves was an indication of bad management. According to one slaveholder, "The best evidence of the good management of slaves, is the keeping up of good discipline with little or no punishment."[40] The use of coercion was an indication that the slave did not identify with the master's interest and refused to play the submissive role. One planter noted this when he observed: "The master should make it his business to show his slaves, that the advancement of his individual interest, is at the same time an advancement of theirs. Once they feel this, it will require but little compulsion to make them act as becomes them."[41] The extent of the planters' failure is revealed in their frequent resort to compulsion.

Because the evidence is so fragmentary and contradictory, scholars have not been able to determine how frequently planters and overseers flogged slaves in the antebellum South. But if planters throughout the Americas acted on similar disciplinary principles, some highly suggestive data can be obtained from reports on slavery in the British West Indies. Planters in St. Lucia, for example, flogged between 7.2 and 21 per cent of their slaves annually in the period 1826 to 1829. In Trinidad, between 33 and 46 per cent of the slaves received floggings during the period 1826 to 1830. On the island of Berbice, between 42 and

38. "Plantation Life—Duties and Responsibilities," *DeBow's Review* XXXIX (Sept. 1860), 362.

39. John Perkins, "Relation of Master and Slave in Louisiana and the South," *DeBow's Review* XV (Sept. 1853), 275-77; F. A. Shoup, "Has the Southern Pulpit Failed?" *North American Review*, CXXX (June 1880), 585-603; A Mississippi Planter, "Management of Negroes Upon Southern Estates," *DeBow's Review* X (June 1851), 621-27; "Instruction of Slaves," *Littell's Living Age* (Jan. 24, 1846), 179-81; "Management of Cotton Estates," *DeBow's Review* XXVI (May 1859), 579-80.

40. *Southern Agriculturalist* VII (July 1834), 368.

41. *Southern Agriculturalist* IX (Dec. 1836), 626.

50 per cent of the total slave population received floggings annually during the years 1827 and 1829. The West Indian planters made no bones about the role of the whip in managing slaves. The Trinidad *Gazette* spoke for many planters when it declared in 1825: "We did, and do declare, the WHIP to be ESSENTIAL to West Indian discipline. . . . The comfort, welfare, and happiness of our laboring classes cannot subsist without it." It is possible that Southern planters, acting on identical principles, flogged their slaves as frequently as West Indian planters did.[42]

Inasmuch as the planters defined the roles and applied the sanctions to ensure conformity, practically all advisers on plantation management insisted that the behavior of the slaves was a reflection of the way planters treated them. A Maryland slaveholder observed in 1837:

> The character of the negro is much underrated. It is like the plastic clay, which may be moulded into agreeable or disagreeable figures, according to the skill of the moulder. The man who storms at, and curses his negroes, and tells them they are a parcel of infernal rascals, not to be trusted, will surely make them just what he calls them; and so far from loving such a master, they will hate him. Now, if you be not suspicious, and induce them to think, by slight trusts, that they are not unworthy of some confidence, you will make them honest, useful, and affectionate creatures.[43]

How, exactly, did the planters characterize slaves? For the most part, they felt that there was great variability among them. Most advisers admonished overseers and planters to try to determine the range of personality types in the quarters. One Virginia planter, for example, noted:

> In the management of slaves, the temper and disposition of each negro should be particularly consulted. Some require

42. Appendix III, table 19; *Gazette* quoted in (British) *Anti-Slavery Reporter* I (Aug. 31, 1825), 19; see Robert W. Fogel and Stanley Engerman, *Time on the Cross: The Economics of American Negro Slavery* (2 vols., Boston, 1974), I, 144-45, for speculations about the extent of slave punishment based on the diary of a single planter (Bennett Barrow).

43. *Farmer's Register* V (Sept. 1837), 302.

Figure 44. The Flogging

> spurring up, some coaxing, some flattering, and others nothing but good words. When an overseer first goes upon a plantation to live, He should study their dispositions well, before he exerts too much rigor. Many a noble spirit has been broken down by injudicious management, and many a lazy cunning fellow has escaped, and put his work on the shoulders of the industrious. Give me a high spirited and even a high tempered negro, full of pride, for easy and comfortable management. Your slow sulky negro although he may have an even temper, is *the devil* to manage.
>
> The negro women are all harder to manage than the men. The only way to get along with them is by kind words and flattery. If you want to cure a sloven, give her something nice occasionally to wear, and praise her up to skies whenever she has on any thing tolerably decent.[44]

If there is any validity at all in the essays on plantation management and publicly held stereotypes, there was a great variety of personality types in the quarters. The first premise of the planter was that there were so many different kinds of slaves that he had to combine several techniques in order to manage them. When the slaveholder considered the best way to get the maximum labor from his slaves he did not assume that a majority of them were Sambos; there was little room for romanticizing when there was cotton to be picked. Even in the publicly held stereotypes, slave behavior ran the whole gamut from abject docility to open rebellion. The predominance of the Sambo and Nat stereotypes explain a great deal more about the white man's character than about the behavior of most slaves.

44. *Southern Agriculturalist* VIII (July 1834), 368.

7

Plantation Realities

> And in this society in which the infant son of the planter was commonly suckled by a black mammy, in which gray old black men were his most loved story-tellers, in which black stalwarts were among the chiefest heroes and mentors of his boyhood, and in which his usual, often practically his only, companions until he was past the age of puberty were the black boys (and girls) of the plantation, in this society in which by far the greater number of white boys of whatever degree were more or less shaped by such companionship and in which nearly the whole body of whites, young and old, had constantly before their eyes the example, had constantly in their ears the accent, of the Negro, the relationship between the two groups was, by the second generation at least, nothing less than organic. Negro entered into white man as profoundly as white man entered into Negro—subtly influencing every gesture, every word, every emotion and idea, every attitude.
>
> Wilbur J. Cash

The behavior of the black slave was intimately bound up with the nature of the antebellum plantation, the behavior of masters, the white man's perceptions and misperceptions, and a multitude of factors which influenced personal relations. In the final analysis, the character of the antebellum plantation was one of the major determinants of the attitudes, perceptions, and behavior of the slave. There was so much variation in plantations, overseers, and masters, however, that the slave had much more freedom from restraint and more independence and autonomy than his institutionally defined role allowed. Consequently, the slave did not have to be infantile or abjectly docile in order to remain alive. It was primarily because of the variegated pattern of plantation life that Sambo did not emerge as the dominant slave personality in the quarters.[1]

The plantation did, however, give a certain uniform pattern to the slave's life, especially in terms of labor requirements. According to the black autobiographers, most field hands rose before dawn, prepared their meals, fed the livestock, and then rushed to the fields before sunrise. Failure to reach the field on time often brought the overseer's lash into play. Depending upon the season or the crop, the laborer would grub and hoe the field, pick worms off the plants, build fences, cut down trees, construct dikes, pull fodder, clear new land, plant rice, sugar, tobacco, cotton, and corn, and then harvest the crop.

Frequently, after working from dawn to sunset, the weary slaves then had to care for the livestock, put away tools, and cook their meals before the horn sounded bedtime in the quarters. During the cotton-picking season, the men sometimes ginned cotton until nine o'clock at night. For the hapless slaves on the sugar plantation, the work of boiling the sugar cane continued far into the night: they often worked eighteen hours a day during the harvest season; some sugar factories ran in shifts seven days and nights each week. The work, while varying in tempo, seemed almost endless. Cotton-planting started the last of March or first of April, cotton-picking lasted from August to Christmas and frequently until January or February. The corn was harvested after cotton-picking ended. During slack periods, the slaves cleared forest land, built fences, repaired the slave cabins, killed hogs, and engaged in a multitude of other tasks.

While the mass of slaves followed this routine, the domestic servants formed part of the plantation elite. They usually ate

1. John Q. Anderson, "Dr. James Green Carson, Ante-Bellum Planter of Mississippi and Louisiana," *Journal of Mississippi History* XVIII (Oct. 1956), 243-67; Winthrop M. Daniels, "The Slave Plantation in Retrospect," *Atlantic Monthly* CVII (March 1911), 363-69; Edwin A. Davis, "Bennett H. Barrow, Ante-Bellum Planter of the Felicianas," *Journal of Southern History* V (Nov. 1939), 431-46; Rosser H. Taylor, "The Gentry of Antebellum South Carolina," *North Carolina Historical Review* XVII (April 1940), 114-31; George C. Osborne, "Plantation Life in Central Mississippi as Revealed in the Clay Sharkey Papers," *Journal of Mississippi History* III (Oct. 1941), 277-88.

better food and wore better clothes than the field slaves because they received leftovers from the planter's larder and hand-me-downs from his wardrobe. In spite of this, their position was no sinecure. They ran errands, worked as part-time gardeners, cooked, served meals, cared for the horses, milked the cows, sewed simple clothes, cared for the master's infant, wove, carded and spun wool, did the marketing, churned the milk, dusted the house, swept the yard, arranged the dining room, cut the shrubbery, and performed numerous other tasks. With the exception of the plantation cook, each domestic servant was responsible not for one but for several of these tasks.[2]

At the beck and call of his master day and night, the domestic servant had no regular hours. Added to the long hours was the discomfiture of constantly being under the watchful eyes of the whites and being subject to their every capricious, vengeful, or sadistic whim. Domestic servants frequently had their ears boxed or were flogged for trifling mistakes, ignorance, delinquent work, "insolent" behavior, or simply for being within striking distance when the master was disgruntled. Lewis Clarke, who felt the domestic servants' lot was worse than that of the field slaves, described the problems which beset them:

> We were constantly exposed to the whims and passions of every member of the family; from the least to the greatest their anger was wreaked upon us. Nor was our life an easy one, in the hours of our toil or in the amount of labor performed. We were always required to sit up until all the family had retired; then we must be up at early dawn in summer, and before day in winter.[3]

The quantity, quality, and variety of food, clothing, housing, and medical care the slave received rarely satisfied him. The fact that another man determined how much and what kind of food,

2. Charles Ball, *Slavery in the United States* . . . (New York, 1849), 156-68, 245-300; Lewis G. Clarke, *Narrative of the Sufferings of Lewis Clarke* . . . (Boston, 1845), 10-22; Henry Watson, *Narrative of Henry Watson, a Fugitive Slave* (Boston, 1848), 5-17; Elizabeth Keckley, *Behind the Scenes* (New York, 1868), 17-28.

3. Clarke, *Sufferings*, 17.

Figure 45. Field Hand

Figure 46. Domestic Servant

clothing, and shelter he needed to survive posed a serious problem for him. Equally serious was his dependence on the "average" amount of food and clothing his master decided was sufficient for *all* slaves. Obviously, an allotment of food or clothing sufficient for one man was not necessarily enough for another man. Most of the black autobiographers complained that they had at least one owner who did not give them enough food. Sometimes, even when slaves generally received enough food, provisions ran low. When the slaves did not receive enough to eat, they stole food. James Watkins, Annie L. Burton, Andrew Jackson, Josiah Henson, and Peter Randolph reported that, in spite of the risks involved, the slaves on their plantations stole food when it was denied them. Other slaves trapped animals and fished at night and on Sundays in order to augment their meager diet.[4]

The slaves often complained bitterly about what their masters described as "adequate" housing. Most of the autobiographers reported that they lived in crudely built one-room log cabins with dirt floors and too many cracks in them to permit much comfort during the winter months. John Brown complained that in the log cabins: "The wind and rain will come in and the smoke will not go out." Austin Steward felt that the slave cabins were "not as good as many of our stables at the north."[5] Not only were the slave cabins uncomfortable, they were often crowded. Most of the cabins contained at least two families. The 260 slaves on Charles Ball's plantation shared 38 cabins, an average of 6.8 slaves per cabin. The 160 slaves on Louis Hughes's plantation lived in 18 cabins or an average of 8.8 slaves per cabin. Josiah Henson declared that from 10 to 12 people shared each cabin on his plantation. Some lived not in cabins but in sheds. William

4. James L. Smith, *Autobiography of James L. Smith* (Norwich, Conn., 1881), 1-9; John Brown, *Slave Life in Georgia* (London, 1855), 170-80; Austin Steward, *Twenty-two Years a Slave, and Forty Years a Freeman* (Rochester, N.Y., 1861), 13-19; Annie L. Burton, *Memories of Childhood's Slavery Days* (Boston, 1909), 3-9; Josiah Henson, *The Life of Josiah Henson* (Boston, 1849), 6-7.

5. J. Brown, *Slave Life*, 191; Steward, *Twenty-two Years*, 19.

Green, for example, lived in a long low shed with 29 others. Some slaves, of course, lived in more spacious and comfortable cabins. Henry Watson's owner, for instance, had 27 cabins for his 100 slaves, an average of 3.7 slaves per cabin. Few slaves were as fortunate as Sam Aleckson whose master's slave cabins were not only neat and commodious, but also had flower gardens in front of them. Usually the slaves had to make what furniture and utensils they used. They built tables, beds, and benches and sometimes carved wooden spoons. Generally the cabins contained beds made of straw covered boards, and tables of packing boxes. Some slaves slept on the ground or on mattresses of corn shucks without blankets.[6]

The physical condition of the slaves has often been compared to that of other laborers and members of other total institutions. Southern propagandists generally argued that slaves were better fed, housed, and clothed than European peasants or factory operatives. Abolitionists drew the opposite conclusion and produced statistics showing that the inmates of Northern prisons, sailors, and soldiers received greater quantities of and more nutritious food than slaves. Twentieth-century economists and cliometricians, using mathematical models, theorized that slaves not only received a relatively adequate return on their labor, but also were well fed, clothed, and housed when compared to Northern free laborers.[7] Despite contrary theories, the return the slave received for his work was in no wise comparable to that received by free laborers. The planters admitted the distinctions. In a carefully reasoned economic treatise written in 1844, for instance, Nathaniel Ware observed:

6. J. Smith, *Autobiography*, 1-9; J. H. Banks, *A Narrative of Events of the Life of J. H. Banks* (Liverpool, 1861), 42-63; Allen Parker, *Recollections of Slavery Times* (Worcester, Mass., 1895), 7-20; James W. C. Pennington, *The Fugitive Blacksmith* (London, 1849), 66.

7. Theodore Dwight Weld, ed., *American Slavery as It Is: Testimony of a Thousand Witnesses* (New York, 1839), 28-35, Robert W. Fogel and Stanley Engerman, *Time on the Cross: The Economics of American Negro Slavery* (2 vols., Boston, 1974), I, 109-26. The best discussion of slave diet, clothing, and housing appears in Todd L. Savitt, *Medicine and Slavery* (Urbana, 1978), 57-110.

> the free laborers are in families, and useless mouths are to be fed, houses, rents, furniture, taxes, doctors' bills, all amounting to some style and a considerable amount, have to be sustained. The slaves live without beds or houses worth so calling, or family cares, or luxuries, or parade, or show; have no relaxations, or whims, or frolics, or dissipations; instead of sun to sun in their hours, are worked from daylight till nine o'clock at night. Where the free man or laborer would require one hundred dollars a year for food and clothing alone, the slave can be supported for twenty dollars a year, and often is. This makes the wages of the one forty cents a day, of the other six cents only. . . . A slave consumes in meat two hundred pounds of bacon or pork, costing, in Kentucky, Ohio, Indiana, Illinois, Missouri, Tennessee, and Western Virginia, $8; thirteen bushels of Indian corn, costing $2; this makes up his food. Now for salt and medicines add $1, and it runs thus: a year's food is $11. Their clothing is of cottons—fifteen yards of Lowell, $1.50; ten yards linsey, $4; one blanket, $2; one pair of shoes, $1—making $7.50. Now this sum of $18.50, say $20, divided among the working days, is six cents. This is not fancy, but every day's practice. So the wages of a slave is one-sixth part of the wages of free laborers.[8]

Whatever their treatment of slaves, most planters worked consistently to make them submissive and deferential. While the lash was the linchpin of his regime, the slaveholder adopted several practices to assure the slave's submissiveness. A master started early trying to impress upon the mind of the young black the awesome power of whiteness: he made the slave bow upon meeting him, stand in his presence, and accept floggings from his young children; he flogged the slave for fighting with young whites. The ritual of deference was required at every turn: the slave was flogged for disputing a white man's word, kicked for walking between two whites on a street, and not allowed to call his wife or mother "Mrs."[9] He had to approach the overseer or

8. [Nathaniel Ware], *Notes on Political Economy, As Applicable to the United States, by a Southern Planter* (New York, 1844), 201-2.

9. Ball, *Slavery*, 40-74; Watson, *Narrative*, 28-38; John Thompson, *The Life of John Thompson, a Fugitive Slave* (Worcester, Mass., 1856), 10-26;

master with great humility. For example, on Charles Ball's plantation the slaves "were always obliged to approach the door of the mansion, in the most humble and supplicating manner, with our hats in our hands, and the most subdued and beseeching language in our mouths. . . ."[10]

Many masters tried first to demonstrate their own authority over the slave and then the superiority of all whites over blacks. They continually told the slave he was unfit for freedom, that every slave who attempted to escape was captured and sold further South, and that the black man must conform to the white man's every wish. The penalties for non-conformity were severe; the lessons uniformly pointed to one idea: the slave was a thing to be used by the "superior" race. Jermain Loguen, for instance, wrote that he "had been taught, in the severest school, that he was a thing for others' uses, and that he must bend his head, body and mind in conformity to that idea, in the presence of a superior race. . . .' Likewise, Austin Steward had since his childhood "been taught to cower beneath the white man's frown, and bow at his bidding, or suffer all the rigor of the slave laws."[11]

Planters insisted that their slaves show no signs of dissatisfaction. Instead, they were to demonstrate their humility by cheerful performance of their tasks. Elizabeth Keckley's master, for instance, "never liked to see one of his slaves wear a sorrowful face, and those who offended in this particular way were always punished." Anxiously scanning the faces of his slaves, the master made them reflect, in their countenances, what he wanted rather than what they felt. Henry Watson asserted that "the slaveholder watches every move of the slave, and if he is downcast or sad,—in fact, if they are in any mood but laughing and singing, and manifesting symptoms of perfect content at heart,—they are said to have the devil in them. . . ."[12]

Sam Aleckson, *Before the War and After the Union* (Boston, 1929), 51-65; William Wells Brown, *Narrative of William W. Brown, a Fugitive Slave* (Boston, 1847), 95-98.

10. Ball, *Slavery*, 41.

11. Jermain Wesley Loguen, *The Rev. J. W. Loguen, as a Slave and as a Freedman* (Syracuse, N.Y., 1859), 165; Steward, *Twenty-two Years*, 97-98.

12. Keckley, *Scenes*, 29; Watson, *Narrative*, 32.

Lest the edifice he was building should fall, the master enlisted the aid of some black men to help him control the others. The most diligent slaves were rewarded and pointed to as models for the others to emulate. Black drivers were forced, on pain of punishment themselves, to keep the slaves at their tasks and to flog them for breaking the plantation rules.

Caught in the no-man's-land between management and labor, the driver suffered the consequences: he was almost literally shot at from all sides. When he earned praise from the master for a job well done, he earned the undying hatred of the slaves for pushing them too hard. Demotion and flogging greeted the driver who allowed the slaves to dawdle at their work, who failed to keep order in the quarters, or who could not account for plantation equipment. While drivers tried to walk the tightrope between the masters who gave them material rewards (money, passes, presents) and the slaves who gave them social rewards (love, respect, companionship), most of them failed. Because masters correctly perceived them as being the most loyal of slaves, the bondsmen treated the drivers as spies and collaborators. The driver was the best example in the quarters of the oppressed identifying with the enemy. The ambiguities some scholars have seen in the driver's role were similar to those of foremen and noncommissioned officers. Like his industrial and military counterparts, the driver was ground relentlessly between the upper (masters) and nether (slaves) millstones. From the perspective of the bondsmen, however, whenever there was a conflict in loyalties the driver acted out his primary role as the master's man. Using the self-serving testimony of a few remarkable drivers, historians have tried to demonstrate that he was the classic man caught in the middle who went to unusual lengths to protect his fellows, that he ranked high in the social order of the quarters, and that he was as rebellious as other slaves.[13] The

13. Leslie Howard Owens, *This Species of Property* (New York, 1976), 121-35; Eugene Genovese, *Roll, Jordan, Roll* (New York, 1974), 365-88; Thomas H. Patten, Jr., *The Foreman: Forgotten Man of Management* (n.p., 1968), 17-33, 106-8, 123-47; Alan Fox, *A Sociology of Work in Industry* (London, 1971), 84-89; David Dunkerley, *The Foreman: Aspects of Task and Structure* (London, 1975), 28-39, 53-58, 85-87, 120-29; Samuel A.

evidence from the blacks themselves contradicts this portrait.

Since most plantations were small, slave owners did not employ enough drivers for them to represent significant personages in the community of the slaves.[14] Called whipping man, overlooker, whipping boss, foreman, and overseer by the slaves, the driver was generally described by bondsmen as being as "mean as the devil." Significantly, the more sympathetic (or neutral) assessments of the drivers come from the drivers themselves, their relatives, or their owners. Rare indeed is the testimony of a field hand that drivers tried in any way to protect the bondsmen or hide their indiscretions from owners.[15] The slaves complained instead of the driver's sexual exploitation of black women, his alacrity in meting out punishment, and his favoritism in giving rewards. In slave interviews and autobiographies, the driver appears as the embodiment of cruelty. Henry Cheatam of Mississippi gave a typical description:

> Old Miss had a nigger overseer and dat was de meanest devil dat ever lived on de Lord's green earth. I promise myself when I growed up dat I was a-goin' to kill dat nigger if it was de last thing I ever done. Lots of times I'se seen him beat my mammy, and one day I seen him beat my auntie who was big with a

---

Stouffer *et al., The American Soldier: Adjustment During Army Life* (4 vols., Princeton, 1949), I, 401-10.

14. Even when one discounts the comments of those too young to remember much about slavery, the driver is an extremely rare figure compared with the ubiquitous overseer in the WPA interviews.

15. John W. Blassingame, ed., *Slave Testimony* (Baton Rouge, 1977), 405, 498, 640; Randall Miller, ed., *"Dear Master": Letters of a Slave Family* (Ithaca, N.Y., 1978), 139-82; Owens, *Species*, 121-35; Genovese, *Roll, Jordan, Roll*, 365-88; George P. Rawick, *The American Slave: A Composite Autobiography* (31 vols., Westport, Conn., 1972-77), VI (Alabama), 63, 155, 169, 426, (Indiana), 199, VII (Oklahoma), 67-70, 98-101, 124, 129, 192, 224, 227, 251-53, 288, 292, 303 (Mississippi), 69, 78, VII, pt. 1:301, IX pt. 3:139, pt. 4:298, X pt. 5:35, 120, 339, pt. 6:49, 82; (Supplement), I, 87, 156-59, 167, 305, 450, II, 11, 106, IV, 471, XII, 13, 82, 111, 361; Charles L. Perdue *et al.*, eds., *Weevils in the Wheat: Interviews with Virginia Ex-Slaves* (Charlottesville, 1976), 26-27, 110, 290; Ronnie C. Tyler and Lawrence R. Murphy, eds., *The Slave Narratives of Texas* (Austin, 1974), 63; Orland K. Armstrong, ed., *Old Massa's People: The Old Slaves Tell Their Story* (Indianapolis, 1931), 98-99, 217-19.

> child, and dat man dug a round hole in de ground and put her stomach in it, and beat and beat her for a half hour straight till de baby come out right dere in de hole.
>
> Mistis allow such treatment only 'cause a heap of times she didn't know nothin' about it, and de slaves better not tell her, 'cause dat overseer whip 'em if he finds out dat dey done gone and told. . . . When de slaves would try to run away our overseer would put chains on deir legs with big long spikes between deir feets, so dey couldn't get away.[16]

The key to the slaves' assessment of the driver was whether or not he had the power to flog them. When masters prohibited drivers from flogging, they had to work out a number of compromises in order to get slaves to labor. Without the whip, the driver spurred his fellows on by example and threats to tell the master when they did not labor conscientiously. Though the size of the plantation, the number of slaves, the crop, the presence or absence of owners, managerial style of masters, and the resort to the task system or gang labor all affected the role of the driver in a variety of ways, the presence or absence of the whip in his hands largely determined his relationship with other slaves and his standing in the quarters.

While the drivers provided part of the coercion necessary to keep the plantation machinery humming, the domestic servants often represented an extension of the master's eyes and ears: the plantation's secret police. Flattered and materially rewarded, the domestic servant kept the master informed of activities in the slave quarters. Trained to speak of his good treatment to Northern visitors and sometimes forced to spy on his fellows, the domestic servant was a valuable adjunct to the slaveholder's security and public relations staff.

Ritual deference and obedience to plantation rules could only

16. Norman R. Yetman, ed., *Voices from Slavery* (New York, 1970), 55; see also: Blassingame, *Slave Testimony*, 65-73, 219-20, 277-79, 359, 524, 586; Rawick, *American Slave*, VI (Alabama), 2, 52, 66, 158, 181, 212, 224, 416, (Indiana), 156, 199-200, VII (Oklahoma), 21, 50-51, 77-78, 216, 233, 296 (Mississippi), 4, 13, VIII, pt. 1:34, IX, pt. 4:85; (Supplement), I, 89-92, III, 261, XII, 29, 37, 142, 369; Perdue, *Weevils*, 156, 266-67, 274; Tyler and Murphy, *Slave Narratives*, 53-55; Armstrong, *Old Massa's People*, 218.

be enforced by most planters by constant floggings. William Wells Brown spoke for many slaves when he wrote that on his plantation the whip was used "very frequently and freely, and a small offence on the part of a slave furnished an occasion for its use."[17] The slaves were flogged most frequently for running away and for failure to complete the tasks assigned them. Slaveholders often punished them for visiting their mates, learning to read, arguing or fighting with whites, working too slowly, stealing, fighting or quarreling with other slaves, drunkenness, or for trying to prevent the sale of their relatives. They were occasionally punished for impudence, asking their masters to sell them, claiming they were free men, breaking household articles, or for giving sexual favors to persons other than their masters.[18]

Nowhere does the irrationality of slavery appear as clearly as in the way that slaves were punished. While generally speaking a slaveholder had no desire to punish his slave so severely as to endanger his life, the master was only a man, subject, like most men, to miscalculations, to anger, to sadism, and to drink. When angry, masters frequently kicked, slapped, cuffed, or boxed the ears of domestic servants, sometimes flogged pregnant women, and often punished slaves so cruelly that it took them weeks to recover.[19] Many slaves reported that they were flogged severely, had iron weights with bells on them placed on their necks, or were shackled. Recalcitrant slaves received more stripes and were treated more cruelly by exasperated planters than were any other blacks. Moses Roper, an incorrigible runaway, regularly received 100 to 200 lashes from his owner. Once his master poured tar on his head and set it afire. On another occasion, after Roper had escaped from leg irons, his master had the nails of his fingers and toes beaten off. Since every white man considered himself

17. W. W. Brown, *Narrative,* 15.

18. Ball, *Slavery,* 160-68, 372-480; Thomas Jones, *The Experience of Thomas Jones, Who Was a Slave for Forty-three Years* (Boston, 1850), 16-20; J. Brown, *Slave Life,* 21-30, 62-68, 127-36.

19. Steward, *Twenty-two Years,* 22-30; W. W. Brown, *Narrative,* 37-41; Clarke, *Sufferings,* 14-20; J. Brown, *Slave Life,* 127-36; Watkins, *Narrative,* 9-10; Loguen, *Freedman,* 78-98; New Orleans *True Delta,* Dec. 7, 1845; New Orleans *Daily Delta,* Sept. 28, Oct. 7, 1858, Jan. 14, April 20, 1859.

the slave's policeman, the black also suffered at the hands of non-slaveholders. Josiah Henson, for example, accidentally pushed a white man who later broke his arm and shoulder blades.[20]

Uncompromisingly harsh, the portrait which the slaves drew of cruel masters was filled with brutality and horror. On the plantations of these masters, strong black men suffered from overwork, abuse, and starvation; and the overseer's horn usually sounded before sleep could chase the fatigue of the last day's labor. Characteristically, stocks closed on hapless women and children, mothers cried for the infants torn cruelly from their arms, and whimpering black women fought vainly to preserve their virtue in the face of the lash or pleaded for mercy while blood flowed from their bare buttocks. A cacophony of horrendous sounds constantly reverberated throughout such plantations: nauseated black men vomited while strung up over slowly burning tobacco leaves, vicious dogs tore black flesh, black men moaned as they were hung up by the thumbs with the whip raising deep welts on their backs and as they were bent over barrels or tied down to stakes while paddles with holes in them broke blisters on their rumps. Frequently, blacks called God's name in vain as they fainted from their master's hundredth stroke or as they had their brains blown out. The slaves described masters of this stripe as besotted, vicious, deceitful, coarse, licentious, bloodthirsty, heartless, and hypocritical Christians who were pitiless fiends.[21]

The first impulse of the historian is to reject the slave's portrait as too harsh. There is, however, a great deal of evidence in antebellum court records, newspapers, memoirs, and plantation diaries which suggests that this is not the case. However much it is denied by Southern romantics, there were many slaveholders who were moral degenerates and sadists. Quite frequently, even the most cultured of planters were so inured to brutality that they thought little about the punishment meted out to slaves.

20. W. W. Brown, *Narrative,* 21-30; J. Brown, *Slave Life,* 21-30, 82-109; Loguen, *Freedman,* 122-36; Clarke, *Sufferings,* 22-30; Henson, *Life,* 15-18.

21. W. W. Brown, *Narrative,* 21-26; Clarke, *Sufferings,* 11-12; Steward, *Twenty-two Years,* 91-93; Henson, *Life,* 15-18.

Floggings of 50 to 75 lashes were not uncommon. On numerous occasions, planters branded, stabbed, tarred and feathered, burned, shackled, tortured, maimed, crippled, mutilated, and castrated their slaves. Thousands of slaves were flogged so severely that they were permanently scarred. In Mississippi a fiendish planter once administered 1000 lashes to a slave.[22]

At the opposite extreme from the fiend was Dr. James Green Carson of Mississippi. Carson, although he inherited 200 slaves, early in life expressed an abhorrence of slavery on religious grounds. Unable to free his slaves because of Mississippi law, Carson felt a moral responsibility to treat them humanely. Consequently, he hired a plantation physician, paid white missionaries to preach to his slaves every Sunday, conducted prayer meetings in the quarters during the week, purchased labor-saving machinery to lighten the slaves' work, punished his children for being discourteous to blacks, and never used the lash. James Carson was a rare man among Southern planters. Still, there were many others who were enough like him to be described as generally kind and humane in their treatment of slaves.[23]

According to antebellum whites, there were many planters who dealt with their slaves in a humane fashion. Walter Peterson, for example, recalled that in Alabama "many slaveholders were kind masters."[24] Philip H. Jones of Louisiana asserted that "Many owners were humane and kind and provided well for them [slaves]."[25] According to Amanda Washington, among the planters "*Noblesse oblige* was recognized everywhere, and we felt bound to treat kindly the class dependent on us."[26]

22. Charles S. Sydnor, *Slavery in Mississippi* (Baton Rouge, 1966), 86-94; Kenneth Stampp, *The Peculiar Institution* (New York, 1956), 171-91.

23. Fletcher M. Green, ed., *Ferry Hill Plantation Journal, January 4, 1838-January 15, 1839* (Chapel Hill, 1961), vii-xxi; Osborne, "Plantation," 277-88; Anderson, "Carson," 243-67; Mary W. Highsaw, "A History of Zion Community in Maury County, 1806-1860," *Tennessee Historical Quarterly* V (June 1946), 111-40.

24. Walter F. Peterson, "Slavery in the 1850's: Recollections of an Alabama Unionist," *Alabama Historical Quarterly* XXX (Fall and Winter 1968), 221.

25. Philip H. Jones, "Reminiscences of Philip H. Jones," 4, Southern Historical Collection, University of North Carolina.

26. Amanda Washington, *How Beauty Was Saved* (New York, 1907), 64.

The testimony of the white witnesses is borne out by that of former slaves. A majority of the slaves, at one time, had one or two masters whom they considered kindly men. Josiah Henson described his master as a "kind-hearted, liberal, and jovial" man. Grimes felt that Dr. Collock of Savannah "was the best and most humane man I ever lived with, or worked under." Sam Aleckson's South Carolina master was "kind and generous." Isaac Jefferson recalled that his master, Thomas Jefferson, was of a similar stripe: "Old master [was] kind to servants." Elijah Marrs declared: "Our master was not hard on us." The slaveholders earned these encomiums in various ways. Sparing use of the lash, provision of adequate shelter, clothing, and food, and maintenance of the family unit all led the slaves to think of their masters as kindly men.[27]

However kind his master, the slave had no guarantee of benevolent treatment. The kindest masters were sometimes crotchety, often wreaking their anger on their slaves.[28] Austin Steward reported that his owner "was not a very hard master; but generally was kind and pleasant. Indulgent when in good humor, but like many of the southerners, terrible when in a passion." Grimes's master was of the same temperament. He was, according to Grimes, "a very kind master, but exceedingly severe when angry."[29]

Most masters were neither pitiless fiends nor saints in their relationships with slaves. Whenever possible, planters hired physicians for slaves when they were ill, gave them what the planter defined as "adequate" food, clothing, and shelter, and flogged them for lying, stealing, fighting, breaking tools, and numerous other "offenses." While ready to give the slave from 10 to 50 lashes for most offenses, the typical planter preferred to punish slaves in other ways (withholding passes, demotion, extra work, humiliation, solitary confinement, etc.). Less violent means of

27. Henson, *Life*, 2; Grimes, *Life*, 36-48; Aleckson, *Union*, 35; Isaac Jefferson, *Life of Isaac Jefferson of Petersburg, Virginia, Blacksmith* (Charlottesville, 1951), 23; Elijah P. Marrs, *Life and History* (Louisville, 1885), 11.

28. Leonard Black, *The Life and Sufferings of Leonard Black, a Fugitive from Slavery* (New Bedford, 1847), 11; Pennington, *Blackmith*, 9.

29. Steward, *Twenty-two Years*, 33; Grimes, *Life*, 33.

punishment were preferred because they were not morally reprehensible, involved no physical harm to valuable property, and were often more effective in preserving discipline than floggings.[30]

In spite of the institutionally defined roles, the treatment of slaves varied from plantation to plantation. Differences in family life, childhood experiences, and religious beliefs caused the planters to treat their slaves in a great variety of ways. A few masters were so brutal and sadistic that they could crush the slave's every manly instinct. Others were too humane, too lazy, or too stupid to make child-like dependents of their slaves. While the normal planter extracted all of the labor he could from blacks, there were several conflicting forces which made him at the same time callous toward the slaves' sufferings and impelled him to recognize their humanity.

One of the most important institutions which influenced the planter's treatment of the slave was the white family. The white child grew up in a society which stressed formalized courtship, romanticized women as angelic, made a fetish of the family, frowned on public displays of affection, encouraged prolific childbearing, and promoted early marriages. The planter's family was patriarchal, deeply religious, and filio-pietistic. Males were given religious and moral lessons as well as being taught to be aggressive, proud, independent, courteous, courageous, chivalrous, honorable, and intelligent.[31]

Although fathers were venerated and children were frequently dependent on them until adulthood, rural isolation sometimes promoted spontaneous and affectionate family relations. Disci-

30. J. Carlyle Sitterson, "The McCollams: A Planter Family of the Old and New South," *Journal of Southern History* VI (Aug. 1940), 347-67; Noah Davis, *A Narrative of the Life of Rev. Noah Davis, a Colored Man* (Baltimore, 1859), 1-14.

31. Susan Dabney Smedes, *Memorials of a Southern Planter* (Baltimore, 1887), 29, 108-15, 135-38; Edmund S. Morgan, *Virginians at Home* (Williamsburg, 1952), 5-8, 36, 45-48; Julia Cherry Spruill, *Women's Life and Work in the Southern Colonies* (Chapel Hill, 1938), 43-50; Rosser H. Taylor, *Ante-Bellum South Carolina: A Social History* (Chapel Hill, 1942), 59-73; Arthur W. Calhoun, *A Social History of the American Family* (New York, 1960), II, 311-55.

pline was unsystematic, and parents overindulged their children. In spite of this, the formalized manners often militated against parents displaying deep affection for their children. Susan Dabney Smedes, for example, reported that her father "did not readily express his affections for his children . . ."[32] The child's relations with his mother were hedged in by his almost religious veneration of her as a genteel, delicate, saintly being. His father's circumspection in his contacts with white women reinforced the picture of her as an untouchable. The situation was complicated even more by the frequent remarriages of widows and widowers and the subsequent strains on their children.

One of the key figures in the white child's socialization was the ubiquitous black mammy to whom he frequently turned for love and security. It was the black mammy who often ran the household, interceded with his parents to protect him, punished him for misbehavior, nursed him, rocked him to sleep, told him fascinating stories, and in general served as his second, more attentive, more loving mother. The mammy's influence on her white charge's thought, behavior, language, and personality is inestimable.[33] One Englishman wrote that in the Carolinas: "Each child has its *Momma,* whose gestures and accent it will necessarily copy, for children, we all know, are imitative beings. It is not unusual to hear an elegant lady say, *Richard always grieves when Quasheehan is whipped, because she suckled him.*"[34] Often the child formed a deep and abiding love for his mammy and as an adult deferred to her demands and wishes.

Black childhood playmates had only a little less influence on the white child than the mammy. As a result of enduring friendships formed during their impressionable childhood, many white youngsters intervened to prevent the punishment or sale of their black favorites, demanded of them far less conformity to the slave role, or preferred the company of slaves to that of their

32. Smedes, *Memorials,* 115.

33. Smedes, *Memorials,* 20, 32-33, 116; Virginia Clay-Clopton, *A Belle of the Fifties* (New York, 1905), 4; Taylor, *South Carolina,* 22-34; Morgan, *Virginians,* 63-65; Calhoun, *Family,* II, 311-55.

34. Quoted in Spruill, *Women,* 56.

white neighbors.[35] William Wells Brown's master held Brown's father in such high esteem that he refused to sell the boy to New Orleans even after he had tried to escape. Similarly, William Green's mother prevented his separation from her by appealing to his young master whom she had nursed. Jacob Stroyer wrote that one intemperate white man terrorized his white neighbors but never abused his forty slaves because of the control his old mammy exercised over him. Rarely could a planter punish a slave with impunity if he were the favorite of his wife and children. The son of John Thompson's master, for instance, threatened to shoot an overseer for flogging the slave fiddler. The regard in which Andrew Jackson was held by his master's sons was so great that they refused to tell their father where he went when he escaped from Kentucky. Even if the slave were not a favorite, a member of the master's family might prevent unusually cruel treatment.[36]

The early association with blacks, and especially his black mammy, had a profound influence on the white Southerner. His constant exposure to the cruelties perpetrated upon slaves led to a sense of detachment which conflicted with his love and respect for his close black associates. Similarly, the demeanor of all slaves toward his parents and his parents' insistence that he demand deference from blacks taught the child to exercise authority. He soon observed that his strict moral code conflicted with the apparently more desirable loose morality, irresponsibility, and happiness of his black associates. He envied the slave his apparent freedom from social restraints and projected all of his own desires to break through these restraints onto the black. Often he internalized the love ideal of the black mammy but later learned that she was a hated, black thing. His intimate relation with the mammy, his observation of the casual sexual contacts among slaves, the idealization of white women and the pur-

35. Smedes, *Memorials,* 116, 162; Taylor, *South Carolina,* 22-34.

36. Henry Box Brown, *Narrative of Henry Box Brown* (Boston, 1851), 1-21, 23-38; Samuel Hall, *47 Years a Slave* (Washington, Iowa, 1912), n.p.; Monroe F. Jamison, *Autobiography and Work of Bishop M. F. Jamison, D.D.* (Nashville, 1912), 17-23; Andrew Jackson, *Narrative and Writings of Andrew Jackson* (Syracuse, N.Y., 1847), 20-23.

suit of black women by white males, convinced him that sexual joy lay in the arms of a black paramour. The white male frequently resolved his love-hate complex by pursuing the allegedly passionate black woman. At the same time, he exaggerated the sexual prowess and desire of the black male for liaisons with angelic white women and reacted with extreme cruelty to any challenge to his monopoly of white women.[37]

The slaveholder's sadistic impulses were frequently restrained by the fear of public disapproval. Sympathetic whites often prevented the cruel punishment of slaves. An innkeeper once prevented Moses Roper's drunken master from flogging him. One of Charles Ball's masters never flogged him because he wanted to retain his public reputation as a benevolent slaveholder. Much to his embarrassment, Memphis city officials upbraided Louis Hughes's master when his overseer almost flogged a slave to death.[38] Frederick Douglass felt that public opinion was "an unfailing restraint upon the cruelty and barbarity of masters, overseers, and slave-drivers, whenever and wherever it can reach them . . ."[39]

One of the strongest forces operating against cruel treatment of slaves was religion. Although it is impossible to determine how many slaveholders were deeply religious, it is obvious from the sources that a number of them tried to apply Christian principles in their relations with slaves. The important thing, however, is that ministers continually reminded masters of their duties to their slaves. One example of the interest in this subject was the response to an essay contest sponsored by the Baptist State Convention in Alabama. In 1849 forty men submitted essays on "The Duties of Christian Masters" in an effort to win the $200 prize the convention offered. Some of the essays went through several editions.

The relationship of the minister to the planter was a complex

37. Grimes, *Life,* 15; Watson, *Narrative,* 5-17; Loguen, *Freedman,* 19-25; Ball, *Slavery,* 238-300.

38. Ball, *Slavery,* 23-40; W. W. Brown, *Narrative,* 21-26.

39. Frederick Douglass, *My Bondage and My Freedom* (New York, 1968 [1855]), 61.

one. Frequently dependent on wealthy planters for his livelihood, the white minister almost never questioned the morality of the master-slave relationship. In fact, a majority of the ministers insisted on slavery's divine origin and encouraged slaves to be obedient to their masters. Even so, in spite of the role the minister played in preserving the peculiar institution and his refusal to castigate the planters for their treatment of slaves, he often preached about an ideal master-slave relationship and the duties and responsibilities planters had toward their slaves.

The first duty of the Christian master was to recognize the slave's humanity. This recognition entailed a respect for the feelings of the slave. Southern divines argued that the slave was also created in God's image. The Reverend J. H. Thornwell testified that

> the Negro is of one blood with ourselves—that he has sinned as we have, and that he has an equal interest with us in the great redemption. Science, falsely so called, may attempt to exclude him from the brotherhood of humanity . . . but the instinctive impulses of our nature, combined with the plainest declarations of the word of God, lead us to recognize in his form and lineaments—his moral, religious and intellectual nature—the same humanity in which we glory as the image of God. We are not ashamed to call him our brother.[40]

While the Reverend George W. Freeman was not as certain of the link between master and slave, he was more insistent on the necessity of respecting the black's feelings. Freeman exhorted masters, in their relations with slaves, "never forget that, as low as they are in the scale of humanity, they are yet *human beings, and have the feelings of human beings*—feelings too with many of them, as delicate and sensitive as your own, and which demand to be respected, and carefully preserved from outrage."[41]

Ministers quoted the Bible freely to prove the obligations masters had to their slaves. They reminded them that Paul had ad-

40. J. H. Thornwell, *The Rights and Duties of Masters, A Sermon Preached at the Dedication of a Church* (Charleston, 1850), 11.

41. George W. Freeman, *The Rights and Duties of Slave-Holders* (Charleston, 1837), 27.

vised masters to forbear threatening slaves "knowing that your Master also is in Heaven; neither is there respect of persons with him" (Ephesians 6:9). The most frequently quoted Biblical admonition was Colossians 4:1: "Masters, give unto *your* servants that which is just and equal; knowing that ye also have a Master in heaven." How was the master to determine justice and equity? Most Southern divines translated the terms into the Golden Rule. The Reverend T. A. Holmes summed up the general view when he observed: "Equity pleads the right of humanity. . . . and, in the conscientious discharge of duty, prompts the master to such treatment of his servant as would be desired on his part, were their positions reversed."[42] Ministers asserted that cruel treatment of slaves would lead to Divine censure. The Reverend H. N. McTyeire of New Orleans declared, "As you treat your servants on earth, so will your Master in heaven treat you."[43] The Reverend T. A. Holmes was more direct. He cautioned slaveholders that "the exercise of right and authority on the part of the master, with reference only to his interest, uninfluenced by kindness to his servant, must incur the displeasure of Him with whom there is no respect of persons."[44]

According to the ministers, Christian masters had several duties to their slaves. They had to maintain the slaves properly, care for them in old age, require no more than a reasonable amount of labor from them, give them adequate leisure time, and respect their humanity. Many ministers repeated the question John Wesley asked slaveholders in 1774: "Have you tried what mildness and gentleness would do?" Holmes told planters that "the master should be the friend of his servant, and the servant should know it. Friendship implies good will, Kindness, a desire for the welfare of him for whom it is entertained." Freeman was just as insistent on mild treatment. He declared: "It is the duty of mas-

42. H. N. McTyeire *et al.*, *Duties of Masters of Servants: Three Premium Essays* (Charleston, 1851), 136.

43. H. N. McTyeire, *Duties of Christian Masters* (Nashville, 1859), 125-26.

44. McTyeire *et al.*, *Essays*, 133.

ters not only to be merciful to their servants, but to do everything in their power to make their situation comfortable, and to put forth all reasonable effort to render them contented and happy."[45]

In addition to several personal and social forces which prevented planters from practicing the kind of cruelty necessary for the systematic extinction of every trace of manhood in the slave, there were certain features of the plantation that militated against abject docility on the part of the slaves. Although legally the planter had absolute authority over the slave, there were many restraints on his use of that authority. Dependent on the slave's labor for his economic survival, the planter ordinarily could not afford to starve, torture, or work him to death. Whatever the regimen on the plantation, the planter never had a supervisory staff which was large enough to extract the kind of labor that killed men in a few months. Consequently, in spite of the slave's constant labor, there was an absolute limit beyond which he was not pushed. The most important factor in this limitation was the size of most plantations and the consequent insurance of a low level of surveillance of many of the slave's activities. Since more than half of the slaves in 1860 lived on plantations containing twenty or more slaves, it is obvious that only a small minority of planters could personally supervise every detail of the work. Besides, many masters were too lazy, too stupid, or away too often visiting spas during the summer to maintain a strict surveillance over their slaves. The editor of the *Southern Quarterly Review* recognized this when he wrote that as a result of "the apathy of the master; his love of repose; his absence from his estates . . . the slave . . . acquires a thousand habits and desires all inconsistent with subordination, labour, decency, sobriety, and all virtues of regularity, humility and temperance."[46]

Seeking to ensure regular labor and humility, most planters

45. McTyeire, *Duties*, 84; McTyeire *et al.*, *Essays*, 143; Freeman, *Rights*, 25.

46. N.P.B., "The Treatment of Slaves in the Southern States," *Southern Quarterly Review* XXI (Jan. 1852), 212.

hired overseers to manage their slaves. The job of the overseer was unbelievably difficult.[47] One overseer indicated this plainly when he complained:

> If there ever was or ever will be a calling in life as mean and contemptible as that of an overseer—I would be right down glad to know what it is, and where to be found. . . . If there be . . . a favorable crop, the *master* makes a splendid crop; if any circumstances be unpropitious and an inferior crop is made, it is the overseer's fault, and if he flogs [the slaves] to keep them at home, or locked up . . . he is a brute and a tyrant. If no meat is made, the overseer *would* plant too much cotton. . . . If hogs are taken good care of the overseer is wasting corn, and "the most careless and thriftless creature alive." If he does not "turn out" hands in time, he is *lazy;* if he "rousts" them out as your dad and mine had to do, why he is a brute. . . .[48]

Planters insisted that the overseer spend all of his time on the plantation, especially if the owner himself did not reside there. George Washington was characteristic in this regard. He informed one of his overseers:

> I do in explicit terms, enjoin it upon you to remain constantly at home, unless called off by unavoidable business, or to attend divine worship, and to be constantly with your people when there. There is no other sure way of getting work well done, and quietly, by negroes; for when an overlooker's back is turned, the most of them will slight their work, or be idle altogether; in which case correction cannot retrieve either, but often produces evils which are worse than the disease. Nor is there any other mode than this to prevent thieving and other disorders, the consequence of opportunities.[49]

47. John E. Moore, ed., "Two Documents Relating to Plantation Overseers of the Vicksburg Region, 1831-1832," *Journal of Mississippi History* XVI (Jan. 1954), 31-36; Lucille Griffith, ed., "The Plantation Record Book of Brookdale Farm, Amite County, 1856-57," *Journal of Mississippi History* VII (Jan. 1945), 25-31.

48. James C. Bonner, "The Plantation Overseer and Southern Nationalism as Revealed in the Career of Garland D. Harmon," *Agricultural History* XIX (Jan. 1945), 2.

49. William K. Scarborough, *The Overseer* (Baton Rouge, 1966), 73.

While constant surveillance of slaves was mandatory for successful management, this was one of the most onerous of the overseer's duties. One overseer complained in May 1858 that his work was so time consuming that "I don't get time scarcely to eat or sleep. I have not been off the plantation since the 3rd of Oct[.] . . . The truth is no man can begin to attend to such a business with any set of negros, without the strictest vigilance on his part."[50]

The disciplining of slaves was the major factor in the success or failure of an overseer. Expected to make a large crop while guarding the welfare of the slaves, the overseer often came into conflict with the planter. If the overseer used unusual force in driving the slaves, he incurred the wrath of the owner for damaging his property. On the other hand, if he were easygoing, the planter might dismiss him for making a small crop. In fact, planters often dismissed overseers for cruelty, drunkenness, absenteeism, and lax discipline.

In order for the overseer to retain his job he had to be adept at managing slaves. There were many pitfalls in the endeavor. If on the one hand the overseer became too familiar with the slaves or had sexual relations with the black women, the slaves extracted favors from him and did little work. On the other hand, if the overseer was too cruel and hard driving, the slaves did everything they could to discredit him. It was often impossible for the overseer to find a happy medium between these two extremes. Whenever the slaves were dissatisfied with the overseer, they informed the owner of his transgressions, or ran away to escape heavy work or to avoid punishment. Often the slaves refused to return to work until they had spoken to their masters about their treatment. One harried overseer indicated the impact of this tactic when he complained that "if I donte please every negro on the place they run away rite strate."[51] If the overseer somehow managed to please the master *and* the slaves, he was guaranteed a long tenure on the plantation. For example, John

50. Quoted in Scarborough, *Overseer,* 46.

51. John S. Bassett, *The Southern Plantation Overseer* (Northampton, Mass., 1925), 64.

Figures 47, 48, 49, 50. Cotton Plantation

B. Lamar wrote in 1844 that he was anxious to retain his overseer because "the negroes like him too."[52]

As the visible symbol of authority, the overseer was the most frequent target of rebellious slaves disgruntled over their work load, food allotment, or punishment. According to one observer, "An over-seer has to plan all the business and be with the negroes all the time. The negroes have great spite and hatred towards them and frequently fight them, when the over-seer pretends to whip them. The negroes think as meanly of the poor white people, as the rich white people do themselves and think anybody that is so poor as to be an overseer mean enough."[53] Hundreds of overseers were beaten, poisoned, stabbed, and shot by rebellious slaves.[54]

The overseer was the weakest link in the chain of plantation management. Whatever his character, it was impossible for the overseer to supervise every detail of the slave's life. Most men were unwilling to lead the kind of solitary life that plantation management demanded. Consequently, most overseers left the plantations periodically at night or on the weekends in order to find some recreation for themselves. Overwhelmed by a multitude of duties, the overseer could not be everywhere at once and consequently could not keep the slaves under constant surveillance. If he happened to be lazy, the level of surveillance was even lower.[55]

As a result of the differences in the characters of overseers and masters, many plantations deviated strikingly from the ideal outlined in the rules of management. According to the investigations of H. Herbemont of South Carolina, "there are very few planters who have anything like a regular system for either the moral

52. Ulrich B. Phillips, ed., *Plantation and Frontier* (2 vols., Cleveland, 1910), I, 170.

53. Martha Van Briesen, ed., *The Letters of Elijah Fletcher* (Charlottesville, 1965), 23.

54. Herbert Aptheker, *American Negro Slave Revolts* (New York, 1943); Phillips, *Plantation,* II, 117-25.

55. Charles S. Sydnor, "A Slave Owner and His Overseers," *North Carolina Historical Review* XIV (Jan. 1937), 31-38.

or physical government of their slaves." A writer in the *American Farmer* agreed: "There is in fact little or no '*system*' of management in regard to our slaves—they are insubordinate and *unmanageable.*"[56]

Even when attempts were made to govern the slaves in some systematic fashion, the planters realized that since the slaves had not internalized their ideals they had to make several compromises in order to maintain the facade of absolute control.[57] First, they recognized that their slaves differed in temperament and intelligence. For instance, one planter asserted: "In every servants' quarters there are the strong and the weak, the sagacious and the simple." Second, since they differed so much in character, all slaves could not be treated in the same manner. The most strong-willed and shrewdest slaves received better treatment than most others and were given positions of power in the plantation hierarchy. The intractable slave was either sold or never molested. Planters spotted him quickly, and, inevitably, they were forced by him to be wary. There were certainly many masters who were cautious with slaves like Louis Manigault's Jack Savage. According to Manigault, Jack "was the only negro ever in our possession who I considered capable of murdering me or burning my dwelling at night or capable of committing any act."[58]

Planters often maintained the appearance of strict obedience by making it relatively easy for the slave to obey. Regardless of their desires, most masters realized that the slaves, like soldiers, were adept at "goldbricking." Once the slaves decided how much labor they were going to perform, they refused to work any harder. One slaveholder observed: "Experience has long since taught masters, that every attempt to force a slave beyond the limits that he fixes as a sufficient amount of labor to render his

56. *Southern Agriculturalist* IX (Feb. 1836), 71; *American Farmer,* II (March 16, 1821), 402.

57. J. Brown, *Slave Life,* 82-109; William Green, *Narrative of Events in the Life of William Green* (Springfield, O., 1863), 13.

58. *DeBow's Review* XXIX (Sept. 1860), 362; Manigault quoted in Taylor, *South Carolina,* 177.

Figures 51, 52, 53, 54. Sugar Plantation

master, instead of extorting more work, only tends to make him unprofitable, unmanageable, a vexation and a curse."[59]

It was primarily because the planters recognized that slaves voluntarily limited their work that many of them set the standard of labor so low that every slave could meet it. Even when every allowance is made for different strains of certain crops, it is impossible to explain the variations in labor performed from plantation to plantation without recognition of the slave's role in restricting his output. Examine, for instance, the average amount of cotton picked per day by an adult slave. Between 1825 and 1860 slaves in Mississippi generally picked between 130 and 150 pounds of cotton per day. On Charles Whitmore's delta plantation, however, few slaves picked more than 100 pounds of cotton daily. The slave's limitation on the labor he performed appears clearly in the results of races arranged by planters. In a race on a Mississippi plantation in 1830 fourteen slaves picked an average of 323 pounds of cotton, twice their normal average.[60] Many planters gave prizes to the best cotton pickers in an effort to speed up the work. While this was often effective, many slaves still refused to exert themselves.[61]

The slaveholder also kept up the pretense of absolute control by refusing to take note of every deviation from the rules. In effect, each planter had to learn to be selectively inattentive to rules infractions. A group of Alabama planters gave sound advice on this point: "Negroes lack the motive of self interest to make them careful and diligent, hence the necessity of great patience in the management of them. Do not, therefore, notice too many small omissions of duty."[62]

The personal relations between master and slave were strained. Rarely did their interests coincide. Because of this, the master

59. "Negro Slavery at the South," *DeBow's Review* VII (Sept. 1849), 220.

60. Mark Swearingen, "Thirty Years of a Mississippi Plantation: Charles Whitmore of Montpelier," *Journal of Southern History* I (May 1935), 198-211; Davis, "Barrow," 431-46; Kathryn T. Abbey, ed., "Documents Relating to El Destino and Chemonie Plantations, Middle Florida, 1828-1868," *Florida Historical Quarterly* VII (Jan. 1929), 179-213.

61. *American Farmer* VII (Jan. 13, 1826), 338.

62. *DeBow's Review* XVIII (June 1855), 718.

Figures 55, 56. Rice Plantation

used physical force to make the slave obedient. The personal relations on the plantation, however, were much more complicated than a simple relationship between subordinate and superordinate. In the first place, all masters did not demand ritual deference at all times to bolster their self-esteem. Second, the same obsequious behavior was not demanded of ordinary slaves and those in positions of trust. Sir Charles Lyell observed that the latter group of slaves were "involuntarily treated more as equals by the whites." Even when all slaves had to be deferential, whites did not require them to go through the ritual at all times. For example, Susan Dabney Smedes wrote that during Christmas "there was an affectionate throwing off of the reserve and decorum of every-day life."[63]

While a planter could demand obedience, he could not always obtain the slave's respect. Samuel Meredith complained in 1774 that one of his slaves had told a group of whites that "I am not worthy to be his Master." Sir Charles Lyell reported that frequently in conversing with an intelligent black driver, "This personage, conscious of his importance, would begin by enlarging, with much self-complacency, on the ignorance of his master. . . ." Such slaves gave deference only as a result of fear. They refused to identify with the planter's interest or to work unless they were watched. One of John B. Lamar's carpenters, Ned, was typical of this class. Lamar refused to send Ned off the plantation to construct buildings because of "his general character for intemperance, & disobedience, & quarrelsomeness. . . . He is an eye servant. If I was with him I could have the work done soon and cheap, but I am afraid to trust him off where there is no one he fears."[64]

The Southern white man's perceptions of slave behavior make one point quite clear: the planter recognized the variability of slave personality in his day-to-day relationships. In reality, he had to make several compromises in order to maintain the facade of absolute control. He often "bought off" the strongest slaves by

63. Charles Lyell, *A Second Visit to the United States of North America* (2 vols., New York, 1850), II, 19-20; Smedes, *Memorials*, 162.

64. Quoted in Phillips, *Plantation*, II, 82; Lyell, *Second Visit*, II, 19.

placing them in the plantation hierarchy, was selectively inattentive to rules infractions, and accepted the slave's definition of how much labor he would perform. There was so little identification with the master's interest in the quarters that he frequently had to resort to coercion and to more and more oppressive laws. There were so many differences among slaveholders and the legal sanctions of slavery were applied in so many different ways that the regimen to which the slave was subjected varied considerably. If the masters' portrait of actual slave behavior is any guide, there was considerable variation in slave personalities.

8

Slave Personality Types

> Blows and insults he bore, at the moment, without resentment; deep but suppressed emotion, rendered him insensible to their sting; but it was afterward, when the memory of them went seething through his brain, breeding a fiery indignation at his injured self-hood, that the resolve came to resist, and the time fixed to resist, and the time fixed when to resist, and the plot laid, how to resist; and he always kept his self-pledged word. In what he undertook, in this line, he looked fate in the face, and had a cool, keen look at the relation of means to ends.
>
> James McCune Smith

The plantation was a battlefield where slaves fought masters for physical and psychological survival. Although unlettered, unarmed, and outnumbered, slaves fought in various ways to preserve their manhood. Several factors exerted a powerful influence on this struggle. The slave's parents, relatives, conjurers, religion, and the size of his master's plantation—all played some role in the formation of his character and affected behavior in the quarters.

In analyzing slave behavior, it is possible to utilize several psychological theories. The most useful of them, however, is Harry Stack Sullivan's "interpersonal theory." Sullivan argued that the "significant others," or persons with most power to reward and punish, are primarily responsible for the way people behave. Crucial to Sullivan's theory is the concept of the self which he defined as "the content of consciousness at all times when one is thoroughly comfortable about one's self-respect, the prestige that one enjoys among one's fellows, and the respect and deference which they pay one."[1] Interpersonal theorists argue that behavioral patterns are determined by the characteristics of the situation, how the person perceives them, and his behavioral dispositions at the time.[2] Despite the emphasis on variability, in interpersonal theory childhood is the most crucial of the personality eras. The general style of behavior adopted in childhood tends to be self-perpetuating. The person's first, most important, and enduring concept of himself develops during childhood as a result of his parents treating him as a unique, thoroughly lovable individual.

From the outset, the most important component of personality is self-esteem. Our sense of self-esteem is heightened or lowered by our perception of the images others have of us. Few adults, however, are solely dependent on the way others see them for their conception of themselves. In other words, one enters into every adult interpersonal relationship with some preconceived ideas of what kind of person he is. The most favorable aspect of this is the high opinion of ourselves which we have formed from interacting with our parents.[3] Sullivan, for example, observed that when everything else fails to preserve one's self-esteem, "membership in that family, which makes one unique and distinguishes one on the basis of the very early valuation, would be a treasured possession."[4]

Interpersonal behavior generally revolves around the dominant-submissive, hate-love axes. One form of behavior tends to elicit its complement: dominance leads to submission and vice versa. The extent of submissiveness often depends on the structure of the group to which the person belongs. The unique norms or subculture of the group, its size, the spatial arrange-

1. H. S. Sullivan, "A Theory of Interpersonal Relations: The Illusion of Personal Individuality," in Hendrik M. Ruitenbeek, ed., *Varieties of Personality Theories* (New York, 1964), 140.

2. Robert C. Carson, *Interaction Concepts of Personality* (Chicago, 1969), 26; Ruitenbeek, *Varieties*, 139-40.

3. Carson, *Interaction*, 8-57; Michael Argyle, *The Psychology of Interpersonal Behavior* (Baltimore, 1967), 117-32; Peter B. Warr and Christopher Knapper, *The Perception of People and Events* (New York, 1968), 245-54.

4. Ruitenbeek, *Varieties*, 148.

ments, frequency of interaction, and the superordinate's ability to observe the subordinates all affect the degree of submission. In institutions there is a formal pattern for exercising authority (tone of voice, facial expressions, phrases, physical violence) and giving deference (obsequious behavior, bowing, tipping hat, downcast look, etc.) Studies of industrial organizations have shown that members of smaller groups tend to internalize more of the expectations of those in power and to comply more fully with their demands than members of larger ones. Behavior in these organizations varies from friendly to aggressive dominance, and from hostile submissiveness to docility. A person may identify with the dominant person either because of affection or fear. In the latter case the identification or internalization of the ideals of the dominant person is directed toward avoiding punishment and is on a rather shallow level.

The extent of surveillance is the key to internalization. If the superordinate feels that the subordinate has internalized the submissive role, he feels no compulsion to continue surveillance beyond the initial stage ("Though I'm not around my daughter will not drink because I have taught her to abstain from alcoholic beverages"). On the other hand, if the superordinate believes that the subordinate has not internalized the role, he is compelled to continue surveillance indefinitely.[5]

The same pattern holds for the exercise of coercive power. Initially the superordinate threatens and punishes the subordinate to ensure behavioral conformity to the submissive role. If the subordinate internalizes the submissive role in the initial stages, the superordinate does not have to rely on threats and punishments later. In other words, the frequent resort to coercion in interpersonal relations indicates that the low power person has not fully accepted his submissive role. Peter Blau noted this when he declared that "coercive force, which can hardly be

5. Stanley Milgram, "Behavioral Study of Obedience," in Warren G. Bennis *et al.*, eds., *Interpersonal Dynamics* (Homewood, Ill., 1964), 110; Abraham Zaleznik and David Moment, *The Dynamics of Interpersonal Behavior* (New York, 1964), 179-213, 256-86; Carson, *Interaction*, 57-92, 122-71; Erving Goffman, *Interaction Ritual: Essays on Face-to-Face Behavior* (Garden City, N.Y., 1967), 60.

resisted, is important as a last resort for exercising power over individuals who cannot otherwise be made to yield."[6] An illustration of this appears in the parent-child relationship. Parents frequently punish their young children for lying and stealing but later, when the parental value of honesty has been internalized, they no longer have to rely on coercive power. But, if the values have not been internalized, the parents have to threaten and punish the child continually to ensure behavioral conformity.[7] Such a situation reveals a diminution in power. Blau clearly demonstrates this:

> If an individual has much power over others, which means that they are obligated to and dependent on him for greatly needed benefits, they will be eager to do his bidding and anticipate his wishes in order to maintain his good will, particiularly if there are still others who compete for the benefits he supplies them. If an individual has little power over others, however, they will be less concerned with pleasing him, and he may even have to remind them that they owe it to him to follow his requests. Such reminders demonstrate to them that he really needs the services they render him, just as they need his services, which implies that the relation between him and them is not one of unequal power but one of egalitarian exchange. Great inequality of power typically obviates the need for such reminders. . . .[8]

While psychologists have found that a superordinate's reliance on coercive power (threats and violent punishment) generally leads to the subordinate's compliance, they have been unable to show that compliant behavior is necessarily an indication of internalization or of inner feelings. Feelings and attitudes, of

6. Peter M. Blau, *Exchange and Power in Social Life* (New York, 1967), 125.

7. Herbert C. Kelman, "Compliance, Identification, and Internalization: Three Processes of Attitude Change," in Harold Proshansky and Bernard Seidenberg, eds., *Basic Studies in Social Psychology* (New York, 1965), 140-48; Amitai Etzioni, "Organization Dimensions and Their Interrelationships: A Theory of Compliance," in Bernard P. Indik and F. Kenneth Berrien, eds., *People, Groups, and Organizations* (New York, 1968), 94-109; Rose Laub Coser, "Insulation from Observability and Types of Social Conformity," *American Sociological Review* XXVI (Feb. 1969), 28-39.

8. Blau, *Exchange*, 134-35.

course, are private and only partially communicable. Still, most powerless individuals comply with the demands of the powerful persons with whom they interact (parent-child, boss-employee). The need to internalize the submissive role, however, may be limited by several factors. First, the superordinate may be more interested in the behavior than in the inner feelings of the subordinate ("I don't care what you think as long as you do as I tell you"). Second, and most important, if the subordinate is not kept under constant surveillance, he can "play at" the role during the superordinate's rare direct observations and, when free of surveillance, behave in a decidedly different manner.

The subordinate may give deference at no emotional cost. He may, for instance, truly believe the superordinate worthy of his respect. If not, he may feign respect through the ritual of deference in spite of his low opinion of the superordinate. The subordinate is able to practice this deception because the superordinate frequently demands submission and deferential behavior more for an audience than for himself. For this reason, and often to maintain his belief in himself as a person worthy of respect, the superordinate may read more into a deferential act than the subordinate means to convey (misperception) or overlook minor lapses (selective inattention) in the submissive role played by the subordinate.[9] Taking advantage of the superordinate's misperception, the subordinate may overact, being very submissive and deferential, to deceive or to show his inner contempt for the superordinate and to preserve his own autonomy.[10] In this regard, Erving Goffman argues: "By easily showing a regard that he does not have, the actor (subordinate) can feel that he is preserving a kind of inner autonomy." The rituals of deference are fleeting, highly formalized, almost unconscious acts which are

9. Goffman, *Ritual*, 5-95; Richard M. Emerson, "Power-Dependence Relations," *American Sociological Review* XXVII (Feb. 1962), 31-41; Edgar F. Borgatta, "Role-Playing Specification, Personality and Performance," *Sociometry* XXIV (Sept. 1961), 218-33; R. D. Laing, H. Phillipson, and A. R. Lee, *Interpersonal Perception* (New York, 1966), 3-8.

10. Emerson, "Power-Dependence Relations," 31-41; Carl W. Backman and Paul F. Secord, "Liking, Selective Interaction, and Misperception in Congruent Interpersonal Relations," *Sociometry* XXV (Dec. 1962), 321-35.

often performed without too much psychological cost to the subordinate. This is especially true in institutions. Goffman asserts: "Where ceremonial practices (of deference) are thoroughly institutionalized . . . it would appear easy to be a person."[11]

The subordinate, often having to curb or repress his anger, may become excessively submissive, or he may focus his hostile feelings on a scapegoat, or make jokes which express his aggressive feelings toward the superordinate to avoid total dependency. Throughout this discussion, it must be remembered that every individual, however submissive he may be in one interpersonal relationship, interacts with other people where he is the dominant one. The greater the number of the latter, the less impact any one submissive stance makes on his personality.[12] In this regard, Sullivan has correctly observed that "every human being has as many personalities as he has interpersonal relations. . . ."[13]

Practically all interpersonal relationships leave the subordinate with some independence, some power, some resources as long as he possesses something valued by the superordinate, whether it be labor or deference. McCall and Simmons noted this fact in their study of social interaction: "there are always some resources and choices open even to the most abject slave."[14]

In order to understand the resources and choices theoretically open to Southern slaves, it is necessary to examine "total" institutions. A total institution is a complex organization in which permanent or semi-permanent personal relationships are determined primarily by the demands, rules, and objectives of the organization, institutional roles are reinforced by ritual deference, rewards, and punishments, most of the needs of members are satisfied, and members are set apart (spatially and socially) in various ways from non-members. Psychological studies of com-

11. Goffman, *Ritual*, 58, 91.

12. Carson, *Interaction*, 93-171; Zaleznik and Moment, *Behavior*, 173-372; Bruce J. Biddle and Edwin J. Thomas, *Role Theory: Concepts and Research* (New York, 1966), 144-48, 195-200, 282-87, 313-17.

13. Ruitenbeek, *Varieties*, 143.

14. George J. McCall and J. L. Simmons, *Identities and Interactions* (New York, 1966), 157.

pliance in such total institutions as concentration camps, prisons, and armies have shown that there is a close relationship between the kind of coercion, pain, torture, or threat of bodily harm that men are exposed to and their ability to resist the institutional norms. On the one hand, the "cruel" treatment (starvation, daily torture, and murder) that concentration camp inmates received caused them to be extremely submissive, infantile, and docile. On the other, the "mild" treatment (relatively adequate food and rare punishment) of prisoners and soldiers led them to be deferential toward their superordinates while rejecting their norms and participating in underground resistance to them. In fact, in institutions where superordinates are not so devoid of moral sense and so free of societal restraints that they can frequently kill subordinates, it would appear virtually impossible to crush all dissent, insubordination, rebellion, independence, and manhood in the organization's members. When the plantation is viewed as a total institution, it is obvious that the slave's personality was intimately bound up with the use of coercive power by his master.[15]

According to the black autobiographers, one of the most important factors affecting their struggle for personal autonomy was the frequency and the nature of the punishment meted out by masters and overseers. In his lifetime a slave usually had several owners; the black autobiographers included in this study had an average of three. While eight of the autobiographers had only one master, Charles Ball and William Grimes had eight and Moses Roper a phenomenal fourteen. As a consequence of having an average of three masters, the slaves were extremely conscious of the differences in human character and contended that there was great variety among slaveholders. Henry Clay Bruce was typical. He wrote that his experience with many slaveholders: "taught him that all masters were not cruel. . . . While

15. Paul de Berker, ed., *Interaction: Human Groups in Community and Institution* (Oxford, Eng., 1969), 7-30; Amitai Etzioni, *A Comparative Analysis of Complex Organizations* (New York, 1961); Erving Goffman, *Asylums* (Garden City, N.Y., 1961), 1-74; see appendix I.

some masters cruelly whipped, half fed and overworked their slaves, there were many others who provided for their slaves with fatherly care, saw that they were well fed and clothed, would neither whip them themselves, nor permit others to do so."[16] Differences in severity of treatment affected behavior on the plantation in the same way that they determined the degree of docility and infantilism in prisons, armies, and concentration camps. Cruel masters caused one kind of behavioral pattern while kind or benevolent masters caused another in the quarters.

The slaves reacted in various ways to humane treatment. Generally, the master's kindness, confidence, and trust was repaid by faithful work on the part of the slave.[17] Bruce argued that a good master made slaves industrious and trustworthy: "The master who treated his slaves humanely had less trouble, got better service from them, and could depend upon their doing his work faithfully, even in his absence, having his interest in view always."[18] Robert Anderson agreed; on his plantation the slaves "were willing to put our best into the tasks when we were treated humanely."[19] Often the slaves were content with such masters. William Grimes demonstrated this clearly when he asserted: "Those slaves who have kind masters are, perhaps, as happy as the generality of mankind. They are not aware that their condition can be better, and I don't know as it can. . . ."[20]

Many slaves identified their own interests with that of a kind master and worked diligently for him. They respected him and

16. Henry Clay Bruce, *The New Man. Twenty-nine Years a Slave. Twenty-nine Years a Free Man* (York, Pa., 1895), iii.

17. Samuel Hall, 47 *Years a Slave* (Washington, Iowa, 1912), n.p.; Solomon Northup, *Twelve Years a Slave* (London, 1853), 78-104; Charles Ball, *Slavery in the United States: A Narrative of the Life and Adventures of Charles Ball* (Lewiston, Pa., 1836), 250-300; Jermain Wesley Loguen, *The Rev. J. W. Loguen, as a Slave and as a Freedman* (Syracuse, N.Y., 1859), 136-62, 178-211; William Wells Brown, *Narrative of William W. Brown, a Fugitive Slave* (Boston, 1847), 102-3; John Brown, *Slave Life in Georgia* (London, 1855), 158.

18. Bruce, *New Man,* 88.

19. Robert Anderson, *From Slavery to Affluence* (Hemingford, Neb., 1927), 32.

20. William Grimes, *Life of William Grimes the Runaway Slave, Brought Down to the Present Time* (New Haven, 1855), 36-48.

refused to steal from him or to lie to him. Lucius H. Holsey exemplified the slave's sense of identity with a kind master. His last owner was very kind, he wrote, and "had great confidence in me and trusted me with money and other valuables. In all things I was honest and true to him and his interests. Though young, I felt as much interest in his well being as I have felt since in my own. . . . I made a special point never to lie to him or deceive him in any way."[21]

Slaves identified with their owners for several reasons. Many, for example, worked faithfully for their masters because they expected to be freed at some future date. They were sometimes loyal because masters catered to their vanity or desire to stand out from the mass of slaves. With house servants this was often a matter of receiving fancy clothes. Louis Hughes, for instance, declared when his master gave him some new clothes, "I had known no comforts, and had been so cowed and broken in spirits, by cruel lashings, that I really felt light-hearted at this improvement in my personal appearance, although it was merely for the gratification of my master's pride; and I thought I would do all I could to please Boss."[22] One of the most frequent reasons for the slave's industriousness was the feeling that he had a stake in the successful completion of his work. Many slaves developed this feeling because the planters promised them money, gifts, dinners, and dances if they labored faithfully.[23]

Simple kindness did much to engender respect. John Mercer Langston's father, for instance, "gained the respect and confidence of all, and might very well trust his people, as was his habit, to govern and direct, largely, their own movements."[24] Robert Anderson recalled that his master "was a very easy going man, kind and generous, and loved by all the plantation people.

21. Lucius H. Holsey, *Autobiography, Sermons, Addresses, and Essays* (Atlanta, 1898), 10.

22. Louis Hughes, *Thirty Years a Slave* (Milwaukee, 1897), 63-64.

23. Ball, *Slavery*, 112-56; Henry Box Brown, *Narrative of Henry Box Brown* (Boston, 1851), 23-38; Hughes, *Thirty Years*, 39-58.

24. John Mercer Langston, *From the Virginia Plantation to the National Capitol* (Hartford, 1894), 17.

We colored folks did what he ask us to because we liked him."[25] On plantations where they were treated humanely, the slaves sometimes looked upon their master almost as a kindly father. Richard Allen described his master as "more like a father to his slaves than anything else. He was a very tender, humane man."[26] W. H. Robinson asserted that one of his masters "was a very kind, fatherly acting man."[27] One of Frederick Douglass's mistresses was so "kind, gentle and cheerful" that he "soon learned to regard her as something more akin to a mother, than a slave-holding mistress."[28]

Rarely did the slave identify with a master who frequently flogged and abused him. Even so, on plantations where masters and overseers were almost as morally insensitive, cruel, and sadistic as the guards in the German concentration camps, many of the slaves became docile, submissive, and Sambo-like. At the same time, unless the slave belonged to a planter who was mentally deranged, he had more elbow room than the German concentration camp inmates. In contrast to the camp inmate, the slave had greater freedom from the threat of death and had less need for abject servility in order to avoid it. Besides, unlike the camp inmate, the slave's life was worth considerably more than a bullet. Ultimately, this fact set limits on the amount of cruelty to which a slave was subjected. Within these limits, however, on many plantations abuse, constant floggings, cruelty, overwork, and short rations were part of the slave's daily life.

Faced with unrelenting cruelty and depressed at every turn, many of the slaves despaired of resisting abuse, lived in deadly fear of all whites, and soon lost all feeling of independence, self-respect, and sympathy for others.[29] Henry Bibb spoke for many

25. Anderson, *From Slavery*, 19.

26. Richard Allen, *The Life, Experience, and Gospel Labors of the Rt. Rev. Richard Allen* . . . (Philadelphia, 1887), 6.

27. W. H. Robinson, *From Log Cabin to the Pulpit* (Eau Claire, Wis., 1913), 73.

28. Frederick Douglass, *My Bondage and My Freedom* (New York, 1968 [1855]), 142.

29. Elizabeth Keckley, *Behind The Scenes* (New York, 1868), 29-38; Moses Roper, *A Narrative of the Adventures and Escape of Moses Roper from*

Figure 57. Frederick Douglass

when he declared that "It is useless for a poor helpless slave to resist a white man in a slaveholding state." The slave, subjected to the will of others "in all respects whatsoever," had, he declared, a feeling "of utter helplessness."[30] After describing an extremely cruel beating, Thomas Jones asked: "Is it any wonder that the spirit of self-respect of the poor, ignorant slave is broken

American Slavery (London, 1840), 56-61, 70-99; Austin Steward, *Twenty-two Years a Slave, and Forty Years a Freeman* (Rochester, N.Y., 1861), 13-19; James Watkins, *Narrative of the Life of James Watkins* (Bolton, Eng., 1852), 12-18.

30. Henry Bibb, *Narrative of the Life and Adventures of Henry Bibb, an American Slave* (New York, 1849), 317-19.

Figure 58. Austin Steward

down by such treatment of unsparing and persevering cruelty?"[31]

The lash, frequently applied, was an awesomely successful fear-inducing instrument. James Mars received many floggings from his master of whom he "thought a great deal," but he also "stood greatly in fear of him and dreaded his displeasure, for I did not like the lash."[32] Henry Watson testified that all of his

31. Thomas Jones, *The Experience of Thomas Jones, Who Was a Slave for Forty-three Years* (Boston, 1850), 17.

32. James Mars, *Life of James Mars, a Slave Born and Sold in Connecticut* (Hartford, 1864), 21-22.

fellow slaves feared his mistress because of her frequent use of the lash, and, "as for myself, I was perfectly terrified when she approached."[33] Frederick Douglass asserted that slaves were "accustomed from childhood and through life to cower before a driver's lash."[34] Sometimes the fear of punishment became unbearable. Lewis Clarke reported that he was so afraid of being flogged that he often walked in his sleep. Other slaves mutilated themselves or committed suicide rather than submit to painful floggings.[35]

Unremitting cruelty often subdued the slave and broke his will to resist. Charles Ball saw one slave whose spirit was so broken by the lash "that he was ready to suffer and to bear all his hardships; not indeed without complaining, but without attempting to resist his oppressors, or to escape from their power." The lash, frequently applied, often drained every ounce of manhood, of resistance, of self-respect, and of independence from the slave. Six months under a Negro breaker, Frederick Douglass declared, "succeeded in breaking me. I was broken in body, soul and spirit." William Wells Brown saw one proud black turned into a "degraded and spirit-crushed" man by three months of daily floggings and unremitting labor. Austin Steward contended that slavery was such a cruel institution that it "crushes and brutalizes the wretched slave." Josiah Henson argued that the slaveholders' tyrannical treatment turned "the slave into the cringing, treacherous, false, and thieving victim of tyranny."[36]

Often when his own punishment or the flogging of his fellows was practically an everyday occurrence, the slave grew indifferent to human sufferings. Sometimes he taunted those slaves who made unsuccessful attempts to escape or who were punished.

33. Henry Watson, *Narrative of Henry Watson, a Fugitive Slave* (Boston, 1848), 23.

34. Douglass, *Bondage,* 120.

35. Ball, *Slavery,* 40-74, 245-58; Keckley, *Scenes,* 29-34; Grimes, *Life,* 24-33; Lewis G. Clarke, *Narrative of the Sufferings of Lewis Clarke* (Boston, 1845), 107-22.

36. Ball, *Slavery,* 89; Douglass, *Bondage,* 219; W. W. Brown, *Narrative,* 29; Steward, *Twenty-two Years.* 26; Josiah Henson, *The Life of Josiah Henson* (Boston, 1849), 5.

Henry Watson, after years of service under cruel masters, finally reached the point where "his heart began to grow less feeling for the sufferings of others, and even indifferent to my own punishment."[37] Jermain Loguen gave a perfect description of the slave's lot under a cruel master. Under his master, he

> had been driven along from day to day by dread of physical suffering, and the hope of escape from it. His affections were not allowed a moment's repose. It was ever a fearful looking for outrage of some kind, attended by an impractical determination not to bear it. His highest aim was to dodge the lash of a tyrant—his daily prayer, that his mother, sisters and brothers might not be subjects of new wrongs. So habited was he to wrongs, that he met them without disappointment, and endured them without complaint.[38]

Added to the slave's fear of the lash was the dread of being separated from loved ones. To be sold away from his relatives or stand by and see a mother, a sister, a brother, a wife, or a child torn away from him was easily the most traumatic event of his life. Strong men pleaded, with tears in their eyes, for their master to spare their loved ones. Mothers screamed and clung grimly to their children only to be kicked away by the slave trader. Others lost their heads and ran off with their children or vainly tried to fight off overseer, master, and slave trader. Angry, despondent, and overcome by grief, the slaves frequently never recovered from the shock of separation. Many became morose and indifferent to their work. Others went insane, talked to themselves, and had hallucinations about their loved ones. A few slaves developed suicidal tendencies. William Wells Brown described one slave woman who was so despondent over being forced to leave her husband that she drowned herself. Separation in many cases caused the slave to decide to run away and obtain his freedom. For most of the slaves, however, there was no recourse but to accept the inevitable.[39] Samuel Hall's reaction was probably typi-

37. Watson, *Narrative*, 32.

38. Loguen, *Freedman*, 162.

39. John Quincy Adams, *Narrative of the Life of John Quincy Adams, When in Slavery, and Now as a Freeman* (Harrisburg, Pa., 1872), 22-30;

cal. When he was sold away from his wife and children, he wrote that "His soul rebelled against such subservience to men who called themselves masters and his temper was aroused to such a pitch that he was like a wild animal in a cage, conscious, in a way, of the hopelessness of his situation, but none the less tamed, or willing to admit that he was justly restrained."[40]

The hopelessness of slavery occasionally caused mental illness in the quarters and led to the inclusion of bondsmen among the insane and idiotic persons enumerated in the United States censuses. Throughout the South the insane and idiotic were under reported during the antebellum period. But since masters had less shame in noting the insane and idiotic among their slaves than in their own families, the blacks may have been more completely enumerated than whites. Required to guarantee that slaves were of sound mind when selling them, the planters kept a close watch on the quarters in an effort to detect mental illness. They were all the more interested in recording mental defectives among slaves because mental diseases affected a slave's capacity for work and posed a danger to the life and property of the planter. Consequently, bondsmen who were of "unsound mind," or "deranged," "insane," and "demented" appear in wills, succession papers, sales receipts, judicial proceedings, and planter lists of slaves. Most mentally ill slaves were not committed to asylums or prisons unless they were especially dangerous. As a result of the general exclusion of insane bondsmen from institutions, the census takers found most of them on their masters' plantations.[41]

Although some slaves feigned insanity, enough reports of ac-

John Anderson, *The Story of the Life of John Anderson, a Fugitive Slave* (London, 1863), 8-20; William Green, *Narrative of Events in the Life of William Green* (Springfield, O., 1863), 6-8; Peter Randolph, *Sketches of Slave Life* (Boston, 1855), 16-19; Jacob Stroyer, *My Life in the South* (Salem, 1890), 41-44.

40. Hall, 47 *Years*, n.p.

41. Kenneth Stampp, *The Peculiar Institution* (New York, 1956), 305; Leslie Howard Owens, *This Species of Property* (New York, 1976), 3-4, 44-46; Joe Gray Taylor, *Negro Slavery in Louisiana* (Baton Rouge, 1963), 121-22; William D. Postell, *The Health of Slaves on Southern Plantations* (Baton Rouge, 1951), 86-87; Todd L. Savitt, *Medicine and Slavery* (Urbana, 1978), 247-54, 274-79.

Figure 59. Solomon Northup

tual cases have survived to suggest some causal linkages between the treatment slaves received and mental disease in the quarters. Birth defects resulting from inadequate prenatal care, organic diseases, and dietary deficiencies took their toll on the mental health of slaves. The greatest causes of mental illness in the quarters, however, were excessive punishment and the separation of family members. Susan Boggs, a former Virginia slave, recalled in 1863 a slave woman "who went crazy because her two sons were sold and sent to the trader's jail. She went up and down the streets, crying like an animal." A Kentucky slave reported that after his mother was sold her new master

> sent her to prison, and had her flogged, and punished in various ways, so that at last she began to have crazy turns. . . . She tried to kill herself several times, once with a knife and once by hanging. She had long, straight black hair, but after this it all turned white, like an old person's. When she had her raving turns she always talked about her children. The jailer told the owner that if he would let her go to her children, perhaps she would get quiet.
>
> They let her out one time, and she came to the place where we were. I might have been seven or eight years old. . . . I was not at home when she came. I came in and found her in one of the cabins near the kitchen. She sprung and caught my arms, and seemed going to break them and then said, "I'll fix *you* so they'll never get you!" I screamed, for I thought she was going to kill me; they came in and took me away. They tied her, and carried her off.

The Reverend Francis Hawley described a similar case in North Carolina:

> One of my neighbors sold to a speculator a negro boy, about 14 years old. It was more than his poor mother could bear. Her reason fled, and she became a perfect *maniac*, and had to be kept in close confinement. She would occasionally get out and run off to the neighbors. On one of these occasions she came to my house. She was indeed a pitiable object. With tears rolling down her cheeks, and her frame shaking with agony, she would cry out, *"don't you hear him—they are whipping him now, and he is calling for me!"*[42]

Systematic cruelty, repeated blows to the head, and frequent floggings often led to temporary or permanent insanity among slaves. Christopher Nichols described the effect of the numerous floggings he received in Virginia. After a sheep was stolen, he

42. John Blassingame, ed., *Slave Testimony* (Baton Rouge, 1977), 421, 696; Theodore Weld, ed., *Slavery as It Is: The Testimony of a Thousand Witnesses* (New York, 1839), 97; Norman R. Yetman, ed., *Voices from Slavery* (New York, 1970), 117; see also Savitt, *Medicine and Slavery*, 247-54.

Figure 60. Scars

was among those flogged: "I went up and pulled off my jacket,—they stripped me and whipped me until I fainted. . . . I was out of my head two or three days. . . . All the time I was in slavery, I lived in dead dread and fear. If I slept it was in dread—and in the morning it was dread—dread, night and day." The holocaust that was slavery never let the bondsmen rest easy at night; they were plagued with nightmares about the floggings they received. In Maryland, Nancy Howard reported that she "was frequently punished with raw hides,—was hit with tongs and poker and any thing. I used when I went out, to look up at the sky, and say, 'Blessed Lord, oh, do take me out of this!' It seemed to me I could not bear another lick. I can't forget it. I sometimes dream that I am pursued, and when I wake, I am scared almost to death."[43]

In spite of the psychological traumas the slaves endured, they consistently represented a smaller percentage of the insane and idiotic than they did of the total number of inhabitants in the South. For example, while constituting 32 per cent of the total population in the South in 1860, slaves constituted only 14.2 per cent of the insane and idiotic persons enumerated in the census. Even if we assume that there were *twice* as many insane and idiotic slaves as were enumerated, or 28.4 per cent of the total, the percentage of insane bondsmen would have been lower than the percentage of slaves in the total population. The probability of the reliability of the 1860 ratio when doubled is increased when the 1880 census is examined. With far more complete enumeration of blacks and whites than for the antebellum censuses, in 1880 blacks represented 24 per cent of the insane and idiotic persons enumerated in the South while representing 33 per cent of the total population in the region.[44]

Although comparatively few of the bondsmen were officially designated as being insane, the cruel separations and constant floggings created a sense of despair among many of the slaves that was all consuming. They saw no hope of improving their condition. As a young man, Frederick Douglass wrote: "To my bondage I saw no end. It was a terrible reality, and I shall never be able to tell how sadly that thought chafed my young spirit." Feeling that even God had forgotten them, the slaves tried to resign themselves to their bleak fate. Certainly many of them must have felt what Jermain Loguen expressed: "no day dawns

43. Benjamin Drew, ed., *The Refugee: A North-Side View of Slavery* (Reading, Mass., 1969), 35, 47-49.

44. Appendix III, tables 20, 21, 22, 23.

for the slave, nor is it looked for. It is all night—night forever."[45]

A number of the slaves were so oppressed that they accepted their master's claims about the rightness, the power, and the sanctity of whiteness and the degradation, the powerlessness, and the shame of blackness. As a result, some blacks wished passionately that they were white. James Watkins was treated so cruelly by his master that eventually, he declared: "I felt as though I had been unfortunate in being born black, and wished that I could by any means change my skin into a white one, feeling certain that I should then be free."[46]

The idea of the superiority of whites was etched into the slave's consciousness by the lash and the ritual respect he was forced to give to every white man. The impact of the planter's credo is revealed in the slave's reaction to kind and egalitarian treatment from whites. Jermain Loguen, who cried the first time he heard kindly words from whites, could not bear the thought of interacting with them on equal terms. Asked to play blind man's buff with a white girl, he was horrified: "Under any circumstances he could not address Alice but as a superior being. For so humble and degraded a thing as he, purposely to put his hand on her person, seemed to him like trespassing on an angel." Many others were uncomfortable interacting with whites on terms of equality. The first time this occurred it was especially traumatic for the slave. Famished John Brown was unable to eat the delicious meal offered to him by a Quaker family when he escaped from slavery because they insisted that he eat at the table with them: "I was so completely abashed, and felt so out of my element, that I had no eyes, no ears, no understanding. I was quite bewildered. As to eating, it was out of the question."[47]

Regardless of how the slave felt about white supremacy, he reacted to cues from whites. He had to be a lifelong student of the white man's moods, ideas, and actions and then conduct himself according to the changes in the white man's behavior. John Brown reported that as a slave he "had been forced to

45. Douglass, *Bondage,* 156; Loguen, *Freedman,* 329.
46. Watkins, *Narrative,* 11.
47. Loguen, *Freedman,* 187; J. Brown, *Slave Life,* 158.

watch the changes of my master's physiognomy, as well as those of the parties he associated with, so as to frame my conduct in accordance with what I had reason to believe was their prevailing mood at any given time." Jermain Loguen felt that all whites believed in maintaining the rituals of white supremacy, but "Whether they did or did not, it was all the same—for they ever acted upon that absurdity, and he was compelled to shape his life to it."[48]

Some slaves were compelled to shape their behavior so completely to the white man's moods that they became Sambos. Nowhere was Sambo more ubiquitous than among house servants and slaves on small plantations who lived in almost constant contact with whites. Because of the continual surveillance, these slaves had to go through the ritual of deference so often that they frequently internalized the submissive role. Often the master and slave lived and worked together on such intimate terms that they developed an affection for each other, and the slave identified completely with his master. Even if the slave initially had no affection for his master, the uninterrupted surveillance led so often to swift punishment for the smallest deviation from the submissive role that the domestic servant became extremely deferential and obsequious.[49]

It is no accident that the Sambo of Southern novels and plays was usually a house servant. Because the planters often had little contact with field hands, in white autobiographies it is almost always the house servant who is portrayed as the epitome of loyalty. While the personal history of a number of house servants appears in white autobiographies, the field slaves are usually por-

48. J. Brown, *Slave Life,* 106; Loguen, *Freedman,* 165.

49. Robert S. Starobin, ed., *Blacks in Bondage: Letters of American Slaves* (New York, 1974), 62-83; Orland K. Armstrong, ed., *Old Massa's People: The Old Slaves Tell Their Story* (Indianapolis, 1931), 35, 76, 100-121; Robert S. Starobin, "Privileged Bondsmen and the Process of Accommodation: The Role of Houseservants and Drivers as Seen in Their Own Letters," *Journal of Social History* V (Fall 1971), 46-70; Mrs. George P. Coleman, ed., *Virginia Silhouettes: Contemporary Letters Concerning Negro Slavery in the State of Virginia* (Richmond, 1934), 14-15, 27, 36, 38-40, 45-46; "A Peculiar People," *Southern Magazine,* XIII (Aug. 1873), 172-76.

trayed as an anonymous mass. One reflection of the faithfulness of house servants and the low level of contact between field hands and whites is that, in an overwhelming majority of the cases where masters manumitted individual slaves, they were house servants.[50]

Unlike the house servant, the typical field slave was sullenly obedient and hostilely submissive. He escaped from total dependency, infantilism, and abject docility, however, because the plantation, unlike the German concentration camp, was not a rationally organized institution capable of crushing all discontent, guaranteeing identification of the subordinate with superordinates, completely abolishing family life and alternative referents of self-esteem to those provided by the institution. Whatever stance the slave was forced to adopt, his master could not watch him all of the time or control his thoughts. Having a variety of relationships, besides that with his master, the slave was able to preserve his self-esteem in spite of the cruel punishment he received. The docility of the slave was a sham, a mask to hide his true feelings and personality traits. Since masters recognized the contradiction between how they wanted the slave to act and the slave's true personality, they often resorted to coercion to obtain the semblance of submission. Rarely did this coercion cause the slave to identify with the master. Whatever his behavior, the slave did not passively accept the portrait whites painted of him.

In spite of the ritual deference they gave to whites, the slaves frequently rejected the arguments of the Negro's inferiority and tried to prove that they were false. As a young slave, Austin Steward felt such charges were "utterly false." Jermain Loguen constantly heard claims about white superiority, but "Of course, he never believed in anything of the sort. . . ." Some blacks, distressed by the allegations of the Negro's dishonesty, stupidity, and indolence, tried to counter the charges by their own actions.

50. Letitia M. Burwell, *Plantation Reminiscences* (Owensboro, Ky., 1878), 4, 37, 159-61; J. G. Clinkscales, *On the Old Plantation* (Spartanburg, S.C., 1916), 8, 40-41; James Stirling, *Letters from the Slave States* (London, 1857), 287-88; Kemp P. Battle, *Memories of an Old-Time Tar Heel* (Chapel Hill, 1945), 125-31; George Lewis, *Impressions of America* (Edinburgh, 1845), 129, 144, 160.

Figure 61. Moses Roper Figure 62. Josiah Henson

Noah Davis was characteristic of many: "Nothing would mortify me as much, as to hear it said, 'A Negro can't be trusted.' This saying would always nerve me with a determination *to be trustworthy.*"[51]

The nature of Southern society prevented the slave's acceptance of all whites as superior beings. The poor whites, looked down upon and treated with contempt by the slaveholders, were viewed by the slave as lower in the scale of humanity than he was. Belonging to wealthy masters themselves, and frequently better fed, housed, and clothed than the poor whites, the slaves considered them far from superior beings. Instead, poor whites were the objects of ridicule, pity, and scorn in the quarters.[52] Henry Bibb felt that they were "generally ignorant, intemperate, licentious, and profane." Robinson reported that they were as il-

51. Steward, *Twenty-two Years,* 21; Loguen, *Freedman,* 165; Noah Davis, *A Narrative of the Life of Rev. Noah Davis, a Colored Man* (Baltimore, 1859), 16.

52. J. Brown, *Slave Life,* 62-68; R. Anderson, *From Slavery,* 26-30; Bibb, *Adventures,* 20-24; Steward, *Twenty-two Years,* 101-2; Robinson, *Pulpit,* 21-26; J. H. Banks, *A Narrative of Events of the Life of J. H. Banks* (Liverpool, 1861), 16.

literate and as oppressed as the Negroes: "When they went before their employer they put their hats under their arms, as any Negro would do, and usually they were as afraid of him as the Negro was of the overseer." Douglass declared that the poor whites were "the laughing stock" of the slaves. Robert Anderson wrote that in the quarters "the colored person who would associate with the 'po' white trash' were practically outcasts, and held in very great contempt." Henry Clay Bruce revealed the depth of this contempt when he slapped the son of a poor white, to whom he had been hired, for "saucing" him and then refused to let the man flog him. Many years later he wrote: "I would be ashamed of myself, even now, had I allowed that poor white man to whip me."[53]

Some slaves did not have to look to the poor whites to discover the false base of the white supremacy argument; they found it, instead, in the ignorance, indolence, and dissolution of their masters. Josiah Henson, for example, frequently carried his drunken master home "with the pride of conscious superiority" and increasingly, as he ran the plantation practically unaided, he came to feel that his master was "absolutely dependent upon his slave."[54]

Several factors prevented the slaves from regressing to infantilism and abject docility. First of all, most of them lived on plantations containing twenty or more slaves. On such plantations it was impossible for the planters or their overseers to supervise every detail of slave life, and many of the slaves on these plantations had few personal contacts with whites as long as their work was generally satisfactory. Consequently, these slaves (especially field hands) rarely had to go through the ritual of deference. Even when planters spent all of their time on the plantations they only saw the field slaves at work.[55]

53. Bibb, *Adventures,* 24; Robinson, *Pulpit,* 21; Douglass, *Bondage,* 344; R. Anderson, *From Slavery,* 29; Bruce, *New Man,* 66.

54. Henson, *Life,* 15, 21.

55. Stirling, *Letters,* 288; Alexander Mackay, *The Western World: Or Travels in the United States in 1846-47* (3 vols., Philadelphia, 1849), I, 282-87; Margaret Devereux, *Plantation Sketches* (Cambridge, Mass., 1906), 9-10, 34.

Figure 63. J. W. C. Pennington   Figure 64. Henry Bibb

Often slaves did not have to be docile because it was more important to a planter that they adhere strictly to the rules of deference when other whites were around than when he was alone with them. Henry Clay Bruce reported that his owner, for instance, was a kind master who rarely required his slaves to assume a deferential posture. Yet, "he tried to appear to his neighbors what he was not, a hard master . . . in the presence of a neighbor he always scolded more, acted more crabbed, and he was harder to please than when alone with us, for as soon as the neighbor left, we could get along with him very well."[56]

It is obvious that many of the slaves recognized the customary deferential act for what it was, a ritual. It was so customary for many of them that they thought little about it. Since it was a habitual mode of behavior, many did not view the deferential act as a symbol of their degradation. Sometimes, in fact, they viewed it as one means of influencing their masters. Charles Ball, for example, reported that the slaves always had to approach their masters humbly, "but, in return, we generally received words of kindness, and very often a redress of our grievances." When

56. Bruce, *New Man*, 84.

Israel Campbell thought that his master was going to punish him, he became very humble. "I knew," he wrote, "that the best way to get around master was to be very humble . . . I set my wits to work to find out something that would please him."[57]

Another factor which sometimes contributed to the slave's self-esteem was his relationship with whites other than his master. Even when he had a cruel master, he might associate with other whites who treated him with kindness. Such associations elevated his self-respect and confidence.[58] While working in his master's store, Thomas Jones developed a very close relationship with one of the white clerks. "I seemed to be lifted up by this noble friend at times, from the dark despair which settled down upon my life, and to be joined once more to a living hope of future improvement in my sad lot." Jermain Loguen's employment by an unusually egalitarian white family, he wrote, "cultivated my self-respect—brought forth the manly qualities of his nature— . . . refined his manners—elevated his aspirations. . . ."[59]

Many of the slaves survived almost indescribable cruelties because they were resigned to their fate. They simply had to make the best of the situation in which they found themselves. Henry Clay Bruce contended that there were many slaves, "who, though they knew they suffered a great wrong in their enslavement, gave their best services to their masters, realizing, philosophically, that the wisest course was to make the best of their unfortunate situation." Such slaves were determined to survive however cruel their masters were. They were brutally realistic. Frederick Douglass spoke for many of them when he asserted: "A man's troubles are always half disposed of when he finds endurance his only remedy." William Grimes indicated the brutal realism and the will to survive of many slaves when he declared that slavery was a cruel institution, "but being placed in that situation, to repine is useless; we must submit to our fate, and bear

57. Ball, *Slavery*, 41; Israel Campbell, *An Autobiography* (Philadelphia, 1861), 62.

58. H. B. Brown, *Narrative*, 23-38; Loguen, *Freedman*, 149-64; Jones, *Experience*, 8-15.

59. Jones, *Experience*, 12; Loguen, *Freedman*, 157.

Figure 65
Isaac Jefferson

up, as well as we can, under the cruel treatment of our despotic tyrants."[60]

One of the primary reasons the slaves were able to survive the cruelty they faced was that their behavior was not totally dependent on their masters. The slave had many referents for self-esteem, for instance, other than his master. In religion, a slave exercised his own independence of conscience. Convinced that God watched over him, the slave bore his earthly afflictions in

60. Bruce, *New Man,* iii; Douglass, *Bondage,* 65; Grimes, *Life,* 35.

order to earn a heavenly reward. Often he disobeyed his earthly master's rules to keep his Heavenly Master's commandments because he had greater fear for his immortal soul than for the pain which could be inflicted on his body. Religious faith gave an ultimate purpose to his life, a sense of communal fellowship and personal worth, and reduced suffering from fear and anxiety. In short, religion helped him to preserve his mental health. Trust in God was conducive to psychic health insofar as it excluded all anxiety-producing preoccupations by the recognition of a loving Providence.[61]

In the quarters the slave was rarely under the direct surveillance of his master. Here, he could be a man. He could express his true feelings and gain respect and sympathy in his family circle. Friendship, love, sexual gratification, fun, and values which differed from those of the master were all found in the quarters.

Many were able to maintain their self-esteem because of their status in the quarters. This status was based on several factors. Generally, those slaves who held some important post in the plantation hierarchy were ascribed higher status in the quarters. Those bondsmen whose jobs took them away from the plantation frequently (drovers, steamboatmen, draymen) or those who supplied the slaves with shoes, clothes, and housing (seamstresses, shoemakers, carpenters) stood high in the social hierarchy of the quarters. Lowest on the social ladder were those who lived and worked closely with the master (house servants, drivers, concubines), mulattoes, and informants. Occasionally, slaves in this proscribed group gained confidence and respect in the quarters because they demonstrated their commitment to their fellows. Some also gained status and self-esteem by adding bright new clothes to the coarse, ill-fitting wardrobe that most slaves had, or

61. Seward Hiltner, "The Contributions of Religion to Mental Health," *Mental Hygiene* XXIV (July 1940), 366-67; P. E. Johnson, "Religious Psychology and Health," *Mental Hygiene* XXXI (Oct. 1947), 556-66; "Symposium on Relationships Between Religion and Mental Health," *American Psychologist* XIII (Oct. 1958), 565-79; Chapter 3.

because they were strong, intelligent, comely, religious, creative, rebellious, or were musicians, conjurors, preachers, and midwives.[62]

The wealth of his owner enhanced the slave's status when dealing with whites and other slaves outside the plantation because it allegedly assured him better food, clothing, housing, and treatment. Then, too, whites were less likely to mistreat the slaves of wealthy than of poor planters.

The few slaves who learned to read gained immeasurable status in the quarters because they had a secret mirror on the outside world and could keep the others informed of events which were transpiring there. Henry Clay Bruce, for instance, wrote that among the slaves: "A Colored man who could read was a very important fellow." In addition, education elevated the slave's sense of personal worth in the midst of his afflictions. After Thomas Jones secretly started learning to read, he wrote that, "I felt at night, as I went to my rest, that I was really beginning to be a *man,* preparing myself for a condition in life better and higher and happier than could belong to the ignorant *slave.*"[63] Since whites put so many restrictions upon slaves obtaining an education, the slaves themselves invested it with almost magical qualities.

So few slaves learned how to read and write that they had to develop other skills to maintain their personal autonomy. Most did this by carefully masking their true personality traits from whites, while adopting "sham" characteristics when interacting with them. According to Lucy Ann Delaney, slaves lived behind an "impenetrable mask . . . how much of joy, of sorrow, of misery and anguish have they hidden from their tormentors!"[64]

62. Ball, *Slavery,* 15; J. Anderson, *Story,* 29-30; Hughes, *Thirty Years,* 59-63; John W. Blassingame, "Status and Social Structure in the Slave Community," in Harry P. Owens, ed., *Perspectives and Irony in American Slavery* (Jackson, Miss., 1976), 137-51; George Rawick, ed., *The American Slave: A Composite Autobiography* (31 vols., Westport, Conn., 1972-77), XII, pt. 1:198, XIII, pt. 4:124, VI (Alabama), 329.

63. Bruce, *New Man,* 86; Jones, *Experience,* 18.

64. Lucy Ann Delaney, *From the Darkness Cometh the Light: Or Struggles for Freedom* (St. Louis, n.d.), 18.

Many masters knew their slaves wore impenetrable masks in their presence. The Georgia planter Charles C. Jones conceded in 1842 that "Persons live and die in the midst of Negroes and Know comparatively little of their real character. . . . The Negroes are a distant class in community, and keep very much to *themselves*. They are one thing before the whites, and another before their own color." Similarly, the South Carolina planter and former slaveholder Edward A. Pollard wrote in 1871: "It is astonishing how little the slaveholders of the South, despite their supposed knowledge of the negro, really knew of what was in him. . . . The difficulty was that slavery was a perpetual barrier to an intimate acquaintance with the negro; it regarded him as a *thing*, and was never concerned to know what was in the sodden and concealed mind of a creature that represented only so much of productive force, and was estimated, body and soul, in dollars and cents."[65]

On innumerable occasions the slaves' public behavior contradicted their private attitudes. For instance, they frequently pretended to love their cruel masters. Lewis Clarke argued that this was "the hardest work that slaves have to do. When any stranger is present we have to love them very much . . . [But when they were sick or dying] Then they all look glad, and go to the cabin with a merry heart." Austin Steward discovered the same practice among his fellow slaves when his mistress died: "The slaves were all deeply affected by the scene; some doubtless truly lamented the death of their mistress; others rejoiced that she was no more. . . . One of them I remember went to the pump and wet his face, so as to appear to weep with the rest." Similarly, when Jacob Stroyer's cruel master died, the slaves shed false tears: "Of course the most of them were glad that he was dead . . . [and some said,] 'Thank God, massa gone home to hell.' "[66]

The slaves dissembled, they feigned ignorance and humility. If their masters expected them to be fools, they would play the

65. Charles C. Jones, *The Religious Instruction of the Negroes in the United States* (Savannah, 1842), 110; *American Missionary* XV (1871), 242.

66. Clarke, *Sufferings*, 113; Steward, *Twenty-two Years*, 86; Stroyer, *My Life*, 31.

fool's role. Frederick Douglass described this trait of the slave. He asserted: "as the master studies to keep the slave ignorant, the slave is cunning enough to make the master think he succeeds." The slave frequently pretended to be much more humble than he actually was. When Jermain Loguen returned after an absence of several months to his rather despicable master, for example, he pretended to be happy. He wrote that he "went through the ceremony of servile bows and counterfeit smiles to his master and mistress and other false expressions of gladness." Later, Loguen fought with his master.[67]

The more the slaves yearned for freedom, the more passionately did they show disdain for it. They walked circumspectly for fear of arousing the wrath of the whites. Lunsford Lane revealed how the slave balanced on a tight rope between revealing his true character and incurring the anger of whites and masking his feelings and surviving:

> Ever after I entertained the first idea of being free, I had endeavored so to conduct myself as not to become obnoxious to the white inhabitants, knowing as I did their power, and their hostility to the colored people. . . . First, I had made no display of the little property or money I possessed. . . . Second, I had never appeared to be even so intelligent as I really was. This all colored people at the south, free and slaves, find it peculiarly necessary for their own comfort and safety to observe.[68]

Often the slaves had to mask their feelings in their relations with their masters because of their attitudes toward whites. Most slaves hated and were suspicious of all whites. William Wells Brown contended: "The slave is brought up to look upon every white man as an enemy to him and his race. . . ." The treatment the slave received verified this suspicion and left him angry. For example, upon conversing with one group of regularly flogged and continuously mistreated slaves, William Webb "saw

67. Douglass, *Bondage*, 81; Loguen, *Freedman*, 226.
68. Lunsford Lane, *The Narrative of Lunsford Lane* (Boston, 1848), 31.

there was great anger among them about the way they were treated."[69]

Many slaves tried to drown their anger in the whiskey bottle,[70] and if not drowned, the anger welling up was translated into many other forms. Sometimes the slave projected his aggression onto his fellow slaves: he might beat up, stab, or kill one of his fellow sufferers. Generally, however, he expressed his resentment in rebellious language in the quarters. William Webb, for instance, frequently heard the slaves talking about wreaking vengeance on their masters, killing them, and appropriating their homes, food, clothes, and women. In addition to their empty threats of vengeance, the slaves customarily gave contemptible nicknames to their masters.[71]

Since the slave viewed all whites as enemies, his master as a tyrant, and himself as being without protection before the law, he generally developed a strong sense of loyalty to all blacks. Douglass wrote that the slaves on his plantation: "were as true as steel, and no band of brothers could have been more loving. There were no mean advantages taken of each other, as is sometimes the case where slaves are situated as we were, no tattling; no giving each other bad names . . . ; and no elevating one at the expense of the other. . . . We were generally a unit, and moved together."[72]

Masters frequently noted the sense of community in the quarters; they reported that slaves usually shared their few goods, rarely stole from each other, and the strong helped the weak. Whitemarsh Seabrook asserted in 1834 that "between slaves on the same plantation there is a deep sympathy of feeling which binds them so closely together that a crime committed by one of their number is seldom discovered through their instrumental-

69. W. W. Brown, *Narrative,* 95-96; William Webb, *The History of William Webb* (Detroit, 1873), 21.

70. Douglass, *Bondage,* 251-56; Allen Parker, *Recollections of Slavery Times* (Worcester, Mass., 1895), 65.

71. James W. C. Pennington, *The Fugitive Blacksmith* (London, 1849), 72; Campbell, *Autobiography,* 31, 41, 67.

72. Douglass, *Bondage,* 269.

ity."[73] Virginian G. W. Gooch contended that among the slaves, "the vice which they hold in the greatest abhorrence is that of telling upon one another." Writing in 1842, the Georgia planter Charles C. Jones repeatedly noted the common front slaves presented when dealing with their masters:

> the Negroes are scrupulous on one point; they make common cause, as servants, in concealing their faults from their owners. Inquiry elicits no information; no one feels at liberty to disclose the transgressor; all are profoundly ignorant; the matter assumes the sacredness of a "professional secret": for they remember that they may hereafter require the same concealment of their own transgressions from their fellow servants, and if they tell upon them *now,* they may have the like favor returned *them;* besides, in the meanwhile, having their names cast out as evil from among their brethren, and being subjected to scorn, and perhaps personal violence or pecuniary injury.[74]

The code, of course, was not perfect; some blacks, especially house servants, could not be trusted. Those who violated the code, while currying the favor of their masters, became outcasts in the quarters and faced retaliation from their fellows. Consequently, often the elite slaves—drivers and house servants—were, in spite of the part they played in policing the plantation, extremely effective in protecting their fellows from the rigors of bondage. Domestic servants were the field slave's most important windows on the outside world and aides in trying to fathom the planter's psyche. Although forced to flog his fellows, a driver frequently allowed them to rest when the overseer was not around, or made his whip create more sound than pain. If he were especially trusted by his master, he doled out much more food than the master or overseer did.

73. Seabrook and Gooch quoted in Jones, *Religious Instruction,* 143-44; see also: John Dixon Long, *Pictures of Slavery in Church and State* (Philadelphia, 1857), 194; Henry W. Ravenel, "Recollections of Southern Plantation Life," *Yale Review* XXV (June 1936), 757, 761-64.

74. William P. Harrison, *The Gospel Among the Slaves* (Nashville, 1893), 103; Jones, *Religious Instruction,* 130-31.

Group solidarity in the quarters enabled the slaves to unite in their struggle against their masters.[75] The ideals in the quarters dictated hostility to and contempt for cruel masters and overseers. The slaves refused to work diligently when cruel masters and overseers were not watching them. Under the lash, the slave became an "eye servant." Robert Anderson asserted that when an overseer treated the slaves cruelly: "we . . . used our wits to escape from all the work we could, and would lag behind, or shirk when he was not looking." Bruce declared that cruel treatment caused the slaves to work against the planter's best interests: "a mean and cruel master made shiftless, careless, and indolent slaves, who, being used to the lash as a remedy for every offense, had no fears of it, and would not go without it." They schemed to get revenge on their masters without incurring the risk of death. Their offensive weapons included the slowdown, riding their master's horses to death, stealing from him, and breaking his plows and hoes. They tried to avoid the lash by being inconspicuous: working neither too fast nor too slow, acting neither too intelligent nor too stupid. The relationship between master and slave was one continual tug of war. According to Allen Parker, "There was always a kind of strife between master and slave, the master on the one hand trying to get all the work he possibly could out of the slaves . . . and the slaves . . . trying to get out of all the work they could, and to take every possible advantage of their master. . . ." As a result of this strife, most slaves grudgingly labored for their masters and tried to repress their anger. They were at least restrained by the lash.[76]

Strong-willed blacks were restrained, but were not broken by the lash. William H. Heard declared that in spite of the cruel treatment meted out to the slaves, "many of them were never conquered." Rather than cower before the overseer's lash, they often cursed the man who inflicted the pain on them. Frederick

75. Northup, *Twelve Years*, 223-62; Henson, *Life*, 15-25; J. Brown, *Slave Life*, 137-70.

76. R. Anderson, *From Slavery*, 32; Bruce, *New Man*, 41; Parker, *Recollections*, 62.

Douglass reported that one slave woman, after being flogged severely: "was not subdued, for she continued to denounce the overseer, and to call him every vile name. He had bruised her flesh, but had left her invincible spirit undaunted." On many occasions the slaves proved their indomitability by refusing to cry out under the lash. Elizabeth Keckley, for instance, resisted the effort of her master to flog her and when he succeeded in doing so, she recalled that it was agonizing but did not break her spirit: "Oh God! I can feel the torture now—the terrible, excruciating agony of those moments. I did not scream; I was too proud to let my tormentor know what I was suffering."[77]

In spite of the slave's general submissiveness, he might at any time resist his master or overseer. In every daily confrontation with his master violence threatened to erupt. Any spark could set off the reaction: carping criticisms for work the slave knew had been done well, or a clearly unjustified flogging, or almost anything else. The slave might submit to any and all abuse for years, then, suddenly fed up, fight any man who attempted to punish him. In many instances the slaves fought with or killed their masters and overseers when their temporary anger overcame their customary caution.

Many of the strongest, most industrious and intelligent slaves refused to submit passively to floggings.[78] Approaching the master or overseer directly, the slaves informed them that they would do the labor required of them, but that no man would whip them. William Wells Brown recalled that there was one strong and valuable slave on his plantation who had never been flogged and had often declared: "that no white man should ever whip him—that he would die first." With such slaves, the gun was an effective and necessary instrument of discipline. Young W. H. Robinson, for instance, wrote that although he wanted to obey

77. William H. Heard, *From Slavery to the Bishopric in the AME Church: An Autobiography* (Philadelphia, 1924), 26; Douglass, *Bondage*, 95; Keckley, *Scenes*, 34.

78. R. Anderson, *From Slavery*, 17-23; Bruce, *New Man*, 32-35, 88-96; Randolph, *Sketches*, 16-19; Isaac Mason, *Life of Isaac Mason as a Slave* (Worcester, Mass., 1893), 13-18; Mars, *Life*, 1-13.

his father's admonition that he "never pull off your shirt to be whipped," the sight of a gun in his master's hand, "knocked all of the manhood out of me." Generally, one white man could not whip such a slave.[79]

The relationship of the planters and overseers to the recalcitrant slave was a strange one. Generally, they feared him, particularly if he were noted for his strength. On innumerable occasions they refused to punish such a slave unless they could get him drunk, surprise him, or get other slaves or whites to overpower him. In most cases the masters tried to avoid trouble with the intractable slave because of his value as a worker. The only way he could be punished was to shoot him. Realizing this, many slaves parlayed it into better treatment: they threatened to run away, to fight, or to stop work if they were flogged. William Green, after fighting his master to a standstill when the latter tried to flog him for disobedience, declared that no man would whip him and if he were flogged, he would cease work. His master relented, Green declared, and "after this we made up and got along very well for almost a year." James Mars wrote that he refused to permit his master to flog him when he was sixteen, and from that time until he was twenty-one he had no more trouble with his master: "I do not remember that he ever gave me an unpleasant word or look."[80] Similarly, when Samuel Hall, Solomon Northup, and Jermain Loguen fought rather than permit their owners to whip them their masters let them alone.[81] Frederick Douglass asserted that after he fought the Negro breaker, Covey, to prevent a flogging: "During the whole six months that I lived with Covey after this transaction, he never laid on me the weight of his finger in anger." According to Douglass, when a man resisted a flogging "Such floggings are seldom repeated by the same overseer. They prefer to whip those who are most easily whipped . . . and that slave who has the

79. W. W. Brown, *Narrative*, 18; Robinson, *Pulpit*, 25, 40.

80. Green, *Events*, 13; Mars, *Life*, 24.

81. Loguen, *Freedman*, 230-43; Northup, *Twelve Years*, 105-61; Hall, *47 Years*, n.p.

courage to stand up for himself against the overseer . . . becomes, in the end, a freeman, even though he sustain the formal relation of a slave."[82]

It is obvious from the discussion above that there was great variety in slave behavior. Some slaves were always docile; others were docile most of the time and rebellious at other times. Likewise, some resisted bondage throughout their lives in various ways, while others, generally docile, might be rebellious only once. In other words, the slave was no different in most ways from most men. The same range of personality types existed in the quarters as in the mansion. The slaves, it is true, were generally submissive and obedient in most of their relations with whites. Obviously, slavery could not have survived had it been otherwise.

While slaves were generally submissive, they did not regress to the infantile dependency, extreme obsequiousness, unquestioning obedience, and abject docility of the concentration camp inmate primarily because they were not treated as harshly as the inmates. Whatever the cruelty inherent in slavery, the slaves were not systematically starved, forced to stand naked for hours in freezing weather, worked eighteen hours daily, and customarily tortured and murdered as the concentration camp inmates were. While the German camp was such an efficient instrument of destruction that the monthly mortality rate was often 20 per cent and less than one per cent of the inmates in some camps survived, there was a natural *increase* in the slave population in the South. However much the black slave was overworked and underfed, he was not systematically starved and worked to death: between 1830 and 1860 there was a 23 per cent natural increase in the slave population every decade. Because masters had a greater sense of morality and a greater interest in protecting their laborers than camp guards had toward inmates, the slave did not live in the shadow of death and did not have to center all of his energies on and tailor all of his behavior toward survival.

The important fact which emerges from the black autobiog-

82. Douglass, *Bondage,* 95, 246.

raphies and interviews is that the master-slave relationship was not the only factor that determined the slave's behavior. Even when it was crucial, this relationship varied from master to master. The slave's behavior, attitudes, and degree of self-esteem also changed as he changed hands. Frequently, since he changed masters often and the behavior expected of him also changed, the impression that an individual owner made on his personality was minimal. In the end, the slave's personality was a composite of the effects on him of cruel and kind owners, of those who demanded ritual deference at all times and of those who demanded it occasionally, and of several other factors. Most slaves lived on such large plantations, had such little contact with their masters and overseers, or went through the ritual of deference so infrequently, that no master made an important impression on their personalities.

While the slave was customarily obedient and deferential to his master, this was not necessarily an innate character trait. He went through the ritual of deference in some cases because he recognized that it was mandatory for his survival. In most cases, he went through the ritual the way that most men perform habitual acts: with little thought about their symbolic significance. Besides, the deferential posture was not the only one the slave assumed. At the same time that he was deferential to his master, he also interacted with other human beings on other levels: he viewed poor whites with contempt, enjoyed the love, respect, and companionship of his family; thought of himself as superior to besotted, licentious masters; won praise, inspired admiration, acquired status, found companionship, obtained sexual gratification, dominated others, and played and relaxed in the quarters. Most importantly, he had a great deal of time free from observation by whites.

The resiliency of the slave was such that the infrequent occasions when he went through the ritual of deference were not sufficient to blot out the numerous other roles he played. Because of this there was a great variety of personality types among slaves. Henry Clay Bruce summed up this phenomenon perfectly:

> There were different kinds of slaves, the lazy fellow, who would not work at all unless forced to do so, and required to be watched, the good man, who patiently submitted to everything . . . and then there was the one who would not yield to punishment of any kind. . . . Then there was the unruly slave, whom no master particularly wanted for several reasons: first, he would not submit to any kind of corporal punishment; second, it was hard to determine which was the master or which the slave; third, he worked when he pleased to do so. . . . This class of slaves were usually industrious, but very impudent. There were thousands of that class, who spent their lives in their master's service doing his work undisturbed, because the master understood the slave . . . there were thousands of high-toned and high spirited slaves, who had as much self-respect as their masters, and who were industrious, reliable, and truthful, and could be depended on by their masters in all cases. . . . These slaves knew their own helpless condition. . . . But . . . they did not give up in abject servility. . . .[83]

The typical slave used his wits to escape from work and punishment, preserved his manhood in the quarters, feigned humility, identified with masters and worked industriously only when he was treated humanely, simulated deference, was hostilely submissive and occasionally obstinate, ungovernable, and rebellious.

83. Bruce, *New Man*, 36-37.

Appendix I:
Comparative Examination of Total Institutions

A comparison of such total institutions as armies, prisons, and concentration camps suggests several ways of examining slave behavior and the range of options open to the slave. From the comparison, it would appear that there is no deterministic relationship between institutional sanctions, roles, and subordinate status and submissiveness. Authorities in total institutions often maintain the facade of absolute control by setting behavioral standards so low that everyone can meet them, ignoring breaches of rules, and accommodating the strongest members of the subordinate group with better treatment. Those officials in closest contact with the subordinate group rarely apply the sanctions rigidly. Consequently, large numbers of individuals pretend to be submissive while preserving their own personalities. While authorities are misled by the outward pattern of deference, group conformity is based on fear rather than internalization of the institutional roles. Subordinate members are able to reject institutional expectations when they hold rigid religious beliefs, expect or accept their treatment as a sign of martyrdom, or can turn to their peer group or subculture for self-esteem, or values and expectations which differ from those of the institution.

The degree to which the members of institutions are able to avoid becoming abjectly docile is dependent on the kinds of power exercised, the level of surveillance, and the frequency of interaction. The ways in which these and other factors operate in large institutions similar to the plantation can be seen by examining armies, prisons, and concentration camps.

Scholarly studies of the army show that it is a closed, highly stratified, authoritarian, neo-feudal, paternalistic institution providing all the biological and psychological needs of its members except sex and family life. Rules control every aspect of the highly routinized existence and failure to obey all rules leads to punishment. Although the army uses the sanctions of personal humiliation, physical abuse, imprisonment, and death to enforce the rules, it tries to make its members internalize them. The most powerful group in the army consists of the aristocratic officers who expect deference, honor, and obedience from enlisted men and use their power to maintain status and to obtain special privileges. The non-commissioned officer, second in the army hierarchy, serves as an intermediary between officers and men, a channel of communications, and helps to enforce rules. At the bottom of the army hierarchy stands the enlisted man.[1]

Army life for the common soldier is a succession of deprivations and frustrations, which begins with the "shock" of basic training, his first weeks in the army. The new recruit is a helpless, insecure, scared, lone individual in a complex, bewildering new environment. One recruit asserted that in basic training "The recruit is warned and threatened, shouted at and sworn at, punished and promised further punishments, with such frequency and from so many sides that he gets to be like the rat in the neurosis production experiment."[2] Exploited by veterans, physically exhausted, constantly repeating his actions, the recruit often loses his initiative and develops a sense of infantile dependency and personal degradation. He soon fears the army and internalizes some of its rules.[3]

Although the soldier internalizes some of the ideals of the army, fear of punishment is the primary inducement to obedience. Moreover, there is general contempt for the soldier who lives by the rules. The average soldier tries to be inconspicuous. He "goldbricks," doing just enough of the boring, nonsensical tasks to avoid punishment. He deprecates but bitterly accepts authority while rejecting the army's degrading image of himself.

1. Hugh Mullian, "The Regular-Service Myth," *American Journal of Sociology* LIII (Jan. 1948), 276-81; Samuel Andrew Stouffer *et al., The American Soldier: Adjustment During Army Life* (4 vols., Princeton, 1949), I, 54-57; Arnold Rose, "The Social Structure of the Army," *American Journal of Sociology* LI (March 1946), 361-64; "Life in the U.S. Army; Fantasy-Land, Peace-Time Variety," *Commentary* XXVI (Sept. 1958), 227-38.

2. Stouffer, *Soldier,* I, 412.

3. Stouffer, *Soldier,* I, 410-13; August B. Hollingshead, "Adjustment to Military Life," *American Journal of Sociology* LI (March 1946), 439-50; "Life in the U.S. Army," 227-37; Howard Brotz and Everett Wilson, "Characteristics of Military Society," *American Journal of Sociology* LI (March 1946), 371-75.

Psychologist Dearborn Spindler argued that American society does not prepare young American males for the strict obedience demanded in the army. In fact, he asserted, the female-dominated American family leads to an "inflation of the growing child's ego, to the extent that he may always be reluctant to surrender it to any group or interest not for his direct personal benefit or be placed in a subordinate position."[4] Whatever the reason, enlisted men do not completely accept the army as a substitute parent. Instead, during his free time the soldier asserts his independence and seeks to regain his pride through rebellious language, drinking, bragging, cursing his officers, and uninhibited sexual exploits. In spite of frequent turnover in personnel, face-to-face contacts, common grievances, and a special language bind the enlisted men together in their underground resistance to the formal control of the officers. According to one sociologist, "The informal social group of enlisted men may supplement, interpret, or even effectively negate the directives of the formal social organization."[5] The norms of the soldier's peer group are often more important than those of his officers.[6] Contrary to army ideals, these norms, according to Samuel Stouffer, may require him "to curb his desire to be industrious or efficient, desire to compete or get ahead, from fear of his fellows. . . ."[7]

Officers neither communicate with the soldiers nor understand how they feel. The great social distance between the two groups frequently causes the officers to misinterpret the troops' actions. For instance, officers almost uniformly grossly overestimate the respect enlisted men have for them.[8] Samuel Stouffer concluded in his four-year study of the army: "Officers could easily be misled by the rituals of deference exacted from all enlisted men. . . . It is easy to under-

4. G. Dearborn Spindler, "American Character as Revealed in the Military," *Psychiatry* XI (Aug. 1948), 280.

5. "Informal Social Organization in the Army," *American Journal of Sociology* LI (March 1946), 365.

6. Frederick Elkin, "The Soldier's Language," *American Journal of Sociology* LI (March 1946), 414-22; Stouffer, *Soldier*, I, 413-29; "Informal Social Organization," 365-70; Spindler, "Character," 275-78; Henry Elkin, "Aggressive and Erotic Tendencies in Army Life," *American Journal of Sociology* LI (March 1946), 408-13; Douglass Scott, "The Negro and the Enlisted Man: An Analogy," *Harper's Magazine* CCXXV (Oct. 1962), 19, 21.

7. Stouffer, *Soldier*, I, 413.

8. Stouffer, *Soldier*, I, 391-95; Spindler, "Character," 275-81; Rose, "Social Structure," 361-64.

stand how during the course of time they could come to mistake these compulsory outward symbols of deference for voluntary respect and fail to perceive underlying hostilities and resentments."[9] Similarly, the non-com, subjected to the resentment and pressure of the enlisted men with whom he socializes and shares the inequalities of army life, also misleads the officers. He conforms to the soldiers' demand for sympathy behind a façade of strict obedience to his officers.[10]

Another total institution is the prison. Subject to absolute authority, playing a restricted number of roles, physically isolated from loved ones, uncertain about the future, prisoners sometimes lose their initiative, show extreme dependency, and are indifferent to other prisoners. Life is routinized and impersonalized. Prisoners are often described as lazy and stupid.[11]

Although theoretically prisoners are under absolute control, the institution, according to an anthropologist who served two years in prison, is divided into two "enemy camps [that] coexist in an atmosphere of mutual fear and hostility." Consequently, there is "the appearance of conformity within the official system, and an underground pattern of nonconformity by which the individual inmate tries to live by his own codes, preserving as best he can his personal preferences and habits."[12] The inmate's personal adjustment is bolstered by group acceptance. The code of the group dictates hostility to the administration, rejection of the administration's myths of justice and equality, and places high values on group loyalty, courage, and power.[13]

The officials recognize the higher status of some prisoners by giving them better jobs as a means of control. Two prison officials, McCorkle and Korn, report that in giving the best jobs to the most

9. Stouffer, *Soldier*, I, 396.

10. Stouffer, *Soldier*, I, 401-10; "Informal Social Organization," 365-70.

11. A. J. W. Taylor, "Social Isolation and Imprisonment," *Psychiatry* XXVI (Nov. 1961), 373-76.

12. M. Arc, "The Prison 'Culture'—From the Inside," *New York Times Magazine* (Feb. 28, 1965), 52.

13. Lloyd W. McCorkle and Richard Korn, "Resocialization Within Walls," *Annals of the American Academy of Political and Social Science* CCXCIII (May 1954), 88-98; Donald Clemmer, *The Prison Community* (New York, 1965 [1940]), 83-133; Robert C. Atchley and M. Patrick McCabe, "Socialization in Correctional Communities: A Replication," *American Sociological Review* XXXIII (Oct. 1968), 774-85; Arc, "Prison 'Culture,'" 52-63.

powerful inmates "the institution buys peace with the system by avoiding battle with it."[14] This same pattern of avoidance is reflected in the euphemistic "hard labor" of prisons. Generally inmates not only refuse to work more than the prison tradition requires, but take reprisals on prisoners who do more work than others.[15]

Among total institutions, the German concentration camp stands in stark contrast to armies and prisons. First, the inmates went through the "shock" of arrest and imprisonment for unknown reasons and under the most painful and bewildering conditions. Jammed into railroad cars and transported hundreds of miles often in freezing weather, they were forced to stand sometimes for seventeen hours without food or water, and were systematically whipped, shot, and bayonetted. Totally isolated from their usual cultural surroundings, family, and the opposite sex, the inmates worked from twelve to eighteen hours daily. There was no privacy and they were under the constant surveillance of the guards. Prisoners were deliberately degraded, starved, tortured, and exterminated. One of the strongest forces ruling them was the anarchy of accident: they could be suddenly killed for doing or not doing almost anything; punishment was completely arbitrary. As a result of the torture, physical deprivation, and unremitting labor, 75 per cent of the new prisoners died within six months; the monthly mortality rate was about 20 per cent; and in some camps the survival rate was less than one per cent.[16]

The objectives of the camps were to make inmates docile, to train the Gestapo in the best terror-producing devices, and to exterminate an "undesirable" population group. The prisoners received the kind of punishment from the guards that helpless children receive from cruel fathers and led an extremely routinized existence. According to one survivor, Bruno Bettelheim, "Every single moment of their lives was strictly regulated and supervised."[17] The guards aimed at a total

14. McCorkle and Korn, "Walls," 91.

15. McCorkle and Korn, "Walls," 91-92.

16. Peter Phillips, *The Tragedy of Nazi Germany* (London, 1969), 185-205; Christopher Burney, *The Dungeon Democracy* (London, 1945); Leon Szalet, *Experiment "E"* (New York, 1945); David Rousset, *The Other Kingdom* (New York, 1947); Elie Cohen, *Human Behavior in the Concentration Camp* (New York, 1953); Olga Lengyel, *Five Chimneys: The Story of Auschwitz* (Chicago, 1947), 7-22; Eugen Kogon, *The Theory and Practice of Hell* (New York, 1946), 66-90.

17. Bruno Bettelheim, "Individual and Mass Behavior in Extreme Situations," *Journal of Abnormal Psychology* XXXVIII (Oct. 1943), 417.

regression of the inmate to infantilism. In the process they played on cultural determinants of disgust and guilt. While German culture placed a high value on cleanliness, filth was the enforced norm in the camps. Prisoners were often tortured or forced to fight each other for food. Sometimes they had to drink water or eat their food from toilet bowls.

With death and starvation as their constant companions, the prisoners naturally centered practically all of their energies on self-preservation. The concentration camp, rationally organized by a powerful national government as an instrument of pain and death, systematically tried to crush the inmate's will. As a result, many prisoners became child-like, boastful, and dishonest; they identified with their oppressors, developed a sense of detachment to the cruelties inflicted on fellow prisoners, lost control of bodily functions, did not resist their guards, and had no hatred for their oppressors after liberation. The inmate's sole interest was apparently in self-preservation. Not only was there practically no concern with sex, but as a result of starvation, fatigue, trauma, and fear of death, males became impotent, women stopped menstruating, and the beginning of menstruation was delayed several years for most young girls. The psychical shock of the concentration camp experience was so great that many previous physiological and psychosomatic diseases became dormant.[18]

In spite of the barbaric treatment they received, the reaction of the German concentration camp inmates was not simply submission. Often living with the daily odors from the crematoria, many prisoners lost their fear of death. According to Bettelheim, because of the arbitrary punishment of the inmates "all rules were broken."[19]

18. Bruno Bettelheim, *The Informed Heart* (Glencoe, Ill., 1960); Peter Oswald and Egon Bittner, "Life Adjustment After Severe Persecution," *American Journal of Psychiatry* CV (Feb. 1949), 601-5; Wolfgang Lederer, "Persecutions and Compensations," *Archives of General Psychiatry* XII (May 1965), 464-74; V. A. Kral, "Psychiatric Observation Under Severe Chronic Stress," *American Journal of Psychiatry* CVIII (Sept. 1951), 185-92; G. W. Allport, J. S. Bruner, and E. M. Jandorff, "Personality Under Social Catastrophe: Ninety Life Histories of the Nazi Revolution," *Character and Personality* X (Sept. 1941), 1-22; Curt Bondy, "Problems of Internment Camps," *Journal of Abnormal Psychology* XXXVIII (Oct. 1943), 453-75; Paul Friedman, "Some Aspects of Concentration Camp Psychology," *American Journal of Psychiatry* CV (Feb. 1949), 601-5; *Commentary* XXV (Jan. 1958), 80-83.

19. Bettelheim, "Individual," 422.

Losing their status, suffering from lack of affection, unable to leave the camp, the inmates envied, hated, and were contemptuous of the guards. Hatred sometimes led to intra-group fights, insubordination, and a few rebellions and attempts to escape.

Among the old prisoners, and especially criminals, a number accepted the guards as father figures and identified with them. The highest ranking inmates (prominents) in the camp hierarchy were more likely to accept the values of the guards and copy their verbal and physical aggressions than were other prisoners. The number of ordinary prisoners who identified completely with their aggressors, however, was small. Hilde Bluhm's study of a large number of the narratives of concentration camp inmates confirms this fact.[20] Those individuals who had a prior love object with whom they identified strongly were least likely to identify with the guards. Even among the old inmates, the identification was apparently not complete. Bettelheim observed in his camp that "these same old prisoners who identified with the Gestapo at other moments defied it, demonstrating courage in doing so."[21]

As Bluhm has observed, it is easy to explain death and infantilism among the camp inmates. The difficult thing is to explain how some of them survived psychologically. The degree of psychological damage depended on the physical stamina of the inmate, his nationality, his social position in the camp, food, kind of work, and condition of the camp. The duration and brutality of imprisonment also strongly affected behavioral patterns. It must be remembered that the German camps ranged from forced labor to extermination centers. Several investigators noted that the degree of regression to childhood depended on the kind of treatment (frequency and nature of torture, amount of food, etc.) that the inmates received. While the very old and the very young fared worse physically and psychologically, children and adolescents were not as deeply affected by the camp experience. Women adjusted more easily than men and very religious people had a higher psychological survival rate than non-religious ones.[22]

20. Hilde O. Bluhm, "How Did They Survive? Mechanisms of Defense in Nazi Concentration Camps," *American Journal of Psychotherapy* II (Jan. 1948), 25.

21. Bettelheim, "Individual," 451.

22. Kral, "Stress," 185-92; Bondy, "Problems," 453-75; Bettelheim, "Individual," 417-22; Cohen, *Camp*, 115-210; Szalet, *Experiment*, 69-73; Rousset, *Kingdom*, 52-62.

Those persons who belonged to groups with ideals differing greatly from those of the Nazis survived with their prior personalities relatively intact. The Jehovah's Witnesses, Gypsies, political prisoners, non-Germans, and members of primary groups who had been imprisoned at the same time cooperated to protect each other and refused to abandon entirely the prior cultural determinants of their status and behavior. In fact, members of these groups regarded themselves as martyrs, gained some esteem because they had been considered dangerous enough to be imprisoned, and considered themselves superior to their oppressors. The individual's previous character, group consciousness, and sense of responsibility often prevented personality disintegration. The earlier in life one's struggle for survival had begun, the easier it was to withstand the trauma of the camp experience. Those persons, for instance, who had some previous experience with prisons adjusted better than non-criminals because they had some idea of what to expect. Those inmates with prior referents of self-esteem suffered less than middle-class prisoners. For example, in spite of the fact that one's previous status had no relationship to status inside the camp, upper-class persons often developed a greater sense of superiority after being imprisoned.[23]

In comparing the behavioral patterns of concentration camp inmates, prisoners, and soldiers, it would appear that the most important factor in causing infantilism, total dependency, and docility in the camps was the real threat of death which left few, if any, alternatives for the inmates. Undoubtedly, the fact that soldiers and prisoners were not systematically starved or worked until they were totally exhausted left them with enough energy to engage in covert resistance and group practices which were at variance with institutional norms.[24] In other words, it is easier to maintain personal autonomy in organizations where deviations from the institutionally defined behavioral patterns are not met swiftly and invariably by brutal punishment, torture, and death than in organizations where inmates are continuously faced with cruel and inhuman treatment and death. Without the frequent use of coercive power, it is impossible to force

23. See note 22; Bluhm, "Survive," 3-32; Allport, "Catastrophe," 1-22; Burney, *Dungeon*, 36-49.

24. One important difference among total institutions is that the soldiers and prisoners are often "attached" to them for a short time. Certainly the behavior of soldiers might also be affected by their sense of patriotism.

the subordinate to regress to infantile dependency, where his sole concern is to insure his self-preservation through abject docility.

Placed on a continuum of total institutions, the concentration camp is far removed from the Southern plantation. Still, an examination of the camp is useful for it illustrates several things. Based on the analysis of the camp experience, it is obvious that a rationally planned, relatively fully staffed twentieth-century organization utilizing all of the scientific knowledge available, could make helpless, child-like dependents of large numbers of people through a variety of techniques. In contrast, the plantation was irrationally organized and understaffed with bureaucrats and guards; it was not aimed at the extermination of its laborers, it emerged when the science of psychology was in its infancy, and could not keep its laborers under constant surveillance, could not survive if it systematically tortured, starved, or exterminated its inmates; it permitted some form of sex and family life to inmates who performed a valuable service and did not live with the daily smell of death. While the concentration camp differed significantly from the plantation, it illustrates how, even under the most extreme conditions, persecuted individuals can maintain their psychical balance because of group solidarity, prior experience in similar institutions, religious ideals, a culture differing greatly from that of their oppressors, prior referents for self-esteem, and physical stamina. If some men could escape infantilism in a murderous institution like the concentration camp, it may have been possible for the slave to avoid becoming abjectly docile in a much more benign institution like the plantation.

Appendix II: African Words, Numerals, and Sentences Used by Former Slaves in Georgia and South Carolina in the 1890s

(Compiled from Charles J. Montgomery, "Survivors from the Cargo of the Negro Slave Yacht *Wanderer*," *American Anthropologist* n.s. X (Oct. 1908), 611-23. All notes are Montgomery's; the geographical references are to Africa.)

TABLE 1. African Words

alligator	*ngändo*	cat	*boomba;*
baby	*mauna*		*mboomba*
back	*nēma*	chickens	*sū̇sū̇*
banana	*bitēba*[1]	cities	*mbämbä*
beads	*nzeembo*	cloth	*nlilly*
bear	*nzow*	clouds	*mä tū̇te*
beard	*njāvo*	coon	*bungee*
belly	*vomo*	corn	*mässä;*
bench[2]			*massängo*[3]
bird	*noonā*	coconut	*lombo*
boat	*coombay*	cow	*gomby*
boy	*mauna tucka*	dance	*zaccomma*
bread	*dimpa*	dead	*fuēdy*
butterbeans	*mongongo*	deer	*păccăsä;*
butterfly	*lūmpūngo*		*mibū̇ngā*[4]

[1] This is the kind of banana we have in this country, while *maconda* is a similar fruit, but much larger.

[2] There is no strict equivalent of bench, as these Africans knew nothing of either benches or chairs, but their nearest idea to this word is expressed by *cando,* or *conda,* which was the skin of an animal spread on the ground as a seat.

[3] The latter term is used more by those living farther south, while *muendā* is more familiar to those coming from the eastern coast.

[4] There seems to be lack of agreement respecting this word.

TABLE 1. (*Continued*)

devil	*doky*	moon	*gonda*
dirt	*ntoto*	partridges	*goomba; kimbimbe*
doctor	*gängä*		
dog	*boa*[5]	peach	*ncēpho*
ear	*kootoo*	peanuts	*gooba drängay*[10]
eyes	*mäso*		
fire	*bäzo; tuvia*[6]	peas	*madăza; zängy*
fish	*golla*[7]	pipe	*torida*
fly	*pĕssĕ*	pot	*cānzo*
foot	*tämby*	rabbit	*loomba*
fox	*coomba*	rain	*mvoola*
give me	*kälä*	rock	*matäde*
gun	*cully*	sense	*gängu*
hair	*sū̇ky; trūky*	sheep	*mamämy*
hand	*corko*	shoulder	*vämbo*
head	*ntu*	sky	*zū̇lū̇*
hoe	*sengo*	snakes	*nēoka*
hog	*gooloo*	spider	*sembe*
horse	*välo*	squirrel	*gemo; conka*
house	*dro; nzo; bindū̇*	stars	*birtity*
		steel	*wēēr*
knife	*mbālā*	sun	*tängo; muāny*
land	*nte; nsetu*	sweet potatoes	*bällä; zeembala*
lie	*gänge*		
love	*zola*	teeth	*mäno*
man (young)	*tucka; mayŭc'kala*	tobacco	*soonga*
		water	*längo; mäza*
man (white)	*fēata*	watermelon	*malengy*
man (colored)	*fēta*	whiskey	*mălăvo*[11]
		women	*cänto*
meat	*zimbēzy*[8]	women (old)	*bauba*
money	*nzeembo*[9]	women (young)	*ndoomba*
monkey	*cäwah*		

[5] *Zeembänga*, having the same meaning, seems to have been brought from the east.

[6] The latter perhaps more common.

[7] Or *tsängo*, while *zimbēzy* we get from the east.

[8] This word, from the eastern coast, is the same as that for fish, this perhaps being their chief animal food.

[9] This is the term for beads, these having been their only medium of exchange.

[10] These are different kinds of peas, while *zin'casa* comes from the eastern coast.

[11] This was made from what they called the "whiskey tree," or in their language *myä'*, doubtless the palm-oil tree referred to by Livingstone.

TABLE 2. African Numerals

1, corsē.	20, makamorly.
2, corla.	21, makamorly enwäno.
3, kootätoo.	22, makamorly ēzoly.
4, kooyä.	23, makamorly etätoo.
5, kootäno.	24, makamorly eyä'.
6, koosambäno.	25, makamorly etäno.
7, tambwody.	26, makamorly esämbäno.
8, nänä.	27, makamorly ensämbody.
9, ĕvwä.	28, makamorly enänä.
10, koomē.	29, makamorly ĕvwä.
11, koomē emorsē.	30, makomatätoo.
12, koomē enzolē.	40, makomäyä.
13, koomē entätē.	50, makomatäno.
14, koomē ēyä'.	60, makomasämbäno.
15, koomē entäno.	70, lusämbody.
16, koomē ensämbäno.	80, luovwä.
17, koomē ensämbody.	90, lunänä.
18, koomē ĕnänä.	100, kämä.
19, koomē ĕvwä.	

Table 3. Sentences Employing African Words

Ukola?	How do you do?
Quer quenda?	Where are you going?
Pahnam bēzy.	Give me some meat.
Wēnda twäs mona kona kēämvo.	Carry me across the river.
Vo vonda ngondo.	Kill that alligator.
Shēka.	Shoot him.
Borkäla.	Call him.
Weeza.	Come here.
Zola änä äku?	Do you love your children?
Inga (or yinga).	Yes.
Gogomby.	No (or, Go away).
Yālä käyāla.	He is very sick.
Wēnda bäkä gänga.	Go bring the doctor.
Fuēdy.	He is dead.
Ä cänto änä yäku?	How many wives have you?
Kū̇tatū̇.	Three.
Ungāya muānā ngo?	Have you seen any lions?
Noka kūnoka.	It is going to rain.
Wenda bängä tēvia.	Go build a fire.
Muāny yäma.	The sun is hot.
Ungā gwäku wōnä yäku ungāyi?	Are you living with your mother?
Yālä?	Where pains you?
Ntu bwänga.	My head aches.
Nzäla.	I am hungry.
Mäno gänzē.	My tooth aches.
Ruākä mbālā.	I cut him with a knife.
A kway tukiddy?	How far away does he live?
Wū̇to Coonawany.	I was born in Coonawany.
Mäzo Mäzēma.	He is blind.

Appendix III: Statistics on Slaves and Slavery: Observations and Tables

Contemporaries often have a greater appreciation of the strengths and weaknesses of statistics than do the scholars who utilize them decades after they are compiled. "Numbers" and "accuracy" are not two interchangeable words: Statistical truths are no more self-evident than literary ones. In fact, statistical analyses rely so heavily on inferences that one must carefully examine the data bases to evaluate the conclusions based on them. Whether compiled by planters, doctors, clergymen, army officers, or census takers, statistics on slavery mean little until combined with literary material. The dry bones of historical analysis, statistics acquire life when filtered through the accounts left by eyewitnesses. Always, the scholar must begin with the shortcomings of the statistical data he utilizes. Compilers of statistics on antebellum slavery often discussed the strengths and weaknesses of the data they presented. Indeed, it was a rare occasion when the publication of statistics on the South did not lead to extended political debate and intricate polemical attacks and defenses.

Among the more useful and complicated statistics on slave life and culture are those compiled by Southern churches. Fortunately, the clergy recognized the problems presented by the data they compiled. For instance, in 1851 the committee examining the parochial reports of the Episcopal Church in Virginia aptly characterized the weaknesses of church statistics when it reported that it was

> desirable that more accuracy and system should distinguish this portion of the labors of the Convention. Among other things which cannot be ascertained from the reports, and which it would be generally interesting to know, is the number of colored communicants and of colored persons confirmed. At present they are so reported with the white communicants, that it is hardly if at all possible to ascertain what the proportion is. The number of teachers and scholars in Sunday Schools is very seldom mentioned.

While the reports of individual ministers leave much to be desired, the cumulative statistics compiled from them when the annual conventions met are often not much better. During the annual meetings the delegates had to transact a great deal of business in a very short time. Usually a committee spent one or two days examining reports from specific churches and compiling cumulative statistics. Often presented in tabular form as an appendix to the convention proceedings, the cumulative statistics were not always complete or accurate. Sometimes the numbers reported by bishops and individual ministers varied considerably. A few harassed ministers estimated the number of communicants in their churches. Occasionally, reports from specific churches came in too late to be included in the cumulative statistics. When some churches did not report at all, the committee sometimes estimated how many communicants they had from the preceding report and included these figures in the cumulative statistics. The estimates (generally conservative) did not, however, represent the greatest problem for the committees. With frequent changes in ministerial charges, some congregations went for years without making reports.

Considered from almost any vantage point, data on marriages, baptisms, burials, communicants, catechumens, and Sunday School scholars in the annual reports of antebellum Southern churches are a statistician's nightmare. Although tabular reports began appearing in many convention proceedings in the 1850s, the figures in them do not always add up to the same totals represented in the reports of specific churches. The chronological periods covered by the reports also varied from state to state and within the same state. Some denominations began by reporting statistics as of 31 December each year. Then, inexplicably, they compiled statistics from May of one year to May of the next. Despite the receipt of repeated epistles from bishops and elders, busy pastors did not always submit reports to the annual conferences. Consequently, fluctuations in total figures sometimes reflect as much about the reporting procedures as they do about changes in congregations. Sometimes the inconsistencies in reporting procedures are so great that no meaningful statistics can be compiled from the journals of the proceedings of the annual conventions.

The problems increase when attempts are made to compare the statistics of one denomination for one or more states, or different denominations in the same state. All too often, different denominations compiled data on different things. Baptists and Methodists, the largest denominations in the South, rarely made racial distinctions in any categories in their reports; the Episcopalians, one of the South's smallest denominations, frequently made such distinctions for almost all categories. But even the Episcopal Church was inconsistent. While the South Carolina and Alabama dioceses regularly distinguished between blacks and whites, for instance, the dioceses of Tennessee, Missouri, and Kentucky combined blacks and whites in the totals they reported. The Southern synods of the Presbyterian Church made few statistical reports of any kind. Baptists, divided into myriad intrastate associations, rarely systematically compiled statistics, and state, regional, and national associations of Baptists almost never published figures on their black members. Consequently, in many states data on black Baptists remain buried in the manuscript records of thousands of churches. Occasionally religious magazines published such data.

The weaknesses of the data on communicants, funerals, marriages, baptisms, catechumens, and confirmations appearing below will be recognized by anyone reading annual parochial reports of any of the conferences, dioceses, associations, or synods. First, all pastors did not always distinguish between black and white. Consequently, since I have counted as "white" all figures not specifically reported as black, there may be an undercount of blacks in every category. Second, none of the churches made a distinction between free Negroes and slaves in their tabular reports. In some states the presence of relatively large numbers of free Negroes suggests the possibility of some distortion of the data. If we did not know that free Negroes, by and large, attended their own churches, this would represent a serious problem. The small number of free Negroes in such states as Arkansas (144), Texas (355), Mississippi (773), Florida (932), and Alabama (2690) in 1860, however, removes the possibility that their presence seriously distorts the data for those states. Those states whose free Negro population nearly equalled or surpassed their slave population in 1860—Maryland and Delaware—have generally been excluded from consideration in order to decrease the possibility of distortion of the data. Since most of the churches directed their energies primarily to the slaves, the distortion of these statistics is probably not significant in most of the categories. In those states such as Georgia and South Carolina where large numbers of plantation slaves were included in missions, the number of free Negroes represented in the statistics probably could not have been great. With the exception of Maryland, Delaware, and Virginia, in no state did free Negroes constitute as much as 10 per cent of the black population in 1860.

In the final analysis, the statistics compiled by the churches must be approached with the same caution scholars normally use when relying on nineteenth-century census reports. The margin of error in each class of statistics is so large that one can only talk confidently about general trends, not absolute numbers. Whatever their weaknesses, however, both kinds of statistics give us the best figures we can obtain.

Unlike the census, many of the problems presented by the church statistics can be resolved. A careful check of the cumulative statistics, for instance, usually reveals most computation errors. Parochial reports received after the cumulative statistics were compiled are usually appended to the published proceedings of the annual conferences and the figures included in them can be added to the cumulative statistics. The key to insuring reliability in the statistics is a perusal of the reports of all of the parishes, missions, and churches. Often when there are no racial distinctions made in the cumulative statistics, they are made in the reports of specific churches reprinted in the annual proceedings. The proceedings also frequently indicate which churches free Negroes attended in large numbers.

Although it is not possible to overcome all of the weaknesses of the statistics, they reveal much about the nature of slave life and culture. Suggesting probabilities and possibilities rather than providing certainties, they differ little from most statistics upon which scholars rely. The most accurate statistics are probably those of the Episcopalians. Beginning in the 1840s many dioceses required detailed parochial reports. When ministers conscientiously filled out such reports, they created a record rich in details.

Despite the detail in some of the records, the lack of symmetry in the data suggests caution in drawing conclusions. The Southern denominations with the largest number of slave members rarely reported statistics on the most significant aspects of life in the quarters. Consequently, one searches, often in vain, for statistical reports of intrastate associations of Baptists and Methodists. For the former, the paucity of even the most elemental statistics leads to a focus on single churches in local areas in the hope they may have cumulative statistical reports on black-white marriages, funerals, and Sunday School scholars. Despite literary evidence of common concerns of the various denominations, extrapolations from the statistics of one to the practices of another are difficult.

Statistical data on many aspects of slave life are so rare that historians have either ignored the topics or utilized local records limited in general applicability. For example, much of the debate on the punishment of slaves has centered on varying interpretations of the notations of floggings in the diary of the Alabama planter Bennet Barrow. Even in the highly unlikely event that Barrow was a typical planter, it is difficult to accept generalizations based on his diary without examining some comparative data. Barrow was among the few planters who apparently consistently noted the floggings on their plantations. Without the diaries of the overseers and mistresses for the same plantations, we can never be certain that we have a record of every slave who was flogged. Seasons, crops, and temperament of the slaves probably determined in some way the number of times slaves were whipped, but the causal links are difficult to establish.

The most revealing data on floggings appears in British Parliamentary reports on West Indian slavery. In 1823 Parliament passed a resolution requiring colonial assemblies to enact laws ameliorating the conditions of servitude and requiring plantation owners to keep a record of all floggings. The colonial assemblies responded to the resolution in a variety of ways. Some of the colonial laws did not require owners to record floggings involving fewer than ten lashes or from owners of fewer than six slaves. Crown colonies appointed a "Protector of the Slaves" who gathered statistics on marriages, manumissions, and punishments and submitted his reports to Parliament.

The parliamentary reports on flogging are among the most remarkable of antebellum records. Unique because they were reported to a colonial official, the statistics on floggings are immediately suspect because they were public. Did the West Indian planters and overseers flog their slaves more in order to show how rebellious bondsmen were with the hope of defeating the plans for emancipation? Under close public scrutiny, did the planters whip the slaves less than they had previously? Although the evidence is contradictory, it is clear that the number of floggings which occurred during this period were under reported. The royal officials monitoring the treatment of the slaves complained repeatedly that planters and overseers consistently refused to obey the law and report all of the times they flogged their bondsmen. West Indian missionaries joined in the chorus of complaints.

Contemporaries registered few complaints about another set of remarkable statistics: the records of slave marriages compiled by U.S. Army Chaplains and officers of the Bureau of Refugees, Freedmen and Abandoned Lands between 1864 and 1866. During the Civil War chaplains began marrying slaves in Union-occupied territory using a certificate containing questions about age, prior marriages, number of children from prior unions, and reasons for the dissolution of prior unions. The data has been preserved in two forms. Most chaplains simply kept the loose certificates. Others transferred the data on the certificates to books entitled, "Marriage Registers." Herbert Gutman utilized the latter records in his study, *The Black Family in Slavery and Freedom* (1976), while I relied upon the original marriage certificates in the table below. Gutman's registers contained data on about 8700 slave unions in two Mississippi counties (Adams and Warren). When the clerks copied the data into the bound volumes, they destroyed the original certificates. This was unfortunate because the clerks were sometimes inconsistent in transferring data from the original marriage certificates to the bound volumes, especially ages.

Although the bound volumes contain a record of more slave unions than the marriage certificates which have been preserved, I have utilized the latter primarily for two reasons. First, the marriage certificates are more representative geographically than the bound volumes: the marriage certificates contain data on slaves in six counties in three states. Second, by utilizing the original marriage certificates, one avoids the replication of the copyists' errors in the bound volumes.

Among the indices of slave life, few are as reliable as judicial records, especially on discontentment in the quarters. In contrast to the other major index of slave rebelliousness, fugitive slave notices, the court records begin early in the seventeenth century. Judicial records also include a greater range of rebelliousness than the runaway slave notices. The data presented below is, however, limited for a number of reasons. First, it is based only on cases which reached the state or colonial supreme courts and necessarily reflects only a fraction of those involving slaves. Second, the cases frequently contained relatively little testimony from blacks. In the final analysis, data drawn from court cases can only suggest a restricted dimension of the black response to bondage.

If one established a descending order of reliability for the statistics on slave life, census data on population, sex, and age would head the list. Another class of census data would, however, be at the very bottom of the list: the insane and idiotic. Becoming a political football in the 1840s, statistics on mental defectives were manipulated and distorted in efforts to prove that blacks were better off in slavery. In 1840 the directors of the census falsely inflated the number of insane free blacks in the North (occasionally making the mistake of counting more blacks who were insane in a town than there were blacks in the town's total population) to "prove" that freedom produced more mental defectives than slavery did. Consequently, the data on Northern blacks are practically worthless. Of course, the relative absence of public facilities for treating the insane in the South (and especially for blacks), necessarily led to an undercount of Southern mental defectives, black and white. But there apparently was far less deliberate distortion of the data on black mental defectives in the South than in the North after 1840.

The 1840 census was an embarrassment. The American Statistical Association (ASA) submitted a memorial to Congress in 1844 noting the "various and gross errors" in the printed census report: the marshals exaggerated the number of colleges and students, and recorded employment haphazardly. After comparing the manuscript returns with the printed census report, the ASA concluded that both the printers and the marshals had exaggerated the number of insane blacks in the North. Complaining of "glaring and remarkable errors," the ASA found "extraordinary contradictions and improbabilities" in the report of the black insane. After detailing eight pages of errors made in the enumeration of the insane in Northern states, the ASA concluded that the census "statements respecting the number of colored insane in these towns and counties carries on its very face its own refutation."

The complaints of the ASA and other groups led to considerable debate in Congress and eventually to more professional practices in the U.S. census office. Louisianian J. B. DeBow, director of the census of 1850, made every effort to ensure its reliability. Moreover, he readily admitted the shortcomings of data on mental defectives: inhabitants refused to report them, idiots and the insane were sometimes listed as belonging to the same category. The same problems are evident in the 1860 census. While the differentials in the number of institutions for mental defectives in the North and the South practically rule out the possibility of comparing the two regions, intraregional and interracial comparisons may be of some value. Masters, responsible for noting slaves who were insane, blind, idiotic, or deaf-mutes, may not have systematically revealed this information to the census takers. At the same time, the planters did not experience the same degree of shame about mental defectives among their slaves as they did about those in their own families. In all probability the major reason for the underenumeration of mental defectives among Southern blacks was the paucity of public institutions to care for them. Provisions for Southern whites were, however, little better than those for slaves. The aggregate figures for both groups, therefore, probably fall far below the actual numbers. Nonetheless, the 1850 and 1860 enumerations suggest some trends in differentials in insanity among blacks and whites in the South.

Historians rarely utilize perfect records; none of the statistical data I have relied upon in the tables below is free of shortcomings. Still, keeping in mind the observations of contemporaries, the statistics provide some useful information on slave life.

TABLE 1. Southern Churches, Accommodations, and Clergymen, 1850*

State	Whites	Slaves	Free Negroes	Clergy-men	Churches	Seating capacity
Alabama	426,514	342,844	2,265	702	1,375	440,155
Arkansas	162,189	47,100	608	233	362	60,226
Delaware	71,169	2,290	18,073	79	180	55,741
Florida	47,203	89,310	932	83	177	44,960
Georgia	521,572	381,682	2,931	715	1,862	632,992
Kentucky	761,413	210,981	10,011	931	1,849	673,528
Louisiana	255,491	244,809	17,462	229	307	109,615
Maryland	417,943	90,368	74,723	453	909	379,465
Mississippi	295,718	309,878	930	471	1,016	294,104
Missouri	592,004	87,422	2,618	814	909	264,979
North Carolina	553,028	288,548	27,463	747	1,787	574,924
South Carolina	274,563	384,984	8,960	474	1,182	460,450
Tennessee	756,836	239,459	6,422	1,081	2,027	628,495
Texas	154,034	58,161	397	308	328	64,155
Virginia	894,800	472,528	54,333	1,087	2,386	858,086
Totals	6,184,477	3,250,364	228,128	8,407	16,656	5,541,875

* Compiled from *Statistical View of the United States . . . A Compendium*

TABLE 2. Southern Churches, Accommodations, and Clergymen, 1860*

State	Whites	Slaves	Free Negroes	Clergy-men	Churches
Alabama	526,271	435,080	2,690	877	1,875
Arkansas	324,143	111,115	144	494	1,008
Delaware	90,589	1,798	19,829	110	220
Florida	77,747	61,745	932	159	319
Georgia	591,550	462,198	3,500	1,015	2,393
Kentucky	919,484	225,483	10,684	1,150	2,179
Louisiana	357,456	331,726	18,647	333	572
Maryland	515,918	87,189	83,942	731	1,016
Mississippi	353,899	436,631	773	693	1,441
Missouri	1,063,489	114,931	3,572	1,280	1,577
North Carolina	629,942	331,059	30,463	907	2,270
South Carolina	291,300	402,406	9,914	586	1,267
Tennessee	826,722	275,719	7,300	1,186	2,311
Texas	420,891	182,566	355	758	1,034
Virginia	1,047,299	490,865	58,042	1,437	3,105
Totals	8,036,700	3,950,511	250,787	11,716	22,587

* Compiled from *Statistics of the United States in 1860* (Washington, D.C., 1864), 598-99, 660-61.

Church to every 100 sq. mi.	Churches per 1000 inhabitants	Seats per 1000 inhabitants	Total Population	Inhabitants per clergyman	Slaves per clergy-man
2.71	1.78	575	771,623	1,099	488
.69	1.72	324	209,897	900	202
8.49	1.97	609	91,532	1,158	28
.30	2.02	514	87,445	1,053	1,076
3.21	2.05	707	906,185	1,267	533
4.91	1.88	689	982,405	1,055	226
.74	.59	214	517,762	2,260	540
8.17	1.56	651	583,084	1,286	199
2.15	1.68	485	606,526	1,500	657
1.35	1.33	396	682,044	837	107
3.52	2.06	664	869,039	1,163	386
4.02	1.77	689	668,507	1,410	812
4.45	2.02	631	1,002,717	927	118
.14	1.54	350	212,592	690	188
3.89	1.68	604	1,421,661	1,326	434
—	1.73	—	9,613,019	1,143	385

of the Seventh Census (Washington, D.C., 1854), 133-39.

Seating capacity	Inhabitants per clergyman	Slaves per clergyman	Seats per slave	Slaves per church	Total Population
550,494	1,099	496	1.26	232	964,201
216,183	899	224	1.94	110	435,450
68,560	1,020	17	38.13	88	112,216
68,990	883	388	1.11	193	140,424
763,812	1,041	455	1.65	193	1,057,286
778,025	1,004	190	3.45	103	1,155,684
206,196	2,126	996	.62	579	708,002
377,022	939	119	4.32	119	687,049
445,965	1,141	630	1.02	303	791,305
500,616	923	89	4.35	72	1,182,012
811,423	1,094	365	2.45	145	992,622
451,256	1,200	686	1.12	317	703,708
728,661	935	232	2.64	119	1,109,801
271,196	797	240	1.48	176	604,215
1,067,840	1,110	341	2.17	158	1,596,318
7,306,239	1,044	337	1.85	174	12,240,293

1866), 500-501; *Population of the United States in 1860* (Washington, D.C.,

TABLE 3. Black Members of the Methodist Episcopal Church, South, Selected Conferences, 1846-1860*

	1860			1855			1850-51			1846-47		
Conference	*Black*	*Total*	*% Black*	*Black*	*Total*	*% Black*	*Black*	*Total*	*% Black*	*Black*	*Total*	*% Black*
Kentucky	5,069	25,511	19.8	6,092	24,618	24.7	5,391	23,643	22.8	5,151	26,710	19.2
Louisville	4,150	28,906	14.3	4,008	24,982	16.0	3,072	19,733	15.5	3,081	18,210	16.9
Missouri	2,006	23,451	8.5	1,458	15,582	9.3	1,215	12,470	9.7	1,025	10,636	9.6
St. Louis	1,375	25,360	5.4	1,200	16,958	7.0	978	12,802	7.6	1,303	13,890	9.3
Tennessee	8,071	49,353	16.3	7,640	41,879	18.2	7,343	42,937	17.1	8,036	41,255	19.4
Holston	4,156	52,787	7.8	4,031	44,252	9.1	3,542	39,230	9.0	4,083	38,605	10.5
Memphis	7,002	42,396	16.5	7,164	38,438	18.6	7,055	36,191	19.4	6,003	29,114	20.6
Mississippi	12,684	37,976	33.4	10,729	26,116	41.0	7,801	20,887	37.3	5,854	15,949	36.7
Louisiana	5,834	17,915	32.5	5,235	11,761	44.5	4,435	9,204	48.1	3,329	8,044	41.3
Virginia	7,070	48,098	14.6	6,294	39,592	15.8	6,312	37,478	16.8	4,781	30,373	15.7
Western Virginia	276	12,663	2.1	232	7,315	3.1	149	5,457	2.7	—	—	—
North Carolina	12,043	45,306	26.5	12,071	42,613	28.3	10,375	35,865	28.9	6,705	26,648	25.1
South Carolina	42,469	90,116	47.1	45,261	80,258	56.3	37,840	68,716	55.0	40,475	73,124	55.3
Georgia	22,339	84,951	26.2	22,552	73,590	30.6	17,399	63,690	27.3	14,958	54,521	27.4
Alabama	21,856	74,696	29.2	19,775	59,684	33.1	15,484	48,272	32.0	14,440	42,431	34.0
Florida	6,589	19,376	34.0	4,381	11,136	39.3	3,165	8,956	35.3	2,570	6,558	39.1
Rio Grande	166	2,168	7.6	—	—	—	—	—	—	—	—	—
Texas	3,196	17,614	18.1	1,855	8,448	21.9	939	4,473	20.9	500	2,545	19.6
East Texas	1,993	19,055	10.4	1,488	11,824	12.5	908	7,863	11.5	764	4,386	17.4
Arkansas	1,013	15,160	6.6	833	10,150	8.2	1,769	13,068	13.5	1,702	9,068	18.7
Wachita	2,158	14,777	14.6	1,975	9,487	20.8	—	—	—			
TOTALS	171,515	747,635	22.9	164,274	598,683	27.4	135,172	510,935	26.4	124,760	452,067	27.5

* Compiled from *Minutes of the Annual Conferences of the Methodist Episcopal Church, South,* 1846-1860.

TABLE 4. Methodist Missions to the Slaves, 1831-1860*

Conference	1860			1850			1845			1840			1835			1831		
	Members	*Missions*	*Missionaries*	*Members*	*Missions*	*Missionaries*	*Members*	*Missions*	*Missionaries*	*Members*	*Missions*	*Missionaries*	*Members*	*Missions*	*Missionaries*	*Members*	*Missions*	*Missionaries*
St. Louis	431	2	2	—	—	—	—	—	—	—	—	—	—	—	—	—	—	—
Louisville	983	5	5	—	—	—	—	—	—	—	—	—	—	—	—	—	—	—
Tennessee	3,417	13	12	1,156	5	4	3,311	12	14	3,251	7	8	621	2	3	—	—	—
Holston	593	4	4	197	1	1	—	—	—	—	—	—	—	—	—	—	—	—
Memphis	4,093	24	23	2,804	10	11	3,383	11	12	769	4	4	—	—	—	—	—	—
Mississippi	7,659	46	48	2,750	16	18	3,022	11	12	3,908	8	10	—	1	1	—	—	—
Louisiana	2,957	16	18	1,381	4	5	—	—	—	—	—	—	—	—	—	—	—	—
Virginia	4,587	20	20	1,297	3	3	481	3	3	—	—	—	—	—	—	—	—	—
North Carolina	3,259	12	12	621	3	3	187	3	3	—	—	—	—	—	—	—	—	—
South Carolina	10,231	33	38	8,326	16	24	8,314	17	22	7,631	18	24	3,134	8	9	1,242	3	3
Georgia	11,071	38	41	3,908	11	13	3,106	10	12	3,972	15	17	1,266	6	7	115	1	1
Alabama	9,208	40	40	3,021	10	10	2,900	11	12	2,691	9	9	—	—	—	—	—	—
Florida	2,913	11	10	585	5	5	563	3	3	—	—	—	—	—	—	—	—	—
Texas	1,761	29	29	217	2	2	—	—	—	—	—	—	—	—	—	—	—	—
East Texas	824	8	8	213	1	1	—	1	1	—	—	—	—	—	—	—	—	—
Arkansas	674	8	7	369	3	3	113	1	1	—	—	—	—	—	—	—	—	—
Wachita	1,226	20	18	—	—	—				—	—	—	—	—	—	—	—	—
TOTALS	65,887	329	335	26,845	90	103	25,380	83	95	22,222	61	72	5,021	17	20	1,357	4	4

* Compiled from William P. Harrison, *The Gospel Among the Slaves* (Nashville, 1893), 194-95.

TABLE 5. Black Probationers in the Methodist Episcopal Church, South, Selected Conferences, 1856-60*

	1860			1859			1858			1856		
Conference	*Black*	*Total*	*% Black*	*Black*	*Total*	*% Black*	*Black*	*Total*	*% Black*	*Black*	*Total*	*% Black*
Kentucky	542	2,517	21.5	416	2,121	19.6	604	2,452	24.6	720	5,987	12.0
Louisville	469	2,952	15.8	310	2,417	12.8	415	2,482	16.7	272	1,954	13.9
Missouri	282	3,457	8.1	302	2,299	13.1	347	2,621	13.2	—	—	—
St. Louis	318	3,956	8.0	250	2,874	8.6	140	2,518	5.5	—	—	—
Tennessee	1,034	6,382	16.2	868	5,242	16.5	926	7,154	12.9	709	4,910	14.4
Holston	670	6,714	9.9	614	6,592	9.3	632	7,407	8.5	377	4,455	8.4
Memphis	1,364	5,996	22.7	1,248	5,143	24.2	858	4,942	17.3	371	3,687	10.0
Mississippi	4,845	9,374	51.6	4,106	8,154	50.3	3,642	7,523	48.4	2,825	5,541	50.9
Louisiana	1,655	4,116	40.2	1,251	3,145	39.7	970	2,706	35.8	702	1,924	36.4
Virginia	497	3,924	12.6	967	5,369	18.0	589	4,490	13.1	—	2,949	—
Western Virginia	101	2,553	3.9	46	2,228	2.0	70	2,311	3.0	—	—	—
North Carolina	1,139	4,123	27.6	1,347	4,476	30.0	1,429	5,059	28.2	1,400	4,780	29.2
South Carolina	7,305	12,889	56.6	7,336	12,332	59.4	7,020	12,007	58.4	5,755	10,100	56.9
Georgia	5,046	15,143	33.5	4,515	11,444	39.4	4,992	14,342	34.8	3,341	8,890	37.5
Alabama	6,045	15,055	40.1	5,871	13,633	43.0	5,414	14,636	36.9	3,489	9,466	36.8
Florida	1,521	3,829	39.7	1,594	3,442	46.3	1,289	2,983	43.2	780	2,368	32.9
Rio Grande	83	574	14.4	58	435	13.3	—	—	—	—	—	—
Texas	1,162	3,814	30.4	1,412	4,369	32.3	1,116	5,063	22.0	839	3,460	24.2
East Texas	851	4,038	21.0	543	4,093	13.2	739	4,309	17.1	413	3,188	12.9
Arkansas	341	2,708	12.5	428	3,104	13.7	309	2,831	10.9	—	—	—
Wachita	639	3,426	18.6	660	3,391	19.4	603	3,080	19.5	685	2,368	28.9
TOTALS	35,908	117,540	30.5	34,142	106,303	32.1	32,104	110,916	28.9	22,678	76,027	29.8

* Compiled from *Minutes of the Annual Conferences of the Methodist Episcopal Church, South,* 1856-1860.

TABLE 6. Black Catechumens in the Protestant Episcopal Church in Selected States, 1841-1860*

	South Carolina			North Carolina		
Year	*Black*	*Total*	*% Black*	*Black*	*Total*	*% Black*
1860	399	1,070	37.2	365	1,123	32.5
1859	1,381	1,964	70.3	351	1,294	27.1
1858	2,564	3,175	80.7	728	—	—
1857		N R D		488	1,593	30.6
1855	1,371	1,790	76.5	769	1,527	50.3
1854	949	1,468	64.6	506	—	—
1853	1,004	1,426	70.4	294	1,022	28.7
1852	821	1,289	63.6	220	—	—
1851	1,273	1,904	66.8	275	—	—
1850	1,649	2,132	77.3	259	790	32.7
1849	1,421	2,191	64.8	208	631	32.9
1848	791	1,381	57.2	—	—	—
1847	638	1,049	60.8	—	—	—
1846	567	1,081	52.4	—	—	—
1845	480	955	50.2	—	—	—
1844	930	1,785	52.1	—	—	—
1843	868	1,818	47.7	—	—	—
1842	779	1,777	43.8	—	—	—
1841	580	1,071	54.1	—	—	—

* Compiled from journals of annual proceedings, Protestant Episcopal Church, South Carolina and North Carolina, 1841-1860.
N R D = no reported data.

TABLE 7. Black Sunday School Scholars in the Protestant Episcopal Church in Selected States, 1841-1860*

	South Carolina			Alabama			Georgia			Florida		
Year	*Black*	*Total*	*% Black*	*Black*	*Total*	*% Black*	*Black*	*Total*	*% Black*	*Black*	*Total*	*% Black*
1860	604	2,167	27.8	107	972	11.0	621	1,641	37.8	121	709	17.0
1859	935	2,245	41.6	86	930	9.2	592	1,526	38.7	—	—	—
1858	1,213	2,545	47.6	209	860	24.3	430	1,569	27.4	63	586	10.7
1857		NRD		135	698	19.3	201	1,412	14.2	—	—	—
1856	1,014	2,072	48.9	223	912	24.4	734	1,499	48.9	200	506	39.5
1855	591	1,716	34.4	120	898	13.3	571	1,204	47.4	138	520	26.5
1854	1,149	2,086	55.0	41	651	6.2	515	1,436	35.8	—	—	—
1853	1,038	1,889	54.9	83	524	15.8	467	1,495	31.2	70	410	17.0
1852	721	1,628	44.2	—	—	—	315	1,292	24.3	—	—	—
1851	792	1,911	41.4	58	418	13.8	39	773	5.0	55	241	22.8
1850	1,295	2,331	55.5	—	—	—	236	856	27.5	—	—	—
1849	1,134	2,165	52.3	221	644	34.3	—	—	—	25	206	12.1
1848	1,077	2,203	48.8	200	525	38.0	—	—	—	30	213	14.0
1847	1,051	1,999	52.5	90	491	18.3	—	—	—	41	149	27.5
1846	753	1,554	48.4	—	—	—	—	—	—	—	115	—
1845	929	1,829	50.7	—	—	—	—	—	—	40	292	13.6
1844	1,454	2,455	59.2	—	—	—	—	—	—	—	—	—
1843	1,219	2,271	53.6	—	—	—	—	—	—	—	—	—
1842	1,454	2,648	54.9	—	—	—	—	—	—	—	—	—
1841	1,632	2,632	62.0	—	—	—	—	—	—	—	—	—

* Compiled from journals of annual proceedings, Protestant Episcopal Church, South Carolina, Alabama, Georgia, and Florida, 1841-1860.

N R D = no reported data.

TABLE 8. Black Confirmations in the Protestant Episcopal Church in Selected States, 1841-1860*

Year	South Carolina			North Carolina			Alabama			Virginia		
	Black	Total	% Black	Black	Total	% Black	Black	Total	% Black	Black	Total	% Black
1860	173	389	44.4	34	247	13.7	55	227	24.2	22	688	3.1
1859	296	445	66.5	20	358	5.5	23	141	16.3	64	671	9.5
1858	550	807	68.1	65	336	19.3	40	258	15.5	11	625	1.7
1857		NRD		63	313	20.1	9	182	4.9	11	532	2.0
1856	365	563	64.8	61	272	22.4	0	90	0	47	452	10.3
1855	414	624	66.3	55	280	19.6	35	211	16.5	17	429	3.9
1854	520	756	68.7	32	190	16.8	21	205	10.2	31	519	5.9
1853	349	473	73.7	0	41	0	0	113	0	9	348	2.5
1852	18	69	26.0	31	—	—	—	—	—	—	—	—
1851	180	391	46.0	32	182	17.5	4	75	5.3	2	345	0.5
1850	113	218	51.8	24	168	14.2	—	—	—	—	287	—
1849	124	259	47.8	31	233	13.3	39	108	36.1	—	—	—
1848	178	315	56.5	—	—	—	6	33	18.1	—	—	—
1847	73	198	36.8	—	—	—	0	106[a]	0	—	—	—
1846	125	219	57.0	—	—	—	—	—	—	—	—	—
1845	233	308	75.6	—	—	—	—	—	—	—	—	—
1844	60	104	57.6	—	—	—	—	—	—	—	—	—
1843	144	313	46.0	—	—	—	—	—	—	—	—	—
1842	166	313	53.0	—	—	—	—	—	—	—	—	—
1841	120	211	56.8	—	—	—	—	—	—	—	—	—

* Compiled from journals of annual proceedings, Protestant Episcopal Church, South Carolina, North Carolina, Alabama, and Virginia, 1841-1860.

NRD = no reported data.

[a] Listed incorrectly as 325 in the tabular report.

TABLE 9. Black Baptisms in the Protestant Episcopal Church in Selected States, 1841-1860*

Year	South Carolina			Georgia			Alabama			North Carolina			Florida			Virginia		
	Black	Total	% Black	Black	Total	% Black	Black	Total	% Black	Black	Total	% Black	Black	Total	% Black	Black	Total	% Black
1860	1,156	1,644	70.3	93	391	23.7	213	608	35.0	208	616	33.7	49	231	21.2	178	1,216	14.6
1859	843	1,286	65.5	117	399	29.3	213	515	41.3	352	799	44.0		NRD		301	1,332	22.5
1858	1,576	2,148	73.3	81	366	22.1	128	453	28.2	236	584	40.4	29	123	23.5	210	1,150	18.2
1857		NRD		89	291	30.5	94	374	25.1	253	642	39.4	—	—	—	164	1,115	14.7
1856	918	1,315	69.8	187	369	50.6	78	356	21.9	389	837	46.4	64	160	40.0	224	836	26.7
1855	975	1,399	69.6	115	349	32.9	141	489	28.8	—	870	—	111	249	44.5	108	847	12.7
1854	1,022	1,387	73.6	96	288	33.3	150	567	26.4	—	518	—	—	—	—	131	1,002	13.0
1853	739	1,099	67.2	202	416	48.5	48	355	13.5	—	438	—	15	103	14.5	167	944	17.6
1852	826	1,172	70.4	128	359	35.6	—	—	—	—	—	—	—	—	—	—	—	—
1851	825	1,216	67.8	18	236	7.6	45	295	15.2	—	521	—	19	91	20.8	117	945	12.3
1850	981	1,207	81.2	78	227	34.3	—	—	—	—	589	—	—	—	—	167	849	19.6
1849	906	1,279	70.8	—	—	—	57	331	17.2	—	604	—	19	103	18.4	—	—	—
1848	1,448	2,063	70.1	—	—	—	31	139	22.3	—	—	—	7	110	6.3	—	—	—
1847	694	992	69.9	—	—	—	132	325	40.6	—	—	—	5	75	6.6	—	—	—
1846	534	703	75.9	—	—	—	—	—	—	—	—	—	13	106	12.2	—	—	—
1845	816	1,108	73.6	—	—	—	—	—	—	—	—	—	7	126	5.5	—	—	—
1844	665	1,031	64.5	—	—	—	—	—	—	—	—	—	—	101	—	—	—	—
1843	727	1,132	64.2	—	—	—	—	—	—	—	—	—	—	—	—	—	—	—
1842	564	892	63.2	—	—	—	—	—	—	—	—	—	—	—	—	—	—	—
1841	321	596	53.8	—	—	—	—	—	—	—	—	—	—	—	—	—	—	—

* Compiled from journals of annual proceedings, Protestant Episcopal Church, South Carolina, Georgia, Alabama, North Carolina, Florida, and Virginia, 1841-1860.

NRD = no reported data.

TABLE 10. Black Communicants in the Protestant Episcopal Church in Selected States, 1841-1860*

Year	South Carolina			Alabama			North Carolina			Virginia		
	Black	*Total*	*% Black*	*Black*	*Total*	*% Black*	*Black*	*Total*	*% Black*	*Black*	*Total*	*% Black*
1860	2,960	6,126	48.3	112	1,761	6.3	366	2,792	13.1	114	7,876	1.4
1859	2,819	5,672	49.7	131	1,673	7.8	353	3,036	11.6	444	7,184	6.1
1858	2,715	5,552	48.9	104	1,485	7.0	342	2,789	12.2	270	6,129	4.4
1857		NRD		89	1,240	7.1	345	2,685	12.8	33	6,315	0.5
1856	2,735	5,453	50.1	78	1,461	5.3	305	2,575	11.8	235	6,527	3.6
1855	3,022	5,993	50.4	52	1,336	3.8	282	2,324	12.1	224	6,017	3.7
1854	2,720	5,620	48.3	23	1,123	2.0	277	2,165	12.7	203	6,055	3.3
1853	2,827	5,456	51.8	16	1,019	1.5	179	1,778	10.0	124	5,299	2.3
1852	2,272	5,000	45.4	—	—	—	229	—	—	—	—	—
1851	2,313	5,043	45.8	19	775	2.4	198	2,219	8.9	111	5,412	2.0
1850	3,168	5,919	53.5	—	—	—	216	2,137	10.1	75	5,347	1.4
1849	2,247	4,916	45.7	36	723	4.9	242	2,129	11.3	—	—	—
1848	2,081	4,531	45.9	25	657	3.8	—	—	—	113	—	—
1847	1,989	4,229	47.0	53	663	7.9	—	—	—	—	—	—
1846	2,116	4,324	48.9	—	—	—	—	—	—	—	—	—
1845	1,779	3,879	45.8	—	—	—	—	—	—	—	—	—
1844	1,636	3,964	41.2	—	—	—	—	—	—	—	—	—
1843	1,404	3,535	39.7	—	—	—	—	—	—	—	—	—
1842	1,379	3,466	39.7	—	—	—	—	—	—	—	—	—
1841	1,314	3,337	39.3	—	—	—	—	—	—	—	—	—

* Compiled from journals of annual proceedings, Protestant Episcopal Church, South Carolina, Alabama, North Carolina, and Virginia, 1841-1860.

NRD = no reported data.

TABLE 11. Black Marriages in the Protestant Episcopal Church

	South Carolina			Alabama			North Carolina		
Year	*Black*	*Total*	*% Black*	*Black*	*Total*	*% Black*	*Black*	*Total*	*% Black*
1860	209	314	66.5	35	112	31.2	31	101	30.6
1859	113	206	54.8	13	84	15.4	22	90	24.4
1858	165	276	59.7	23	82	28.0	25	80	31.2
1857		NRD		26	79	32.9	20	95	21.0
1856	96	185	51.8	14	67	20.8	19	80	23.7
1855	96	195	49.2	20	96	20.8	16	77	20.7
1854	89	198	44.9	15	80	18.7	21	79	26.5
1853	102	178	57.3	0	57	0	21	73	28.7
1852	100	182	54.9	—	—	—	20	91	21.9
1851	106	179	59.2	11	50	22.0	14	73	19.1
1850	87	192	45.3	—	—	—	16	67	23.8
1849	94	165	56.9	14	49	28.5	14	72	19.4
1848	82	153	53.5	5	22	22.7	—	—	—
1847	52	107	48.5	2	24	8.3	—	—	—
1846	46	90	51.1	—	—	—	—	—	—
1845	58	131	44.2	—	—	—	—	—	—
1844	75	155	48.3	—	—	—	—	—	—
1843	58	113	51.3	—	—	—	—	—	—
1842	38	105	36.1	—	—	—	—	—	—
1841	39	101	38.6	—	—	—	—	—	—

* Compiled from journals of annual proceedings, Protestant Episcopal Mississippi, and Virginia, 1841-1860.

NRD = no reported data.

in Selected States, 1841-1860*

Georgia			Louisiana			Mississippi			Virginia		
Black	*Total*	*% Black*	*Black*	*Total*	*% Black*	*Black*	*Total*	*% Black*	*Black*	*Total*	*% Black*
25	77	32.4	53	224	23.6	17	68	25.0	99	332	29.8
39	72	54.1	37	230	16.0	—	—	—	109	409	26.6
18	73	24.7	59	243	24.2	19	58	32.7	76	344	22.0
29	70	41.4	43	278	15.4	16	50	32.0	66	281	23.4
28	81	34.5	16	159	10.0	17	52	32.6	81	366	22.1
41	89	46.0	7	236	2.9	16	—	—	71	327	21.7
31	59	52.5	—	—	—	—	—	—	82	330	24.8
32	75	42.6	16	289	5.5	6	—	—	80	445	17.9
45	87	51.7	—	—	—	—	—	—	80	445	17.9
7	48	14.5	35	209	16.7	—	—	—	28	348	8.0
9	42	21.4	—	—	—	5	—	—	9	275	3.2
—	—	—	6	191	3.1	7	—	—	—	—	—
—	—	—	—	214	—	21	—	—	20	—	—
—	—	—	—	—	—	—	—	—	—	—	—
—	—	—	—	—	—	—	—	—	—	—	—
—	—	—	—	—	—	—	—	—	—	—	—
—	—	—	—	—	—	—	—	—	—	—	—
—	—	—	—	—	—	—	—	—	—	—	—
—	—	—	—	—	—	—	—	—	—	—	—
—	—	—	—	—	—	—	—	—	—	—	—

Church, South Carolina, Alabama, North Carolina, Georgia, Louisiana,

TABLE 12. Black Funerals in the Protestant Episcopal Church in Selected States, 1841-1860*

	South Carolina			Alabama			Virginia		
Year	*Black*	*Total*	*% Black*	*Black*	*Total*	*% Black*	*Black*	*Total*	*% Black*
1860	118	369	31.9	25	319	7.8	97	691	14.0
1859	122	475	25.6	15	214	7.0	128	718	17.8
1858	206	536	38.4	9	154	5.8	93	667	13.9
1857		NRD		25	169	14.7	86	634	13.5
1856	140	393	35.6	4	138	2.8	112	822	13.6
1855	145	437	33.1	10	163	6.1	109	708	15.3
1854	96	403	23.8	14	212	6.6	81	626	12.9
1853	128	329	38.9	2	106	1.8	55	520	10.5
1852	124	407	30.4	—	—	—	—	—	—
1851	108	330	32.7	7	85	8.2	—	—	—
1850	102	328	31.0	—	—	—	—	—	—
1849	89	344	25.8	4	97	4.1	—	—	—
1848	54	269	20.0	1	50	2.0	—	—	—
1847	44	209	21.0	5	59	8.4	—	—	—
1846	42	198	21.2	—	—	—	—	—	—
1845	33	193	17.0	—	—	—	—	—	—
1844	57	219	26.0	—	—	—	—	—	—
1843	63	228	27.6	—	—	—	—	—	—
1842	42	213	19.7	—	—	—	—	—	—
1841	35	203	17.2	—	—	—	—	—	—

* Compiled from journals of annual proceedings, Protestant Episcopal Church, South Carolina, Alabama, and Virginia, 1841-1860.

N R D = no reported data.

TABLE 13. Black Members of the Baptist Church in Georgia, Selected Associations, 1845-1846*

Association	Members			*Ministers*	*Churches*
	Black	*Total*	*% Black*		
Bethel	392	2,439	16.0	30	39
Central	405	1,632	24.8	19	19
Columbus	504	3,534	14.2	21	40
Coosa	63	2,094	3.0	21	44
Flint River	312	2,152	14.4	26	30
Georgia	3,382	7,560	44.7	45	49
Hepzibah	489	2,632	18.5	20	25
Rehoboth	507	1,736	29.2	14	22
Sunbury	3,764	4,283	87.8	13	21
Western	571	3,013	18.9	28	38
Elijah	7	588	1.1	17	18
Hightower	75	1,498	5.0	16	29
Houston	40	894	4.4	16	20
Rock Mountain	163	1,160	14.0	13	17
Valley River	42	939	4.4	14	21

* Compiled from Jesse H. Campbell, *Georgia Baptists: Historical and Biographical* (Richmond, 1847), 286-88.

TABLE 14. Black Members of Selected Churches of the Ebeneezer Missionary Baptist (Georgia) Association, 1848-68*

		1848		1858		1868	
Church	*County*	*Black*	*Total*	*Black*	*Total*	*Black*	*Total*
Antiock	Twiggs	5	85	17	145	105	320
Bethel	Wilkinson	4	79	20	166	—	123
Big Sandy	"	9	75	16	102	82	219
Blue Water	Laurens	1	57	8	89	32	171
Clear Creek	Wilkinson	—	30	3	78	1	54
Dublin	Laurens	7	52	39	90	98	175
Ebeneezer	Wilkinson	—	54	4	37	11	85
Evergreen	Pulaski	—	118	101	186	84	147
Hawkinsville	"	40	130	Dismissed		—	—
Hopewell	"	7	61	—	—	—	—
Jeffersonville	Twiggs	—	—	88	131	109	154
Irwinton	Wilkinson	6	29	—	15	—	—
Laurens Hill	Laurens	15	81	38	100	27	57
Liberty	Wilkinson	25	157	43	196	65	199
Limestone	Pulaski	—	50	4	43	—	127
Mt. Calvary	"	—	67	14	97	—	40
New Hope	Laurens	—	—	5	21	10	41
New Providence	Wilkinson	—	93	48	98	122	155
Parkinson	Laurens	—	—	2	60	—	61
Pleasant Spring	Montgomery			9	53	—	—
Poplar Spring	Laurens	61	224	72	176	—	103
Richland Creek	Twiggs	123	257	165	254	265	339
Rocky Creek	Laurens	—	64	57	84	89	122
Stone Creek	Twiggs	93	212	163	313	184	324

* Compiled from Billy Walker Jones, *History of Ebeneezer Missionary Baptist Association of Georgia, 1814-1964* (Macon, Ga., 1965), 62.

TABLE 15. Black Members, Welsh Neck Baptist Association, South Carolina, 1841-1860*

Year	*Churches*	*Whites*	*Blacks*	*Total*	*% Black*
1841	37	1,275	1,145	2,420	47.3
1842	37	1,277	2,198	3,475	63.2
1843	38	1,252	2,014	3,266	61.6
1844	38	1,255	2,113	3,368	62.7
1845	38	1,341	1,845	3,186	57.9
1846	38	1,514	1,896	3,410	55.6
1847	—	—	—	—	—
1848	38	1,758	2,059	3,817	53.9
1849	38	1,828	2,202	4,030	54.6
1850	40	1,895	2,483	4,378	56.7
1851	43	2,394	2,618	5,012	52.2
1852	—	—	—	—	—
1853	44	2,437	2,619	5,056	51.7
1854	45	2,200	2,604	4,804	54.2
1855	45	2,219	2,435	4,654	52.3
1856	46	2,311	2,658	4,969	53.4
1857	46	2,430	2,900	5,330	54.4
1858	47	2,716	3,035	5,751	52.7
1859	48	3,004	3,242	6,246	51.9
1860	47	3,157	3,319	6,476	51.2

* Compiled from Welsh Neck Baptist Association, annual *Minutes,* 1841-1860.

TABLE 16. Black Members, Selected Virginia Baptist Associations, 1838-1846*

	Dover			Salem Union			Middle District			Rappahannock		
Year	*Black*	*Total*	% *Black*	*Black*	*Total*	% *Black*	*Black*	*Total*	% *Black*	*Black*	*Total*	% *Black*
1838	9,142	19,118	47.8	—	—	—	—	—	—	—	—	—
1839	9,415	19,082	49.3	441	810	54.4	—	—	—	—	—	—
1841	—	—	—	383	794	48.2	1,469	2,118	69.3	—	—	—
1844	—	—	—	—	—	—	—	—	—	8,207	14,037	58.4
1845	8,355	12,710	65.7	—	—	—	—	—	—	8,164	14,065	58.0
1846	8,698	12,945	67.1	510	1,390	36.6	1,900	3,100	61.2	—	—	—

* Compiled from *Minutes of the Dover Baptist Association*, 1838, 1839, 1845, 1846; Richmond *Religious Herald*, 1839-1846.

TABLE 17. Slave Families*

	Mississippi		Tennessee		Louisiana		Totals	
Unions	*No.*	*Per Cent*	*No.*	*Per Cent*	*No.*	*Per Cent*	*No.*	*Per Cent*
Totals	1225	—	1123	—	540	—	2888	—
Unbroken	78	6.3	226	20.1	90	16.6	394	13.6
Broken	1147	93.6	897	79.8	450	83.3	2494	86.3
by: Master	477	38.9	302	26.8	158	29.2	937	32.4
Personal choice	145	11.8	106	9.4	58	10.7	309	10.6
Death	509	41.5	418	37.2	226	41.8	1153	39.9
War	16	1.3	71	6.3	8	1.4	95	3.2

* Compiled from unbound "Marriage Certificates," Bureau of Refugees, Freedmen and Abandoned Lands, Record Group 105, National Archives.

TABLE 18. Slave Discontent, 1640-1865*

	Suits for Freedom						
State	*Won*	*Lost*	*Unresolved*	*Total*	*Runaway*	*Violence*	*Discontent and Insubordination*
Va.	41	24	6	71	24	4	3
Ky.	41	32	10	83	49	3	5
N.C.	10	6	3	19	56	44	18
S.C.	13	6	4	23	62	33	17
Tenn.	28	4	3	35	27	18	11
Ga.	2	1	2	5	27	11	11
Fla.	1	2	—	3	3	1	—
Ala.	2	5	1	8	33	43	13
Miss.	2	2	1	5	31	28	9
La.	43	38	9	90	160	63	33
Md.	35	45	10	90	24	96	4
D.C.	34	34	20	88	16	16	—
Del.	13	4	1	18	5	—	—
Mo.	11	16	12	39	24	18	8
Ark.	1	5	4	10	11	6	5
Texas	2	—	2	4	9	5	7
Totals	279	224	88	591	561	389	144

* Compiled from Marion Russell, "American Slave Discontent in Records of the High Courts," *Journal of Negro History* XXXI (Oct. 1946), 411-34.

TABLE 19. Floggings, West Indies, 1826-30*

Place	Slave Population, 1828-29			Punishments			Period covered by report	Percentage of slaves flogged
	Males	Females	Total	Males	Females	Total		
Berbice	11,284	10,035	21,319	6,270	4,508	10,778	1829	50.5
Berbice	—	—	—	6,374	4,088	10,462	1828	49.0
Berbice	—	—	—	5,939	3,173	9,112	1827-28	42.7
St. Lucia	6,280	7,381	13,661	—	—	1,125	1829	8.2
St. Lucia	—	—	—	—	—	1,012	1828	7.4
St. Lucia	—	—	—	—	—	2,876	1826-27	21.0
Trinidad	13,141	10,865	24,006	5,064	2,860	7,924	1828-30	33.0
Trinidad	—	—	—	6,223	4,908	11,131	1826-27	46.3

* Compiled from *Anti-Slavery Reporter* II (Nov. 1827), 129-30; III (Nov. 1829), 137, 139; IV (July 25, 1831), 349 (Aug. 1831), 372, 374; V (Sept. 1, 1832), 259, 263.

TABLE 20. The Blind, Insane, and Idiotic in the South, 1850*

	Blind			Insane			Idiotic		
State	*White*	*Slave*	*Free Negroes*	*White*	*Slave*	*Free Negroes*	*White*	*Slave*	*Free Negroes*
Delaware	25	—	14	48	—	20	74	4	14
Maryland	215	45	63	477	25	44	275	68	48
Virginia	197	299	85	864	59	47	891	201	90
North Carolina	379	155	27	467	33	10	615	151	28
South Carolina	150	134	14	224	21	4	249	94	5
Georgia	224	129	4	294	28	2	515	148	1
Florida	15	14	1	9	2	—	28	8	—
Alabama	156	138	2	201	30	2	343	133	—
Mississippi	112	93	—	105	24	—	136	84	2
Louisiana	72	122	20	144	45	11	106	62	6
Texas	61	11	1	37	—	—	93	11	—
Arkansas	78	13	1	60	3	—	103	10	2
Tennessee	383	82	9	380	22	5	756	85	5
Kentucky	419	113	20	502	23	2	796	91	20
Missouri	191	38	3	249	11	2	325	32	—
Totals	2,677	1,386	264	4,061	326	149	5,305	1,182	221

* Compiled from U. S. Census Office, *Seventh Census of the United States, 1850* (Washington, D.C., 1853), L. Racial distinctions were not consistently made in statistics on the deaf and dumb.

TABLE 21. The Insane, Idiotic, Deaf and Dumb, and Blind in the South, 1860*

State	Insane			Idiotic			Deaf and Dumb			Blind		
	White	*Slave*	*Free Black*	*White*	*Slave*	*Free Black*	*White*	*Slave*	*Free Black*	*White*	*Slave*	*Free Black*
Alabama	223	32	2	398	134	5	207	67	1	198	114	6
Arkansas	81	5	1	152	24	0	116	15	0	117	26	1
Delaware	52	0	8	53	0	14	54	1	1	32	0	10
Florida	17	5	3	50	16	2	15	9	0	15	21	0
Georgia	447	44	0	535	183	6	304	83	1	285	187	12
Kentucky	588	33	2	892	155	11	574	75	3	516	144	14
Louisiana	125	37	7	135	104	8	198	38	3	102	118	10
Maryland	495	14	51	174	62	69	177	35	25	196	34	68
Mississippi	236	36	0	192	86	1	152	55	1	147	117	0
Missouri	750	20	0	457	63	3	450	46	2	380	60	8
North Carolina	576	63	21	708	241	31	354	106	8	372	189	20
South Carolina	297	18	2	270	121	12	142	59	2	161	120	10
Tennessee	609	28	3	727	149	3	361	73	2	432	117	5
Texas	112	13	0	164	37	0	157	24	0	119	31	0
Virginia	1,088	58	33	1,009	214	56	676	121	19	520	232	37
Totals	5,696	406	133	5,916	1,589	221	3,937	808	68	3,592	1,510	201

* Compiled from U. S. Census Office, *Population of the United States in 1860* (Washington, D.C., 1864), 624-49.

TABLE 22. The Insane, Idiotic, Blind, and Deaf-Mutes in the South, 1880*

State	Insane		Idiots		Blind		Deaf-Mutes		Total Population	
	White	*Black*	*White*	*Black*	*White*	*Black*	*White*	*Black*	*White*	*Black*
Alabama	1,110	411	1,354	869	755	644	405	288	662,185	600,103
Arkansas	629	160	1,050	324	759	213	417	72	591,531	210,666
Delaware	150	48	214	55	101	26	72	12	120,160	26,442
Florida	168	85	213	156	94	121	55	63	142,605	126,690
Georgia	1,286	411	1,499	934	861	773	499	320	816,906	725,133
Kentucky	2,439	345	3,026	487	1,777	339	1,107	168	1,377,179	271,451
Louisiana	698	304	587	466	366	479	328	196	454,954	483,635
Maryland	1,598	259	959	360	694	252	515	156	724,693	210,230
Mississippi	715	432	801	778	468	603	317	289	479,398	650,291
Missouri	3,165	145	3,130	242	2,082	176	1,523	75	2,022,826	145,350
North Carolina	1,591	437	2,134	1,008	1,161	712	724	308	867,242	531,277
South Carolina	651	461	806	782	434	666	301	263	391,105	604,332
Tennessee	2,040	364	2,817	716	1,542	484	868	240	1,138,831	403,151
Texas	1,258	306	1,636	640	1,017	358	614	157	1,197,237	393,384
Virginia	1,719	692	1,839	955	897	813	705	293	880,858	631,616
TOTALS	19,217	4,860	22,065	8,772	13,008	6,659	8,450	2,900	11,867,710	6,013,751

* Compiled from U.S. Census Office, *Report on the Defective, Dependent, and Delinquent Classes of the Population of the United States, 1880* (Washington, D.C., 1888), xvii-xviii.

TABLE 23. Ratio of Insane to 1,000,000 of Population, by Race, 1850, 1860, 1880*

	1850		1860		1880	
State	*Whites*	*Blacks*	*Whites*	*Blacks*	*Whites*	*Blacks*
Alabama	471	93	424	78	1,676	685
Arkansas	370	63	250	54	1,063	758
Delaware	48	20	52	8	150	48
Florida	9	2	17	8	168	85
Georgia	294	30	447	44	1,286	411
Kentucky	502	25	588	35	2,439	345
Louisiana	144	56	125	44	698	304
Maryland	477	69	495	65	1,598	259
Mississippi	105	24	236	36	715	432
Missouri	249	13	750	20	3,165	145
North Carolina	467	43	576	84	1,591	437
South Carolina	224	25	297	20	651	461
Tennessee	380	27	609	31	2,040	364
Texas	37	—	112	13	1,258	306
Virginia	864	106	1,088	91	1,719	692

* Compiled from U.S. Census Office, *Report on the Defective, Dependent, and Delinquent Classes of the Population in the United States, 1880* (Washington, D.C., 1888), 4-7.

Critical Essay on Sources

Sources left by slaves, and especially the autobiography, have been utilized more heavily in this study than others primarily because there is no better way to investigate the slave's personality than through his personal records. Since slaves have left so few letters and diaries, the autobiography provides the interested observer with the largest body of life histories dealing with the intimate details of their lives. If historians seek to provide some understanding of the past experiences of slaves, then the autobiography must be their point of departure; in the autobiography, more clearly than in any other source, we learn what went on in the minds of black men. It gives us a window into the "inside half" of the slave's life which never appears in the commentaries of "outsiders." Autobiographers are generally so preoccupied with conflict, those things blocking their hopes and dreams, that their works give a freshness and vitality to history which is often missing in other sources.

Autobiographies are especially important in any study of the slave's personality development. There is generally so much ego involvement in the autobiographies that they are invaluable for studies of black self-concepts. Since these works focus on the mental life of the authors (fear, love, pain, dreams, insecurity, frustrations), they provide the scholar with numerous insights into the nature of interpersonal relations during slavery. At the same time, such works place the general conditions under which slaves existed in America in the context where they have the most meaning, the slaves' personal lives. While other sources are important in any general description of the institution of slavery, they rarely tell us much about how blacks *perceived* their experiences. Yet, psychologists have constantly pointed out that how people perceive objective conditions, is, under most circumstances, more important in determining their attitudes and how they act than the "reality" of the situation. The chief value of the autobiography lies in the fact that it is subjective, that it tells us a great deal about how blacks felt about the conditions under which they lived. Since no other large body of material written by blacks is so profoundly introspective, and since no one can know as much about blacks as they themselves knew, black autobiographies are crucial for an understanding of the slave experience.

There are, of course, several problems involved in the use of them. Even so, it is possible to examine autobiographies systematically by applying the rules of evidence rigidly. Four works which are especially helpful in establishing a framework for using autobiographies are: Ernest S. Bates, *Inside Out: An Introduction to Autobiography* (1936), G. W. Allport, *The Use of Personal Documents in Psychological Science* (1942), Roy Pascal, *Design and Truth in Autobiography* (1960), and John H. Wigmore, *The Principles of Judicial Proof* (1931).

One of the major shortcomings of autobiographies (though common to other sources) is that few men are able to tell the *whole* truth about themselves. Almost inevitably they exaggerate the difficulties they faced and make themselves more heroic than they were in real life. The unconscious plays tricks on the conscious; some things are either too painful to recall or to reveal to others. Undoubtedly this was a serious problem for black men as they contemplated the hostile audience to which they were addressing themselves. Could they really strip themselves bare before white America? Even if they had been able to overcome these problems, however, the black autobiographers were confined by the conventions of the genre they were using. In nineteenth-century autobiographies, a discussion of sex was taboo and family secrets were too sacred to reveal. For those accustomed to twentieth-century canons of literary taste, these limitations would almost rule out analysis altogether. While they certainly make the task more difficult, the problems are not insurmountable. Some men, of course, violated the conventions; and when they did not, an unguarded slip of the pen here and an innuendo there often provide clues to topics not explored in depth.

The usefulness of any autobiography is affected by the objectives, age, and memory of the author. Generally speaking, the black autobiographies were written to leave records for relatives and historians, to raise money, and as polemical attacks on the institution of slavery. With the objectives clearly stated, it is usually possible to separate fact from opinion, myth, and propaganda. On the other hand, it is often impossible to determine the impact of the age of the author on the reliability of his autobiography. While it is true that old age distorts memory, psychologists have found that old people tend to have far less difficulty in recalling events which occurred in the remote than the recent past. Then, too, the aging process operates differently in different individuals; some eighty-year-old men have more vivid memories than some fifty-year-old men. Consequently, every autobiography must be evaluated on its own merit. At the same time, it is obvious that if a majority of the authors in a sample of autobiographies were senile, the chances of error and distortion would be great. In regard to the black autobiographers included in this study, it would appear that they wrote their accounts long before the age at which senility usually occurs: 41 per cent published their books before they reached the age of fifty, and 71 per cent before they were sixty. The average age of the authors when they published their accounts was about fifty-two years.

Because an autobiography is the record of what one person has seen and experienced, the stories of the men and women included in this study have been verified by investigating several independent sources. Since the autobiographies were often concerned with things which rarely, if ever, appeared in other sources, however, it was often impossible to check the experiences of an individual narrator against independent records. Consequently, it was generally more fruitful to compare the experiences of one autobiographer with those of others, and to accept exceptional events as truthful if everything else in the individual's account appeared to be true.

The inevitable question which arises in connection with autobiographies is: "Are they representative?" It must be admitted, of course, that the black autobiographers were unique in that they were either literate enough to describe their experiences or lucky enough to get sympathetic whites to do so. While recognizing this fact, it must be remembered that this is not peculiar to this genre. Autobiographies are just as representative as other kinds of literary material (perhaps more so). Any historian who deals with such material is forced to ignore the illiterate masses and recognize that many of these sources have been preserved only by accident. Probably no historian, for example, will ever know how much our portrayal of Southern society would have been altered if small planters and poor whites had left as many records as the large planters have. In a sense, all studies based on literary records are selective, the people they describe are "atypical," and their generalizations apply only to that small percentage of the population which has left written records.

Like most personal documents, the autobiography provides a window to the larger world. In this sense, the slave writers present a participant observer's comments on the larger slave society. As an eyewitness, the autobiographer brings the historian into contact with almost all kinds of slaves. When the autobiographies are accepted both as records of the unique experiences of each individual author and as eyewitness accounts of several slave communities, they are clearly "representative."

The crux of the matter, of course, is what is meant by "representative." Whether explicit or implicit, the representative slave for many Americans is a composite of myths long perpetuated by historians and the white man's stereotypes of blacks. Since blacks have been the invisible men of American scholarship, certainly real black men have as much claim to representativeness as the mythological slave. This is especially true because the historian has ignored blacks for so long that we have few objective facts to use to construct a profile of the "average" or representative slave. Rather than testing the autobiographers against the mythological average slave, it may be better to reverse the procedure. Historians must use autobiographies the same way they have used other kinds of literary sources, recognizing both their uniqueness and their representativeness.

A more serious question than representativeness is the reliability of that which is revealed in the autobiography. This is especially true in regard to the autobiographies of fugitive slaves. Many historians refuse to use these accounts because they have felt the fugitive, as the primary sufferer in the institution, was unable to give an objective account of bondage. This is obviously true. At the same time, most historians realize that few individuals are able to give completely objective accounts of things and persons with whom they were associated intimately. Inasmuch as all commentators were prejudiced in some way, slaves cannot be dismissed because of their biases. Historians can no longer discount the narratives while using other material from even more biased witnesses. Stanley Elkins, for example, in his study of slavery illogically rejected the slaves' accounts because of their alleged bias while relying heavily on Bruno Bettelheim's concentration camp narrative which several American psychological journals rejected because it lacked objectivity. Significantly, Bettelheim's answer to his critics was that in regard to the concentration camps "the persons most able to discuss them are former prisoners, who obviously are more interested in what happened to them than why it happened." (Bruno Bettelheim, "Individual and Mass Behavior in Extreme Situations," *Journal of Abnormal Psychology* XXXVIII [Oct. 1943], 418; Bruno Bettelheim, *The Informed Heart* [1960], 118.) Instead of rejecting the narratives *in toto*, investigators must use those which pass the tests commonly applied to historical documents. The slave, like the master, gave *his* view of the institution. Both distorted reality as they viewed the world through their respective lenses. In a sense, their views represent two sides of a coin. The distortions cancel themselves out and we are left, if we study both views, with a clear impression of the institution. If nothing else, both views reveal how the participants felt about the institution.

One cannot concede, however, that there is no validity in the slave narratives. Most of them have the ring of truth. Many of the writers, for instance, analyzed slavery in relatively dispassionate terms. The portrait of the institution of slavery which emerges from the narratives is not the simple picture of hell on earth that most historians have led us to believe they contain. Instead, the fugitives' plantations are peopled with the same range of heroes and villains, black and white, which one generally finds in the human race. The narratives add an important dimension to the story of slavery: the black's life within, and reaction to, the institution. There is, of course, no better way to explore this important facet of bondage than through the words of the slave himself.

Many historians refuse to accept the narratives as the actual words of the slaves. They point to the well-known fact that some of the fugitives had abolitionist amanuenses as sufficient reason to discount the narratives. Unfortunately, since they have not read many of the narratives, these historians have no way of knowing what percentage of them were, in fact, edited by the abolitionists. Many of the fugitives had received enough education and had associated long enough with educated whites to have written their *own* stories. On the other hand, such narratives as those of Solomon Bayley, G. W. Offley, and Andrew Jackson are so lacking in style, so woefully ungrammatical, and so straightforward that they could only have been written by relatively uneducated men. In other instances, a check of the narrative against other writings of the fugitives reveals unmistakable similarities in style. I have compared, for example, the narratives with numerous antebellum letters, speeches, sermons, and books published by such fugitives as James W. C. Pennington, Henry Bibb, Jermain Loguen, Henry Box Brown, William and Ellen Craft, Lewis and

Milton Clarke, Andrew Jackson, John Anderson, William Wells Brown, Levin Tilmon, Austin Steward, Richard Allen, Noah Davis, and Solomon Bayley.

Probably a little more than half of the fugitive slave narratives were written by abolitionists. Often these were not distorted, but rather written as dictated by the fugitive or copied from court and church records. Believing that truth alone could destroy slavery, many of the editors felt no need to embellish the story. Fabrications, of course, would not help the anti-slavery cause. The abolitionists were seriously embarrassed, for instance, when a Negro, passing himself off as a fugitive, manufactured a story and tricked John Greenleaf Whittier into editing it for him—the slaveholders had a field day exposing the fraudulent *Narrative of James Williams*. It is significant that the abolitionists checked the authenticity of the other accounts so thoroughly that there were no comparable exposés during the antebellum period. Instead of exaggerating the horrors of slavery, it is clear in some instances that the editors toned down the accounts. The editor of Charles Ball's narrative, for example, asserted that he had excluded the slave's bitterness and that "Many of his opinions have been cautiously omitted" (p. ii).

There were, of course, some narratives which were edited heavily by the abolitionists. These, however, can be identified relatively easily. In fact, one can often discover the points in the narratives where the editor interpolated his own views. His literary flourish, sweeping condemnation, and stirring appeals generally contrast sharply with the monotonous details of daily routine supplied by the slave. The most heavily edited narratives are generally very short, stress generalization rather than details, focus on the escape from, rather than the routine of, slavery, and are diatribes on unbelievably fiendish masters who terrorized the perfectly angelic slave. These furnished little evidence for this study.

It is perhaps even easier to detect the fictional and largely fictional slave narratives than the heavily edited ones. Richard Hildreth's *Archy Moore: Or the White Slave* (1836), and Peter Nielson's *The Life of Zamba* (1850), for example, were among the best antebellum fictional narratives. While Hildreth almost knew enough about slavery to palm off his novel as a true account of a fugitive slave, none of the other novels approach the verisimilitude of the real narratives. Frequently, for instance, the novelists had their heroes engaging in practices almost totally foreign to slavery. The best example of this is the story of a fugitive slave written by the Englishman, Charles Lee. In the story, purportedly narrated by Francis Fedric, *Slave Life in Virginia and Kentucky* (1863), all of the slaves are chaste, cunning, and courageous. The reader begins to question the validity of the account when Lee records the slaves frequently shaking hands with slaveholders, talking about running off to Canada in the presence of their masters, using such expressions as "fie" and "bid you fare you well," and offering high opinions of Great Britain and of Englishmen.

In some of the fictional accounts, the major character may have been a real fugitive, but the narrative of his life is probably false. *Aunt Sally: Or the Cross the Way to Freedom* (1858), distributed by the American Reform Tract and Book Society as a Sunday School reader for children, is a good example of the type. Aunt Sally is so Christ-like, suffers so patiently all of the horrors of slavery, draws a religious moral from so many of her sufferings, and speaks so directly to the children, that only children could have believed her account. Similarly, in spite of Lydia Maria Child's insistence that she had only revised the manuscript of Harriet Jacobs "mainly for purpose of condensation and orderly arrangement," the work is not credible. In the first place, *Incidents in the Life of a Slave Girl* (1861), is too orderly; too many of the major characters meet providentially after years of separation. Then, too, the story is too melodramatic: miscegenation and cruelty, outraged virtue, unrequited love, and planter licentiousness appear on practically every page. The virtuous Harriet sympathizes with her wretched mistress who has to look on all of the mulattoes fathered by her husband, she refuses to bow to the lascivious demands of her master, bears two children for another white man, and then runs away and hides in a garret in her grandmother's cabin for seven years until she is able to escape to New York. In the meantime, her white lover has acknowledged his paternity of her children, purchased their freedom, and been elected to Congress. In the end, all live happily ever after.

Fortunately, historians do not have to rely solely on internal evidence to determine the validity of the narratives. A number of scholars have investigated plantation records, manuscript census returns, diaries and letters of whites, local records, newspapers, and city directories in an effort to determine if the slave narratives were true. Joseph Logsdon and Sue Eakin's painstaking check of Solomon

Northup's story, and Paul Edward's investigation of the narrative of Gustavus Vassa are just two examples of successful efforts to verify the slave narratives.

Frequently, one autobiography which was undoubtedly true confirmed the validity of others of less credibility. The paths of the fugitive slaves, for example, often crossed those of free Negroes and of those men and women who wrote their autobiographies after the Civil War. For instance, Henry Box Brown's account of his escape from bondage in a small box appears at first glance to be a tall tale. Yet Brown was able to demonstrate to a group of Englishmen how he did this. The most convincing evidence, however, was supplied by Miflin Gibbs, a free Negro who was at the Philadelphia railroad depot when the box containing Brown arrived.

Even if one is unable to untangle the question of the validity of the fugitive slave narratives, it is still possible to present the Negro's view of bondage. Many Negroes who were born in slavery either purchased their freedom, or were manumitted by their owners, or emancipated by the Civil War, and later wrote their autobiographies. Seventy-eight of the black autobiographies included in this study were written by slaves or by black men or women who had direct knowledge of the institution. Twenty of these accounts were written by slaves who were manumitted by their masters, or who purchased their freedom. Thirty-four of these autobiographies were written before 1860 and forty-four after 1860. Only twenty-six of them were written by fugitive slaves. Consequently, the description of slavery in this volume rests primarily upon the accounts of men and women who had no abolitionist amanuenses. The diversity in the descriptions of slavery in the autobiographies is, perhaps, the greatest testament to their validity. The most informative of the autobiographies were those written by Louis Hughes, Henry Clay Bruce, Jermain Loguen, William Wells Brown, Robert Anderson, Frederick Douglass, Sam Aleckson, Jacob Stroyer, Austin Steward, Solomon Northup, Elizabeth Keckley, and Henry Bibb.

Slave interviews rival autobiographies in their revelations about the internal dynamics of bondage. Like the autobiographies, the interviews must be used with caution. One of the keys to utilizing them was presented in 1937 by ninety-four-year-old Amy Chapman who informed an interviewer for the Writers Project of the Work Progress Administration: "I kin tell you things about slavery times dat would make yo' blood bile, but dey's too turrible." Though an overwhelming majority of the more than 3,000 blacks interviewed by the WPA in the 1930s had been children when the Civil War began, they told Southern white interviewers so many things to make the blood boil that much of what they said was deleted. The heavy editing of the WPA interviews makes them far more difficult to utilize than black autobiographies. Since Southern white interviewers often deleted material contrary to the paternalistic image of the Old South they wanted to present, the WPA stories are least reliable as indices of planter treatment of the blacks. Because the informants had generally only known bondage as children, however, the interviews present a revealing portrait of slave childhood. Slave folk tales, religion, medicine, recreation, and songs also emerge clearly in the WPA interviews. By comparing the few verbatim interviews with the edited ones, those conducted by blacks with those conducted by white interviewers, and the accounts of blacks who lived on the same plantations, it is possible to overcome some of the shortcomings of the WPA interviews.

It is mandatory, when reading the WPA interviews, to remember the observation of ninety-year-old Martin Jackson of Texas: "Lot of old slaves close the door before they tell the truth about their days of slavery. When the door is open, they tell how kind their masters were and how rosy it all was. You can't blame them for this because they had plenty of early discipline, making them cautious about saying anything uncomplimentary about their masters." Perhaps the best way of getting behind the closed door of the WPA stories and correcting their distortions is to read them in tandem with earlier interviews of blacks who had been adults before the Civil War, were not senile when interviewed, and were not seventy years removed from bondage. Thousands of interviews antedating those of the WPA can be found in nineteenth-century periodicals and Benjamin Drew, ed., *A North-Side View of Slavery* (1856), James Redpath, *The Roving Editor* (1859), Octavia Albert, ed., *The House of Bondage* (1891), Orland Kay Armstrong, ed., *Old Massa's People* (1931), S. G. Howe, *The Refugees from Slavery in Canada West* (1864), and James McKaye, *The Mastership and Its Fruits* (1864).

The herculean labors of George P. Rawick made the WPA interviews readily accessible to scholars beginning in 1972 with the publication of a multi-volume compilation entitled *The American Slave: A Composite Autobiography*. A most talented researcher, Rawick subsequently located thousands of other interviews (published in twelve volumes in 1977). As a result of the work of Rawick, Charles Perdue, editor of *Weevils in the Wheat* (1976), and other researchers, there are now more easily accessible interviews of American slaves than of all other bondsmen in the New World. Judiciously edited selections from the WPA interviews can be found in Norman R. Yetman, ed., *Voices from Slavery* (1970), Ronald Killion and Charles Waller, eds., *Slavery Time When I Was Chillun down on Marster's Plantation* (1973), and Ronnie C. Tyler and Lawrence R. Murphy, eds., *The Slave Narratives of Texas* (1974).

In spite of the hazy memory of the aged informants and the deliberate distortion by many of the white interviewers, the WPA stories contain much valuable data about slavery. A great deal of this material supports or expands the portrait of the institution drawn from black autobiographies. Though generally too short to contain much on slave personality development beyond childhood, the WPA interviews clearly delineate the cultural milieu of the quarters. Supplemented with the speeches, interviews, letters, and autobiographies from the eighteenth and nineteenth centuries published in John Blassingame, ed., *Slave Testimony: Two Centuries of Letters, Speeches, Interviews, and Autobiographies* (1977), Robert Starobin, *Blacks in Bondage: Letters of American Slaves* (1974), and Randall Miller, ed., *"Dear Master": Letters of a Slave Family* (1978), the WPA interviews add an important dimension to the data drawn from black autobiographies.

Because there is no published equivalent of the WPA interviews for whites enslaved in Africa, the interested student must turn to their autobiographies to obtain personal testimony about their servitude. Unfortunately, historians analyzing white servitude have not systematically explored the strengths and weaknesses of the slave narratives they used. The historians' faith in the validity of the narratives was not, however, matched by contemporaries of the white slaves. The editors of the white slave narratives tried to convince incredulous readers of the validity of the stories by indicating that they had questioned the illiterate freedmen in minute detail about the experiences they recounted, checked their accounts against historical works and traveler's reports, and tried to locate white merchants, ship captains, or other ex-slaves who could verify their stories. Reviewers of the narratives often consulted a staggering array of other works and discussed them with knowledgeable people before accepting them as valid autobiographies. Though a number of European writers wrote novels about white servitude in Africa and presented them as true accounts, most of these tales lacked the verisimilitude of the actual autobiographies. The fictional stories were quickly recognized as novels by reviewers shortly after they were published, and pose few problems for the historian interested in finding the white slave's own description of his bondage.

Though often marred by religious, national, and racial biases, an overwhelming majority of the white slave narratives appear to be accurate. Some of the narrators (especially women) resorted to such heavy use of metaphors or wrote such brief accounts that it is almost impossible to reconstruct in detail the psychological impact of their captivity and bondage on them. Occasionally, when clerics edited the stories, they contain little more than diatribes on heathens and infidels and constant reminders of the evidences of the Divine presence in the white's captivity, servitude, and redemption. Fortunately, many of the former slaves wrote their own narratives soon after their redemption and long before they became senile. Wanting to acquaint their countrymen with what they had endured, raise money for themselves, or to contribute to the abolition of black servitude, the narrators tried to describe, as accurately as possible, what it meant when white sailors, merchants, women, doctors, and craftsmen were captured and enslaved in Africa. Since there are few autobiographies of manumitted whites who remained in Africa, those who were slaves for life, or African slaveholders, it is difficult to determine how representative the narratives are of white servitude. Travel accounts, diplomatic records, church archives, periodicals, and historical works written or compiled over a period of 1200 years all suggest, however, that the narratives provide characteristic views of the physical and psychological world of the white slave in Africa.

However important traditional records are in delineating the Southern white man's political, social, economic, and racial ideology, they are inferior to the slave narratives and interviews in explaining slave behavior. Traditional sources (plantation records, newspapers, letters, travel accounts) have been used in this study primarily to verify some details of the narratives and interviews, to amplify topics not explored in depth by the black writers, and to analyze the master's perception of interpersonal relations on the plantation. In regard to the latter point, the autobiographies written by antebellum Southern whites, and especially the manuscript ones, were most helpful. Among the more revealing ones were those written by Rebecca Felton, Susan

Smedes, Robert Q. Mallard, Jane Swisshelm, J. G. Clinkscales, Virginia Clayton, Letitia Burwell, Philip H. Jones, Norman Wood, Charles Hutson, Elizabeth Pringle, and Walter F. Peterson.

Periodicals representing planter interests, such as the *American Farmer, DeBow's Review, Southern Agriculturalist, Southern Cabinet, Southern Cultivator,* and the *Farmer's Register,* furnish data on plantation management philosophies and techniques. The impact of those philosophies and techniques on the bondsman is often revealed in the newspaper in the form of runaway slave notices, grand jury charges, criminal proceedings against masters and slaves, letters, petitions, and reports of the proceedings of religious bodies, agricultural societies, and governmental agencies. The New Orleans *Picayune* and New Orleans *Delta* are representative of Southern newspapers giving relatively full coverage of the most significant aspects of bondage. Ulrich B. Phillips, ed., *Plantation and Frontier* (1910) contains a good collection of runaway slave notices from various newspapers. The best analysis of the runaway notices appears in Daniel Meaders's essay in the *Journal of Negro History* (1975), "South Carolina Fugitives as Viewed Through Local Colonial Newspapers with Emphasis on Runaway Notices, 1732-1801."

No examination of the periodical literature on slavery would be complete without systematically exploring Northern abolitionist compilations from the Southern press. Especially rewarding because of their thoroughness are Theodore Weld, ed., *Slavery as It Is: The Testimony of a Thousand Witnesses* (1839) and Lydia M. Child, comp., *The Patriarchal Institution* (1860). Within the pages of the *Liberator, National Anti-Slavery Standard, Pennsylvania Freeman, Anti-Slavery Bugle,* and other abolitionist periodicals are a staggering number of slave interviews, autobiographies, and letters. Abolition journals gave even more coverage to white Southerners than to slaves and frequently reprinted articles, letters, and proceedings from a large number of Southern newspapers.

The Southern abolition press was especially prominent in the coverage it gave to the lives of planters. Consequently, such journals as the Shelbyville (Ky.) *Abolition Intelligencer,* Jonesboro (Tenn.) *Emancipator,* and the Baltimore *Genius of Universal Emancipation* provide singularly illuminating glimpses of Southern life.

Supporters of African colonization rivalled and sometimes surpassed abolition journals in publishing slave interviews, autobiographies, and letters. The colonization periodicals also had more interest in West African society, the actions of Southern white churches, and planter ideology than did abolition journals. The long-running *African Repository* and *Maryland Colonization Journal* furnish details on aspects of slavery largely unavailable in other sources. Denominational journals also supply important data. Such religious periodicals as the *Literary and Evangelical Magazine, Christian Intelligencer and Southern Methodist, Southern Christian Advocate, Southern Presbyterian Review, Religious Herald, Southern Episcopalian,* and *Charleston Gospel Messenger* contain a wide array of sermons, reports, and essays on practically every aspect of slavery.

Travel accounts were among the most important sources used in this study. Xenophobia, class and race bias, age, sex, intelligence, routes, mode of travel, and numerous other things have to be considered in reading the travel accounts. By and large, the travelers' observations are much more trustworthy in regard to the attitudes of whites than their opinions of slaves. Even so, many of the accounts are extremely illuminating if they are used cautiously. The most reliable accounts were written by businessmen, soldiers, scientists, journalists, teachers, and persons who either spent several months in one location or several years in one or more states, recorded their observations soon after the trip, and habitually gave detailed descriptions of people and institutions. A number of the more famous travelers have not been included in the bibliography because they were so long on generalization and so short on details.

Many historians have been so preoccupied with the attitudes of travelers toward slavery that they have not considered the accounts on their merits. Often profoundly ignorant of American institutions, many foreign travelers made facile generalizations about the plantations based on data gathered in fashionable salons and from gossip. Others rarely left their steamboat, train, or stagecoach and yet spoke with great "authority" on the South. The most misleading of the lot, however, were those gullible travelers who reported as fact whatever the planters told them, or judged the institution of slavery from what they saw of the relationship between house servants and slaveholders.

If one discounts the haphazardly formed generalizations and studies instead the descriptions of events the travelers actually saw, the accounts can be extremely useful. This is especially true because much of what the traveler saw was new to him. Consequently, he was much more likely to comment on things which resident whites accepted as commonplace (religious services, singing, dancing, dress, and language patterns in the quarters) than natives. Viewed from this perspective, even the most rabid abolitionist or pro-slavery zealot provides the investigator with some useful information. The most illuminating accounts were written by Oscar Comettant, Timothy Flint, Charles Lyell, Charles Lanman, Francis and Theresa Pulszky, Mathilda Houston, George Lewis, Frederick Law Olmsted, Basil Hall, Fredrika Bremer, S. A. O'Ferrall, Thomas Nichols, James K. Paulding, and Robert Sutcliff.

Secondary works on slavery are numerous. Several of them formed an indispensable part of my background reading. Three studies of slave narratives, Charles Nichols, *Many Thousand Gone* (1963), Stanley Feldstein, *Once A Slave* (1971), and Marion W. Starling, "The Slave Narrative: Its Place in American Literary History" (Ph.D. diss., New York University, 1946), although primarily literary analyses or compendiums, contain good bibliographies. The most extensive treatment of the masters appears in Ulrich B. Phillips, *American Negro Slavery* (1918) and *Life and Labor in the Old South* (1929). Eugene Genovese's *The Political Economy of Slavery* (1965) reiterates many of the points Phillips makes and places the plantation economy within a Marxian framework. Kenneth Stampp's *Peculiar Institution* (1956), free of the racial antipathy of Phillips, presents the clearest picture of the slave laborer and planter exploitation. Stanley Elkins' *Slavery* (1959) contains some interesting hypotheses about slave personality development. Since this pioneering book is not based on primary sources and many of its weaknesses are well known, I did not feel that it was necessary to write a critique. Instead, I have accepted the book the way that Elkins hoped that it would be received, as a "proposal," or series of hypotheses to be tested. For the most part this meant a refinement of or additions to Elkins' questions with new answers. Ann Lane's *The Debate Over Slavery* (1971) contains a good collection of essays critical of Elkins's hypotheses. The most perceptive comments on the slave appear in such studies of slavery as Charles Sydnor, *Slavery in Mississippi* (1933); Albert J. Raboteau, *Slave Religion* (1978); Orville Taylor, *Negro Slavery in Arkansas* (1958); George P. Rawick, *From Sundown to Sunup* (1972); Leslie Howard Owens, *This Species of Property* (1976); Herbert Gutman, *The Black Family in Slavery and Freedom* (1976); Lawrence Levine, *Black Culture and Black Consciousness* (1977); Eugene Genovese, *Roll, Jordan, Roll* (1974); Julia Floyd Smith, *Slavery and Plantation Growth in Antebellum Florida* (1973);

Peter Wood, *Black Majority* (1974); and James B. Sellers, *Slavery in Alabama* (1950). All of the secondary accounts should be supplemented with sophisticated articles on specific topics in the *Journal of Negro History, Phylon, North Carolina Historical Review, Journal of Southern History, Journal of Mississippi History, Louisiana Historical Quarterly,* and the *Georgia Historical Quarterly.* James C. Bonner, "Plantation and Farm: The Agricultural South," and Bennett H. Wall, "African Slavery," in Arthur S. Link and Rembert W. Patrick, eds., *Writing Southern History* (Baton Rouge, 1965), are good historiographical essays on plantation slavery.

Secondary works on religion in the South usually contain some account of the conversion and treatment of bondsmen by the churches, the abolition controversy, and the clerical defense of slavery. Often written by ministers, the general analytical level of the books is not very high. The best general works on Southern religion are the heavily researched, analytically sophisticated, and well written studies of Walter B. Posey, Donald S. Mathews, and Shelton Smith. Posey's *The Presbyterian Church in the Old Southwest* (1952), Smith's *In His Image* (1972), and Mathews' *Slavery and Methodism* (1965) and *Religion in the Old South* (1977), unravel many of the complexities of religion in the South and the ways it affected masters and slaves.

The only comprehensive, detailed, and generally objective volume on white servitude in Africa is Stephen Clissold, *The Barbary Slaves* (1977). Though primarily a diplomatic study, H. G. Barnby's *The Prisoners of Algiers* (1966) contains much information on American whites enslaved in Africa. Bibliographical guides to the narratives (published in many European languages) of white slaves are few. Clissold cites many of the most important ones, but his list should be supplemented by William Mathews' *American Diaries* (1945) and *British Autobiographies* (1955) where many more can be discovered. The Library of Congress and Yale's Bienecke Rare Book Library have copies of white slave narratives generally unavailable elsewhere.

Many of the misconceptions about Latin American slavery created and perpetuated by Gilberto Freyre, Frank Tannenbaum, and Stanley Elkins in the 1940s and the 1950s have been corrected by subsequent studies of servitude in Cuba, Brazil, Columbia, Venezuela, Haiti, and Mexico. Among the best of the accounts of Latin American slavery are Stanley Stein, *Vassouras* (1957), Franklin W.

Knight, *Slave Society in Cuba During the Nineteenth Century* (1970), Warren Dean, *Rio Claro* (1976), and Frederick Bowser, *The African Slave in Colonial Peru* (1974). Richard Greenleaf's *The Roman Catholic Church in Colonial Latin America* (1971), J. Lloyd Meacham, ed., *Church and State in Latin America* (1966), and Frederick Pike's *The Conflict Between Church and State in Latin America* (1964) explore many aspects of the Catholic Church's role in Latin American society.

A necessary but unsatisfactory introduction to interpersonal theory is the collected manuscripts, books, essays, memoranda, and lecture notes of Harry Stack Sullivan edited by his students and published posthumously as *The Collected Works of Harry Stack Sullivan* (1953-56). The founder of the interpersonal school, Sullivan died before he had the opportunity to elaborate fully on the theory he first enunciated in an essay in 1948. Consequently, the interested student has to turn to the work of Sullivan's disciples for discussions of the fully developed theory of interpersonal relations.

A good introduction to theories of personality development can be found in Henry Clay Lindgren, ed., *Contemporary Research in Social Psychology* (1969) and Hendrik M. Ruitenbeek, ed., *Varieties of Personality Theories* (1964). The most important works, however, are the monographs and reports of experiments which appear in such journals as *Sociometry* and the *American Journal of Psychiatry*. Erving Goffman's *Asylums* (1961) and Amitai Etzioni's *A Comparative Analysis of Complex Organizations* (1961) contain the best analyses of total institutions.

Select Bibliography

I. *Primary Sources, Unpublished*

Louisiana State University

Bond, Priscilla, Diary
De Clouet, Alexandre, Papers
Hephzibah Church Books, 1813-1840
McKinney, Jeptha, Papers
Pugh, Alexander F., Plantation Diaries, 1850-65
Risley, Alice C., Diary
Ryland, Robert H., Journals
Tibbetts, John C., Correspondence
Town, Clarissa, Diary

National Archives

Records of the Bureau of Freedmen and Abandoned Lands, Record Group 105

University of North Carolina

Aiken, David Wyatt, Autobiography
Allan, William, Memoirs
Asbury, Samuel E., Papers
Bateman, Mary E., Diary
Bayne, Hugh A., Memoirs
Berry, Mrs. John, Reminiscences
Blanchard, Elizabeth, Papers
Bondurant, Emily M., Reminiscences
Boyd, John, Diary
Bradbury, Charles W., Papers
Broidrick, Annie L., Recollections
Burnley, Edwina and Bertha, Recollections
Carmouche, Annie Jeter, Papers
Chotard, Eliza W., Autobiography
Clitherall, Eliza B., Diary
Colcock, William F., Autobiography
Comer, John Fletcher, Farm Journal
Foster, Elmina, Reminiscences
Gale and Polk Family Papers
Grimball, Meta M., Journal
Hardaway, Robert A., Book
Herbert, Hilary A., Reminiscences
Hutson, Charles W., Reminiscences
Jones, Philip H., Reminiscences
Killebrew, Joseph B., Autobiography
King, William Henry, Papers
Lawton, Alexander Robert, Diary
Mallet, Peter, Papers
Mayo, Peter H., Recollections

Meriwether, Elizabeth A., Recollections
Miller, Letitia D., Recollections
Milner Papers
Morrison, Columbus, Autobiography
Pharr, Louise Taylor, Book
Pilsbury, Rebecca, Diary
Polk, George W., Reminiscences
Rainey-Wren Papers
Ramsey, James Gettys, Autobiography
Stuart, James R., Recollections
Tazewell, Littleton Waller, Book
Wilson, Thomas B., Reminiscences

II. *Primary Sources, Published*

A. Black Autobiographies and Memoirs

Adams, John Quincy, *Narrative of the Life of John Quincy Adams, When in Slavery, and Now as a Freeman* (Harrisburg, Pa., 1872)
Aleckson, Sam, *Before the War, and After the Union* (Boston, 1929)
Allen, Richard, *The Life, Experience, and Gospel Labors of the Rt. Rev. Richard Allen* . . . (Philadelphia, 1887)
Anderson, John, *The Story of the Life of John Anderson, a Fugitive Slave* (London, 1863)
Anderson, Robert, *From Slavery to Affluence* (Hemingford, Neb., 1927)
Arter, Jared M., *Echoes from a Pioneer Life* (Atlanta, 1922)
Ball, Charles, *Slavery in the United States: A Narrative of the Life and Adventures of Charles Ball* (Lewistown, Pa., 1836)
Banks, J. H., *A Narrative of Events of the Life of J. H. Banks* (Liverpool, 1861)
Bayley, Solomon, *A Narrative of Some Remarkable Incidents, in the Life of Solomon Bayley, Formerly a Slave* (London, 1825)
Bibb, Henry, *Narrative of the Life and Adventures of Henry Bibb, an American Slave* (New York, 1849)
Black, Leonard, *The Life and Sufferings of Leonard Black, a Fugitive from Slavery* (New Bedford, 1847)
Branham, Levi, *My Life and Travels* (Dalton, Ga., 1929)
Brown, Henry Box, *Narrative of Henry Box Brown* (Boston, 1851)
Brown, John, *Slave Life in Georgia* (London, 1855)
Brown, William Wells, *Narrative of William W. Brown, a Fugitive Slave* (Boston, 1847)
———, *My Southern Home* (Boston, 1880)
Bruce, Henry Clay, *The New Man. Twenty-nine Years a Slave. Twenty-nine Years a Free Man* (York, Pa., 1895)
Bruner, Peter, *A Slave's Adventures Toward Freedom* (Oxford, O., 1918?)

Burton, Annie L., *Memories of Childhood's Slavery Days* (Boston, 1909)
Campbell, Israel, *An Autobiography* (Philadelphia, 1861)
Clarke, Lewis G., *Narrative of the Sufferings of Lewis Clarke . . .* (Boston, 1845)
Craft, William, *Running a Thousand Miles for Freedom: Or the Escape of William and Ellen Craft from Slavery* (London, 1860)
Davis, Noah, *A Narrative of the Life of Rev. Noah Davis, a Colored Man* (Baltimore, 1859)
Delaney, Lucy Ann, *From the Darkness Cometh the Light: Or Struggles for Freedom* (St. Louis, n.d.)
Douglass, Frederick, *My Bondage and My Freedom* (New York, 1855)
Grandy, Moses, *Narrative of the Life of Moses Grandy* (London, 1843)
Green, Elisha W., *Life of the Rev. Elisha W. Green* (Maysville, Ky., 1888)
Green, William, *Narrative of Events in the Life of William Green* (Springfield, O., 1853)
Grimes, William, *Life of William Grimes, the Runaway Slave, Brought Down to the Present Time* (New Haven, 1855)
Hall, Samuel, *47 Years a Slave* (Washington, Iowa, 1912)
Heard, William H., *From Slavery to the Bishopric in the A.M.E. Church: An Autobiography* (Philadelphia, 1924)
Henson, Josiah, *The Life of Josiah Henson* (Boston, 1849)
———, *Father Henson's Story of His Own Life* (New York, 1962 [1858])
Holsey, Lucius H., *Autobiography, Sermons, Addresses, and Essays* (Atlanta, 1898)
Hughes, Louis, *Thirty Years a Slave* (Milwaukee, 1897)
Jackson, Andrew, *Narrative and Writings of Andrew Jackson* (Syracuse, N.Y., 1847)
Jamison, Monroe F., *Autobiography and Work of Bishop M. F. Jamison, D.D.* (Nashville, 1912)
Jefferson, Isaac, *Life of Isaac Jefferson of Petersburg, Virginia, Blacksmith* (Charlottesville, 1951)
Johnson, Thomas L., *Twenty-eight Years a Slave: Or the Story of My Life in Three Continents* (London, 1909)
Jones, Thomas, *The Experience of Thomas Jones, Who Was a Slave for Forty-three Years* (Boston, 1850)
Keckley, Elizabeth, *Behind the Scenes* (New York, 1868)
Lane, Isaac, *Autobiography* (Nashville, 1916)
Lane, Lunsford, *The Narrative of Lunsford Lane* (Boston, 1848)
Langston, John Mercer, *From the Virginia Plantation to the National Capital* (Hartford, 1894)
Lewis, J. Vance, *Out of the Ditch* (Houston, 1910)

Loguen, Jermain Wesley, *The Rev. J. W. Loguen, As a Slave and as a Freedman* (Syracuse, N.Y., 1859)

Lowery, I. E., *Life on the Old Plantation in Ante-Bellum Days: Or a Story Based on Facts* (Columbia, S.C., 1911)

Marrs, Elijah P., *Life and History* (Louisville, 1885)

Mason, Isaac, *Life of Isaac Mason as a Slave* (Worcester, Mass., 1893)

Newton, A. H., *Out of the Briars* (Philadelphia, 1910)

Northup, Solomon, *Twelve Years a Slave* (London, 1853)

Offley, G. W., *A Narrative of the Life and Labors of the Rev. G. W. Offley, a Colored Man* (Hartford, 1860)

O'Neal, William, *Life and History of William O'Neal* (St. Louis, 1896)

Parker, Allen, *Recollections of Slavery Times* (Worcester, Mass., 1895)

Pennington, James W. C., *The Fugitive Blacksmith* (London, 1849)

Randolph, Peter, *Sketches of Slave Life* (Boston, 1855)

Roberts, James, *The Narrative of James Roberts* (Hattiesburg, Miss., 1945 [1858])

Robinson, W. H., *From Log Cabin to the Pulpit* (Eau Clare, Wis., 1913)

Roper, Moses, *A Narrative of the Adventures and Escape of Moses Roper from American Slavery* (London, 1840)

Smith, Amanda, *An Autobiography* (Chicago, 1893)

Smith, James L., *Autobiography of James L. Smith* (Norwich, Conn., 1881)

Smith, Venture, *A Narrative of the Life and Adventures of Venture, a Native of Africa* (New London, Conn., 1798)

Steward, Austin, *Twenty-two Years a Slave, and Forty Years a Freeman* (Rochester, N.Y., 1861)

Stroyer, Jacob, *My Life in the South* (Salem, 1890)

Thompson, John, *The Life of John Thompson, a Fugitive Slave* (Worcester, Mass., 1856)

Vassa, Gustavus, *The Interesting Narrative of the Life of Olaudah Equiano, or Gustavus Vassa, the African* (London, 1794)

Veney, Bethany, *The Narrative of Bethany Veney, a Slave Woman* (Worcester, Mass., 1889)

Washington, Booker T., *Up from Slavery* (Cambridge, 1928)

Watkins, James, *Narrative of the Life of James Watkins* (Bolton, Eng., 1852)

Watson, Henry, *Narrative of Henry Watson, a Fugitive Slave* (Boston, 1848)

Webb, William, *The History of William Webb* (Detroit, 1873)

White, George, *A Brief Account of the Life, Experience, Travels and Gospel Labours of George White, an African* (New York, 1810)

Wilkerson, James, *Wilkerson's History of His Travels & Labors, in the United States* (Columbus, O., 1861)

Williams, Isaac D., *Sunshine and Shadow of Slave Life* (East Saginaw, Mich., 1885)

B. Slave Interviews and Letters

Albert, Octavia, ed., *The House of Bondage; or Charlotte Brooks and Other Slaves* (New York, 1891)

Armstrong, Orland Kay, ed., *Old Massa's People: The Old Slaves Tell Their Story* (Indianapolis, 1931)

Blassingame, John W., ed., *Slave Testimony: Two Centuries of Letters, Speeches, Interviews, and Autobiographies* (Baton Rouge, 1977)

Botkin, Benjamin A., ed., *Lay My Burden Down* (Chicago, 1945)

Cade, John B., "Out of the Mouths of Ex-Slaves," *Journal of Negro History* XX (July 1935), 294-337

Drew, Benjamin, ed., *The Refugee: A North-Side View of Slavery* (Reading, Mass., 1969 [1856])

Howe, S. G., *The Refugees from Slavery in Canada West* (Boston, 1864)

Hurston, Zora Neale, "Cudjo's Own Story of the Last African Slaver," *Journal of Negro History* XII (Oct. 1927), 648-63

Jones, J. Ralph, "Portrait of Georgia Slaves," *Georgia Review* XXI (Spring 1967), 126-32 (Summer 1967), 268-73 (Fall 1967), 407-11, (Winter 1967), 521-25, XXII (Spring 1968), 125-27, (Summer 1968), 254-57

Killion, Donald and Charles Waller, eds., *Slavery Time When I Was Chillun down on Marster's Plantation: Interviews with Georgia Slaves* (Savannah, 1973)

McKaye, James, *The Mastership and Its Fruits* (New York, 1864)

Miller, Randall, ed., *"Dear Master": Letters of a Slave Family* (Ithaca, N.Y., 1978)

Montgomery, Charles J., "Survivors from the Cargo of the Negro Slave Yacht *Wanderer*," *American Anthropologist*, n.s. X (Oct. 1908), 611-23

Murphy, Lawrence R., and Ronnie C. Tyler, eds., *The Slave Narratives of Texas* (Austin, 1974)

Perdue, Charles L., *et al.*, eds., *Weevils in the Wheat: Interviews with Virginia Ex-Slaves* (Charlottesville, 1976)

Rawick, George, ed., *The American Slave: A Composite Autobiography* (31 vols., Westport, Conn., 1972-78)

Redpath, James, *The Roving Editor: or, Talks with Slaves in the Southern States* (New York, 1859)

Roche, Emma Langdon, *Historic Sketches of the South* (New York, 1914)

Starobin, Robert S., ed., *Blacks in Bondage: Letters of American Slaves* (New York, 1974)
Troy, William, *Hair-Breadth Escapes from Slavery to Freedom* (Manchester, Eng., 1861)
Yetman, Norman R., ed., *Voices from Slavery* (New York, 1970)

C. White Slave Narratives

Adams, Robert, *The Narrative of Robert Adams, a Sailor Who Was Wrecked on the Western Coast of Africa in the Year 1810* (London, 1816)
Bradley, Eliza, *An Authentic Narrative of the Shipwreck and Sufferings of Mrs. Eliza Bradley* (Boston, 1821)
De Brisson, M., *An Account of the Shipwreck and Captivity of M. De Brisson* (London, 1789)
Drury, Robert, *Madagascar; or, Robert Drury's Journal, During Fifteen Years' Captivity on That Island* (London, 1890)
Foss, John, *A Journal, of the Captivity and Sufferings of John Foss* (Newburyport, Mass., 1798)
Gee, Joshua, *Narrative of Joshua Gee of Boston Mass., While He Was Captive in Algeria of the Barbary Pirates, 1680-1687* (Hartford, 1943)
Laranda, Viletta, *Interesting Narrative of the Captivity and Sufferings of Miss Viletta Laranda* (New York, 1830)
Okeley, William, *Eben-Ezer; or a Small Monument of Great Mercy* (London, 1675)
Paddock, Judah, *A Narrative of the Shipwreck of the Ship Oswego* (New York, 1818)
Pananti, Filippo, *Narrative of a Residence in Algiers* (London, 1818)
Pellow, Thomas, *The Adventures of Thomas Pellow* (London, 1890)
Pfeiffer, G. S. F., *The Voyages and Five Years' Captivity in Algiers of Doctor G. S. F. Pfeiffer* (Harrisburg, Pa., 1836)
Price, Howell, *A Genuine Account of the Life and Transactions of the Howell ap David Price, Gentleman of Wales* (London, 1752)
Ray, William, *Horrors of Slavery: or, the American Tars in Tripoli* (Troy, N.Y., 1808)
Riley, James, *Loss of the American Brig Commerce* (London, 1817)
Voyages to the Coast of Africa, by Messrs. Saugnier and Brisson (London, 1792)

D. White Autobiographies and Memoirs

Anderson, John Q., *Brockenburn: The Journal of Kate Stone* (Baton Rouge, 1955)

Andrews, Charles Wesley, *Memoir of Mrs. Anne R. Page* (Philadelphia, 1844)
Andrews, Garnett, *Reminiscences of an Old Georgia Lawyer* (Atlanta, 1870)
Avirett, James Battle, *The Old Plantation: How We Lived in Great House and Cabin Before the War* (New York, 1901)
Bailey, Robert, *The Life and Adventures of Robert Bailey* (Richmond, 1822)
Banks, Mary Ross, *Bright Days in Old Plantation Times* (Boston, 1882)
Battle, Kemp P., *Memories of an Old-Time Tar Heel* (Chapel Hill, 1945)
Brackenridge, H. M., *Recollections of Persons and Places in the West* (Philadelphia, 1868)
Burke, Emily P., *Reminiscences of Georgia* (Oberlin, 1850)
Burwell, Letitia M., *Plantation Reminiscences*, by Page Thacker, Pseud. ([Owensboro?, Kentucky], 1878)
Candler, Mrytil Lon, "Reminiscences of Life in Georgia During the 1850's and 1860's," *Georgia Historical Quarterly* XXXIII (June 1949), 110-23
Chester, Samuel, *Pioneer Days in Arkansas* (Richmond, 1927)
Clayton, Victoria Virginia, *White and Black Under the Old Regime* (Milwaukee, 1899)
Clinkscales, J. G., *On the Old Plantation* (Spartanburg, S.C., 1916)
De Saussure, Mrs. Nancy (Bostick), *Old Plantation Days, Being Recollections of Southern Life Before the Civil War* (New York, 1909)
Devereux, Mrs. Margaret, *Plantation Sketches* (Cambridge, Mass., 1906)
Drake, Daniel, *Pioneer Life in Kentucky 1795-1800* (New York, 1948)
DuBose, John W., "Recollections of the Plantations," *Alabama Historical Quarterly* I (Spring 1930), 63-75, (Summer 1930), 107-18
Duke, Basil W., *Reminiscences of General Basil W. Duke, CSA* (Garden City, N.Y., 1911)
Etzenhouser, Elder R., *From Palmyra, N.Y., 1830, to Independence, Mo., 1894* (Independence, Mo., 1894)
Felton, Rebecca Latimer, *Country Life in Georgia in the Days of My Youth* (Atlanta, 1919)
Fulkerson, H. S., *Random Recollections of Early Days in Mississippi* (Vicksburg, 1885)
Gilmer, George R., *Sketches of Some of the First Settlers of Upper Georgia, of the Cherokees, and the Author* (New York, 1855)
Gordon, William S., *Recollections of the Old Quarter* (Lynchburg, Va., 1902)
Hallum, John, *Diary of an Old Lawyer* (Nashville, 1895)
Joyce, John A., *A Checkered Life* (Chicago, 1883)

Kemble, Frances Anne, *Journal of a Residence on a Georgian Plantation in 1838-1839* (New York, 1863)

Le Conte, Joseph, *The Autobiography of Joseph Le Conte* (New York, 1903)

Macon, T. J., *Life's Gleanings* (Richmond, 1913)

Mallard, Robert Q., *Plantation Life Before Emancipation* (Richmond, 1892)

Maury, Dabney H., *Recollections of a Virginian* (New York, 1894)

Meade, Anna Hardeman, *When I Was a Little Girl: The Year's Round on the Old Plantation* (Los Angeles [1916])

Meek, A. B., *Romantic Passages in Southwestern History* (Mobile, 1857)

Michaux, R. R., *Sketches of Life in North Carolina* (Cutler, N.C., 1894)

Milburn, William H., *Ten Years of Preacher Life: Chapters from an Autobiography* (New York, 1859)

Morton, Marmaduke, B., *Kentuckians Are Different* (Louisville, 1938)

Paschal, George W., *Ninety-four Years—Agnes Paschal* (Washington, D.C., 1871)

Pendleton, James M., *Reminiscences of a Long Life* (Louisville, 1891)

Peterson, Walter F., "Slavery in the 1850's: The Recollections of an Alabama Unionist," *Alabama Historical Quarterly* (Fall and Winter 1968), 219-27

Redd, John, "Reminiscences of Western Virginia, 1770-1790," *Virginia Magazine of History and Biography* VI (April 1899), 337-46

Shaler, Nathanel Southgate, *Autobiography* (Boston, 1909)

Sims, J. Marion, *The Story of My Life* (New York, 1884)

Smedes, Susan Dabney, *Memorials of a Southern Planter* (Baltimore, 1887)

Stafford, G. M., ed., "The Autobiography of George Mason Graham," *Louisiana Historical Quarterly* XX (Jan. 1937), 43-57

Stoney, Samuel G., ed., "The Memoirs of Frederick Augustus Porcher," *South Carolina Historical and Genealogical Magazine* XLIV (July 1943), 135-47, XLV (April 1944), 80-98

Swisshelm, Jane Grey, *Half a Century* (Chicago, 1880)

Torian, Sarah H., ed., "Ante-Bellum and War Memories of Mrs. Telfair Hodgson," *Georgia Historical Quarterly* XXVII (Dec. 1943), 350-56

Washington, Amanda, *How Beauty Was Saved* (New York, 1907)

Wilkinson, Eliza, *Letters of Eliza Wilkinson* (New York, 1839)

Wood, Norman B., *The White Side of a Black Subject* (Chicago, 1899)

E. Travel Accounts

"A St. Joseph Diary of 1839," *Florida Historical Quarterly* XVII (Oct. 1938), 132-51

Alexander, James Edward, *Transatlantic Sketches* (2 vols., London, 1833)

Anburey, Thomas, *Travels Through the Interior Parts of America* (London, 1789)

Arfwedson, Carl D., *The United States and Canada in 1832, 1833 and 1834* (2 vols., London, 1834)

Ashworth, Henry, *A Tour in the United States* . . . (London, 1861)

Baxter, W. E., *America and the Americans* (London, 1855)

Benwell, J., *An Englishman's Travels in America* (London, 1853)

Berquin-Duvallon, *Vue de colonie espagnole du Mississippi* (Paris, 1803)

Birkbeck, Morris, *Notes on a Journey to America* (Philadelphia, 1817)

Boucher, Jonathan, *Reminiscences* (Boston, 1923)

Bremer, Fredrika, *The Homes of the New World* (2 vols., New York, 1853)

Brickell, John, *The Natural History of North Carolina* (Dublin, 1737)

Bryant, William C., *Letters of a Traveller* (London, 1850)

Buni, Andrew, ed., "Rambles Among the Virginia Mountains: The Journal of Mary Jane Boggs, June 1851," *Virginia Magazine of History and Biography* LXXVII (Jan. 1969), 78-111

Candler, Isaac, *A Summary View of America* (London, 1824)

Chastellux, François Jean, *Travels in North America in the Years 1780, 1781 and 1782* (Chapel Hill, 1963)

Comettant, Jean Pierre O., *Trois Ans aux Etats-Unis* (Paris, 1857)

———, *L'Amerique telle qu'elle est* (Paris, 1864)

Cresswell, Nicholas, *The Journal of Nicholas Cresswell, 1774-1777* (New York, 1924)

Daubeny, Charles, *Journal of a Tour Through the United States, and Canada, Made During the Years 1837-38* (Oxford, 1843)

Davis, John, *Travels in the United States of America, 1798 to 1802* (Boston, 1910)

De Montulé, Edouard, *Travels In America, 1816-1817* (Bloomington, 1950)

Denny, Collins, ed., "Diary of John Early, Bishop of the Methodist Episcopal Church, South," *Virginia Historical Magazine* XXXIII (April 1925), 166-74

Descourtilz, Miguel Esteban, *Voyages d'un naturaliste* (3 vols., Paris, 1809)

Drayton, John, *A View of South Carolina* (Charleston, 1802)

Dureau, Jean Baptiste, *Les Etats-Unis en 1850* (Paris, 1891)

Du Roi, August, *Journal of Du Roi the Elder* (Philadelphia, 1911)

Easterby, J. H., ed., "South Carolina Through New England Eyes: Almira Coffin's Visit to the Low Country in 1851," *South Carolina Historical and Genealogical Magazine* XLV (July 1944), 127-36

Eddis, William, *Letters from America, Historical and Descriptive Comprising Occurrences from 1769 to 1777, Inclusive* (London, 1792)

Evarts, Jeremiah, *Through the South and West* (Lewisburg, Pa., 1956)

Faux, W[illiam], *Memorable Days in America* (London, 1823)

Feltman, William, *The Journal of Lieut. William Feltman, of the First Pennsylvania Regiment, 1781-82* (Philadelphia, 1853)

Ferguson, William, *America by River and Rail* (London, 1856)

Finch, John, *Travels in the United States of America and Canada* (London, 1833)

Fithian, Philip V., *Journal and Letters of Philip Vickers Fithian, 1773-1774* (Williamsburg, 1943)

Flint, Timothy, *Recollections of the Last Ten Years, Passed in Occasional Residence and Journeying in the Valley of the Mississippi* (New York, 1968)

Flower, Richard, *Letters from Lexington and Illinois* (London, 1819)

Fontaine, Jaques, *Memoirs of a Hugenot Family* (New York, 1853)

Glen, James, *A Description of South Carolina* (London, 1761) in B. R. Carrol, ed., *Historical Collection of South Carolina* (2 vols., New York, 1836)

Glover, Thomas, *An Account of Virginia* (Oxford, 1907)

Hall, Basil, *Travels in North America in the Years 1827 and 1828* (3 vols., Philadelphia, 1829)

Hall, Francis, *Travels in Canada and the United States in 1816 and 1817* (London, 1818)

Hamilton, Thomas, *Men and Manners in America* (2 vols., Philadelphia, 1833)

Harris, William T., *Remarks Made During a Tour Through the United States of America in the Years 1817, 1818, and 1819* (London, 1821)

Hartwell, Henry, *The Present State of Virginia* (London, 1727)

Herz, Henri, *Mes Voyages en Amerique* (Paris, 1866)

Hewatt, Alexander, *An Historical Account of the Rise and Progress of the Colonies of South Carolina and Georgia* (2 vols., 1779) in B. R. Carrol, ed., *Historical Collection of South Carolina* (2 vols., New York, 1836)

Hinke, William J., ed., "Report of the Journey of Francis Louis Michel from Berne, Switzerland, to Virginia, October, 1701-December 1, 1702," *Virginia Magazine of History and Biography* XXIV (April 1916), 113-41

Hodgson, Adam, *Letters from North America, Written During a Tour of the United States and Canada* (2 vols., London, 1824)

Ingraham, Joseph Holt, *The South-West: By a Yankee* (2 vols., New York, 1835)

Irving, John B., *A Day on Cooper River* (Charleston, 1842)
Johnston, Gideon, *Carolina Chronicle* (Berkeley, 1946)
Jones, Hugh, *The Present State of Virginia* (Chapel Hill, 1956)
Kellar, Herbert A., ed., "A Journey Through the South in 1836: Diary of James D. Davidson," *Journal of Southern History* I (Aug. 1935), 345-77
Knight, Henry C., *Letters from the South and West* (Boston, 1824)
Lanman, Charles, *Haw-He-Noo: Or Records of a Tourist* (Philadelphia, 1850)
Latrobe, Charles J., *The Rambler in North America 1832-33* (2 vols., New York, 1835)
Lawson, John, *A New Voyage to Caroline* (Chapel Hill, 1967)
Lewis, George, *Impressions of America* (Edinburgh, 1845)
Lyell, Charles, *Travels in North America, Canada, and Nova Scotia* (2 vols., London, 1845)
———, *A Second Visit to the United States of North America* (2 vols., New York, 1850)
Mackay, Alexander, *The Western World: Or Travels in the United States in 1846-47* (3 vols., Philadelphia, 1849)
Martineau, Harriet, *Society in America* (3 vols., London, 1837)
———, *Retrospect of Western Travel* (3 vols., London, 1838)
Mead, Whitman, *Travels in North America* (New York, 1820)
Moffatt, L. G., and J. M. Carriere, eds., "A Frenchman Visits Norfolk, Fredericksburg and Orange County, 1816," *Virginia Magazine of History and Biography* LIII (July 1945), 197-214
Murat, Achille, *America and the Americans* (New York, 1849)
Murray, Amelia, *Letters from the United States, Cuba and Canada* (New York, 1856)
Murray, James, *Letters of James Murray* (Boston, 1901)
Nairne, Thomas, *A Letter from South Carolina* (London, 1732)
Nichols, Thomas Low, *Forty Years of American Life, 1821-1861* (New York, 1937)
O'Connor, John, *Wanderings of a Vagabond* (New York, 1873)
O'Ferrall, S. A., *A Ramble of Six Thousand Miles Through the United States of America* (London, 1832)
Padgett, James A., ed., "A Yankee School Teacher in Louisiana, 1835-1837: The Diary of Caroline B. Poole," *Louisiana Historical Quarterly* XX (July 1937), 651-79
Paine, Lewis, *Six Years in a Georgia Prison* (New York, 1951)
Palliser, John, *Solitary Rambles* (London, 1853)
Paulding, James K., *Letters from the South Written During an Excursion in the Summer of 1816* (New York, 1817)
Perrin de Lac, François Marie, *Voyage dans les deux Louisianes* (Lyon, 1805)

Power, Tyrone, *Impressions of America, During the Years 1833, 1834, and 1835* (London, 1836)

Pulszky, Francis and Theresa, *White, Red and Black* (3 vols., London, 1853)

Robinson, Solon, *Solon Robinson, Pioneer and Agriculturalist* (2 vols., Indianapolis, 1936)

Rogers, George, *Memoranda of the Experience, Labors, and Travels of a Universalist Preacher* (Cincinnati, 1845)

Romans, Bernard, *A Concise Natural History of East and West Florida* (New York, 1775)

Rugbaean, A., *Transatlantic Rambles* (London, 1851)

Sealsfield, Charles, *The Americans as They Are, Described in a Tour Through the Valley of the Mississippi* (London, 1828)

Shelley, Fred., ed., "The Journal of Ebeneezer Hazard in Virginia, 1777," *Virginia Magazine of History and Biography* LXII (Oct. 1954), 400-423

Stewart, Catherine, *New Homes in the West* (Nashville, 1843)

Stirling, James, *Letters from the Slave States* (London, 1857)

Stoddard, Amos, *Sketches, Historical and Descriptive of Louisiana* (Philadelphia, 1812)

Story, Thomas, *A Journal of the Life of Thomas Story* (Newcastle-upon-Tyne, 1747)

Stuart-Wortley, Lady Emmeline Charlotte Elizabeth (Manners), *Travels in the United States, Etc., During 1849 and 1850* (3 vols., London, 1851)

Sutcliff, Robert, *Travels in Some Parts of North America in the Years 1804, 1805, & 1806* (York, Eng., 1811)

Tasistro, Louis F., *Random Shots and Southern Breezes* (2 vols., New York, 1842)

Thomson, William, *A Tradesman's Travels* (Edinburgh, 1842)

Tixier, Victor, *Travels on the Osage Prairies* (Norman, Okla., 1940)

Watson, Elkanah, *Men and Times of the Revolution* (New York, 1857)

Whipple, Henry B., *Bishop Whipple's Southern Diary* (Minneapolis, 1937)

Woolman, John, *A Journal of Life* (Dublin, 1776)

Younger, Edward, ed., "A Yankee Reports on Virginia, 1842-1843: Letters from John Adam Kasson," *Virginia Magazine of History and Biography* LVI (Oct. 1948), 408-30

F. Miscellaneous

Abbey, Kathryn T., ed., "Documents Relating to El Destino and Chemonie Plantations, Middle Florida, 1828-1868," *Florida Historical Society Quarterly* VII (Jan. 1929), 179-213

Arrowood, Mary D., and Thomas H. Hamilton, "Nine Negro Spirituals, 1850-61, from Lower South Carolina," *Journal of American Folklore* XLI (Oct.-Dec. 1928), 579-84

Bacon, A. M., "Conjuring and Conjure Doctors," *Southern Workman* XXIV (Nov. 1895), 193-94, (Dec. 1895), 209-11

Brown, John Mason, "Songs of the Slave," *Lippincott's Magazine* II (Dec. 1868), 617-23

Cable, George Washington, "Creole Slave Songs," *Century Magazine* XXXI (April 1886), 807-28

Catterall, Helen, ed., *Judicial Cases Concerning American Slavery and the Negro* (5 vols., Washington, D.C., 1926-37)

Christiensen, A. M. F., ed., *Afro-American Folklore; Told Round Cabin Fires on the Sea Islands of South Carolina* (Boston, 1892)

Dayrell, Elphistone, *Folk Stories from Southern Nigeria, West Africa* (London, 1910)

"Diary of Col. William Bolling of Bolling Hall," *Virginia Magazine of History and Biography* XLIII (Oct. 1935), 330-42

Donnan, Elizabeth, ed., *Documents Illustrative of the History of the Slave Trade in America* (4 vols., Washington, D.C., 1930-35)

Easterby, J. H., ed., "Charles Cotesworth Pinckney's Plantation Diary, April 6-December 15, 1818," *South Carolina Historical and Genealogical Magazine* XLI (Oct. 1940), 135-50

"Eighteenth Century Slaves as Advertized by their Masters," *Journal of Negro History* I (April 1916), 163-216

Ennis, Merlin, ed., *Umbundu: Folk Tales From Angola* (Boston, 1962)

Evans, Gladys C., and Theodora B. Marshall, eds., "Plantation Report from the Papers of Levin R. Marshall of 'Richmond,' Natchez, Mississippi," *Journal of Mississippi History* III (Jan. 1941), 45-55

Fortier, Alcée, *Louisiana Folk-Tales* (Boston, 1895)

Freeman, George W., *The Rights and Duties of Slave-Holders* (Charleston, 1837)

Green, Fletcher M., ed., *Ferry Hill Plantation Journal, January 4, 1838-January 15, 1839* (Chapel Hill, 1961)

Griffith, Benjamin W., "Longer Version of 'Guinea Negro Song,' from a Georgia Frontier Songster," *Southern Folklore Quarterly* XXVIII (June 1964), 117-18

Griffith, Lucille, ed., "The Plantation Record Book of Brookdale Farm, Amite County, 1856-57," *Journal of Mississippi History* VII (Jan. 1945), 23-31

Harrison, William P., *The Gospel Among the Slaves* (Nashville, 1893)

Itgayemi, Phebean, and P. Gurney, eds., *Folk Tales and Fables* (London, 1953)

Jablow, Alta, ed., *An Anthology of West African Folklore* (n.p., 1962)

Jones, Charles C., *The Religious Instruction of the Negroes in the United States* (Savannah, 1842)
"Journal of Col. James Gordon," *William and Mary Quarterly* 1st. ser., XII (July 1903), 1-12
"Journal of John Barnwell," *Virginia Magazine of History and Biography* VI (July 1898), 42-55
MacMaster, Richard K., ed., "Arthur Lee's Address On Slavery," *Virginia Magazine of History and Biography* LXXX (April 1972)
McKim, J. M., "Negro Songs," *Dwight's Journal of Music* XXI (Aug. 9, 1862), 148-49
McKim, Lucy, "Songs of the Port Royal Contrabands," *Dwight's Journal of Music* XXI (Nov. 8, 1862), 254-55
McTyeire, H. N., *et al., Duties of Masters of Servants: Three Premium Essays* (Charleston, 1851)
———, *Duties of Christian Masters* (Nashville, 1859)
Moore, John H., ed., "Two Documents Relating to Plantation Overseers of the Vicksburg Region, 1831-32," *Journal of Mississippi History* XVI (Jan. 1954), 31-36
Morton, Louis, ed., "The Daybook of Robert Wormley Carter of Sabine Hall, 1766," *Virginia Magazine of History and Biography* LXVIII (July 1960), 301-16
Salley, A. S., ed., "Journal of General Peter Horry," *South Carolina Historical and Genealogical Magazine* XXXIX (Oct. 1938), 157-59, XL (July 1939), 91-96, XLI (Jan. 1940), 15-18
Thornwell, J. H., *The Rights and Duties of Masters: A Sermon Preached at the Dedication of a Church* (Charleston, 1850)
Weld, Theodore Dwight, ed., *American Slavery As It Is: Testimony of a Thousand Witnesses* (New York, 1839)

III. *Secondary Sources*

A. Books

Abrahamson, Mark, *Interpersonal Accommodation* (New York, 1966)
Aptheker, Herbert, *American Negro Slave Revolts* (New York, 1943)
Argyle, Michael, *The Psychology of Interpersonal Behavior* (Baltimore, 1967)
Ballagh, J. C., *A History of Slavery in Virginia* (Baltimore, 1902)
Barnby, H. G., *The Prisoners of Algiers* (London, 1966)
Bassett, John S., *History of Slavery in North Carolina* (Baltimore, 1899)
Bennis, Warren G., *et al.*, eds., *Interpersonal Dynamics* (Homewood, Ill., 1964)

Berken, Paul de, ed., *Interaction: Human Groups in Community and Institutions* (Oxford, Eng., 1969)

Berkowitz, Leonard, ed., *Advances in Experimental Social Psychology* (2 vols., New York, 1965)

Berrien, F. Kenneth, and Bernard P. Indik, eds., *People, Groups, and Organizations* (New York, 1968)

Biddle, Bruce J., and Edwin J. Thomas, eds., *Role Theory: Concepts and Research* (New York, 1966)

Bjerstedt, Ake, *Glimpses from the World of the School Child* (Lund, Sweden, 1960)

Blau, Peter M., *Exchange and Power in Social Life* (New York, 1967)

Bowser, Frederick P., *The African Slave in Colonial Peru, 1524-1650* (Stanford, 1974)

Brackett, Jeffrey R., *The Negro in Maryland* (Baltimore, 1889)

Bryk, Felix, *Dark Rapture: The Sex-Life of the African Negro* (New York, 1961)

Burney, Christopher, *The Dungeon Democracy* (London, 1945)

Carson, Robert C., *Interaction Concepts of Personality* (Chicago, 1969)

Clemmer, Donald, *The Prison Community* (New York, 1965)

Clissold, Stephen, *The Barbary Slaves* (London, 1977)

Cohen, Elie A., *Human Behavior in the Concentration Camp* (New York, 1953)

Coulter, E. Merton, *John Jacobus Flournoy* (Savannah, 1942)

Craven, Wesley Frank, *White, Red, and Black: The Seventeenth Century Virginian* (Charlottesville, 1971)

Davis, Charles S., *The Cotton Kingdom in Alabama* (Montgomery, 1939)

Davis, David B., *The Problem of Slavery in Western Culture* (Ithaca, N.Y., 1966)

Dean, Warren, *Rio Claro: A Brazilian Plantation System, 1820-1920* (Stanford, 1976)

Degler, Carl, *Neither Black nor White* (New York, 1971)

Elkins, Stanley, *Slavery: A Problem in American Institutional and Intellectual Life* (Chicago, 1959)

Epstein, Dena J., *Sinful Tunes and Spirituals: Black Folk Music to the Civil War* (Urbana, 1977)

Fickling, Susan M., *Slave Conversion in South Carolina, 1830-1860* (Columbia, S.C., 1924)

Fisher, Allan G. B., and Humphrey J. Fisher, *Slavery and Muslim Society in Africa* (Garden City, N.Y., 1970)

Fisher, Miles Mark, *Negro Slave Songs in the United States* (Ithaca, N.Y., 1953)

Flanders, Ralph B., *Plantation Slavery in Georgia* (Chapel Hill, 1933)

Fogel, Robert W., and Stanley Engerman, *Time On The Cross: The Economics of American Negro Slavery* (2 vols., Boston, 1974)
Freyre, Gilberto, *The Masters and the Slaves* (New York, 1946)
Genovese, Eugene D., *The Political Economy of Slavery* (New York, 1965)
———, *Roll, Jordan, Roll* (New York, 1974)
Goffman, Erving, *Interaction Ritual: Essays on Face-To-Face Behavior* (Garden City, N.Y., 1967)
Gray, Louis C., *History of Agriculture in the Southern United States to 1860* (2 vols., Washington, D.C., 1933)
Gutman, Herbert, *The Black Family in Slavery and Freedom, 1750-1925* (New York, 1976)
Hare, A. Paul, *et al.*, eds., *Small Groups: Studies in Social Interaction* (New York, 1965)
Harris, Marvin, *Patterns of Race in the Americas* (New York, 1964)
Hereven, Tamara K., ed., *Anonymous Americans* (Englewood Cliffs, N.J., 1971)
Herskovits, Melville, *The Myth of the Negro Past* (New York, 1941)
Ichheiser, Gustav, *Appearances and Realities* (San Francisco, 1970)
Johnson, Guion Griffis, *Ante-Bellum North Carolina: A Social History* (Chapel Hill, 1937)
Johnson, Guy B., *Folk Culture on St. Helena Island, South Carolina* (Chapel Hill, 1930)
Jordan, Winthrop D., *White over Black* (Chapel Hill, 1968)
Kardiner, Abram, and Lionel Ovesey, *The Mark of Oppression* (New York, 1951)
Knapper, Christopher, and Peter B. Warr, *The Perception of People and Events* (New York, 1968)
Knight, Franklin W., *Slave Society in Cuba During the Nineteenth Century* (Madison, 1970)
Kogon, Eugen, *The Theory and Practice of Hell* (New York, 1946)
Kopytoff, Igor and Suzanne Meiers, eds., *Slavery in Africa* (Madison, 1977)
Korn, Bertram W., *Jews and Negro Slavery in the Old South* (Elkins Park, Pa., 1961)
Laing, R. D., H. Phillipson, and A. R. Lee, *Interpersonal Perception* (New York, 1966)
Lane, Ann, ed., *The Debate Over Slavery* (Urbana, 1971)
Lauber, Almon W., *Indian Slavery in Colonial Times Within the Present Limits of the United States* (New York, 1913)
Lengyel, Olga, *Five Chimneys: The Story of Auschwitz* (Chicago, 1947)
Lindgren, Henry Clay, ed., *Contemporary Research in Social Psychology* (New York, 1969)

McCall, George J., and J. L. Simmons, *Identities and Interactions* (New York, 1966)
Meacham, J. Lloyd, ed., *Church and State in Latin America* (Chapel Hill, 1966)
Moment, David, and Abraham Zaleznik, *The Dynamics of Interpersonal Behavior* (New York, 1964)
Mooney, Chase C., *Slavery in Tennessee* (Bloomington, 1957)
Mullin, Gerald W., *Flight and Rebellion: Slave Resistance in Eighteenth Century Virginia* (New York, 1972)
Newcomb, Theodore M., *Social Psychology* (New York, 1950)
Nichols, Charles H., *Many Thousand Gone* (Leiden, 1963)
Oraison, Marc, *Being Together: Our Relationships with Other People* (Garden City, N.Y., 1970)
Owens, Leslie Howard, *This Species of Property* (New York, 1976)
Owsley, Frank L., *Plain Folk of the Old South* (Baton Rouge, 1949)
Pepitone, Albert, *Attraction and Hostility* (New York, 1964)
Phillips, Peter, *The Tragedy of Nazi Germany* (London, 1969)
Phillips, Ulrich B., *American Negro Slavery* (New York, 1918)
———, *Life and Labor in the Old South* (Boston, 1929)
Posey, Walter B., *The Presbyterian Church in the Old Southwest, 1788-1838* (Richmond, 1952)
Postell, William D., *The Health of Slaves on Southern Plantations* (Baton Rouge, 1951)
Proshansky, Harold, and Bernard Seidenberg, eds., *Basic Studies in Social Psychology* (New York, 1965)
Rousset, David, *The Other Kingdom* (New York, 1947)
Ruitenbeek, Hendrik, ed., *Varieties of Personality Theories* (New York, 1964)
Sampson, Edward E., ed., *Approaches, Contexts, and Problems in Social Psychology* (Englewood Cliffs, N.J., 1964)
Savitt, Todd L., *Medicine and Slavery* (Urbana, 1978)
Scarborough, William K., *The Overseer* (Baton Rouge, 1966)
Schutz, William C., *The Interpersonal Underworld* (Palo Alto, Cal., 1966)
Sellers, James B., *Slavery in Alabama* (University, Ala., 1950)
Sharp, William F., *Slavery on the Spanish Frontier: The Colombian Choco, 1680-1810* (Norman, Okla., 1976)
Smith, H. Shelton, *In His Image, But . . . Racism in Southern Religion, 1780-1910* (Durham, 1972)
Stampp, Kenneth, *The Peculiar Institution* (New York, 1956)
Stein, Stanley J., *Vassouras: A Brazilian Coffee Country: 1850-1900* (Cambridge, Mass., 1957)
Stouffer, Samuel A., *et al.*, eds., *The American Soldier: Adjustment During Army Life* (4 vols., Princeton, 1949)

Sydnor, Charles S., *Slavery in Mississippi* (New York, 1933)
Tannenbaum, Frank, *Slave and Citizen* (New York, 1947)
Thorpe, Earl E., *Eros and Freedom in Southern Life and Thought* (Durham, 1967)
———, *The Old South: A Psychohistory* (Durham, 1972)
Wood, Peter, *Black Majority: Negroes in Colonial South Carolina* (New York, 1974)

B. Articles

Abel, Theodore, "The Sociology of Concentration Camps," *Social Forces* XXX (Dec. 1951), 150-55
Adler, H. G., "Ideas Toward a Sociology of the Concentration Camp," *American Journal of Sociology* LXIII (March 1958), 513-22
Anderson, Ronald E., "Status Structures in Coalition Bargaining Games," *Sociometry* XXX (Dec. 1967), 393-403
Arc, M., "The Prison 'Culture'—From the Inside," *New York Times Magazine* (Feb. 28, 1965), 52-63
Backman, Carl W., and Paul F. Secord, "Liking, Selective Interaction, and Misperception in Congruent Interpersonal Relations," *Sociometry* XXV (Dec. 1962), 321-35
Backman, Carl W., Paul F. Secord, and Jerry R. Pierce, "Resistance to Change in the Self-Concept as a Function of Consensus Among Significant Others," *Sociometry* XXVI (March 1953), 102-11
Bauer, Raymond A. and Alice H. Bauer, "Day to Day Resistance to Slavery," *Journal of Negro History* XXVII (Oct. 1942), 388-419
Bendix, Reinhard, "Compliant Behavior and Individual Personality," *American Journal of Sociology* LVIII (Nov. 1952), 290-303
Bettelheim, Bruno, "Individual and Mass Behavior in Extreme Situations," *Journal of Abnormal Psychology* XXXVIII (Oct. 1943), 417-52
Bloch, Herbert A., "The Personality of Inmates of Concentration Camps," *American Journal of Sociology* LII (Jan. 1947), 335-41
Bluhm, H. O., "How Did They Survive?" *American Journal of Psychotherapy* II (Jan. 1948), 3-32
Bondy, Curt, "Problems of Internment Camps," *Journal of Abnormal Psychology* XXXVIII (Oct. 1943), 453-75
Brotz, Howard, and Everett Wilson, "Characteristics of Military Society," *American Journal of Sociology* II (March 1946), 371-75
Corlew, Robert E., "Some Aspects of Slavery in Dickson County," *Tennessee Historical Quarterly* X (Sept. 1931), 224-48
Coser, Rose Laub, "Insulation from Observability and Types of Social Conformity," *American Sociological Review* XXVI (Feb. 1969), 28-39

Couch, Carl J., and John S. Murray, "Significant Others and Evaluation," *Sociometry* XXVII (Dec. 1964), 502-9

Elkin, Frederick, "The Soldier's Language," *American Journal of Sociology* II (March 1946), 414-22

Elkin, Henry, "Aggressive and Erotic Tendencies in Army Life," *American Journal of Sociology* II (March 1946), 408-13

Emerson, Richard M., "Power-Dependence Relations," *American Sociological Review* XXVII (Feb. 1962), 31-41

Friedman, Paul, "Some Aspects of Concentration Camp Psychology," *American Journal of Psychiatry* CV (Feb. 1949), 601-5

Galtung, Johan, "The Social Functions of a Prison," *Social Problems* VI (Fall 1958), 127-40

Harvey, O. J., "Personality Factors in Resolution of Conceptual Incongruities," *Sociometry* XXV (Dec. 1962), 336-52

Hayner, Norman S., and Ellis Ash, "The Prison as a Community," *American Sociological Reivew* V (Aug. 1940), 577-83

Hollingshead, August B., "Adjustment to Military Life," *American Journal of Sociology* LI (March 1946), 439-47

Jackson, Luther P., "Religious Development of the Negro in Virginia from 1790 to 1860," *Journal of Negro History* XVI (April 1931), 168-239

Jeltz, Wyatt F., "The Relations of Negroes and Choctaw and Chickasaw Indians," *Journal of Negro History* XXXIII (Jan. 1948), 24-37

Jernegan, Marcus W., "Slavery and Conversion in the American Colonies," *American Historical Review* (April 1916), 504-27

Johnson, Hosmer H., "Some Effects of Discrepancy Level on Responses to Negative Information About One's Self," *Sociometry* XXIX (March 1966), 52-66

Johnson, Hosmer H., and Ivan D. Steiner, "The Effects of Source on Responses to Negative Information About One's Self," *Journal of Social Psychology* LXXIV (April 1968), 215-24

Jordan, Weymouth T., "The Elisha F. King Family, Planters of the Alabama Black Belt," *Agricultural History* XIX (July 1945), 152-63

Knoff, William F., "Roles: A Concept Linking Society and Personality," *American Journal of Psychiatry* CXVII (May 1961), 1010-15

Korn, Richard, and Lloyd W. McCorkle, "Resocialization Within the Walls," *Annals of the American Academy of Political and Social Science* CCXCIII (May 1954), 88-98

Kral, V. A., "Psychiatric Observations under Severe Chronic Stress," *American Journal of Psychiatry* CVIII (Sept. 1951), 185-92

Lederer, Wolfgang, "Persecutions and Compensation," *Archives of General Psychiatry* XII (May 1965), 464-74

Meaders, Daniel, "South Carolina Fugitives as Viewed Through Local

Colonial Newspapers with Emphasis on Runaway Notices, 1732-1801," *Journal of Negro History* LX (April 1975), 288-319

Muffett, D. J. M., "Uncle Remus Was a Hausaman?" *Southern Folklore Quarterly* XXXIX (June 1975), 151-66

Perkins, Haven P., "Religion for Slaves: Difficulties and Methods," *Church History* X (Sept. 1941), 228-45

Pierson, William D., "An African Background for American Negro Folktales," *Journal of American Folklore* LXXXIV (April-June 1971), 204-14

Porter, Kenneth W., "Negroes on the Southern Frontier, 1670-1763," *Journal of Negro History* XXXIII (Jan. 1948), 53-78

Postell, Paul E., "John Hampton Randolph, a Louisiana Planter," *Louisiana Historical Quarterly* XXV (Jan. 1942), 149-223

Read, Allen W., "Bilingualism in the Middle Colonies, 1725-1775," *American Speech* XII (April 1937), 93-99

Rose, Arnold, "The Social Structure of the Army," *American Journal of Sociology* LI (March 1946), 361-64

Scott, Douglass, "The Negro and the Enlisted Man: An Analogy," *Harper's Magazine* CCXXV (Oct. 1962), 19, 21

Sides, Susan D., "Southern Women and Slavery," *History Today* XX (Jan. 1970), 54-60, (Feb. 1970), 124-30

Sitterson, J. Carlyle, "The McCollams: A Planter Family of the Old and New South," *Journal of Southern History* VI (Aug. 1940), 347-67

Southall, Eugene P., "Negroes in Florida Prior to the Civil War," *Journal of Negro History* XIX (Jan. 1934), 77-86

Spindler, G. Dearborn, "American Character as Revealed in the Military," *Psychiatry* XI (Aug. 1948), 275-81

Sullivan, Harry Stack, "Toward a Psychiatry of Peoples," *Psychiatry* XI (May 1948), 105-16

Sykes, Gresham M., "Men, Merchants, and Toughs: A Study of Reaction to Imprisonment," *Social Problems* IV (Oct. 1956), 130-38

Thorpe, Earle, "Chattel Slavery and Concentration Camps," *Negro History Bulletin* XXV (May 1962), 171-76

Vibert, Faith, "The Society for the Propagation of the Gospel in Foreign Parts: Its Work for the Negroes in North America before 1783," *Journal of Negro History* XVIII (April 1933), 171-212

Weinberg, S. Kirson, "Aspects of the Prison's Social Structure," *American Journal of Sociology* XLVII (March 1942), 717-26

White, Alice P., "The Plantation Experience of Joseph and Lavinia Erwin, 1807-1836," *Louisiana Historical Quarterly* XXVII (April 1944), 343-478

Whittington, G. P., "Dr. John Sibley of Nachitoches, 1757-1837," *Louisiana Historical Quarterly* X (Oct. 1927), 468-521

Index

Abolitionists:
literature barred from mails, 234; mob violence against, 234; religion and, 75-82; Southern writers and, 229-30
Abraham, 213
Accomac County, Virginia, 210
Acculturation:
of black slaves, 20; church and, 65; determinants of, 49; in Latin America and U.S., 65; of white slaves, 61-63, 65
Adams, Robert, 51-52, 62
Adultery:
and church, 178; interracial, 154-56; among slaves, 152-53, 162-63, 170; among whites, 154-57
Africa:
culture, 5, 20-24; origins of slaves, 5-6; reminiscences of, 13-17; sexual attitudes in, 161-62; slave trade and, 5-13
African survivals:
courtship, 157-58; dance, 23, 36-39; factors affecting, 47; familial roles, 177-78; folktales, 23-24, 31-33; language, 24-27, 29-30, 98-100; music, 22-23, 33-39; names, 181-83; proverbs, 114; religion, 20-21, 40-41, 71-75; in U.S. and Latin America, 47-48, 65
Africanization:
agricultural practice, 101; crafts, 101; food, 103; friendship, 104; labor, 101; language, 98-100; white children, 100-101
Aggression, slave:
patterns of, 314-20; projection, 314; repression, 317; verbal, 127-30, 315
Alabama, 338
Albert, Octavia, 375
Aleckson, Sam, 184, 186, 255, 264, 374
Algiers, 50, 62
Allah, 31
Allain, Helene, 37
Allen, Richard, 293, 372
Allen, William F., 145
Allport, G. W., 368
American Statistical Association, 342
Anderson, John, 164, 372
Anderson, Robert, 108, 126, 134, 291ff, 374
Arada, 5
Arkansas, 338
Armstrong, Orland Kay, 375
Army:
compared to plantation, 289-90; as total institution, 289-90, 324-26
Ashanti, 5, 32
Assignation:
black men and white women, 156; white men and black women, 154-55, 267-68
Autobiography:
fictional, 372-73; use, 367-78

Bacon, Thomas, 85
Bakongo, 5
Ball, Charles, 30, 31, 133-34, 178, 186, 191, 254, 257, 268, 290ff, 308, 372
Bambara, 5

Baptist State Convention, Alabama, 268
Baptists, 167, 337
Barbados, 18
Barnby, H. G., 381
Barrow, Bennet, 340
Bates, Ernest S., 368
Bayley, Solomon, 371, 372
Beebe, J. A., 91
Behavior:
  and personality, 288; of planters, 254-71; slave, factors affecting, 290-319
Bell, John, 26
Benin, 15
Bentley, George, 133
Berbice, 245
Bettelheim, Bruno, 327ff, 370-71
Biafada, 5
Bibb, Henry, 110, 112, 154-55, 164, 171, 173, 199, 293-94, 306, 371, 374
Bidell, Hosea, 177
Bilingualism of slaves, 24-30
Bishop of London, 71
Blassingame, John, 376
Blau, Peter, 286ff
Blues:
  African origins of, 121; celebration and, 123-24; freedom and, 122; love songs, 124-25; sex and, 124; slave attitudes and, 122-23; slave treatment, 122-23; work songs, 122-23
Bluhm, Hilde, 329
Boggs, Susan, 299-300
Bonner, James C., 381
Bowser, Frederick, 382
Bray's Associates, 71
Brazil:
  literary stereotypes of slaves, 228-29; sex ratio of slaves, 149-50
Breckinridge, Robert J., 76
Bremer, Fredrika, 380
Brewer, John Mason, 127
Broad River Baptist Association, 171
Brown, Henry Box, 171, 187, 371, 374
Brown, John, 159, 199ff, 235, 254, 303
Brown, William Wells, 113, 141, 154, 186, 191, 261, 267, 296ff, 371, 374
Brownlow, William G., 83
Bruce, Henry Clay, 110, 135-36, 290ff, 374
Bruner, Clarence, 97
Bureau of Refugees, Freedmen and Abandoned Lands, 341
Burton, Annie L., 254
Burwell, Letitia, 377

Calhoun, John C., 80
Call and response:
  in African songs, 22; in slave music, 138
Campbell, Israel, 309
Carson, James Green, 263
Cartwright, Samuel A., 227
Castration of slaves, 233
Catholic Church:
  and Indians, 66; in Latin America, 65-70; materialism of, 67, 68; role in slave life, 65-70
Catterall, Helen T., 195
Cervantes, Miguel de, 62
Chapman, Amy, 374
Charleston Presbytery, 174
Cheatham, Henry, 259-60
Chickasaws, 211
Child, Lydia Maria, 373, 378
Childhood:
  of planters, 265-67; racial equality during, 183-84; of slaves, 179-191
Children, slave:
  infant mortality of, 181; and masters, 185, 256; and parents, 186-91; socialization, 181-91; unaware of status, 183-85
Children, white:
  acculturation, 100-101
Choctaws, 211
Christian, Ella, 138
Christian Examiner, 228

Christian masters:
duties, 269; ministers and, 269-71
Church, slave:
desire for freedom, 133-35, 137-47; preachers, 130-33; secrecy in, 133, 145-46; theology, 130-34
Church, white:
christianization of slaves, 72; in Latin America and U.S., 69-72; and planter guilt, 77-80; restricts planter cruelty, 269-71; separation of slave families, 170-71, 174-75; slave marriages, 162-63, 167-70
Clarke, Lewis, 251, 296, 313, 371-72
Clarke, Milton, 372
Clay, Cassius M., 78-79
Clayton, Virginia, 378
Clinkscales, J. G., 378
Clissold, Stephen, 381
Clothing:
and self-esteem, 292; slave, 251-54
Clotide, 27, 29
Cobb, Joseph, 26-27, 39-40
Collock, Dr., 264
Comettant, Oscar, 380
Community, slave:
folktales and, 114-15, 127-29; quarters and, 315-16; rules, 316-17; and self-esteem, 307-14; slave driver and, 258-60; spirituals and, 145; socialization, 181-91
Compliance:
and coercion, 260-63, 293-97; and identification with masters, 286, 291-93; and surveillance, 286
Concentration camp:
behavior in, 327-29; compared to plantation, 289-90, 293, 330-31; factors promoting psychological survival in, 329-30; infantilism in, 327-28; resistance in, 328-29; as total institution, 289-90, 327-30
Conjurer:
African roots, 40-41; effect on whites, 113; impact on slaves, 109-10, 113; role on plantation, 109-10, 113; and slave resistance, 109, 110, 113
Conrad, Robert, 150
Corn songs, 117-18
Corsica, 50
Cotton plantation:
cultivation, 250; labor requirements, 279
Courtship:
African roots, 157-58; among slaves, 156-61
Cowley, Malcolm, 10
Craft, William and Ellen, 371
Creeks, 211
Cresswell, Nicholas, 115
Cuba:
church in, 68-70; rebellion in, 214-15; sex ratio of slaves in, 149
Culture:
effect of, on slave behavior, 105-6; African, 5, 20-24; elements of slave, 105; and self-esteem, 105-6
Cyprus, 50

Dahomey, 5
Damballa, 41
Dance:
African, 23-24, 36-39, 108-9; slave, 37-39, 108-9; white responses to, 23
Davies, Samuel, 90
Davis, Daniel Webster, 160
Davis, David B., 228
Davis, Hugh, 153
Davis, Keith E., 243
Davis, Noah, 179, 306, 372
Dean, Warren, 382
DeBow, J. B., 342
DeBow's Review, 239
De Brisson, M., 53
Decoration of graves, 41-45
Deference:
and personality, 285-89; ritual, 256-58, 260-61; slave, 293-305, 308-9; white slaves and, 56
Delaney, Lucy Ann, 312
De Las Casas, Bartholomew, 66

Delaware, 338
Deslondes, Charles, 216
Discontentment:
manifestations of, 116-17, 192-96; statistics on, 195-96
Dissembling, slave:
and behavior, 313-14; and personality, 200-202
Divorce, 152
Docility:
in concentration camps, 290, 327-29; fear and, 286-90; personality and, 285-89; punishment and, 286-88, 293-303; sham, 288, 313-14
Domestic servants:
aiding other slaves, 316; loyalty to whites, 304-5; role in controlling slaves, 261; as "Sambo," 225, 304-5; work of, 250-51
Dominance:
in interpersonal relations and personality, 285-89; in slave family, 178-79
Don Quixote (Cervantes), 62
Douglass, Frederick, 27, 116, 138-39, 142, 154, 180, 184, 193, 198, 199, 268, 293ff, 374
Drew, Benjamin, 375
Drivers:
role in controlling slaves, 258-60; role in protecting slaves, 316; slaves' view of, 258-60
Drunkenness:
masters' abuse of slaves and, 261; of slaves, 315
Du Bois, W. E. B., 40
DuBose, John W., 29
Dupuis, Mr., 62
Durham, Exter, 166-67

Eakin, Sue, 373
Edwards, Paul, 374
Elkins, Stanley, 231, 380, 381
Ellis, Harrison W., 132-33
England, 50
Enslavement:
of Indians, 4-5; Middle Passage, 7-11; process of, 3-13, 15; reactions of Africans to, 5, 7-20; reactions of whites to, 53-63
Enslavement, of whites:
by Arabs, 50; by West Africans, 51-52
Episcopal Church, 167, 178, 336, 337-38
Equiano, Olaudah, 15-20, 46-47, 74
Escape of slaves:
mass attempts, 206-8; methods of, 196-201; obstacles, 197-200; reasons for, 196
Etzioni, Amitai, 382
Ewe, 5, 32-33, 41, 114, 157
Ezell, Lorenzo, 182

Falconer, James, 26
Fan, 177
Family, African, 13, 15-16, 177-78
Family, planter:
"mammy" and, 266; treatment of slaves and, 265-68
Family, slave:
children, 179-91; courtship, 156-61; marriage, 164-70; planters and, 151-53; role of men, 172-73, 178-79; role of women, 179-81; separation, 170-71, 173-77; sex ratio, 149-50
Faux, William, 115
Favor, Lewis, 132
Fears:
of slaves, 295-98; of whites, 230-32, 267-68
Fedric, Francis, 373
Feldstein, Stanley, 380
Felton, Rebecca, 377
Flint, Timothy, 380
Flogging:
and insanity, 300-302; internalization and, 293-98, 302-3; Parliamentary resolution and, 340; resistance to, 317-19; slave behavior and, 296

Florida, 338
Flournoy, John Jacobus, 231
Folkes, Minnie, 163
Folklore:
African, 23-24, 31-33; aggression in, 127-30; slave, 114-15; socialization and, 127-30; tar-baby tale, 32-33; world view of slaves, 127-30
Fom, 41
Food allotment, 251-54
France, 50
Freedmen's Bureau, 175
Freeman, George W., 269
Frémont, John C., 194
Freyre, Gilberto, 381
Fulani, 5
Funeral rites:
African, 20-21; slave, 41, 45

Genovese, Eugene, 380
Georgia, 338
Gergen, Kenneth, 243
Ghana, 32, 114
Gibbs, Miflin, 374
Glennie, Alexander, 85, 94
Goffman, Erving, 288, 382
Gooch, G. W., 316
Grandy, Moses, 165
Gray, Thomas R., 217ff
Grayson, William, 118
Greece, 50
Green, William, 179, 199, 254-55, 267, 319
Greenleaf, Richard, 382
Grimes, William, 146, 185, 198, 264, 290ff, 309-10
Gullah:
African languages and, 30; slave-white interaction and, 29-30
Gutman, Herbert, 341, 380

Haile, Jesse, 75-76
Haiti, 214
Hall, Basil, 380
Hall, Samuel, 25, 30, 297ff
Hallucinations:
separations and, 297
Hammond, J. H., 236
Haring, Clarence, 69
Harrison, William P., 29-30
Hausa, 5, 32, 99, 161
Hawley, Francis, 300
Heard, William H., 317
Hearn, Lafcadio, 34, 38
Henson, Josiah, 193, 254, 262, 265, 296ff
Herbemont, H., 276
Herndon, Tempie, 166
Hewatt, Alexander, 36
Higginson, Thomas Wentworth, 137
Hildreth, Richard, 372
Hodgson, Mrs. Telfair, 41-42
Holland, Edwin C., 235-36
Holmes, David, 182-83
Holmes, Isaac, 36
Holmes, T. A., 270
Holsey, Lucius, 154, 187, 292ff
Housing, 254-56
Houston, Mathilda, 380
Howard, Nancy, 302
Howe, S. G., 375
Hughes, Louis, 195, 254, 268, 292ff, 374
Humboldt, Alexander, 149
Hunger, 251-54
Hurston, Zora Neale, 129
Hutson, Charles, 378

Ibibio, 5
Ibo, 5, 15, 16-17, 23, 32, 99
Iceland, 50
Ichheiser, Gustav, 226
Identification with masters:
behavior and, 291; domestic servants and, 303-5; factors in, 290-93
Improvisation:
in African music, 22; in slave music, 120

Indians:
  and disease, 4-5; enslavement of, 4-5; enslavement of blacks, 211; intermarriage with slaves, 211; maroons and, 211-14
Infantilism:
  in concentration camps, 289-90; 327-28; factors contributing to, 289-90
Insanity:
  and slave treatment, 298-302; statistics for, 342
Insurrection. *See* Rebellion
Internalization:
  contributing factors, 285-86; factors preventing, 288-89; slaves and, 291-304
Ireland, 50
Islam:
  black slaves and, 73; white slaves and, 57, 59-61
Italy, 50

Jackson, Andrew (General), 212
Jackson, Andrew (slave), 254, 267, 371, 372
Jackson, Edmund, 234
Jackson, Martin, 375
Jacobins, 232, 236
Jacobs, Harriet, 373
Jamison, M. F., 110, 155
Jefferson, Isaac, 264
Jefferson, Thomas, 77, 264
Jehovah's Witnesses, 330
Jesup, Thomas, 213, 214
Jones, Charles C., 73, 133, 138, 174, 313, 316
Jones, Edward E., 243
Jones, Philip H., 263, 378
Jones, Thomas, 185, 294ff, 309
Juba, 125
Judicial Cases Concerning American Slavery and the Negro (Catterall), 195

Keckley, Elizabeth, 181, 257, 318, 374
Kemble, Frances, 229-30
Kennerley, Samuel, 204
Killion, Ronald, 376
Kirk, James, 78
Knight, Franklin W., 381-82
Knight, Henry, 45
Kom, 5
Koran, 56
Korn, Richard, 326-27

Lamar, John B., 273, 276, 282
Lane, Ann, 380
Lane, Isaac J., 91
Lane, Lunsford, 184, 186, 192, 314
Langston, John Mercer, 155, 292
Language:
  African survivals, 47-48; Catholic Gullah, 30; patois, 26-27, 30
Lanier, Sidney, 125
Lanman, Charles, 380
Latin America:
  African survivals, 47-48; Catholic Church, 65-70; rebellions, 214-15; slave trade, 47-48; sex ratio, 149-50
Latrobe, Benjamin, 37, 38, 39
Lee, Arthur, 232
Lee, Charles, 373
Levine, Lawrence, 380
Lewis, George, 380
Lewis, J. Vance, 184, 185
Lexington, Kentucky, Presbytery of, 168
Lindgren, Henry Clay, 382
Link, Arthur S., 381
Logsdon, Joseph, 373
Loguen, Jermain, 155, 186, 257, 297ff, 371, 374
Long, John Dixon, 78, 116, 231-32
Louisiana:
  Africanisms, 36-38; voodoo, 41
Lyell, Charles, 282, 380

McCall, George, 289
McCorkle, Lloyd, 326-27
McKaye, James, 375

Macmillan, Harry, 163-64
McTyeire, H. N., 270
Mallard, Robert Q., 378
Mandingo, 5, 99
Manigault, Louis, 277
Mannix, Daniel, 10
Manumission:
religion and, 77-80; slave loyalty and, 292
Maroons:
attack plantations, 208-10; character of, 208-11; in Seminole wars, 211-14
Marriage, slave:
ceremony, 165, 167-70; Christian, 167-70; encouraged by masters, 151-53; legal status, 151; length, 176-77; number, 169-70; postnuptial ceremony, 166-67; restrictions on, 165; slave respect for, 171-72; statistics for, 341
Marrs, Elijah, 108, 187, 195, 264
Mars, James, 190, 295ff, 319
Maryland, 338
Mason, Isaac, 146
Mathews, Donald S., 381
Mauritius, 32
Meacham, J. Lloyd, 382
Meaders, Daniel, 378
Medical attention for slaves, 263
Meredith, Samuel, 282
Merton, Robert K., 244
Methodists, 167, 337
Middle Passage:
mortality, 7; reaction of Africans to, 7-11
Milburn, William H., 174
Militia, 215, 232
Miller, Randall, 376
Miner, Valentine, 177
Ministers, slave:
desire for freedom and, 133-34; sermons, 130-33; services, 92, 130-35, 137; white ministers and, 91-92
Ministers, white:
defense of slavery, 83, 132-33; denunciation of slavery, 75-77; on duties of masters, 268-71; instruction of black ministers, 91; promote slave obedience, 84-86, 132-33; religious instruction of slaves, 84-89, 92-98, 130-33; separation of slave families and, 174-75; slave life and, 77, 81-86; slave marriage and, 162-63, 167-71
Minor, William J., 152
Miscegenation:
slave family and, 154-56; slave morality and, 154-57; slave traders and, 155; white men and, 154-56, 172-73; white women and, 156
Mississippi, 338
Missionaries:
defense of slavery, 130; promote slave obedience, 130
Mobile, Alabama, 27
Mohamet, 59
Montgomery, Charles, 27
Moore, George W., 101
Murder, of whites by slaves, 195
Murphy, Lawrence R., 376
Music, African, 22-23
Music, slave:
African instruments, 39; African survivals in, 22-23, 33-39; origins of, 33-39; role in slave life, 115-27; secular, 115-26; spirituals, 137-46. *See also* Blues
Mutinies:
during Mid-Passage, 10-11; on Mississippi River, 206

"Nat" stereotype:
fears of whites, 231-33; relation to dominant slave personality, 233-34; "Sambo" stereotype and, 230-33; slave behavior and, 230-37
Neilson, Peter, 372
New Orleans:
African music in, 34, 36-38; voodoo in, 41
New Orleans *Delta*, 203-4
Nichols, Charles, 380

Nichols, Christopher, 300-301
Nichols, Thomas, 380
Nigeria, 15, 161
Northup, Solomon, 125, 126, 155, 194, 319, 373ff
Nupe, 161

Occupation of slaves:
 influence on self-esteem, 311-12; influence on treatment, 250-51
O'Ferrall, S. A., 380
Offley, G. W., 371
Olmsted, Frederick Law, 380
Omens, 114
Osceola, 213
Overseer:
 duties, 271-76; and reaction of slaves, 273-76; and surveillance of slaves, 271-76
Owens, Leslie Howard, 380

Page, Anne Meade, 79-80
Paranoia of whites, 231-33
Parker, Allen, 317
Parliament:
 and conditions of slavery, 340; and floggings, 340
Pascal, Roy, 368
Patrick, Rembert W., 381
Paulding, James K., 380
Paxton, John, 76
Pellow, Thomas, 59
Pennington, James W. C., 371
Perception:
 in interpersonal relations, 226-27; stereotypes and, 226-27; 228
Perdue, Charles, 376
Personality:
 slave, 319-22; stereotypes and, 226-28; theories of, 284-85
Peterson, Walter, 263, 377
Phillips, Ulrich B., 378, 380
Pike, Frederick, 382
Plantation:
 churches on, 130-33; labor routine, 250-51
Planter expectations:
 behavior of slave, 238; overseer and, 273-76; stereotypes and, 238
Planters:
 absenteeism, 271; characterized by slaves, 262, 264; concern for slaves, 263-64; family life, 265-68; guilt of, 77-80; miscegenation, 154-56, 172-73; overseers and, 273; protecting slave health, 263-64; public opinion and, 268; restrictions on power, 265-71; rules for controlling slaves, 238-48; runaways and, 196; selective inattention toward slaves, 280-83; separation of slave families, 173-74, 175-77; use of labor incentives, 239
Pollard, Edward A., 99-100, 313
Polygamy, 13, 171
Poor whites:
 literary stereotypes, 229-30; relations with slaves, 306-7; slave contempt for, 276, 306-7
Portugal, 50
Posey, Walter B., 381
Presbyterian Church, 132, 167, 338
Price, David, 53, 55
Pringle, Elizabeth, 378
Prison:
 behavior in, 289-90; as total institution, 289-90, 326-27
Prosser, Gabriel, 221
Prostitution, 154-55
Protestant Church:
 and Latin American Catholic Church, 70-71; proselytization in, 71-72
Proverbs, 114; African, 177
Pulszky, Francis and Theresa, 380

Quarles, Ralph, 155

Raboteau, Albert J., 380
Randolph, Peter, 196, 254

Rape of slave women, 153-54, 172-73
Rawick, George P., 375-76, 380
Rebellion:
Army and, 232; defined, 215-16; group identification, 222; leaders, 221-22; Louisiana, 216-17; militia and, 215; Nat Turner's, 217-21; New York City, 216; Stono, 206-7; topography and, 214-15; U.S. and Latin America, 214-15
Recalcitrant slaves, masters' accommodation of, 277-79, 319-20
Recreation:
activities, 106-9; attitudes of masters toward, 107-8; frequency of, 106-7; role in slave life, 105-9
Redpath, James, 375
Religion:
defiance of masters and, 147; docility and, 132-33; slave attitudes toward, 130-37; slave practice, 131-37; spirituals, 137-48; treatment of slaves and, 268-71; white missionaries, 130
Rewards:
as means of control, 239; slave labor and, 238-48; slave recreation, 106-7
Rhythm:
in African music, 22-23; in Juba, 125; in slave music, 122, 125, 126-27
Riley, James, 51
Ring shout, 134-35
Robinson, Lucy, 177
Robinson, W. H., 172, 188, 193, 293ff, 318-19
Roche, Emma Langdon, 27
Roles:
overseers, 240, 242; planters, 238-40; relation to personality, 242-44; slaves, 242-43
Role theory, 242-44
Roper, Moses, 155, 156, 261, 268, 290ff
Ruitenbeek, Hendrik M., 382
Rules of plantation management:
slave behavior and, 242-48, 276; slave role and, 242-43; stereotypes and, 238
Runaways:
character of, 198-206; rebellious, 205-6; Sambo, 203-5; statistics on, 200, 202
Russell, Marion J., 195

St. Lucia, 245
"Sambo" personality:
cruel treatment and, 293-98, 302-3; predominant among house servants, 304-5
"Sambo" stereotype:
dominant slave personality and, 224-30; fugitives, 203-5; perception of outsiders, 226-27; projections of whites, 226; rebellious slaves, 230-38; relation to other slave stereotypes, 233-38; roots of, 227-28; similarity to stereotypes of serf and Brazilian slave, 228-30
San Juan de los Remedios, 149
Sardinia, 50
Seabrook, Whitemarsh, 315-16
Selective inattention, 280-83
Self:
concept of, 284-85; as factor in personality and childhood, 285
Self-esteem:
personality factors promoting, 285; slave, 308-14; slave occupation and, 311-12
Self-fulfilling prophecy, and rebellions, 235
Sellers, James B., 381
Seminoles:
maroons and, 211-14; wars, 211-14
Senegal, 32
Separation of slave families:
church and, 170-71, 174-75; extent of, 173-74, 175-77; fear of, 173-74; insanity and, 298-300; laws prohibiting, 174; psychological impact, 297-98

Serer, 5
Sex ratios:
family life and, 149-50; U.S. and Latin America, 149-50
Schultz, Christian, 36-37
Sicily, 50
Significant others:
behavior and, 284-86; conjurers as, 109-10, 113; parents as, 151, 186-88, 190-91; several on plantation, 305, 310-11; Sullivan and, 284-85
Simmons, J. L., 289
Slave behavior:
belief in inferiority, 302-3; contentment, 291-92; courtship, 156-61; cruelty, 261-63; culture, 105-7; desire for freedom, 192-201; dissembling, 313-14; escapes, 192-208; fear of whites, 295-98; fighting masters, 317-18; group solidarity, 315-17; insanity, 298-302; kindly treatment, 263-64; literacy, 312; loyalty, 291-92, 304; overseers, 273-76; plantation management and, 239-48; rebellion, 206-21; religion, 47; self-hatred, 302-3; significant other, 320; stereotypes and, 223-38; submissiveness, 295-303
Slave personality:
African origins and, 4-5; coercion, 246, 261-63; culture and, 105-6; parental models, 186-88, 190-91; rebellions, 215-22; roles, 242-48; stereotypes, 223-38; variety in, 246-48, 286-322
Slave Songs of the United States (Allen), 145
Slave trade:
African reactions, 7-12; character, 5-11; volume, 47
Slave traders:
miscegenation and, 155; rebellious slaves sold to, 277
Slave women:
control of, 248; role in family, 154-55, 179-81, 191
Slaves:
African-born, 3-42; branding, 263; castration, 263; children, 179-91; clothing, 251-54; court decisions regarding, 195-96; courtship, 156-61; culture, 105-48; family life, 149-91; holidays, 106-7; housing, 254-55; influence on white family, 266-68; labor of, 250-51; marriages, 164-70; ministers, 130-33; names, 181-83; number imported, 47; and other labor conditions, 255-56; parents, 151, 186-88, 190-91; punishments, 245-46, 260-62; religion, 130-47; religious instruction, 91-94, 98; separations, 173-77; stereotypes, 223-38; women, 154-56, 179-81, 191
Slaves, white:
acculturation, 61-63, 65; alcohol and, 61; Arab treatment of, 49-65; and Christianity, 53; conversion of, 57-61; escape attempts of, 62; and Islam, 57, 59-61; in North Africa, 50-51, 52; number of, 50; rebellions, 62; shock of enslavement, 53, 55; thievery and, 61; in West Africa, 51-52; women, 56
Smedes, Susan Dabney, 266, 282, 377-78
Smith, Amanda, 185
Smith, Julia Floyd, 380
Smith, Shelton, 381
Smith, Venture, 13, 15
Smyth, J. F. D., 26
Socialization:
of slaves, 181-91; of whites, 98-104, 265-68
Society for Promoting Christian Knowledge, 71
Society for the Propagation of the Gospel in Foreign Parts, 71
South Carolina, 338
Southampton County, Virginia, 206, 217
Southern Evangelical Messenger, 100

Southern Quarterly Review, 271
Southern writers:
Brazilian writers and, 228-29; defense of slavery, 229-30; stereotypes of poor whites, 229-30; stereotypes of slaves, 228-31
Spain, 50
Spaulding, H. G., 134
Spindler, Dearborn, 325
Spirituals:
African origins, 33-34; imagery, 138-46; as means of communication, 139; references to freedom, 141-44; satire in, 120-22; world view, 137-48
Stampp, Kenneth, 380
Starling, Marion W., 380
Starobin, Robert, 376
Statistics:
and British Parliamentary reports, 340; and Bureau of Refugees, Freedmen and Abandoned Lands, 341; denominational records, 336-39; margin of error, 339; problems affecting, 336-43; and U.S. census, 342-43; use of, 336-43
Stein, Stanley, 149, 381
Stereotypes:
comparative, 224-38; factors affecting, 226-29; Jack, 224-25; literary, 224-38; Nat, 224-25, 230-33; poor whites, 229-30; relationship to personality, 226-27; roles, 238; Sambo, 224-26, 227-30; and Southern leaders, 234
Steward, Austin, 108, 172, 187, 190, 194, 195, 254, 257, 264, 296ff, 372, 374
Stone, Kate, 79
Stouffer, Samuel, 325
Stroyer, Jacob, 30, 140, 155, 190, 193, 267, 313, 374
Submissiveness:
coercive power and, 286-87; personality and, 285-88; slave, 295-304; white slave, 53, 55
Suicides:
among Africans, 4, 7-9; separations and, 197
Sullivan, Harry Stack, 284-85, 289, 382
Superstition:
slave, 109-10, 113-14; white, 113
Surinam, 214
Surveillance:
in concentration camps, 327-28; internalization and, 285-86; masters and, 271; obedience and, 286; overseers and, 273; in quarters, 310-11
Sutcliff, Robert, 380
Swisshelm, Jane, 378
Sydnor, Charles, 380
Syncretism:
in language, 24-30, 98-100; in music, 22-23, 33-39; in religion, 20-21, 40-41, 134-35
Szwed, John F., 33

Tannenbaum, Frank, 381
Taylor, Orville, 202, 214, 380
Taylor, Zachary, 214
Temne, 32
Tennant, Thomas, 76
Texas, 338
Thompson, John, 267
Thornwell, J. H., 269
Tilmon, Levin, 372
Tonga, 177
Total institutions:
coercive power in, 230-31, 289-90, 323-24; compared, 323-31; defined, 289-90; plantation and, 289-90
Travis, Joseph, 219
Trinidad, 245
Trinidad *Gazette,* 246
Turner, Benjamin, 217
Turner, Henry McNeal, 91
Turner, Lorenzo, 30
Turner, Nat:
issue in Virginia legislature, 237; rebellion, 144, 217-21
Tyler, Ronnie C., 376

Vassa, Gustavus, 15-20, 374
Vassouras, 149
Virey, Julien, 228
Virginia, 339
Voodoo, 41

Wacamaw, South Carolina, 94
Wall, Bennett, 381
Waller, Charles, 376
Wanderer, 27, 29
Ware, Nathaniel, 255-56
Washington, Amanda, 263
Washington, Booker T., 181
Washington, George, 272
Watkins, James, 190, 254, 303ff
Watson, Henry, 156, 255, 257, 295-96
Watts Hymnal, 90
Webb, William, 107, 110, 130, 146-47, 187, 193, 194, 314-15
Weld, Theodore, 378
Wesley, John, 270
West Africa:
  and Southern periodicals, 378-79; and white slaves, 51-52
West Indies:
  slave treatment in, 340
Whitehead, Margaret, 220
Whitmore, Charles, 280
Whittier, John Greenleaf, 372
Whydah, 41
Wigmore, John H., 368
Williams, James, 372
Wolof, 5, 32
Wood, Norman, 378
Wood, Peter, 381
Work songs:
  in Africa, 22; among slaves, 117-18
Works Progress Administration, 374-76

Yetman, Norman R., 376
Yoruba, 5, 39

Znaniecki, Florian, 243

CPSIA information can be obtained
at www.ICGtesting.com
Printed in the USA
BVHW082307030721
610931BV00002B/3

9 780195 025637